Will Trusts and Equitable Property Rights

WILL TRUSTS AND EQUITABLE PROPERTY RIGHTS

Dr Albert Keating
BCL, LLB, LLM, BL, DLitt

CLARUS PRESS

Published by
Clarus Press Ltd,
Griffith Campus,
South Circular Road,
Dublin 8.
www.claruspress.ie

Typeset by
Gough Typesetting Services,
Dublin

Printed by
CPI Antony Rowe,
Chippenham,
Wiltshire

ISBN
978-1-911611-08-0

A catalogue record for this book is available from the British Library

To my Sisters, Rose and Marion

PREFACE

The law relating to will trusts and equitable property rights is derived from the law of wills, the law of trusts and the formulation of equitable principles by the courts. The law of wills provides the rules for determining the legal validity of wills. The law of trusts provides the rules for determining the validity of trusts. The law of wills and law of trusts provide the rules for determining the legal validity of will trusts. The law of wills also provide the rules for the appointment, removal and liability of executors. The law of trusts provide the rules for the appointment, removal and liability of trustees. The application of equitable principles, such as proprietary estoppel, promissory estoppel and remedial constructive trusts, may result in the acquisition of equitable property rights. The application of an equitable doctrine, such as secret trust or half-secret trusts, may create equitable property rights. The application of a concept, such as a *donatio mortis causa*, may also create property rights once the conditions for establishing it are satisfied. The opening of a joint bank account may give rise contractual and equitable rights to the monies remaining in the account in favour of the surviving account holder. Propositions in relation to the identity, validity and applicability of the rules of law and equity in relation to will trusts, executors and trustees, and equitable property rights, may be presented as an introduction to the material covered by, and dealt with, in the chapters in the book.

Propositions of law and equity relating to wills, trusts and will trusts

- A will in order to be valid must be duly executed.
- A trust to be valid must be created in accordance with the law of trusts.
- A trust must have a subject matter, i.e. property.
- A trust must have objects, i.e. beneficiaries.
- Words creating a trust must be mandatory in purport.
- A trust in a will may be rendered ineffective by the sale of the trust property during the lifetime of the testator under the doctrine of ademption.
- A gift or trust in a will may be rendered ineffective by the predecease of beneficiaries under the doctrine of lapse.
- A gift or trust in a will may be rendered ineffective by the words creating the trust not being expressed in the necessary imperative mood.
- A will not duly executed is invalid.
- A trust not created in accordance with the law of trusts is invalid.
- An invalid will cannot create a valid will trust.
- An invalid trust in a will is an invalid will trust.

- An invalid trust in a will may not render a will invalid.
- An invalid trust in a will may not render a valid will ineffective.
- An invalid will and invalid trust will render a will trust a nullity.
- A will may be revoked.
- A will may be validly revoked in compliance with the statutory rules.
- A will may be revived.
- A will may be validly revived in compliance with the statutory rules.
- A will may be revived by codicil duly executed.
- An invalid will may result in intestacy.
- A will takes effect on the death of the testator.
- A trust created by will takes effect on the death of the testator.

Propositions relating to executors and trustees

- Executors may be appointed by the testator to administer his or her whole estate.
- Trustees may be appointed by the testator to administer the trust estate only.
- Executors who are also appointed trustees by the testator may administer the whole estate, including the trust estate.
- Executors owe a duty of prudence and diligence when administering the estate.
- Trustees owe a duty of prudence and diligence when administering the trust estate.
- Executors who are also trustees owe a duty of prudence and diligence when administering the whole estate, including the trust estate.
- Executors and trustees may be liable for breach of duty for a devastavit caused by them.
- Trustees who are not also executors may be liable for breach of duty for a devastavit caused to the trust estate and/or beneficiaries.
- Executors who are also trustees may be liable for breach of duty for a devastavit caused to the whole estate, including the trust estate.
- Executors and trustees may be personally liable for breach of duty to beneficiaries.
- Trustees may be sued for wilful default and breach of trust.
- Trustees who are also executors may be sued as trustees for wilful default and breach of trust.
- Executors and trustees may be removed.
- Executors may be removed as executors of the whole estate.
- Trustees may be removed as trustees of the trust estate.
- Executors who are also trustees may be removed as executors of the whole estate including the trust estate.
- Executors and/or trustees may be removed for serious misconduct.
- Executors and/or trustees may be removed for conflict of interests.

Propositions relating to the acquisition and creation of equitable property rights

- Equitable property rights may be acquired or created by the application of equitable principles and doctrines, and enforceable by the courts of equity
- Equitable property rights may be acquired by the equitable principle of proprietary estoppel.
- Equitable property rights may be acquired by the equitable principle of promissory estoppel.
- A proprietary estoppel may be established once it is shown by the claimant that the representation or assurance was made to him or her, that he or she relied on it, and suffered a detriment in consequence of his or her reasonable reliance on it.
- The detriment occasioned by the claimant may take the form of a money expenditure on land.
- The claimant may suffer a loss or detriment by working on the land for no wages or an inadequate wage.
- A distinction may be made between claims based on present interests in land and future interests when determining the acquisition of equitable property rights by proprietary estoppel or promissory estoppel.
- The principles of proprietary estoppel and promissory estoppel regarding future claims to interests in land may be assimilated.
- Promissory estoppel traditionally viewed as providing a "shield" only, and proprietary estoppel as both "sword" and "shield", but where future interests in land are concerned promissory estoppel may also be used as a "sword".
- Assimilated principles of proprietary estoppel and promissory estoppel dispel the functional distinction between the two principles in relation to claims to future interests in land.
- The onus of proof rests on the claimant to show that the elements for establishing a proprietary estoppel or promissory estoppel have been satisfied.
- Where a claimant successfully establishes a proprietary or promissory estoppel he or she may acquire equitable rights to property forming part of a deceased's estate.
- Proprietary estoppel and remedial constructive trust may be treated as separate and distinct equitable remedies regarding claims to future interests in land.
- Where the representations are made or assurances given in relation to future interests in land, the principles of remedial constructive trusts are more conceptually acceptable and applicable, than the principles of proprietary estoppel or promissory estoppel.
- Where a claimant successfully establishes the existence of a remedial constructive trust over property forming part of a deceased person's estate he or she may acquire equitable rights to that property.

- Equitable property rights may be created by constructive trusts arising out of pre-testamentary agreements to make mutual wills.
- Equitable property rights may be created by *donationes mortis causa*.
- Equitable property rights may be created by secret trusts.
- Contractual and equitable property rights may be created by contracts to open joint bank accounts.

Actions relating to will trusts on the following grounds

- That the subject matter of the trust was disposed of by the testator during his or her lifetime, resulting in the failure of the trust under the doctrine of ademption.
- That the objects of the trust predeceased the testator, resulting in the failure of the trust under the doctrine of lapse.
- That the property of the lapsed trust forms part of the testator's residuary estate.
- That the object or beneficiary of the trust is a predeceased child of the testator leaves issue him or her surviving and therefore the trust is not subject to the doctrine of lapse.
- The words used by the testator fail to show that the testator intended "to create an obligation," or manifest an intention to create a trust.
- That the words used by the testator in creating the trust do not clearly state that the person appointed as trustee holds the property in trust for the named beneficiaries.
- That the will was not duly executed in compliance with s.78 of the Succession Act 1965.
- That the testator lacked testamentary capacity.
- That the testator was subject to undue influence when he or she made his or her will.
- That the will was procured by a beneficiary.
- That the will was prepared and executed in suspicious circumstances.
- Decisions made by trustees for improper motives.
- Unreasonable decisions by trustees.
- Wilful default by trustees but only where that default can be truly characterised as a conscious breach of duty.

Actions relating equitable property rights on the following grounds

- That a proprietary estoppel over land exists.
- That the defendant made representations or assurances to the plaintiff regarding current or future interests in relation to land owned by the defendant.
- That the plaintiff placed reliance on such representations or assurances.
- That the plaintiff suffered a detriment on foot of his or her reliance on the representations or assurances made by the defendant by

expending monies on the land.

- That the suffered a detriment by working on the land free of charge or at a reduced rate by his or her reliance on the representations or assurances made by the defendant.
- That equitable property rights were acquired by the claimant.
- That a remedial constructive trust exists.
- That representations or assurances were made to the plaintiff by the defendant regarding a future interest in land belonging to the defendant.
- That the plaintiff placed reliance on such representations or assurances.
- That as a result of placing reliance on the defendant's representations or assurances the plaintiff suffered a detriment in the form of money expenditure on the defendant's land.
- That, and in the alternative, the plaintiff suffered a detriment by working free of charge or at a reduced wage on the defendant's land.
- That the defendant by will devised the land to another taking effect on the defendant's death.
- That the testator intended to create a secret trust over property devised by him or her by will.
- That the testator communicated his or her intention to the secret trustee/beneficiary of the devised property.
- That the secret trustee/beneficiary accepted the terms of the secret trust.
- That the donor intended to create a *donatio mortis causa* in favour of the donee.
- That the *donatio mortis causa* was made in contemplation of the donor's death.
- That the subject matter of the *donatio mortis causa* was delivered by the donor or his or her agent to the donee.
- That the deceased during his or her lifetime opened a joint bank account in his or her name and in the name of another person.
- That the deceased died leaving that other person him or her surviving.
- That the surviving account holder was entitled as survivor to the monies remaining in the joint account.
- That a pre-testamentary agreement was entered into by testators to make mutual wills benefitting one another.
- That, on the death of one of the testator, the pre-testamentary agreement took effect, and was enforceable against the surviving testator by the creation of a constructive trust by equity.

All of the foregoing issues and matters are covered and discussed in depth in the four parts and twenty-six chapters of the book by reference to relevant legislation and recent case law.

The author is, as ever, extremely grateful to David McCartney and his staff at Clarus Press for their assistance and hard work in the publication of *Will Trusts and Equitable Property Rights*.

Dr Albert Keating
December 2018

TABLE OF CONTENTS

PART THREE
EQUITABLE PROPERTY RIGHTS

TABLE OF CASES

TABLE OF LEGISLATION

STATUTORY INSTRUMENTS

UK

Part One

WILL TRUSTS

Chapter 1

THE CREATION OF TRUSTS BY WILLS

Introduction

The rules for the creation of trusts by wills are those prescribed by the law of wills and the law of trusts. For a trust in a will to be valid, the trust must satisfy the so-called "three certainties" for the creation of trusts, viz. **1–01**

> the subject-matter must be certain, the objects of the trust must be certain, and the words relied upon as creating the trust must have been used in the imperative mood, so as to show that the testator intended to create an obligation.[1]

The "subject-matter", i.e. the property, must be certain, the "objects", i.e. the beneficiaries, must be identifiable or at least ascertainable, and the words creating the trust must be clear in manifesting the testator's intention to create a trust, and free of any ambiguity or vagueness. The words must also be expressed in the imperative mood so as to make it clear that the person appointed as trustee is holding property in trust for the named beneficiaries [2] Words that merely request something to be done or words that are "precatory" and not mandatory will not be sufficient to create a trust.[3] **1–02**

A testator, for the purposes of his or her will trust, may appoint the same or different persons to act as his or her executors and trustees. It is, however, the normal practice to appoint the same persons to act as executors and trustees for the purposes of the Land and Conveyancing Law Reform Act 2009 and the Conveyancing Acts and s 57 of the Succession Act 1965. **1–03**

> I appoint AB of [address]
>
> and CD of [address]
>
> (hereinafter called "my trustees") to be executors and trustees and appoint them trustees for the purposes of the Land and Conveyancing Law Reform Act 2009 and for the purposes of the Conveyancing Acts and for the purposes of s 57 of the Succession Act 1965.

---

1 *Chambers v Fahy* [1931] IR 17 at 21 *per* O'Byrne J; see A. Keating, *The Law of Wills* (2nd ed, Clarus Press, Dublin, 2018); A. Keating, *Succession Law in Ireland* (Clarus Press, Dublin, 2015); A. Keating, *Keating on Probate* (5th ed, Round Hall, Dublin, 2015); A. Keating, *Succession Law in Ireland: Principles, Cases and Commentary* (Clarus Press, Dublin, 2016); A. Keating, *Irish Wills Precedents Service* (Round Hall, Dublin, 2009), Pt V.

2 *Re Humphrey's Estate* [1916] 1 IR 21; *Re Sweeney* [1976–77] ILRM 88.

3 See *Re Blackwood* [1953] NI 23; *Re Coulson* (1953) 87 ILTR 93.

1–04 It is normal practice to include a survival clause of 30 days in will trusts as follows:

> If my wife/husband/civil partner [name] survives me by thirty days, I give devise and bequeath the whole of my estate to him/her and appoint him/her my executor/executrix. If my wife/husband/civil partner does not survive me by thirty days the following provisions shall apply … .

1–05 The instructions given by a testator may determine the type of trust he or she wishes to create by his or her will. Where the objects of the trust are the testator's spouse, civil partner and/or children with substitutive provisions for children in the event of a spouse or civil partner not surviving the testator by thirty days, such a will trust may be termed a family will trust. The following words will create such a will trust:

> I give devise and bequeath to my trustees the whole of my estate upon trust to sell the same (with power to postpone such sale in whole or in part for such time or times as they shall think fit) and to hold the same or the proceeds of sale thereof on the following trusts:
>
> (a) To pay my debts, funeral expenses, and testamentary expenses;
>
> (b) (Provision for legacies, house and/or contents to, etc., if intended)
>
> (c) To hold the residue (hereinafter called "my Residuary Estate") in trust for my son/daughter until he/she attains the age of 21 years [or 18 years] BUT if my son/daughter should die before me or before attaining a vested interest leaving a child or children then such child or children shall on reaching the age of 21 years (or 18 years) take the share my son/daughter would otherwise have taken, and if more than one, in equal shares absolutely AND I DECLARE that no advancement within the meaning of section 63 of the Succession Act 1965 shall be brought into account in the distribution of my estate;
>
> (d) To pay to my son/daughter on reaching the age of 18 years the annual income of his or her share of my Residuary Estate until he or she reaches the age of 21 years.

1–06 Where the subject matter of the trust is land, it may termed a will trust of land within the meaning of the Land and Conveyancing Law Reform Act 2009. Where a testator decides to create a discretionary trust in his or her will giving the trustees discretionary powers over the operation of the trust provisions, such a will trust may be termed a discretionary will trust. A discretionary trust is one that empowers the trustees to pay or apply any part or parts of the capital and income of the trust fund to "all or any one or more" of the beneficiaries but without giving a beneficiary a right to any part of the capital or income of the trust fund.

1–07 For a will creating a trust to be valid, it must be executed in compliance with s 78 of the Succession Act 1965. Section 78(2) of the 1965 Act provides that the testator's signature must be made or acknowledged in the presence of two witnesses present at the same time when he or she signs his or her name or acknowledges his signature. Under s 78(3) of the 1965 Act

> it is sufficient if the signature is so placed at or after, or following, or under, or beside, or opposite to the end of the will that it is apparent on the face of the will

that the testator intended to give effect by the signature to the writing signed as his will.[4]

The following is a standard form of testimonium and attestation clause: **1–08**

> In witness whereof I have hereunto signed my name the … day of … 20 … .
>
> SIGNED by the said [testator's name] as and for his/her last Will and Testament in the presence of us who at his/her request and in his presence and in the presence of each other (all three being present at the same time) have hereunto subscribed our names as witnesses.

Before the execution of the will trust, the testator must also be given the opportunity to read his or her will, or have it read over to him or her by another, to approve of its contents, and thereby satisfy the principle of knowledge and approval of contents of wills before execution.[5] **1–09**

When using precedents in the preparation of will trusts, it is important to emphasise that a precedent must be adjusted to reflect the testator's wishes, and not vice versa. Or, to put it another way, the precedent provides the form and the testator's wishes provide the essence of a disposition. It is a process akin to *per genus et differentiam*, expressing with precision the testator's wishes regarding the disposition of his or her real and personal estate.[6] **1–10**

Definitions, Prerequisites and Vitiating Elements

Definitions **1–11**

(i) The definition of a will includes joint wills, mutual wills, conditional wills and/or codicils
(ii) The definition of a trust includes family trusts, trusts of land and discretionary trusts
(iii) The definition of a will trust includes all wills and/or codicils creating family trusts, trusts of land or discretionary trusts.

Prerequisites of Will Trusts **1–12**

(i) A trust must have a subject matter, i.e. property
(ii) A trust must have objects, i.e. beneficiaries
(iii) Words creating a trust must be mandatory in purpose
(iv) A will creating trusts must be duly executed
(v) A will takes effect on the death of the testator
(vi) A trust created by will takes effect as a will trust on the death of the testator.

---

[4] See A. Keating, *The Law of Wills* (2nd ed, Clarus Press, Dublin, 2018).
[5] See A. Keating, *The Law of Wills* (2nd ed, Clarus Press, Dublin, 2018).
[6] See A. Keating, *Irish Wills Precedents Service* (Round Hall, Dublin, 2009).

1–13 Vitiating Elements

(i) A trust in a will may be rendered ineffective under the doctrine of ademption by the sale of the trust property during the lifetime of the testator

(ii) A trust in a will may be rendered ineffective under the doctrine of lapse by the predecease of beneficiaries

(iii) A trust in a will may be rendered ineffective by the words creating the trust not being expressed in the necessary imperative mood.

THE CREATION OF WILL TRUSTS

(i) Family Will Trusts

1–14 The following precedent may act as guidelines for the creation of family will trusts:

1–15 ***Will trusts by husband for wife or civil partner with substitutive provisions for son/daughter***

I, [name of testator/testatrix] of [address] make this as and for my last will and testament and hereby revoke all former wills and testamentary dispositions heretofore made by me.

1. If my wife/husband/civil partner [name] survives me by thirty days I give devise and bequeath the whole of my estate to him/her and appoint him/her my executor/executrix. If my wife/husband/civil partner does not survive me by thirty days the following provisions shall apply:
2. I appoint AB of [address]
   and CD of [address]
   (hereinafter called "my trustees") to be executors and trustees and appoint them trustees for the purposes of the Land and Conveyancing Law Reform Act 2009 and for the purposes of the Conveyancing and for the purposes of s 57 of the Succession Act 1965.
3. I appoint my trustees guardians of my infant son/daughter.
4. I give devise and bequeath to my trustees the whole of my estate upon trust to sell the same (with power to postpone such sale in whole or in part for such time or times as they shall think fit) and to hold the same or the proceeds of sale thereof on the following trusts:
   (a) To pay my debts, funeral and testamentary expenses;
   (b) (Provision for legacies, house and/or contents to, etc., if intended)
   (c) To hold the residue (hereinafter called "my Residuary Estate") in trust for my son/daughter until he/she attains the age of 21 years [or 18 years] BUT if my son/daughter should die before me or before attaining a vested interest leaving a child or children then such child or children shall on reaching the age of 21 years [or 18 years] take the share my son/daughter would otherwise have taken, and if more than one, in equal shares absolutely AND I DECLARE that no advancement within the meaning of section 63 of the Succession Act 1965 shall be brought into account in the distribution of my estate;
   (d) To pay to my son/daughter on reaching the age of 18 years the annual income of his or her share of my Residuary Estate until he or she reaches the age of 21 years

In addition to all statutory powers that my trustees may have they shall have the following powers:

(i) To exercise the power of appropriation under section 55 of the Succession Act 1965 without serving any of the notices or obtaining any of the required consents.

(ii) To sell, call in or convert into money at such time or times and in such manner as they shall think fit so much of my estate as shall not be in money form; nevertheless to postpone such sale conversion or calling in indefinitely without being liable for any loss.

(iii) To sell any asset comprised in my estate at its full open market value to any one or more of my trustees.

(iv) To borrow any amount of money on the security of all or any assets comprised in the estate or without security and generally on such terms as they shall decide without limitation of any kind.

(v) To apply income derived from my estate for the benefit of any beneficiary under the trust hereby created.

(vi) To invest and change investments freely as if they were absolute owners beneficially entitled and to invest in unsecured interest free loans or other non-income-producing assets including property for occupation or use by any beneficiary.

(vii) To lease, let, mortgage, charge, licence and generally manage and deal with any land which, or the proceeds of sale of which, may for the time being form part of my estate as they were the beneficial owners thereof absolutely entitled.

(viii) To lend money or property to any one or more of the beneficiaries either free of interest or on such terms as to payment of interest and generally as the Executors shall in their absolute discretion think fit.

(ix) To trade or take part in any venture in the nature of trade whether solely or jointly with any other person and whether or not by way of partnership and for these purposes to make such arrangements as they shall in their absolute discretion think fit and may delegate any exercise of this power to any one or more of their number or to a company or partnership formed for this purpose.

(x) To insure against any loss or damage from any peril of any property for the time being comprised in my estate for any amount and to pay the premiums out of my estate.

(xi) To appoint a new, additional or substitutional trustee or trustees of this my will.

All income received after my death shall be treated as income of my estate regardless of the period to which it relates and the statutory rules concerning apportionment and the rules in *Howe v Dartmouth* and *Allhusen v Whittell* shall not be applied.

I declare that any of my trustees who is/are engaged in a profession shall be entitled to be paid fees for work done by him/her or his/her firm on the basis that he/she were not one of my trustees but employed to act on behalf of my trustees.

I declare that no trustee of this my will shall be liable for loss not attributable to the trustee's own dishonesty or wilful commission by the trustee of any act known to be a breach of trust.

In witness whereof I have hereunto signed my name the … day of … 20…

SIGNED PUBLISHED AND DECLARED by the said … as and for his last Will and Testament in the presence of us who at his request and in his presence and in the presence of each other (all three being present at the same time) have hereunto subscribed our names as witnesses.

Witness 1 (name and address)

Witness 2 (name and address)

(ii) Will Trusts of Land

1–16 The following precedent may be used as guidelines for the creation of will trusts of land:

1–17 ***Will trusts of residuary real estate by father for son/daughter***

I, [name of testator] of [address] make this as and for my last will and testament and hereby revoke all former wills and testamentary dispositions heretofore made by me.

1. I appoint AB of [address]
   and CD of [address]
   (hereinafter called "my trustees") to be executors and trustees and appoint them trustee for the purposes of the Land and Conveyancing Law Reform Act 2009 and for the purposes of the Conveyancing Acts and for the purposes of s 57 of the Succession Act 1965.
2. I Appoint my trustees guardians of my infant son/daughter.
3. I give devise and bequeath to my trustees my residuary real estate upon trust to sell the same (with power to postpone such sale in whole or in part for such time or times as they shall think fit) and to hold the same or the proceeds of sale thereof on the following trusts:
   (a) To pay my debts, funeral and testamentary expenses;
   (b) (Provision for legacies, house and/or contents to, etc., if intended)
   (c) To hold the residue (hereinafter called "my residuary real estate") in trust for my son/daughter until he/she attains the age of 21 years (or 18) BUT if my son/daughter should die before me or before attaining a vested interest leaving a child or children then such child or children shall on reaching the age of 21 years (or 18 years) take the share my son/daughter would otherwise have taken, and if more than one, in equal shares absolutely AND I DECLARE that no advancement within the meaning of section 63 of the Succession Act 1965 shall be brought into account in the distribution of my estate;
   (d) To pay to my son/daughter on reaching the age of 18 years the annual income of his or her share of my residuary estate until he or she reaches the age of 21 years

In addition to all statutory powers that my trustees may have they shall have the following powers:

(i) To exercise the power of appropriation under section 55 of the Succession Act 1965 without serving any of the notices or obtaining any of the required consents.
(ii) To sell, call in or convert into money at such time or times and in such manner as they shall think fit so much of my estate as shall not be in money form but nevertheless to postpone such sale conversion or calling in indefinitely without being liable for any loss.
(iii) To sell any asset comprised in my estate at its full open market value to any one or more of my trustees.
(iv) To borrow any amount of money on the security of all or any assets

comprised in the estate or without security and generally on such terms as they shall decide without limitation of any kind.

(v) To apply income derived from my estate for the benefit of any beneficiary under the trust hereby created.

(vi) To invest and change investments freely as if they were absolute owners beneficially entitled and to invest in unsecured interest-free loans or other non-income-producing assets, including property for occupation or use by any beneficiary.

(vii) To lease, let, mortgage, charge, licence and generally manage and deal with any land which, or the proceeds of sale of which, may for the time being form part of my estate as they were the beneficial owners thereof absolutely entitled.

(viii) To lend money or property to any one or more of the beneficiaries either free of interest or on such terms as to payment of interest and generally as the Executors shall in their absolute discretion think fit.

(ix) To trade or take part in any venture in the nature of trade whether solely or jointly with any other person and whether or not by way of partnership and for these purposes to make such arrangements as they shall in their absolute discretion think fit and may delegate any exercise of this power to any one or more of their number or to a company or partnership formed for this purpose.

(x) To insure against any loss or damage from any peril of any property for the time being comprised in my estate for any amount and to pay the premiums out of my estate.

(xi) To appoint a new, additional or substitutional trustee or trustees of this my will.

All income received after my death shall be treated as income of my estate regardless of the period to which it relates and the statutory rules concerning apportionment and the rules in *Howe v Dartmouth* and *Allhusen v Whittell* shall not be applied.

I declare that any of my trustees who is/are engaged in a profession shall be entitled to be paid fees for work done by him/her or his/her firm on the basis that he/she were not one of my trustees but employed to act on behalf of my trustees.

I declare that no trustee of this my will shall be liable for loss not attributable to the trustee's own dishonesty or wilful commission by the trustee of any act known to be a breach of trust.

In witness whereof I have hereunto signed my name the … day of … 20…

SIGNED, PUBLISHED AND DECLARED by the said … as and for his last Will and Testament in the presence of us who at his request and in his presence and in the presence of each other (all three being present at the same time) have hereunto subscribed our names as witnesses.

Witness 1 (name and address)

Witness 2 (name and address)

(iii) Discretionary Will Trusts

The following precedent may be used as guidelines for the creation of discretionary will trusts: **1–18**

1–19 *Discretionary will trusts by grandfather for grandchildren*

I, [name of testator/testatrix] of [address] make this as and for my last will and testament and hereby revoke all former wills and testamentary dispositions heretofore made by me.

1. I appoint AB of … and CD of … to be the executors and trustees of this my last will (hereinafter called "my trustees") and I direct my trustees to discharge all my just debts, funeral and testamentary expenses
2. I appoint my trustees to be trustees for the purposes of the Land and Conveyancing Law Reform Act 2009 and for the purposes of the Conveyancing Acts and for the purposes of s 57 of the Succession Act 1965 and I DECLARE that a sole trustee for the time being hereof and of every trust fund hereby created shall be competent to act for all the purposes of the said Acts and this my Will including the receipt of capital monies under the Settled Land Acts.
3. To the Secretary for the time being of the … Society (Charity) having its principal offices at [address] I give and bequeath the sum of €5,000.00 (Five Thousand Euro) for the charitable purposes in Ireland of the said Society.
4. To my nephew [name] of [address] I give and bequeath the sum of €5,000.00 (Five Thousand Euro).
5. I give and bequeath to my trustees the sum of €500,000.00 (Five Hundred Thousand Euro) to be held by them in trust for my grandchildren in equal shares absolutely and I DIRECT that if any of my said grandchildren shall be under the age of 21 years [or 18 years] at the date of my death, my trustees shall be empowered to apply, in addition to the income from the said legacy or any investment representing the same, the entire of the capital representing the said legacy for the purposes of the maintenance, benefit, advancement, and in particular the education of my said grandchildren in such manner and at such times as they in absolute discretion shall think fit and any payments made by my trustees may be made by them to the guardian of any of my said grandchildren or to any other person in whose custody or charge any of my said grandchildren may be without my trustees being responsible for seeing to the actual application thereof, and upon my said grandchildren attaining the age of 21 years [or 18 years] the said legacy and the investments representing the same and any accumulated income thereof shall be paid and transferred to them, but if any of my said grandchildren shall die under the age of 21 years [or 18 years], the said legacy and investments and accumulated income therefrom shall revert to and become part of my residuary estate.
6. Any monies requiring investment hereunder may be laid out in or upon the acquisition of security of any property of whatsoever nature and wheresoever situate including in particular, but without prejudice to the generality of the foregoing words, stocks, shares or securities of any kind whatsoever, insurance policies of any description and any house or flat or apartment as a residence for any beneficiary hereunder to the intent that my trustees shall have the same full and unrestricted powers of investing in all respects as if they were absolutely entitled thereto beneficially and subject to no restriction with regard to advice or otherwise in relation to investment.
7. As to all the rest residue and remainder of my estate whatsoever and wheresoever situate I GIVE DEVISE AND BEQUEATH same to my sister [name] of [address] for her own use and benefit absolutely. If my said sister predeceases me, then in that event I GIVE DEVISE AND BEQUEATH all the rest residue and remainder of my estate to my brother [name] of [address] for his own use and benefit absolutely.

In addition to all statutory powers that my trustees may have, they shall have the following powers:

(i) To exercise the power of appropriation under section 55 of the

Succession Act 1965 without serving any of the notices or obtaining any of the required consents.

(ii) To sell, call in or convert into money at such time or times and in such manner as they shall think fit so much of my estate as shall not be in money form, nevertheless to postpone such sale conversion or calling in indefinitely without being liable for any loss.

(iii) To sell any asset comprised in my estate at its full open market value to any one or more of my trustees.

(iv) To borrow any amount of money on the security of all or any assets comprised in the estate or without security and generally on such terms as they shall decide without limitation of any kind.

(v) To apply income derived from my estate for the benefit of any beneficiary under the trust hereby created.

(vi) To invest and change investments freely as if they were absolute owners beneficially entitled, and to invest in unsecured interest-free loans or other non- income-producing assets, including property for occupation or use by any beneficiary.

(vii) To lease, let, mortgage, charge, licence and generally manage and deal with any land which, or the proceeds of sale of which, may for the time being form part of my estate as if they were the beneficial owners thereof absolutely entitled.

(viii) To lend money or property to any one or more of the beneficiaries either free of interest or on such terms as to payment of interest and generally as the executors shall in their absolute discretion think fit.

(ix) To trade or take part in any venture in the nature of trade whether solely or jointly with any other person and whether or not by way of partnership and for these purposes to make such arrangements as they shall in their absolute discretion think fit and may delegate any exercise of this power to any one or more of their number or to a company or partnership formed for this purpose.

(x) To insure against any loss or damage from any peril of any property for the time being comprised in my estate for any amount and to pay the premiums out of my estate.

(xi) To appoint a new, additional or substitutional trustee or trustees of this my will

All income received after my death shall be treated as income of my estate regardless of the period to which it relates and the statutory rules concerning apportionment and the rules in *Howe v Dartmouth* and *Allhusen v Whittell* shall not be applied.

I declare that any of my trustees who is/are engaged in a profession shall be entitled to be paid fees for work done by him/her or his/her firm on the basis that he/she were not one of my trustees but employed to act on behalf of my trustees.

I declare that no trustee of this my will shall be liable for loss not attributable to the trustee's own dishonesty or wilful commission by the trustee of any act known to be a breach of trust.

In witness whereof I have hereunto signed my name the … day of … 20…

SIGNED PUBLISHED AND DECLARED by the said … as and for his last Will and Testament in the presence of us who at his request and in his presence and in the presence of each other (all three being present at the same time) have hereunto subscribed our names as witnesses.

Witness 1 [name and address]

Witness 2 [name and address]

Survival Clauses

1–20 A testator may create a will trust in favour of his or her children to take effect in the event of his or her spouse or civil partner not surviving him or her within thirty days. Such a clause may take the following form:

> If my wife/husband/civil partner [name] survives me by thirty days, I give devise and bequeath the whole of my estate to him/her and appoint him/her my executor/executrix. If my wife/husband/civil partner does not survive me by thirty days the following provisions shall apply:

1–21 Such survival clauses may also involve the application of the *commorientes* rule. Section 5 of the Succession Act 1965 for the purposes of the rule provides that where

> two or more persons have died in circumstances rendering it uncertain which of them survived the other or others, then, for the purposes of the distribution of the estate of any of them, they shall all be deemed to have died simultaneously.

1–22 Section 5 was the subject of interpretation by Kearns J (as he then was) in *In Re Kennedy*[7] when dealing with issues surrounding the simultaneous death of a husband and wife who had driven off Kilgarvan Pier on Lough Derg and were found three days later in about thirty feet from the pier. The post-mortem report concluded that the husband's death was due to acute cardiac-respiratory failure associated with the shock of sudden immersion in water, and under the heading "approximate interval between onset and death" the word "seconds" was inserted. The post-mortem report on the wife concluded that her death was due to drowning, and under a similar heading the words "minutes" was inserted. Both deceased had made mutual wills with each making the other universal devisee and legatee. They had no children. Their assets were all held as joint tenants. The applicant was a sister of the wife and the respondents were seven siblings and nephews and nieces of the husband. Owing to the references to the interval of time between onset and death as being "seconds" in the case of the husband and "minutes" in the case of the wife, the wife's sister applied for a grant of letters of administration with the will annexed to the wife's estate on the basis that she had survived her husband. At the request of the probate officer, further clarification was sought as to the sequence of the deaths. As there was no agreement on the matter between the respective families, the applicant sought liberty to apply for a grant on the basis that the wife had survived her husband. In the course of his judgment Kearns J stated that "the onus of establishing that one deceased survived another remains on the party so asserting." Where clear and cogent evidence is produced

[7] Unreported, High Court, Kearns J, 31 January 2000.

"to establish and prove positively the order of death then, even if the time interval is a matter only of seconds," s 5 is not applicable. Where, however, the evidence adduced falls short of eliminating the uncertainty, s 5 becomes applicable. He went on to say that the standard of proof "is nothing more than the onus of proof necessarily to be derived from the wording of the section". The evidence established an element of uncertainty, and as a result Kearns J found that the husband and wife had died simultaneously.

CHAPTER 2

FAMILY WILL TRUSTS

INTRODUCTION

It is essential to the validity of a trust in a will that the objects of the trust—i.e. the beneficiaries—are clearly identified by its provisions.[1] The beneficiaries may be identified by the provisions in italics in the following will trust: **2–01**

> I give, devise and bequeath to my trustees the whole of my estate upon trust to sell the same (with power to postpone such sale in whole or in part for such time or times as they shall think fit) and to hold the same or the proceeds of sale thereof on the following trusts:
>
> (a) To pay my debts, funeral expenses and testamentary expenses;
>
> (b) [Provision for legacies, house and/or contents to, etc., if intended]
>
> (c) To divide the residue (hereinafter called "my residuary estate") *among such of my children as shall survive me and reach the age of 18 [or 21] years and, if more than one, in equal shares absolutely, BUT if any child of mine dies before me or before attaining a vested interest leaving a child or children, then such child or children shall on reaching the age of 18 years take* per stirpes *the share his/her or their parent would otherwise have taken, and if more than one, in equal shares absolutely.*

THE CREATION OF FAMILY WILL TRUSTS

The following precedents may act as guidelines for the creation of family will trusts: **2–02**

Will Trusts by Husband for Wife or Civil Partner with Substitutive Provisions for Son/Daughter **2–03**

> I, [name of testator] of [address] make this as and for my last will and testament and hereby revoke all former wills and testamentary dispositions heretofore made by me.
>
> 1. If my wife/husband/civil partner [name] survives me by thirty days I give, devise and bequeath the whole of my estate to him/her and appoint him/her my executor/executrix. If my wife/husband /civil partner does not survive me by thirty days, the following provisions shall apply:
> 2. I appoint
>   AB of [address]
>   and CD of [address]
>   (hereinafter called "my trustees") to be executors and trustees and appoint

---

[1] See Albert Keating, *The Law of Wills* Second Edition (Dublin: Clarus Press, 2018); Albert Keating, "The Effect of the Land and Conveyancing Law Reform Act 2009 on Wills Precedents Referring to the Settled Land Acts and Conveyancing Acts (2010) 28 ILT 252; Albert Keating, *Irish Wills Precedents Service* (Dublin: Round Hall, 2009).

them trustees for the purposes of the Land and Conveyancing Law Reform Act 2009 and for the purposes of the Conveyancing Acts and for the purposes of s 57 of the Succession Act 1965.

3. I appoint my trustees guardians of my infant son/daughter.
4. I give, devise and bequeath to my trustees the whole of my estate upon trust to sell the same (with power to postpone such sale in whole or in part for such time or times as they shall think fit) and to hold the same or the proceeds of sale thereof on the following trusts:
   (a) To pay my debts, funeral expenses and testamentary expenses;
   (b) [Provision for legacies, house and/or contents to, etc., if intended]
   (c) To hold the residue (hereinafter called "my residuary estate") in trust for my son/daughter until he/she attains the age of 21 years [or 18 years] BUT if my son/daughter should die before me or before attaining a vested interest leaving a child or children then such child or children shall on reaching the age of 21 years [or 18 years] take the share my son/daughter would otherwise have taken, and if more than one, in equal shares absolutely AND I DECLARE that no advancement within the meaning of section 63 of the Succession Act 1965 shall be brought into account in the distribution of my estate;
   (d) To pay to my son/daughter on reaching the age of 18 years the annual income of his or her share of my residuary estate until he or she reaches the age of 21 years.

In addition to all statutory powers that my trustees may have, they shall have the following powers:

(i) To exercise the power of appropriation under section 55 of the Succession Act 1965 without serving any of the notices or obtaining any of the required consents.
(ii) To sell, call in or convert into money at such time or times and in such manner as they shall think fit so much of my estate as shall not be in money form, nevertheless to postpone such sale conversion or calling in indefinitely without being liable for any loss.
(iii) To sell any asset comprised in my estate at its full open market value to any one or more of my trustees.
(iv) To borrow any amount of money on the security of all or any assets comprised in the estate or without security and generally on such terms as they shall decide without limitation of any kind.
(v) To apply income derived from my estate for the benefit of any beneficiary under the trust hereby created.
(vi) To invest and change investments freely as if they were absolute owners beneficially entitled and to invest in unsecured interest-free loans or other non-income-producing assets including property for occupation or use by any beneficiary.
(vii) To lease, let, mortgage, charge, licence and generally manage and deal with any land which, or the proceeds of sale of which, may for the time being form part of my estate as if they were the beneficial owners thereof absolutely entitled.
(viii) To lend money or property to any one or more of the beneficiaries either free of interest or on such terms as to payment of interest and generally as the executors shall in their absolute discretion think fit.
(ix) To trade or take part in any venture in the nature of trade whether solely or jointly with any other person and whether or not by way of partnership and for these purposes to make such arrangements as they shall in their absolute discretion think fit and delegate any exercise of this power to any one or more of their number or to a company or partnership formed for this purpose.
(x) To insure against any loss or damage from any peril of any property

for the time being comprised in my estate for any amount and to pay the premiums out of my estate.

(xi) To appoint a new, additional or substitutional trustee or trustees of this my will.

All income received after my death shall be treated as income of my estate regardless of the period to which it relates and the statutory rules concerning apportionment and the rules in *Howe v Dartmouth* and *Allhusen v Whittell* shall not be applied.

I declare that any of my trustees who is/are engaged in a profession shall be entitled to be paid fees for work done by him/her or his/her firm on the basis that he/she were not one of my trustees but employed to act on behalf of my trustees.

I declare that no trustee of this my will shall be liable for loss not attributable to the trustee's own dishonesty or wilful commission by the trustee of any act known to be a breach of trust.

In witness whereof I have hereunto signed my name the ... day of ... 20....

SIGNED, PUBLISHED AND DECLARED by the said ... as and for his last will and testament in the presence of us who at his request and in his presence and in the presence of each other (all three being present at the same time) have hereunto subscribed our names as witnesses.

Witness 1 [Name and address]

Witness 2 [Name and address]

Will Trusts by Wife for Husband or Civil Partner with Substitutive Provisions for Son/Daughter 2–04

I, [name of testatrix] of [address] make this as and for my last will and testament and hereby revoke all former wills and testamentary dispositions heretofore made by me.

1. If my wife/husband/civil partner [name] survives me by thirty days I give, devise and bequeath the whole of my estate to him/her and appoint him/her my executor/executrix. If my wife/husband /civil partner does not survive me by thirty days, the following provisions shall apply:
2. I appoint AB of [address]
   and CD of [address]
   (hereinafter called "my trustees") to be executors and trustees and appoint them trustees for the purposes of the Land and Conveyancing Law Reform Act 2009 and for the purposes of the Conveyancing Acts and for the purposes of section 57 of the Succession Act 1965.
3. I appoint my trustees guardians of my infant son/daughter.
4. I give, devise and bequeath to my trustees the whole of my estate upon trust to sell the same (with power to postpone such sale in whole or in part for such time or times as they shall think fit) and to hold the same or the proceeds of sale thereof on the following trusts:
   (a) To pay my debts, funeral expenses and testamentary expenses;
   (b) [Provision for legacies, house and/or contents to, etc., if intended]
   (c) To hold the residue (hereinafter called "my residuary estate") in trust for my son/daughter until he/she attains the age of 21 years [or 18 years] BUT if my son/daughter should die before me, or before attaining a

vested interest, leaving a child or children, then such child or children shall on reaching the age of 21 years [or 18 years] take the share my son/daughter would otherwise have taken, and if more than one, in equal shares absolutely AND I DECLARE that no advancement within the meaning of section 63 of the Succession Act 1965 shall be brought into account in the distribution of my estate;

(d) To pay to my son/daughter on reaching the age of 18 years the annual income of his or her share of my residuary estate until he or she reaches the age of 21 years.

In addition to all statutory powers that my trustees may have, they shall have the following powers:

(i) To exercise the power of appropriation under section 55 of the Succession Act 1965 without serving any of the notices or obtaining any of the required consents.

(ii) To sell, call in or convert into money at such time or times and in such manner as they shall think fit so much of my estate as shall not be in money form, nevertheless to postpone such sale conversion or calling in indefinitely without being liable for any loss.

(iii) To sell any asset comprised in my estate at its full open market value to any one or more of my trustees.

(iv) To borrow any amount of money on the security of all or any assets comprised in the estate or without security and generally on such terms as they shall decide without limitation of any kind.

(v) To apply income derived from my estate for the benefit of any beneficiary under the trust hereby created.

(vi) To invest and change investments freely as if they were absolute owners beneficially entitled and to invest in unsecured interest-free loans or other non-income-producing assets including property for occupation or use by any beneficiary.

(vii) To lease, let, mortgage, charge, licence and generally manage and deal with any land which, or the proceeds of sale of which, may for the time being form part of my estate as if they were the beneficial owners thereof absolutely entitled.

(viii) To lend money or property to any one or more of the beneficiaries either free of interest or on such terms as to payment of interest and generally as the executors shall in their absolute discretion think fit.

(ix) To trade or take part in any venture in the nature of trade whether solely or jointly with any other person and whether or not by way of partnership and for these purposes to make such arrangements as they shall in their absolute discretion think fit and delegate any exercise of this power to any one or more of their number or to a company or partnership formed for this purpose.

(x) To insure against any loss or damage from any peril of any property for the time being comprised in my estate for any amount and to pay the premiums out of my estate.

(xi) To appoint a new, additional or substitutional trustee or trustees of this my will.

All income received after my death shall be treated as income of my estate regardless of the period to which it relates and the statutory rules concerning apportionment and the rules in *Howe v Dartmouth* and *Allhusen v Whittell* shall not be applied.

I declare that any of my trustees who is/are engaged in a profession shall be entitled to be paid fees for work done by him/her or his/her firm on the basis that he/she were not one of my trustees but employed to act on behalf of my trustees.

I declare that no trustee of this my will shall be liable for loss not attributable to the trustee's own dishonesty or wilful commission by the trustee of any act known to be a breach of trust.

In witness whereof I have hereunto signed my name the ... day of ... 20....

SIGNED, PUBLISHED AND DECLARED by the said ... as and for his last will and testament in the presence of us who at his request and in his presence and in the presence of each other (all three being present at the same time) have hereunto subscribed our names as witnesses.

Witness 1 [Name and address]

Witness 2 [Name and address]

Will Trusts by Husband for Wife or Civil Partners with Provisions for Children 2–05

I, [name of testator] of [address] make this as and for my last will and testament and hereby revoke all former wills and testamentary dispositions heretofore made by me.

1. If my wife/husband [name] survives me by thirty days I give, devise and bequeath the whole of my estate to him/her and appoint him/her my executor/executrix. If my wife/husband/civil partner does not survive me by thirty days, the following provisions shall apply:
2. I appoint
   AB of [address]
   and CD of [address]
   (hereinafter called "my trustees") to be executors and trustees and appoint them trustees for the purposes of the Land and Conveyancing Law Reform Act 2009 and for the purposes of the Conveyancing Acts and for the purposes of section 57 of the Succession Act 1965.
3. I appoint my trustees guardians of my infant children.
4. I give, devise and bequeath to my trustees the whole of my estate upon trust to sell the same (with power to postpone such sale in whole or in part for such time or times as they shall think fit) and to hold the same or the proceeds of sale thereof on the following trusts:
   (a) To pay my debts, funeral expenses and testamentary expenses;
   (b) [Provision for legacies, house and/or contents to, etc., if intended]
   (c) To divide the residue (hereinafter called "my residuary estate") among such of my children as shall survive me and reach the age of 18 [or 21] years and, if more than one, in equal shares absolutely BUT if any child of mine dies before me or before attaining a vested interest leaving a child or children then such child or children shall on reaching the age of 18 years take *per stirpes* the share his/her or their parent would otherwise have taken, and if more than one, in equal shares absolutely AND I DECLARE that no advancement within the meaning of section 63 of the Succession Act 1965 shall be brought into account in the distribution of my estate;
   (d) To pay to each child on reaching the age of 18 years the annual income of his or her share of my residuary estate until he or she reaches the age of 21 years.

In addition to all statutory powers that my trustees may have, they shall have the following powers:

(i) To exercise the power of appropriation under section 55 of the Succession Act 1965 without serving any of the notices or obtaining any of the required consents.

(ii) To sell, call in or convert into money at such time or times and in such manner as they shall think fit so much of my estate as shall not be in money form, nevertheless to postpone such sale conversion or calling in indefinitely without being liable for any loss.

(iii) To sell any asset comprised in my estate at its full open market value to any one or more of my trustees.

(iv) To borrow any amount of money on the security of all or any assets comprised in the estate or without security and generally on such terms as they shall decide without limitation of any kind.

(v) To apply income derived from my estate for the benefit of any beneficiary under the trust hereby created.

(vi) To invest and change investments freely as if they were absolute owners beneficially entitled and to invest in unsecured interest-free loans or other non-income-producing assets including property for occupation or use by any beneficiary.

(vii) To lease, let, mortgage, charge, licence and generally manage and deal with any land which, or the proceeds of sale of which, may for the time being form part of my estate as if they were the beneficial owners thereof absolutely entitled.

(viii) To lend money or property to any one or more of the beneficiaries either free of interest or on such terms as to payment of interest and generally as the executors shall in their absolute discretion think fit.

(ix) To trade or take part in any venture in the nature of trade whether solely or jointly with any other person and whether or not by way of partnership and for these purposes to make such arrangements as they shall in their absolute discretion think fit and delegate any exercise of this power to any one or more of their number or to a company or partnership formed for this purpose.

(x) To insure against any loss or damage from any peril of any property for the time being comprised in my estate for any amount and to pay the premiums out of my estate.

(xi) To appoint a new, additional or substitutional trustee or trustees of this my will.

All income received after my death shall be treated as income of my estate regardless of the period to which it relates and the statutory rules concerning apportionment and the rules in *Howe v Dartmouth* and *Allhusen v Whittell* shall not be applied.

I declare that any of my trustees who is/are engaged in a profession shall be entitled to be paid fees for work done by him/her or his/her firm on the basis that he/she were not one of my trustees but employed to act on behalf of my trustees.

I declare that no trustee of this my will shall be liable for loss not attributable to the trustee's own dishonesty or wilful commission by the trustee of any act known to be a breach of trust.

In witness whereof I have hereunto signed my name the ... day of ... 20....

SIGNED, PUBLISHED AND DECLARED by the said ... as and for his last will and testament in the presence of us who at his request and in his presence and in the presence of each other (all three being present at the same time) have hereunto subscribed our names as witnesses.

Witness 1 [Name and address]

Witness 2 [Name and address]

Will Trusts by Husband or Civil Partners with Provisions for Children 2–06

I, [name of testator/testatrix] of [address] make this as and for my last will and testament and hereby revoke all former wills and testamentary dispositions heretofore made by me.

1. If my wife/husband/civil partner [name] survives me by thirty days I give, devise and bequeath the whole of my estate to him/her and appoint him/her my executor/executrix. If my wife/husband/civil partner does not survive me by thirty days, the following provisions shall apply:
2. I appoint AB of [address]
   and CD of [address]
   (hereinafter called "my trustees") to be executors and trustees and appoint them trustees for the purposes of the Land and Conveyancing Law Reform Act 2009 and for the purposes of the Conveyancing Acts and for the purposes of section 57 of the Succession Act 1965.
3. I appoint my trustees guardians of my infant children.
4. I give, devise and bequeath to my trustees the whole of my estate upon trust to sell the same (with power to postpone such sale in whole or in part for such time or times as they shall think fit) and to hold the same or the proceeds of sale thereof on the following trusts:
   (a) To pay my debts, funeral expenses and testamentary expenses;
   (b) [Provision for legacies, house and/or contents to, etc., if intended]
   (c) To divide the residue (hereinafter called "my residuary estate") among such of my children as shall survive me and reach the age of 18 [or 21] years and, if more than one, in equal shares absolutely BUT if any child of mine dies before me or before attaining a vested interest leaving a child or children, then such child or children shall on reaching the age of 18 years take *per stirpes* the share his/her or their parent would otherwise have taken, and if more than one, in equal shares absolutely AND I DECLARE that no advancement within the meaning of section 63 of the Succession Act 1965 shall be brought into account in the distribution of my estate;
   (d) To pay to each child on reaching the age of 18 years the annual income of his or her share of my residuary estate until he or she reaches the age of 21 years.

In addition to all statutory powers that my trustees may have, they shall have the following powers:

(i) To exercise the power of appropriation under section 55 of the Succession Act 1965 without serving any of the notices or obtaining any of the required consents.
(ii) To sell, call in or convert into money at such time or times and in such manner as they shall think fit so much of my estate as shall not be in money form, nevertheless to postpone such sale conversion or calling in indefinitely without being liable for any loss.
(iii) To sell any asset comprised in my estate at its full open market value to any one or more of my trustees.
(iv) To borrow any amount of money on the security of all or any assets comprised in the estate or without security and generally on such terms as they shall decide without limitation of any kind.
(v) To apply income derived from my estate for the benefit of any beneficiary under the trust hereby created.

(vi) To invest and change investments freely as if they were absolute owners beneficially entitled and to invest in unsecured interest-free loans or other non-income-producing assets including property for occupation or use by any beneficiary.

(vii) To lease, let, mortgage, charge, licence and generally manage and deal with any land which, or the proceeds of sale of which, may for the time being form part of my estate as if they were the beneficial owners thereof absolutely entitled.

(viii) To lend money or property to any one or more of the beneficiaries either free of interest or on such terms as to payment of interest and generally as the executors shall in their absolute discretion think fit.

(ix) To trade or take part in any venture in the nature of trade whether solely or jointly with any other person and whether or not by way of partnership and for these purposes to make such arrangements as they shall in their absolute discretion think fit and delegate any exercise of this power to any one or more of their number or to a company or partnership formed for this purpose.

(x) To insure against any loss or damage from any peril of any property for the time being comprised in my estate for any amount and to pay the premiums out of my estate.

(xi) To appoint a new, additional or substitutional trustee or trustees of this my will.

All income received after my death shall be treated as income of my estate regardless of the period to which it relates and the statutory rules concerning apportionment and the rules in *Howe v Dartmouth* and *Allhusen v Whittell* shall not be applied.

I declare that any of my trustees who is/are engaged in a profession shall be entitled to be paid fees for work done by him/her or his/her firm on the basis that he/she were not one of my trustees but employed to act on behalf of my trustees.

I declare that no trustee of this my will shall be liable for loss not attributable to the trustee's own dishonesty or wilful commission by the trustee of any act known to be a breach of trust.

In witness whereof I have hereunto signed my name the … day of … 20….

SIGNED, PUBLISHED AND DECLARED by the said … as and for his last will and testament in the presence of us who at his request and in his presence and in the presence of each other (all three being present at the same time) have hereunto subscribed our names as witnesses.

Witness 1 [Name and address]

Witness 2 [Name and address]

2–07 Will Trusts by Husband to Wife for Life or Civil Partner to Civil Partner with Gifts Over

I, [name of testator/testatrix] of [address] make this as and for my last will and testament and hereby revoke all former wills and testamentary dispositions heretofore made by me.

1. I appoint
   AB of [address] and

CD of [address]
(hereinafter referred to as "my trustees") to be the executors and trustees of this my will and appoint them trustees for the purposes of the Land and Conveyancing Law Reform Act 2009 and for the purposes of the Conveyancing Acts and for the purposes of section 57 of the Succession Act 1965 and in the event of my wife's/husband's/civil partner's death, I also appoint them guardians of my infant children.

2. My trustees shall hold the whole of my estate upon trust either to retain or sell it on the following trusts:
   (a) To pay my debts, funeral expenses and testamentary expenses;
   (b) To pay the income from the residue to my spouse/civil partner during his/her lifetime and after his/her death to divide the residue equally among those of my children who survive me and reach the age of 18 [or 21] years, but if any child of mine dies before me or before attaining a vested interest leaving children, then those children shall on reaching the age of 18 years take equally the share which their parent would otherwise have taken AND I DECLARE that no advancement within the meaning of section 63 of the Succession Act 1965 shall be brought into account in the distribution of my estate;
   (c) To pay to each child on reaching the age of 18 years the annual income of his or her share of my estate until he or she reaches the age of 21 years.

In addition to all statutory powers that my trustees may have, they shall have the following powers:

(i) To exercise the power of appropriation under section 55 of the Succession Act 1965 without serving any of the notices or obtaining any of the required consents.
(ii) To sell, call in or convert into money at such time or times and in such manner as they shall think fit so much of my estate as shall not be in money form, nevertheless to postpone such sale conversion or calling in indefinitely without being liable for any loss.
(iii) To sell any asset comprised in my estate at its full open market value to any one or more of my trustees.
(iv) To borrow any amount of money on the security of all or any assets comprised in the estate or without security and generally on such terms as they shall decide without limitation of any kind.
(v) To apply income derived from my estate for the benefit of any beneficiary under the trust hereby created.
(vi) To invest and change investments freely as if they were absolute owners beneficially entitled and to invest in unsecured interest-free loans or other non-income-producing assets including property for occupation or use by any beneficiary.
(vii) To lease, let, mortgage, charge, licence and generally manage and deal with any land which, or the proceeds of sale of which, may for the time being form part of my estate as if they were the beneficial owners thereof absolutely entitled.
(viii) To lend money or property to any one or more of the beneficiaries either free of interest or on such terms as to payment of interest and generally as the executors shall in their absolute discretion think fit.
(ix) To trade or take part in any venture in the nature of trade whether solely or jointly with any other person and whether or not by way of partnership and for these purposes to make such arrangements as they shall in their absolute discretion think fit and delegate any exercise of this power to any one or more of their number or to a company or partnership formed for this purpose.
(x) To insure against any loss or damage from any peril of any property

for the time being comprised in my estate for any amount and to pay the premiums out of my estate.

(xi) To appoint a new, additional or substitutional trustee or trustees of this my will.

All income received after my death shall be treated as income of my estate regardless of the period to which it relates and the statutory rules concerning apportionment and the rules in *Howe v Dartmouth* and *Allhusen v Whittell* shall not be applied.

I declare that any of my trustees who is/are engaged in a profession shall be entitled to be paid fees for work done by him/her or his/her firm on the basis that he/she were not one of my trustees but employed to act on behalf of my trustees.

I declare that no trustee of this my will shall be liable for loss not attributable to the trustee's own dishonesty or wilful commission by the trustee of any act known to be a breach of trust.

In witness whereof I have hereunto signed my name the ... day of ... 20....

SIGNED, PUBLISHED AND DECLARED by the said ... as and for his last will and testament in the presence of us who at his request and in his presence and in the presence of each other (all three being present at the same time) have hereunto subscribed our names as witnesses.

Witness 1 [Name and address]

Witness 2 [Name and address]

2–08 Will Trusts by Wife to Husband for Life or Civil Partner to Civil Partner for Life with Gifts Over

I, [name of testator/testatrix] of [address] make this as and for my last will and testament and hereby revoke all former wills and testamentary dispositions heretofore made by me.

1. I appoint
   AB of [address] and
   CD of [address]
   (hereinafter referred to as "my trustees") to be the executors and trustees of this my will and appoint them trustees for the purposes of the Land and Conveyancing Law Reform Act 2009 and for the purposes of the Conveyancing Acts and for the purposes of section 57 of the Succession Act 1965 and in the event of my wife's/husband's/civil partner's death, I also appoint them guardians of my infant children.
2. My trustees shall hold the whole of my estate upon trust either to retain or sell it on the following trusts:
   (a) To pay my debts, funeral expenses and testamentary expenses;
   (b) To pay the income from the residue to my spouse/civil partner during his/her lifetime and after his/her death to divide the residue equally among those of my children who survive me and reach the age of 18 [or 21] years but if any child of mine dies before me or before attaining a vested interest leaving children, then those children shall on reaching the age of 18 years take equally the share which their parent would otherwise have taken AND I DECLARE that no advancement within

the meaning of section 63 of the Succession Act 1965 shall be brought into account in the distribution of my estate;

(c) To pay to each child on reaching the age of 18 years the annual income of his or her share of my estate until he or she reaches the age of 21 years.

In addition to all statutory powers that my trustees may have, they shall have the following powers:

(i) To exercise the power of appropriation under section 55 of the Succession Act 1965 without serving any of the notices or obtaining any of the required consents.

(ii) To sell, call in or convert into money at such time or times and in such manner as they shall think fit so much of my estate as shall not be in money form, nevertheless to postpone such sale conversion or calling in indefinitely without being liable for any loss.

(iii) To sell any asset comprised in my estate at its full open market value to any one or more of my trustees.

(iv) To borrow any amount of money on the security of all or any assets comprised in the estate or without security and generally on such terms as they shall decide without limitation of any kind.

(v) To apply income derived from my estate for the benefit of any beneficiary under the trust hereby created.

(vi) To invest and change investments freely as if they were absolute owners beneficially entitled and to invest in unsecured interest-free loans or other non-income-producing assets including property for occupation or use by any beneficiary.

(vii) To lease, let, mortgage, charge, licence and generally manage and deal with any land which, or the proceeds of sale of which, may for the time being form part of my estate as if they were the beneficial owners thereof absolutely entitled.

(viii) To lend money or property to any one or more of the beneficiaries either free of interest or on such terms as to payment of interest and generally as the executors shall in their absolute discretion think fit.

(ix) To trade or take part in any venture in the nature of trade whether solely or jointly with any other person and whether or not by way of partnership and for these purposes to make such arrangements as they shall in their absolute discretion think fit and delegate any exercise of this power to any one or more of their number or to a company or partnership formed for this purpose.

(x) To insure against any loss or damage from any peril of any property for the time being comprised in my estate for any amount and to pay the premiums out of my estate.

(xi) To appoint a new, additional or substitutional trustee or trustees of this my will.

All income received after my death shall be treated as income of my estate regardless of the period to which it relates and the statutory rules concerning apportionment and the rules in *Howe v Dartmouth* and *Allhusen v Whittell* shall not be applied.

I declare that any of my trustees who is/are engaged in a profession shall be entitled to be paid fees for work done by him/her or his/her firm on the basis that he/she were not one of my trustees but employed to act on behalf of my trustees.

I declare that no trustee of this my will shall be liable for loss not attributable to the trustee's own dishonesty or wilful commission by the trustee of any act known to be a breach of trust.

In witness whereof I have hereunto signed my name the ... day of ... 20....

SIGNED, PUBLISHED AND DECLARED by the said ... as and for his last will and testament in the presence of us who at his request and in his presence and in the presence of each other (all three being present at the same time) have hereunto subscribed our names as witnesses.

Witness 1 [Name and address]

Witness 2 [Name and address]

2–09 Will Trusts of Residuary Personal Estate by Father for Children

I, [name of testator] of [address] make this as and for my last will and testament and hereby revoke all former wills and testamentary dispositions heretofore made by me.

1. I appoint
   AB of [address]
   and CD of [address]
   (hereinafter called "my trustees") to be executors and trustees and appoint them trustees for the purposes of the Land and Conveyancing Law Reform Act 2009 and for the purposes of the Conveyancing Acts and for the purposes of section 57 of the Succession Act 1965.
2. I appoint my trustees guardians of my infant son/daughter.
3. I give, devise and bequeath to my trustees all of my residuary personal estate upon trust to sell the same (with power to postpone such sale in whole or in part for such time or times as they shall think fit) and to hold the same or the proceeds of sale thereof on the following trusts:
   (a) To pay my debts, funeral expenses and testamentary expenses;
   (b) [Provision for legacies, house and/or contents to, etc., if intended]
   (c) To divide the residue (hereinafter called "my residuary personal estate") among such of my children as shall survive me and reach the age of 18 [or 21] years and, if more than one, in equal shares absolutely, BUT if any child of mine dies before me, or before attaining a vested interest, leaving a child or children, then such child or children shall on reaching the age of 18 years take *per stirpes* the share his/her or their parent would otherwise have taken, and if more than one, in equal shares absolutely AND I DECLARE that no advancement within the meaning of section 63 of the Succession Act 1965 shall be brought into account in the distribution of my estate;
   (d) To pay to my son/daughter on reaching the age of 18 years the annual income of his or her share of my residuary estate until he or she reaches the age of 21 years.

In addition to all statutory powers that my trustees may have, they shall have the following powers:

(i) To exercise the power of appropriation under section 55 of the Succession Act 1965 without serving any of the notices or obtaining any of the required consents.
(ii) To sell, call in or convert into money at such time or times and in such manner as they shall think fit so much of my estate as shall not be in money form, nevertheless to postpone such sale conversion or calling in indefinitely without being liable for any loss.

(iii) To sell any asset comprised in my estate at its full open market value to any one or more of my trustees.
(iv) To borrow any amount of money on the security of all or any assets comprised in the estate or without security and generally on such terms as they shall decide without limitation of any kind.
(v) To apply income derived from my estate for the benefit of any beneficiary under the trust hereby created.
(vi) To invest and change investments freely as if they were absolute owners beneficially entitled and to invest in unsecured interest-free loans or other non-income-producing assets including property for occupation or use by any beneficiary.
(vii) To lease, let, mortgage, charge, licence and generally manage and deal with any land which, or the proceeds of sale of which, may for the time being form part of my estate as if they were the beneficial owners thereof absolutely entitled.
(viii) To lend money or property to any one or more of the beneficiaries either free of interest or on such terms as to payment of interest and generally as the executors shall in their absolute discretion think fit.
(ix) To trade or take part in any venture in the nature of trade whether solely or jointly with any other person and whether or not by way of partnership and for these purposes to make such arrangements as they shall in their absolute discretion think fit and delegate any exercise of this power to any one or more of their number or to a company or partnership formed for this purpose.
(x) To insure against any loss or damage from any peril of any property for the time being comprised in my estate for any amount and to pay the premiums out of my estate.
(xi) To appoint a new, additional or substitutional trustee or trustees of this my will.

All income received after my death shall be treated as income of my estate regardless of the period to which it relates and the statutory rules concerning apportionment and the rules in *Howe v Dartmouth* and *Allhusen v Whittell* shall not be applied.

I declare that any of my trustees who is/are engaged in a profession shall be entitled to be paid fees for work done by him/her or his/her firm on the basis that he/she were not one of my trustees but employed to act on behalf of my trustees.

I declare that no trustee of this my will shall be liable for loss not attributable to the trustee's own dishonesty or wilful commission by the trustee of any act known to be a breach of trust.

In witness whereof I have hereunto signed my name the ... day of ... 20....

SIGNED, PUBLISHED AND DECLARED by the said ... as and for his last will and testament in the presence of us who at his request and in his presence and in the presence of each other (all three being present at the same time) have hereunto subscribed our names as witnesses.

Witness 1 [Name and address]

Witness 2 [Name and address]

2–10 Residuary Estate in Trust for Testator's Children in Equal Shares

I, [name of testator] of [address] make this as and for my last will and testament and hereby revoke all former wills and testamentary dispositions heretofore made by me.

1. I appoint
   AB of [address]
   and CD of [address]
   (hereinafter called "my trustees") to be executors and trustees and appoint them trustees for the purposes of the Land and Conveyancing Law Reform Act 2009 and for the purposes of the Conveyancing Acts and for the purposes of section 57 of the Succession Act 1965.
2. I appoint my trustees guardians of my infant son/daughter.
3. I give, devise and bequeath to my trustees the whole of my estate upon trust to sell the same (with power to postpone such sale in whole or in part for such time or times as they shall think fit) and to hold the same or the proceeds of sale thereof on the following trusts:
   (a) To pay my debts, funeral expenses and testamentary expenses;
   (b) [Provision for legacies, house and/or contents to, etc., if intended]
   (c) To hold the residue (hereinafter called "my residuary estate") in trust for my son and daughter until he/she attains the age of 21 years [or 18 years] in equal shares absolutely AND I DECLARE that no advancement within the meaning of section 63 of the Succession Act 1965 shall be brought into account in the distribution of my estate;
   (d) To pay to my son/daughter on reaching the age of 18 years the annual income of his or her share of my residuary estate until he or she reaches the age of 21 years.

In addition to all statutory powers that my trustees may have, they shall have the following powers:

(i) To exercise the power of appropriation under section 55 of the Succession Act 1965 without serving any of the notices or obtaining any of the required consents.
(ii) To sell, call in or convert into money at such time or times and in such manner as they shall think fit so much of my estate as shall not be in money form, nevertheless to postpone such sale conversion or calling in indefinitely without being liable for any loss.
(iii) To sell any asset comprised in my estate at its full open market value to any one or more of my trustees.
(iv) To borrow any amount of money on the security of all or any assets comprised in the estate or without security and generally on such terms as they shall decide without limitation of any kind.
(v) To apply income derived from my estate for the benefit of any beneficiary under the trust hereby created.
(vi) To invest and change investments freely as if they were absolute owners beneficially entitled and to invest in unsecured interest-free loans or other non-income-producing assets including property for occupation or use by any beneficiary.
(vii) To lease, let, mortgage, charge, licence and generally manage and deal with any land which, or the proceeds of sale of which, may for the time being form part of my estate as if they were the beneficial owners thereof absolutely entitled.
(viii) To lend money or property to any one or more of the beneficiaries either free of interest or on such terms as to payment of interest and generally as the executors shall in their absolute discretion think fit.
(ix) To trade or take part in any venture in the nature of trade whether solely or jointly with any other person and whether or not by way of partnership

and for these purposes to make such arrangements as they shall in their absolute discretion think fit and delegate any exercise of this power to any one or more of their number or to a company or partnership formed for this purpose.

(x) To insure against any loss or damage from any peril of any property for the time being comprised in my estate for any amount and to pay the premiums out of my estate.

(xi) To appoint a new, additional or substitutional trustee or trustees of this my will.

All income received after my death shall be treated as income of my estate regardless of the period to which it relates and the statutory rules concerning apportionment and the rules in *Howe v Dartmouth* and *Allhusen v Whittell* shall not be applied.

I declare that any of my trustees who is/are engaged in a profession shall be entitled to be paid fees for work done by him/her or his/her firm on the basis that he/she were not one of my trustees but employed to act on behalf of my trustees.

I declare that no trustee of this my will shall be liable for loss not attributable to the trustee's own dishonesty or wilful commission by the trustee of any act known to be a breach of trust.

In witness whereof I have hereunto signed my name the … day of … 20….

SIGNED, PUBLISHED AND DECLARED by the said … as and for his last will and testament in the presence of us who at his request and in his presence and in the presence of each other (all three being present at the same time) have hereunto subscribed our names as witnesses.

Witness 1 [Name and address]

Witness 2 [Name and address]

Residuary Estate in Trust for Testator's Children Jointly **2–11**

I, [name of testator] of [address] make this as and for my last will and testament and hereby revoke all former wills and testamentary dispositions heretofore made by me.

1. I appoint
   AB of [address]
   and CD of [address]
   (hereinafter called "my trustees") to be executors and trustees and appoint them trustees for the purposes of the Land and Conveyancing Law Reform Act 2009 and for the purposes of the Conveyancing Acts and for the purposes of section 57 of the Succession Act 1965.
2. I appoint my trustees guardians of my infant son/daughter.
3. I give, devise and bequeath to my trustees the whole of my estate upon trust to sell the same (with power to postpone such sale in whole or in part for such time or times as they shall think fit) and to hold the same or the proceeds of sale thereof on the following trusts:
   (a) To pay my debts, funeral expenses and testamentary expenses;
   (b) [Provision for legacies, house and/or contents to, etc., if intended]
   (c) To hold the residue (hereinafter called "my residuary estate") in trust

for my son and daughter until he/she attains the age of 21 years [or 18 years] jointly and absolutely.

In addition to all statutory powers that my trustees may have, they shall have the following powers:

(i) To exercise the power of appropriation under section 55 of the Succession Act 1965 without serving any of the notices or obtaining any of the required consents.

(ii) To sell, call in or convert into money at such time or times and in such manner as they shall think fit so much of my estate as shall not be in money form, nevertheless to postpone such sale conversion or calling in indefinitely without being liable for any loss.

(iii) To sell any asset comprised in my estate at its full open market value to any one or more of my trustees.

(iv) To borrow any amount of money on the security of all or any assets comprised in the estate or without security and generally on such terms as they shall decide without limitation of any kind.

(v) To apply income derived from my estate for the benefit of any beneficiary under the trust hereby created.

(vi) To invest and change investments freely as if they were absolute owners beneficially entitled and to invest in unsecured interest-free loans or other non-income-producing assets including property for occupation or use by any beneficiary.

(vii) To lease, let, mortgage, charge, licence and generally manage and deal with any land which, or the proceeds of sale of which, may for the time being form part of my estate as if they were the beneficial owners thereof absolutely entitled.

(viii) To lend money or property to any one or more of the beneficiaries either free of interest or on such terms as to payment of interest and generally as the executors shall in their absolute discretion think fit.

(ix) To trade or take part in any venture in the nature of trade whether solely or jointly with any other person and whether or not by way of partnership and for these purposes to make such arrangements as they shall in their absolute discretion think fit and delegate any exercise of this power to any one or more of their number or to a company or partnership formed for this purpose.

(x) To insure against any loss or damage from any peril of any property for the time being comprised in my estate for any amount and to pay the premiums out of my estate.

(xi) To appoint a new, additional or substitutional trustee or trustees of this my will.

All income received after my death shall be treated as income of my estate regardless of the period to which it relates and the statutory rules concerning apportionment and the rules in *Howe v Dartmouth* and *Allhusen v Whittell* shall not be applied.

I declare that any of my trustees who is/are engaged in a profession shall be entitled to be paid fees for work done by him/her or his/her firm on the basis that he/she were not one of my trustees but employed to act on behalf of my trustees.

I declare that no trustee of this my will shall be liable for loss not attributable to the trustee's own dishonesty or wilful commission by the trustee of any act known to be a breach of trust.

In witness whereof I have hereunto signed my name the … day of … 20….

SIGNED, PUBLISHED AND DECLARED by the said ... as and for his last will and testament in the presence of us who at his request and in his presence and in the presence of each other (all three being present at the same time) have hereunto subscribed our names as witnesses.

Witness 1 [Name and address]

Witness 2 [Name and address]

Residuary Estate in Trust for Testator's Children in Equal Shares 2–12

I, [name of testator] of [address] make this as and for my last will and testament and hereby revoke all former wills and testamentary dispositions heretofore made by me.

1. I appoint
   AB of [address]
   and CD of [address]
   (hereinafter called "my trustees") to be executors and trustees and appoint them trustees for the purposes of the Land and Conveyancing Law Reform Act 2009 and for the purposes of the Conveyancing Acts and for the purposes of section 57 of the Succession Act 1965.
2. I appoint my trustees guardians of my infant son/daughter.
4. I give, devise and bequeath to my trustees the whole of my estate upon trust to sell the same (with power to postpone such sale in whole or in part for such time or times as they shall think fit) and to hold the same or the proceeds of sale thereof on the following trusts:
   (a) To pay my debts, funeral expenses and testamentary expenses;
   (b) [Provision for legacies, house and/or contents to, etc., if intended]
   (c) To hold the residue (hereinafter called "my residuary estate") in trust for my son/daughter until he/she attains the age of 21 years [or 18 years] in equal shares absolutely AND I DECLARE that no advancement within the meaning of section 63 of the Succession Act 1965 shall be brought into account in the distribution of my estate;
   (d) To pay to my son/daughter on reaching the age of 18 years the annual income of his or her share of my residuary estate until he or she reaches the age of 21 years.

In addition to all statutory powers that my trustees may have, they shall have the following powers:

(i) To exercise the power of appropriation under section 55 of the Succession Act 1965 without serving any of the notices or obtaining any of the required consents.
(ii) To sell, call in or convert into money at such time or times and in such manner as they shall think fit so much of my estate as shall not be in money form, nevertheless to postpone such sale conversion or calling in indefinitely without being liable for any loss.
(iii) To sell any asset comprised in my estate at its full open market value to any one or more of my trustees.
(iv) To borrow any amount of money on the security of all or any assets comprised in the estate or without security and generally on such terms as they shall decide without limitation of any kind.
(v) To apply income derived from my estate for the benefit of any beneficiary under the trust hereby created.
(vi) To invest and change investments freely as if they were absolute owners beneficially entitled and to invest in unsecured interest-free loans or

other non-income-producing assets including property for occupation or use by any beneficiary.

(vii) To lease, let, mortgage, charge, licence and generally manage and deal with any land which, or the proceeds of sale of which, may for the time being form part of my estate as if they were the beneficial owners thereof absolutely entitled.

(viii) To lend money or property to any one or more of the beneficiaries either free of interest or on such terms as to payment of interest and generally as the executors shall in their absolute discretion think fit.

(ix) To trade or take part in any venture in the nature of trade whether solely or jointly with any other person and whether or not by way of partnership and for these purposes to make such arrangements as they shall in their absolute discretion think fit and delegate any exercise of this power to any one or more of their number or to a company or partnership formed for this purpose.

(x) To insure against any loss or damage from any peril of any property for the time being comprised in my estate for any amount and to pay the premiums out of my estate.

(xi) To appoint a new, additional or substitutional trustee or trustees of this my will.

All income received after my death shall be treated as income of my estate regardless of the period to which it relates and the statutory rules concerning apportionment and the rules in *Howe v Dartmouth* and *Allhusen v Whittell* shall not be applied.

I declare that any of my trustees who is/are engaged in a profession shall be entitled to be paid fees for work done by him/her or his/her firm on the basis that he/she were not one of my trustees but employed to act on behalf of my trustees.

I declare that no trustee of this my will shall be liable for loss not attributable to the trustee's own dishonesty or wilful commission by the trustee of any act known to be a breach of trust.

In witness whereof I have hereunto signed my name the … day of … 20….

SIGNED, PUBLISHED AND DECLARED by the said … as and for his last will and testament in the presence of us who at his request and in his presence and in the presence of each other (all three being present at the same time) have hereunto subscribed our names as witnesses.

Witness 1 [Name and address]

Witness 2 [Name and address]

2–13 Residuary Estate in Trust for Testator's Children Jointly

I, [name of testator] of [address] make this as and for my last will and testament and hereby revoke all former wills and testamentary dispositions heretofore made by me.

1. I appoint
   AB of [address]
   and CD of [address]
   (hereinafter called "my trustees") to be executors and trustees and appoint them trustees for the purposes of the Land and Conveyancing Law Reform

Act 2009 and for the purposes of the Conveyancing Acts and for the purposes of section 57 of the Succession Act 1965.

2. I appoint my trustees guardians of my infant son/daughter.
3. I give, devise and bequeath to my trustees the whole of my estate upon trust to sell the same (with power to postpone such sale in whole or in part for such time or times as they shall think fit) and to hold the same or the proceeds of sale thereof on the following trusts:
   (a) To pay my debts, funeral expenses and testamentary expenses;
   (b) [Provision for legacies, house and/or contents to, etc., if intended]
   (c) To hold the residue (hereinafter called "my residuary estate") in trust for my son/daughter until he/she attains the age of 21 years [or 18 years], BUT if my son/daughter should die before me or before attaining a vested interest, leaving a child or children, then such child or children shall on reaching the age of 21 years [or 18 years] take the share my son/daughter would otherwise have taken, and if more than one, jointly and absolutely.

In addition to all statutory powers that my trustees may have, they shall have the following powers:

(i) To exercise the power of appropriation under section 55 of the Succession Act 1965 without serving any of the notices or obtaining any of the required consents.
(ii) To sell, call in or convert into money at such time or times and in such manner as they shall think fit so much of my estate as shall not be in money form, nevertheless to postpone such sale conversion or calling in indefinitely without being liable for any loss.
(iii) To sell any asset comprised in my estate at its full open market value to any one or more of my trustees.
(iv) To borrow any amount of money on the security of all or any assets comprised in the estate or without security and generally on such terms as they shall decide without limitation of any kind.
(v) To apply income derived from my estate for the benefit of any beneficiary under the trust hereby created.
(vi) To invest and change investments freely as if they were absolute owners beneficially entitled and to invest in unsecured interest-free loans or other non-income-producing assets including property for occupation or use by any beneficiary.
(vii) To lease, let, mortgage, charge, licence and generally manage and deal with any land which, or the proceeds of sale of which, may for the time being form part of my estate as if they were the beneficial owners thereof absolutely entitled.
(viii) To lend money or property to any one or more of the beneficiaries either free of interest or on such terms as to payment of interest and generally as the executors shall in their absolute discretion think fit.
(ix) To trade or take part in any venture in the nature of trade whether solely or jointly with any other person and whether or not by way of partnership and for these purposes to make such arrangements as they shall in their absolute discretion think fit and delegate any exercise of this power to any one or more of their number or to a company or partnership formed for this purpose.
(x) To insure against any loss or damage from any peril of any property for the time being comprised in my estate for any amount and to pay the premiums out of my estate.
(xi) To appoint a new, additional or substitutional trustee or trustees of this my will.

All income received after my death shall be treated as income of my estate regardless of the period to which it relates and the statutory rules concerning apportionment and the rules in *Howe v Dartmouth* and *Allhusen v Whittell* shall not be applied.

I declare that any of my trustees who is/are engaged in a profession shall be entitled to be paid fees for work done by him/her or his/her firm on the basis that he/she were not one of my trustees but employed to act on behalf of my trustees.

I declare that no trustee of this my will shall be liable for loss not attributable to the trustee's own dishonesty or wilful commission by the trustee of any act known to be a breach of trust.

In witness whereof I have hereunto signed my name the … day of … 20….

SIGNED, PUBLISHED AND DECLARED by the said … as and for his last will and testament in the presence of us who at his request and in his presence and in the presence of each other (all three being present at the same time) have hereunto subscribed our names as witnesses.

Witness 1 [Name and address]

Witness 2 [Name and address]

CHAPTER 3

WILL TRUSTS OF LAND

INTRODUCTION

The subject matter of trusts of land created by wills must be clearly identified, otherwise the trusts may be deemed invalid, although the invalidity of the trust will not affect the validity of the will once it has been duly executed.[1] The following provisions emphasised in italics in a will trust may sufficiently identify the subject matter of a trust in a will: **3–01**

> I give, devise and bequeath to my trustees the whole of my estate upon trust to sell the same (with power to postpone such sale in whole or in part for such time or times as they shall think fit) and to hold the same or the proceeds of sale thereof on the following trusts:
> (a) To pay my debts, funeral expenses and testamentary expenses;
> (b) [Provision for legacies, house and/or contents to, etc., if intended]
> (c) *To hold the residue (hereinafter called "my Residuary Estate") in trust* for my son/daughter until he/she attains the age of 21 years [or 18 years] BUT if my son/daughter should die before me or before attaining a vested interest leaving a child or children, then such child or children shall on reaching the age of 21 years [or 18 years] take the share my son/daughter would otherwise have taken, and if one more than one such child, in equal shares absolutely.

Where the subject matter of the trust is land, it may be termed a will trust of land within the meaning of the Land and Conveyancing Law Reform Act 2009 (the "2009 Act"). Section 11(1) of the 2009 Act provides that the only legal estates which may be created or disposed of are the freehold and leasehold estates specified in s 11(2) of the 2009 Act. Section 18(3) of the 2009 Act also provides that a trust of land is governed by the general law of trusts. **3–02**

Trusts of land may also be varied by the courts under ss 23 and 24 of the 2009 Act. The Rules of the Superior Courts (Land and Conveyancing Law Reform Act 2009) 2010 (SI No 149 of 2010) amended the Rules of the Superior Courts 1986 to take account of ss 22, 23 and 24 of the 2009 Act. **3–03**

THE MEANING OF REAL ESTATE

Section 3(1) of the Succession Act 1965 (the "1965 Act") provides that "real **3–04**

---

1 See *Chambers v Fahy* [1931] IR 17 at 21 *per* O'Byrne J; A. Keating, *The Law of Wills* (2nd ed, Clarus Press, Dublin, 2018); A. Keating, *Succession Law in Ireland* (Clarus Press, Dublin, 2015); A. Keating, *Keating on Probate* (5th ed, Round Hall, Dublin, 2015); A. Keating, *Succession Law in Ireland: Principles, Cases and Commentary* (Clarus Press, Dublin, 2016).

estate" has the meaning assigned to it by s 4 of that Act, and s 4(a) provides that "real estate" includes chattels real, and land in possession, remainder, or reversion, and every estate or interest in or over land. Section 14 of the 1965 Act provides that the estate of a deceased person includes references to both his real and personal estate. As real estate includes freeholds and leaseholds, it is important to point out that the meaning of freehold and leasehold estates is now subject to the provisions of the 2009 Act. The 2009 Act also contains provisions dealing with future interests in land and abolishes a significant number of long-established rules. Section 9(1) of the 2009 Act provides that ownership of land comprises the estates specified in Pt 2 of that Act only. The concept of an estate in land is, however, retained by the Act.[2] Section 11(1) of the 2009 Act provides that the only legal estates which may be created or disposed of are the freehold and leasehold estates specified in s 11(2) of the 2009 Act. Section 11(2) provides that:

> A freehold estate means a fee simple in possession and includes:
> (a) A determinable fee,
> (b) A fee simple subject to a right of entry,
> (c) A fee simple subject only to a power of revocation, an annuity or other payment of capital or income for the advancement, maintenance or other benefit of any person, or a right of residence which is not an exclusive right over the whole land.[3]

3–05 A leasehold estate means the estate which arises when a tenancy is created for any period of time or any recurring period and irrespective of whether or not the estate:

> (a) takes effect in immediate possession, or
> (b) is subject to another legal estate or interest, or
> (c) is for a term which is uncertain or liable to termination by notice, re-entry or operation of law or by virtue of a provision for cessor on redemption or for any other reason.

The Creation of Will Trusts of Land

3–06 Prior to the enactment of the 2009 Act, the Settled Land Acts 1882–1890 governed all settlements and trusts of land created by testators.[4] The Settled Land Acts 1882–1890 have now been repealed and replaced by the 2009 Act, and the various kinds of settlements and trusts relating to land will now comprise a "trust of land" for the purposes of s 18 of the 2009 Act. A trust of land covers every kind of settlement (whether or not the instrument creating it creates an express trust), holding trusts and trusts for sale whereby land is to be held for persons in succession to each other, and any other

---

2 s 10(1) of the 2009 Act.

3 See s 11(2) of the 2009 Act.

4 See A. Keating, *The Law of Wills* (2nd ed, Clarus Press, Dublin, 2018); A. Keating, *Irish Wills Precedents Service* (Round Hall, Dublin, 2009); A. Keating, "The Effect of the Land and Conveyancing Law Reform Act 2009 on Wills Precedents Referring to the Settled Land Acts and Conveyancing Acts" (2010) 28 ILT 252.

situation where land is subject to a trust, including a constructive or resulting trust declared by a court. It also covers the situation where land is owned by a minor which is the same position as that under the Settled Land Acts 1882–1890. The only exception to this rule is in s 18(9), where land is held directly for a charitable purpose. The law relating to charities gives rise to special considerations and they have long been the subject of special legislation such as the Charities Acts 1961 and 1973 and the Charities Act 2009.[5] Section 18(1) of the 2009 Act (replacing ss 2, 59 and 60 of the Settled Land Act 1882) now provides that there is trust of land for purposes of Pt 4 of the 2009 Act where land is:

(a) for the time being limited by an instrument, whenever executed, to persons by way of succession without the interposition of a trust—this is referred to as a "strict settlement", and under s 18(2)(a), a strict settlement exists where an estate or interest in reversion or remainder is not disposed of and reverts to the settlor or the testator's successors in title, but does not exist where a person owns a fee simple in possession—or
(b) held, either with or without other property, on a trust whenever it arises and of whatever kind—under s 18(2)(b), a trust includes an express, implied, resulting, constructive and bare trust and a trust for sale—or
(c) vested, whether before or after the commencement of the 2009 Act, in a minor.

The following precedents may be used as guidelines for the creation of will trusts of land: **3–07**

Will Trusts of Residuary Real Estate by Father for Son/Daughter **3–08**

I [name of testator] of [address] make this as and for my last will and testament and hereby revoke all former wills and testamentary dispositions heretofore made by me.

1. I appoint AB of [address]
   and CD of [address]
   (hereinafter called "my trustees") to be executors and trustees and appoint them trustees for the purposes of the Land and Conveyancing Law Reform Act 2009 and for the purposes of the Conveyancing Acts and for the purposes of s 57 of the Succession Act 1965.
2. I appoint my trustees guardians of my infant son/daughter.
3. I give devise and bequeath to my trustees my residuary real estate upon trust to sell the same (with power to postpone such sale in whole or in part for such time or times as they shall think fit) and to hold the same or the proceeds of sale thereof on the following trusts:
   (a) To pay my debts, funeral expenses and testamentary expenses;
   (b) [Provision for legacies, house and/or contents to, etc., if intended]
   (c) To hold the residue (hereinafter called "my Residuary Real Estate") in trust for my son/daughter until he/she attains the age of 21 years [or 18 years] BUT if my son/daughter should die before me or before attaining a vested interest leaving a child or children, then such child or children shall on reaching the age of 21 years [or 18 years] take the share my son/daughter would otherwise have taken, and if in equal shares absolutely AND I DECLARE that no advancement within the

[5] See Ch 5: Charitable Will Trusts.

meaning of section 63 of the Succession Act 1965 shall be brought into account in the distribution of my estate;

(d) To pay to my son/daughter on reaching the age of 18 years the annual income of his or her share of my Residuary Estate until he or she reaches the age of 21 years.

In addition to all statutory powers that my Trustees may have they shall have the following powers:

(i) To exercise the power of appropriation under section 55 of the Succession Act 1965 without serving any of the notices or obtaining any of the required consents.

(ii) To sell, call in or convert into money at such time or times and in such manner as they shall think fit so much of my estate as shall not be in money form, nevertheless to postpone such sale conversion or calling in indefinitely without being liable for any loss.

(iii) To sell any asset comprised in my estate at its full open market value to any one or more of my trustees.

(iv) To borrow any amount of money on the security of all or any assets comprised in the estate or without security and generally on such terms as they shall decide without limitation of any kind.

(v) To apply income derived from my estate for the benefit of any beneficiary under the trust hereby created.

(vi) To invest and change investments freely as if they were absolute owners beneficially entitled and to invest in unsecured interest free loans or other non-income-producing assets including property for occupation or use by any beneficiary.

(vii) To lease, let, mortgage, charge, licence and generally manage and deal with any land which, or the proceeds of sale of which, may for the time being form part of my estate as they were the beneficial owners thereof absolutely entitled.

(viii) To lend money or property to any one or more of the beneficiaries either free of interest or on such terms as to payment of interest and generally as the executors shall in their absolute discretion think fit.

(ix) To trade or take part in any venture in the nature of trade whether solely or jointly with any other person and whether or not by way of partnership and for these purposes to make such arrangements as they shall in their absolute discretion think fit and delegate any exercise of this power to any one or more of their number or to a company or partnership formed for this purpose.

(x) To insure against any loss or damage from any peril of any property for the time being comprised in my estate for any amount and to pay the premiums out of my estate.

(xi) To appoint a new, additional or substitutional trustee or trustees of this my will.

All income received after my death shall be treated as income of my estate regardless of the period to which it relates and the statutory rules concerning apportionment and the rules in *Howe v Dartmouth* and *Allhusen v Whittell* shall not be applied.

I declare that any of my trustees who is/are engaged in a profession shall be entitled to be paid fees for work done by him/her or his/her firm on the basis that he/she were not one of my trustees but employed to act on behalf of my trustees.

I declare that no trustee of this my will shall be liable for loss not attributable to the trustee's own dishonesty or wilful commission by the trustee of any act known to be a breach of trust.

In witness whereof I have hereunto signed my name the … day of … 20….

SIGNED, PUBLISHED AND DECLARED by the said … as and for his last will and testament in the presence of us who at his request and in his presence and in the presence of each other (all three being present at the same time) have hereunto subscribed our names as witnesses.

Witness 1 [name and address]

Witness 2 [name and address]

Will Trusts of Residuary Real Estate by Mother for Son/Daughter 3–09

I [name of testatrix] of [address] make this as and for my last will and testament and hereby revoke all former wills and testamentary dispositions heretofore made by me.

1. I appoint AB of [address]
   and CD of [address]
   (hereinafter called "my trustees") to be executors and trustees and appoint them trustees for the purposes of the Land and Conveyancing Law Reform Act 2009 and for the purposes of the Conveyancing Acts and for the purposes of s 57 of the Succession Act 1965.
2. I appoint my trustees guardians of my infant son/daughter.
3. I give devise and bequeath to my trustees my residuary real estate upon trust to sell the same (with power to postpone such sale in whole or in part for such time or times as they shall think fit) and to hold the same or the proceeds of sale thereof on the following trusts:
   (a) To pay my debts, funeral expenses and testamentary expenses;
   (b) [Provision for legacies, house and/or contents to, etc., if intended]
   (c) To hold the residue (hereinafter called "my Residuary Real Estate") in trust for my son/daughter until he/she attains the age of 21 years [or 18 years] BUT if my son/daughter should die before me or before attaining a vested interest leaving a child or children, then such child or children shall on reaching the age of 21 years [or 18 years] take the share my son/daughter would otherwise have taken, and if , in equal shares absolutely AND I DECLARE that no advancement within the meaning of section 63 of the Succession Act 1965 shall be brought into account in the distribution of my estate;
   (d) To pay to my son/daughter on reaching the age of 18 years the annual income of his or her share of my Residuary Estate until he or she reaches the age of 21 years.

Variation of Trusts of Land

Sections 23 and 24 of the 2009 Act deal with applications to vary trusts and the jurisdiction of the courts to hear such applications. The Rules of the Superior Courts (Land and Conveyancing Law Reform Act 2009) 2010 (SI No 149 of 2010), amended the Rules of the Superior Courts 1986 to take account of ss 22, 23 and 24 of the 2009 Act. The amended Rules include the provision that: 3–10

2. (1) Proceedings for the following reliefs under the Act shall be commenced by special summons in accordance with Order 3:
  (a) an order to resolve a dispute mentioned in section 22;
  (b) an order to approve an arrangement specified in an application under section 24.

(i) Definitions and Interpretations for the Purposes of the 2009 Act

3–11 Section 23 of the 2009 Act defines "appropriate person", "arrangement", "relevant person" and "relevant trust" for the purposes of variation of trusts, as follows:

'appropriate person', in relation to a relevant trust, means—
  (a) a trustee of, or a beneficiary under, the trust, or
  (b) any other person that the court, to which the application concerned under section 24 is made, considers appropriate;

'arrangement', in relation to a relevant trust, means an arrangement—
  (a) varying, revoking or resettling the trust, or
  (b) varying, enlarging, adding to or restricting the powers of the trustees under the trust to manage or administer the property the subject of the trust;

'relevant person', in relation to a relevant trust, means—
  (a) a person who has a vested or contingent interest under the trust but who is incapable of assenting to an arrangement by reason of lack of capacity (whether by reason of minority or absence of mental capacity),
  (b) an unborn person,
  (c) a person whose identity, existence or whereabouts cannot be established by taking reasonable measures, or
  (d) a person who has a contingent interest under the trust but who does not fall within paragraph (a);

'relevant trust'—
  (a) subject to paragraph (b), means a trust arising, whether before, on or after the commencement of this section, under a will, settlement or other disposition,
  (b) does not include—
    (i) a trust created for a charitable purpose within the meaning of the Charities Acts 1961 and 1973 and the Charities Act 2009,
    (ii) an occupational pension scheme within the meaning of the Pensions Act 1990 established under a trust,
    (iii) a trust created by a British statute,
    (iv) a trust created by a Saorstát Éireann statute, or
    (v) a trust created by an Act of the Oireachtas, whether passed before, on or after the commencement of this section.

(ii) Applications to the Court under Section 24 of the 2009 Act

3–12 Under s 24(1) of the 2009 Act:

(1) An appropriate person may make, in respect of a relevant trust, an application to the court for an order to approve an arrangement specified in the application

for the benefit of a relevant person specified in the application if the arrangement has been assented to in writing by each other person (if any) who—

(a) is not a relevant person,
(b) is beneficially interested in the trust, and
(c) is capable of assenting to the arrangement.

(2) The court shall not hear an application made to it under subsection (1) in respect of a relevant trust unless it is satisfied that the applicant has given notice in writing of the application—

(a) to the Revenue Commissioners, and
(b) to such persons as may be prescribed by rules of court,

at least 2 weeks before the hearing of the application.

(3) The court may hear an application made to it under subsection (1) otherwise than in public if it considers that it is appropriate to do so.

(4) The court shall determine an application made to it under subsection (1) in respect of a relevant trust—

(a) subject to paragraph (b), by making an order approving the arrangement specified in the application if it is satisfied that the carrying out of the arrangement would be for the benefit of—
  (i) the relevant person specified in the application, and
  (ii) any other relevant person,
(b) by refusing to make such an order in any case where—
  (i) the court is not satisfied as referred to in paragraph (a), or
  (ii) the Revenue Commissioners have satisfied the court that the application is substantially motivated by a desire to avoid, or reduce the incidence of, tax.

(5) In determining under subsection (4) whether an arrangement would be for the benefit of a relevant person, the court may have regard to any benefit or detriment, financial or otherwise, that may accrue to that person directly or indirectly in consequence of the arrangement.

(6) Nothing in this section shall be construed as derogating from or affecting the operation of—

(a) the Charities Acts 1961 and 1973 and the Charities Act 2009,
(b) any power of a court, whether under an enactment or rule of law, to—
  (i) vary, revoke or resettle a trust (including a relevant trust), or
  (ii) vary, enlarge, add to or restrict the powers of the trustees under a trust (including a relevant trust) to manage or administer the property the subject of the trust.

CHAPTER 4

DISCRETIONARY WILL TRUSTS

INTRODUCTION

Where a testator decides to create a discretionary trust in his or her will giving the trustees discretionary powers over the operation of the trust provisions, such a will trust may be termed a discretionary will trust. A discretionary trust is one that empowers the trustees to pay or apply any part or parts of the capital and income of the trust fund to "all or any one or more" of the beneficiaries, but without giving a beneficiary a right to any part of the capital or income of the trust fund. **4–01**

THE CREATION OF DISCRETIONARY WILL TRUSTS

The following precedents may be used as guidelines for the creation of discretionary will trusts: **4–02**

(i) Discretionary Will Trusts by Grandfather for Grandchildren **4–03**

I, [name of testator] of [address] make this as and for my last will and testament and hereby revoke all former wills and testamentary dispositions heretofore made by me.

1. I appoint
   AB of [address]
   and CD of [address]
   to be the executors and trustees of this my last will (hereinafter called "my trustees") and I direct my trustees to discharge all my just debts, funeral expenses and testamentary expenses.
2. I appoint my trustees to be trustees for the purposes of the Land and Conveyancing Law Reform Act 2009 and for the purposes of the Conveyancing Acts and for the purposes of section 57 of the Succession Act 1965 and I DECLARE that a sole trustee for the time being hereof and of every trust fund hereby created shall be competent to act for all the purposes of the said Acts and this my will including the receipt of capital monies under the Settled Land Acts.
3. To the Secretary for the time being of the … Society (Charity) having its principal offices at [address], I give and bequeath the sum of €5,000.00 (Five Thousand Euro) for the charitable purposes in Ireland of the said Society.
4. To my nephew [name] of [address], I give and bequeath the sum of €5,000.00 (Five Thousand Euro).
5. I give and bequeath to my trustees the sum of €500,000.00 (Five Hundred Thousand Euro) to be held by them in trust for my grandchildren in equal shares absolutely and I DIRECT that if any of my said grandchildren shall be under the age of 21 years [or 18 years] at the date of my death, my trustees shall be empowered to apply, in addition to the income from the said legacy or any investment representing the same, the entire of the capital representing the said legacy for the purposes of the maintenance, benefit, advancement,

and in particular the education of my said grandchildren in such manner and at such times as they in their absolute discretion shall think fit, and any payments made by my trustees may be made by them to the guardian of any of my said grandchildren or to any other person in whose custody or charge any of my said grandchildren may be without my trustees being responsible for seeing to the actual application thereof and upon my said grandchildren attaining the age of 21 years [or 18 years] the said legacy and the investments representing the same and any accumulated income thereof shall be paid and transferred to them, but if any of my said grandchildren shall die under the age of 21 years [or 18 years] the said legacy and investments and accumulated income therefrom shall revert to and become part of my residuary estate.

6. Any monies requiring investment hereunder may be laid out in or upon the acquisition of security of any property of whatsoever nature and wheresoever situate, including in particular but without prejudice to the generality of the foregoing words, stocks, shares or securities of any kind whatsoever, insurance policies of any description and any house or flat or apartment as a residence for any beneficiary hereunder to the intent that my trustees shall have the same full and unrestricted powers of investing in all respects as if they were absolutely entitled thereto beneficially and subject to no restriction with regard to advice or otherwise in relation to investment.
7. As to all the rest, residue and remainder of my estate whatsoever and wheresoever situate I GIVE, DEVISE AND BEQUEATH same to my sister [name] of [address] for her own use and benefit absolutely. If my said sister predeceases me, then in that event I GIVE, DEVISE AND BEQUEATH all the rest, residue and remainder of my estate to my brother [name] of [address] for his own use and benefit absolutely.

In addition to all statutory powers that my trustees may have, they shall have the following powers:

(i) To exercise the power of appropriation under section 55 of the Succession Act 1965 without serving any of the notices or obtaining any of the required consents.

(ii) To sell, call in or convert into money at such time or times and in such manner as they shall think fit so much of my estate as shall not be in money form, nevertheless to postpone such sale, conversion or calling in indefinitely without being liable for any loss.

(iii) To sell any asset comprised in my estate at its full open market value to any one or more of my trustees.

(iv) To borrow any amount of money on the security of all or any assets comprised in the estate or without security and generally on such terms as they shall decide without limitation of any kind.

(v) To apply income derived from my estate for the benefit of any beneficiary under the trust hereby created.

(vi) To invest and change investments freely as if they were absolute owners beneficially entitled and to invest in unsecured interest-free loans or other non- income-producing assets including property for occupation or use by any beneficiary.

(vii) To lease, let, mortgage, charge, licence and generally manage and deal with any land which, or the proceeds of sale of which, may for the time being form part of my estate as they were the beneficial owners thereof absolutely entitled.

(viii) To lend money or property to any one or more of the beneficiaries either free of interest or on such terms as to payment of interest and generally as the executors shall in their absolute discretion think fit.

(ix) To trade or take part in any venture in the nature of trade whether solely or jointly with any other person and whether or not by way of partnership and for these purposes to make such arrangements as they shall in their absolute discretion think fit and delegate any exercise of this power to any one or more of their number or to a company or partnership formed for this purpose.

(x) To insure against any loss or damage from any peril of any property for the time being comprised in my estate for any amount and to pay the premiums out of my estate.

(xi) To appoint a new, additional or substitutional trustee or trustees of this my will.

All income received after my death shall be treated as income of my estate regardless of the period to which it relates and the statutory rules concerning apportionment and the rules in *Howe v Dartmouth* and *Allhusen v Whittell* shall not be applied.

I declare that any of my trustees who is/are engaged in a profession shall be entitled to be paid fees for work done by him/her or his/her firm on the basis that he/she were not one of my trustees but employed to act on behalf of my trustees.

I declare that no trustee of this my will shall be liable for loss not attributable to the trustee's own dishonesty or wilful commission by the trustee of any act known to be a breach of trust.

In witness whereof I have hereunto signed my name the … day of … 20.…

SIGNED, PUBLISHED AND DECLARED by the said … as and for his last will and testament in the presence of us who at his request and in his presence and in the presence of each other (all three being present at the same time) have hereunto subscribed our names as witnesses.

Witness 1 [name and address]

Witness 2 [name and address]

(ii) Discretionary Will Trusts by Aunt for Nephews 4–04

I, [name of testatrix] of [address] make this as and for my last will and testament and hereby revoke all former wills and testamentary dispositions heretofore made by me.

1. I appoint
   AB of [address] and
   CD of [address]
   to be the executors and trustees of this my last will (hereinafter called "my trustees") and I direct my trustees to discharge all my just debts, funeral expenses and testamentary expenses.
2. I appoint my trustees to be trustees for the purposes of the Land and Conveyancing Law Reform Act 2009 and for the purposes of the Conveyancing Acts and for the purposes of section 57 of the Succession Act 1965 and I DECLARE that a sole trustee for the time being hereof and of every trust fund hereby created shall be competent to act for all the purposes of the said Acts and this my will including the receipt of capital monies under the Settled Land Acts.
3. To the Secretary for the time being of the … Society (Charity) having its principal offices at [address], I give and bequeath the sum of €5,000.00 (Five Thousand Euro) for the charitable purposes in Ireland of the said Society.

4. To my niece [name] of [address], I give and bequeath the sum of €5,000.00 (Five Thousand Euro).
5. I give and bequeath to my trustees the sum of €500,000.00 (Five Hundred Thousand Euro) to be held by them in trust for all my nephews in equal shares absolutely and I DIRECT that if any of my said nephews shall be under the age of 21 years [or 18 years] at the date of my death, my trustees shall be empowered to apply, in addition to the income from the said legacy or any investment representing the same, the entire of the capital representing the said legacy for the purposes of the maintenance, benefit, advancement, and in particular the education of my said nephews in such manner and at such times as they in their absolute discretion shall think fit, and any payments made by my trustees may be made by them to the guardian of any of my said nephews, or to any other person in whose custody or charge any of my said nephews may be, without my trustees being responsible for seeing to the actual application thereof, and upon my said nephews attaining the age of 21 years [or 18 years], the said legacy and the investments representing the same and any accumulated income thereof shall be paid and transferred to them, but if any of my said nephews shall die under the age of 21 years [or 18 years] the said legacy and investments and accumulated income therefrom shall revert to and become part of my residuary estate.
6. Any monies requiring investment hereunder may be laid out in or upon the acquisition of security of any property of whatsoever nature and wheresoever situate, including in particular but without prejudice to the generality of the foregoing words, stocks, shares or securities of any kind whatsoever, insurance policies of any description and any house or flat or apartment as a residence for any beneficiary hereunder to the intent that my trustees shall have the same full and unrestricted powers of investing in all respects as if they were absolutely entitled thereto beneficially and subject to no restriction with regard to advice or otherwise in relation to investment.
7. As to all the rest, residue and remainder of my estate whatsoever and wheresoever situate, I GIVE, DEVISE AND BEQUEATH same to my sister [name] of [address] for her own use and benefit absolutely. If my said sister predeceases me, then in that event I GIVE, DEVISE AND BEQUEATH all the rest, residue and remainder of my estate to my brother [name] of [address] for his own use and benefit absolutely.

In addition to all statutory powers that my trustees may have they shall have the following powers:

(i) To exercise the power of appropriation under section 55 of the Succession Act 1965 without serving any of the notices or obtaining any of the required consents.

(ii) To sell, call in or convert into money at such time or times and in such manner as they shall think fit so much of my estate as shall not be in money form, nevertheless to postpone such sale, conversion or calling in indefinitely without being liable for any loss.

(iii) To sell any asset comprised in my estate at its full open market value to any one or more of my trustees.

(iv) To borrow any amount of money on the security of all or any assets comprised in the estate or without security and generally on such terms as they shall decide without limitation of any kind.

(v) To apply income derived from my estate for the benefit of any beneficiary under the trust hereby created.

(vi) To invest and change investments freely as if they were absolute owners beneficially entitled and to invest in unsecured interest-free loans or other non- income-producing assets including property for occupation or use by any beneficiary.

(vii) To lease, let, mortgage, charge, licence and generally manage and deal with any land which, or the proceeds of sale of which, may for the time being form part of my estate as they were the beneficial owners thereof absolutely entitled.

(viii) To lend money or property to any one or more of the beneficiaries either free of interest or on such terms as to payment of interest and generally as the executors shall in their absolute discretion think fit.

(ix) To trade or take part in any venture in the nature of trade whether solely or jointly with any other person and whether or not by way of partnership and for these purposes to make such arrangements as they shall in their absolute discretion think fit and delegate any exercise of this power to any one or more of their number or to a company or partnership formed for this purpose.

(x) To insure against any loss or damage from any peril of any property for the time being comprised in my estate for any amount and to pay the premiums out of my estate.

(xi) To appoint a new, additional or substitutional trustee or trustees of this my will.

All income received after my death shall be treated as income of my estate regardless of the period to which it relates and the statutory rules concerning apportionment and the rules in *Howe v Dartmouth* and *Allhusen v Whittell* shall not be applied.

I declare that any of my trustees who is/are engaged in a profession shall be entitled to be paid fees for work done by him/her or his/her firm on the basis that he/she were not one of my trustees but employed to act on behalf of my trustees.

I declare that no trustee of this my will shall be liable for loss not attributable to the trustee's own dishonesty or wilful commission by the trustee of any act known to be a breach of trust.

In witness whereof I have hereunto signed my name the … day of … 20 ….

SIGNED, PUBLISHED AND DECLARED by the said … as and for his last will and testament in the presence of us who at his request and in his presence and in the presence of each other (all three being present at the same time) have hereunto subscribed our names as witnesses.

Witness 1 [name and address]

Witness 2 [name and address]

(iii) Discretionary Will Trusts by Uncle for Nieces 4–05

I, [name of testator] of [address] make this as and for my last will and testament and hereby revoke all former wills and testamentary dispositions heretofore made by me.

1. I appoint
   AB of [address] and
   CD of [address]
   to be the executors and trustees of this my last will (hereinafter called "my trustees") and I direct my trustees to discharge all my just debts, funeral expenses and testamentary expenses.
2. I appoint my trustees to be trustees for the purposes of the Land and

Conveyancing Law Reform Act 2009 and for the purposes of the Conveyancing Acts and for the purposes of s 57 of the Succession Act 1965.

3. To the Secretary for the time being of the … Society (Charity) having its principal offices at [address], I give and bequeath the sum of €5,000.00 (Five Thousand Euro) for the charitable purposes in Ireland of the said Society.
4. To my nephew [name] of [address], I give and bequeath the sum of €5,000.00 (Five Thousand Euro).
5. I give and bequeath to my trustees the sum of €500,000.00 (Five Hundred Thousand Euro) to be held by them in trust for all my nieces in equal shares absolutely and I DIRECT that if any of my said nieces shall be under the age of 21 years [or 18 years] at the date of my death, my trustees shall be empowered to apply, in addition to the income from the said legacy or any investment representing the same, the entire of the capital representing the said legacy for the purposes of the maintenance, benefit, advancement, and in particular the education of my said nieces in such manner and at such times as they in their absolute discretion shall think fit, and any payments made by my trustees may be made by them to the guardian of any of my said nieces, or to any other person in whose custody or charge any of my said nieces may be, without my trustees being responsible for seeing to the actual application thereof and upon my said nieces attaining the age of 21 years [or 18 years], the said legacy and the investments representing the same and any accumulated income thereof shall be paid and transferred to them, but if any of my said nieces shall die under the age of 21 years [or 18 years], the said legacy and investments and accumulated income therefrom shall revert to and become part of my residuary estate.
6. Any monies requiring investment hereunder may be laid out in or upon the acquisition of security of any property of whatsoever nature and wheresoever situate, including in particular but without prejudice to the generality of the foregoing words, stocks, shares or securities of any kind whatsoever, insurance policies of any description and any house or flat or apartment as a residence for any beneficiary hereunder to the intent that my trustees shall have the same full and unrestricted powers of investing in all respects as if they were absolutely entitled thereto beneficially and subject to no restriction with regard to advice or otherwise in relation to investment.
7. As to all the rest, residue and remainder of my estate whatsoever and wheresoever situate, I GIVE, DEVISE AND BEQUEATH same to my sister [name] of [address] for her own use and benefit absolutely. If my said sister predeceases me, then in that event I GIVE, DEVISE AND BEQUEATH all the rest, residue and remainder of my estate to my brother [name] of [address] for his own use and benefit absolutely.

In addition to all statutory powers that my trustees may have, they shall have the following powers:

(i) To exercise the power of appropriation under section 55 of the Succession Act 1965 without serving any of the notices or obtaining any of the required consents.

(ii) To sell, call in or convert into money at such time or times and in such manner as they shall think fit so much of my estate as shall not be in money form, nevertheless to postpone such sale, conversion or calling in indefinitely without being liable for any loss.

(iii) To sell any asset comprised in my estate at its full open market value to any one or more of my trustees.

(iv) To borrow any amount of money on the security of all or any assets comprised in the estate or without security and generally on such terms as they shall decide without limitation of any kind.

(v) To apply income derived from my estate for the benefit of any beneficiary under the trust hereby created.

(vi) To invest and change investments freely as if they were absolute owners beneficially entitled and to invest in unsecured interest-free loans or other non-income-producing assets, including property for occupation or use by any beneficiary.

(vii) To lease, let, mortgage, charge, licence and generally manage and deal with any land which, or the proceeds of sale of which, may for the time being form part of my estate as they were the beneficial owners thereof absolutely entitled.

(viii) To lend money or property to any one or more of the beneficiaries either free of interest, or on such terms as to payment of interest and generally as the executors shall in their absolute discretion think fit.

(ix) To trade or take part in any venture in the nature of trade, whether solely or jointly with any other person, and whether or not by way of partnership and for these purposes to make such arrangements as they shall in their absolute discretion think fit and delegate any exercise of this power to any one or more of their number or to a company or partnership formed for this purpose.

(x) To insure against any loss or damage from any peril of any property for the time being comprised in my estate for any amount and to pay the premiums out of my estate.

(xi) To appoint a new, additional or substitutional trustee or trustees of this my will.

All income received after my death shall be treated as income of my estate regardless of the period to which it relates and the statutory rules concerning apportionment and the rules in *Howe v Dartmouth* and *Allhusen v Whittell* shall not be applied.

I declare that any of my trustees who is/are engaged in a profession shall be entitled to be paid fees for work done by him/her or his/her firm on the basis that he/she were not one of my trustees but employed to act on behalf of my trustees.

I declare that no trustee of this my will shall be liable for loss not attributable to the trustee's own dishonesty or wilful commission by the trustee of any act known to be a breach of trust.

In witness whereof I have hereunto signed my name the … day of … 20….

SIGNED, PUBLISHED AND DECLARED by the said … as and for his last will and testament in the presence of us who at his request and in his presence and in the presence of each other (all three being present at the same time) have hereunto subscribed our names as witnesses.

Witness 1 [name and address]

Witness 2 [name and address]

(iv) Discretionary Will Trusts by Uncle for Nephew 4–06

I, [name of testator] of [address] make this as and for my last will and testament and hereby revoke all former wills and testamentary dispositions heretofore made by me.

1. I appoint
   AB of [address] and
   CD of [address]

to be the executors and trustees of this my last will (hereinafter called "my trustees") and I direct my trustees to discharge all my just debts, funeral expenses and testamentary expenses.

2. I appoint my trustees to be trustees for the purposes of the Land and Conveyancing Law Reform Act 2009 and for the purposes of the Conveyancing Acts and for the purposes of section 57 of the Succession Act 1965 and I DECLARE that a sole trustee for the time being hereof and of every trust fund hereby created shall be competent to act for all the purposes of the said Acts and this my will including the receipt of capital monies under the Settled Land Acts.
3. I GIVE AND BEQUEATH the sum of €5,000.00 (Five Thousand Euro) to the Secretary for the time being of the ... Society (Charity) having its principal offices at [address] for the charitable purposes in Ireland of the said Society.
4. I GIVE AND BEQUEATH the sum of €5,000.00 (Five Thousand Euro) to my nephew A.
5. I GIVE AND BEQUEATH €300,000 (Three Hundred Thousand Euro) out of my deposit account in the [Bank, Credit Union or Post Office] to my trustees to be held by them in trust for my nephew B and I DIRECT that if my said nephew shall be under the age of 21 years [or 18 years] at the date of my death, my trustees shall be empowered to apply, in addition to the income from the said legacy or any investment representing the same, the entire of the capital representing the said legacy for the purposes of the maintenance, benefit, advancement, and in particular the education of my said nephew in such manner and at such times as they in their absolute discretion shall think fit, and any payments made by my trustees may be made by them to my nephew's guardian or to any other person in whose custody or charge my said nephew may be, without my trustees being responsible for seeing to the actual application thereof, and upon my said nephew attaining the age of 21 years [or 18 years], the said legacy and the investments representing the same and any accumulated income thereof shall be paid and transferred to him, but if my said nephew shall die under the age of 21 years [or 18 years], the said legacy and investments and accumulated income therefrom shall revert to and become part of my residuary estate.
6. Any monies requiring investment hereunder may be laid out in or upon the acquisition of security of any property of whatsoever nature and wheresoever situate, including in particular but without prejudice to the generality of the foregoing words, stocks, shares or securities of any kind whatsoever, insurance policies of any description and any house or flat or apartment as a residence for any beneficiary hereunder to the intent that my trustees shall have the same full and unrestricted powers of investing in all respects as if they were absolutely entitled thereto beneficially and subject to no restriction with regard to advice or otherwise in relation to investment.
7. As to all the rest, residue and remainder of my estate whatsoever and wheresoever situate I GIVE, DEVISE AND BEQUEATH same to my sister [name] of [address] for her own use and benefit absolutely. If my said sister predeceases me then in that event I GIVE, DEVISE AND BEQUEATH all the rest, residue and remainder of my estate to my brother [name] of [address] for his own use and benefit absolutely.

In addition to all statutory powers that my trustees may have, they shall have the following powers:

(i) To exercise the power of appropriation under section 55 of the Succession Act 1965 without serving any of the notices or obtaining any of the required consents.

(ii) To sell, call in or convert into money at such time or times and in such manner as they shall think fit so much of my estate as shall not be in money form, nevertheless to postpone such sale, conversion or calling in indefinitely without being liable for any loss.

(iii) To sell any asset comprised in my estate at its full open market value to any one or more of my trustees.

(iv) To borrow any amount of money on the security of all or any assets comprised in the estate or without security and generally on such terms as they shall decide without limitation of any kind.

(v) To apply income derived from my estate for the benefit of any beneficiary under the trust hereby created.

(vi) To invest and change investments freely as if they were absolute owners beneficially entitled and to invest in unsecured interest-free loans or other non-income-producing assets including property for occupation or use by any beneficiary.

(vii) To lease, let, mortgage, charge, licence and generally manage and deal with any land which, or the proceeds of sale of which, may for the time being form part of my estate as they were the beneficial owners thereof absolutely entitled.

(viii) To lend money or property to any one or more of the beneficiaries either free of interest or on such terms as to payment of interest and generally as the executors shall in their absolute discretion think fit.

(ix) To trade or take part in any venture in the nature of trade, whether solely or jointly with any other person and whether or not by way of partnership, and for these purposes to make such arrangements as they shall in their absolute discretion think fit and delegate any exercise of this power to any one or more of their number or to a company or partnership formed for this purpose.

(x) To insure against any loss or damage from any peril of any property for the time being comprised in my estate for any amount and to pay the premiums out of my estate.

(xi) To appoint a new, additional or substitutional trustee or trustees of this my will.

All income received after my death shall be treated as income of my estate regardless of the period to which it relates and the statutory rules concerning apportionment and the rules in *Howe v Dartmouth* and *Allhusen v Whittell* shall not be applied.

I declare that any of my trustees who is/are engaged in a profession shall be entitled to be paid fees for work done by him/her or his/her firm on the basis that he/she were not one of my trustees but employed to act on behalf of my trustees.

I declare that no trustee of this my will shall be liable for loss not attributable to the trustee's own dishonesty or wilful commission by the trustee of any act known to be a breach of trust.

In witness whereof I have hereunto signed my name the ... day of ... 20....

SIGNED, PUBLISHED AND DECLARED by the said ... as and for his last will and testament in the presence of us who at his request and in his presence and in the presence of each other (all three being present at the same time) have hereunto subscribed our names as witnesses.

Witness 1 [name and address]

Witness 2 [name and address]

Chapter 5

CHARITABLE WILL TRUSTS

Introduction

While a will trust benefitting a charity must, like all trusts, have certainty of subject matter—i.e. property—certainty of objects—i.e. beneficiaries—and the words creating the trust must be mandatory and expressed in the imperative, and the will creating the trust must be duly executed, a charitable trust must also be for a charitable purpose recognised by law. Charitable purposes include the relief of poverty, the advancement of education, the advancement of religion, or a purpose beneficial to the community at large, and for a charitable trust to be valid and enforceable, it must be created for one or more of these purposes.[1] Furthermore, a charitable will trust must also confer a public benefit. Once a charitable will trust has a charitable purpose and confers a public benefit, an added discretionary element introduced by the testator regarding the administration of the trust by his executors and trustees will not render the charitable trust invalid on that ground only; for instance, a testator may allow his executors to exercise their discretion when choosing the beneficiaries among the poor of a district.[2] **5–01**

A charitable will trust may be created using the following precedent: **5–02**

> I [name of testator] of [address] make this as and for my last will and testament and hereby revoke all former wills and testamentary dispositions heretofore made by me.
>
> 1. I appoint AB of [address]
>   and CD of [address]
>   (hereinafter called "my trustees") to be executors and trustees of this my last will and testament.
> 2. I give devise and bequeath to my trustees all of my residuary estate upon trust:
>   (a) To pay my debts, funeral expenses and testamentary expenses;
>   (b) To divide the residue of my estate equally among the following charities:
>   (i) [Name of charity, address and registered number]; and
>   (ii) [Name of charity, address and registered number].

Once a gift or trust has a charitable purpose, it may still be enforced even though the intended charity is no longer in existence, or the testator's intentions are impossible to carry out, or are impracticable. In such cases, the court may apply the *cy-près* doctrine to use the trust funds or property for a charitable purpose as near as possible related to or resembling the **5–03**

---

1. *Commissioners for Special Purposes of Income Tax v Pemsel* [1891] AC 531; *Re Worth Library* [1994] 1 ILRM 161.
2. *Brett v Attorney General* [1945] IR 526.

purpose intended by the testator, and a so-called "scheme" may be devised accordingly. The Commissioners of Charitable Donations and Bequests also had a limited jurisdiction under the Charities Act 1961 (the "1961 Act") to frame a scheme for the application *cy-près* of the property comprised in a charitable gift or trust.[3]

5–04 The Charities Act 2009 (the "2009 Act") introduced significant reforms of the law relating to charities. Since the enactment of the 2009 Act, a gift or trust must be for a charitable purpose as defined by s 3 of the Act. However, the charitable purposes outlined in *Commissioners for Special Purposes of Income Tax v Pemsel*[4] are apparently retained and given statutory recognition by s 3 of the 2009 Act. The 2009 Act also provides for the establishment of the Charities Regulatory Authority in place of the Commissioners for Charitable Donations and Bequests, and provides for a system of registration of charitable organisations by the Charities Regulatory Authority. It also contains provisions dealing with the financial regulation and protection of charitable organisations, and the regulation of fund-raising by registered charitable organisations. In relation to charity trustees, s 89(1) of the 2009 Act allows for the remuneration of trustees, s 90 empowers the court to grant relief from liability for breach of trust, and s 91 allows for the provision of indemnity insurance in respect of charity trustees. Section 38(1) of the 2009 Act provides that

> all functions relating to charitable organisations or charitable trusts (or otherwise relating to charities) that, immediately before the establishment day, were vested in the Attorney General are transferred to the Authority, and references in any enactment in so far as it relates to charitable organisations or charitable trusts (or otherwise relates to charities) shall be construed as references to the Authority.

5–05 Section 38(2) of the 2009 Act provides that the section comes into operation on the establishment day.

5–06 Section 18(9) of the Land and Conveyancing Law Reform Act 2009 provides at Pt 4 of the Act that the provisions of the Act dealing with trusts of land do not apply to land held directly for a charitable purpose. Part 5 of the Land and Conveyancing Law Reform Act 2009, which deals with the variation of trusts, provides at s 23 that the definition of "relevant trusts" does not include trusts created for a charitable purpose within the meaning of the Charities Acts 1961 and 1973, and the 2009 Act. Section 24 which deals with the jurisdiction of the courts to vary trusts provides at s 24(6) that nothing in the section may be construed as derogating from or affecting the operation of the Charities Acts 1961 and 1973, and the 2009 Act.

---

3 See s 29(2) and s 47(1).
4 [1891] AC 531.

Charitable Trusts

Prior to the enactment of the 2009 Act, for a trust to be charitable it had to be for a purpose that was charitable in the legal sense, and four such categories of charitable purposes were identified in *Commissioners for Special Purposes of Income Tax v Pemsel*[5]: 5–07

(i) Relief of Poverty

While the poor in general may be the beneficiaries of a charitable trust under this heading, other persons who would not be poor in the ordinary sense of the word may be so for this purpose, where, for instance, they are "hard up" or in "genteel poverty", and also taking into account their status in life and their financial inability to maintain the lifestyle to which they are accustomed.[6] A testator may wish to create a trust for his or her "poor relations", and while such a purpose would suggest the existence of a private trust rather than a public one, nevertheless the law has given charitable recognition to such trusts. The beneficiaries of the charitable trust for the relief of poverty may, therefore, be the poor in general, a particular class of persons with limited or reduced means, or "poor relations". Persons, like the widows and children of deceased bank officials and ladies of limited means, have also been held to be beneficiaries of such trusts.[7] However, once the purpose of the trust is the relief of poverty among such persons, the courts are prepared to treat such trusts as exceptions to the general requirement of public benefit and will enforce them as charitable trusts.[8] 5–08

(ii) Advancement of Education

While a trust created for the advancement of education will be viewed as a charitable purpose, for it to be a valid charitable trust, it must also confer some form of public benefit. The two elements of "educational purpose" and "public benefit" must co-exist for the trust to be a valid charitable one. Trusts benefitting schools and colleges, or funding professorships, lectureships and scholarships, were all held to create valid charitable trusts under this heading. Extra-curricular activities organised by educational establishments may also form the subject matter of a valid charitable trust—for instance, providing prizes for sports events—but where there is no connecting factor between education and the trust for providing prizes, it may not be treated as a charitable trust and consequently, a trust providing prizes for a sport only may not create a charitable trust. Trusts for the advancement of education are not confined to trusts for schools, colleges and universities, 5–09

---

5 [1891] AC 531; see also *Re Worth Library* [1994] 1 ILRM 161.

6 *Brett v Attorney General* [1945] IR 526; *Re Segelman* [1996] Ch 171; *Re Coulthurst* [1951] 1 All ER 774.

7 *Re Coulthurst* [1951] 1 All ER 774; *IRC v Baddeley* [1955] AC 572; *Re Gardom* [1914] 1 Ch 662.

8 *Re Compton* [1945] Ch 123; *Re Segelman* [1996] Ch 171; *Dingle v Turner* [1972] AC 601.

and the endowment of a university with chairs and scholarships only. They may also include trusts or gifts "for the establishment of theatres, art galleries and museums and the promotion of literature and music."[9] The public benefit element must also be shown to exist in such trusts, "and if the benefit extends to a section of the community only, that section must not be numerically negligible."[10]

(iii) Advancement of Religion

5–10 Trusts created by testators for the purpose of the advancement of religion are also valid charitable trusts. The term "religion" for this charitable purpose is not confined to Christianity and may include other religious beliefs as well.[11] Prior to the enactment of the 1961 Act, a public element was of vital importance to a trust for the advancement of religion, and even a trust that contained partly charitable and partly non-charitable purposes was not a valid one. Trusts or gifts to religious orders or communities were held by the courts not to be valid charitable trusts or gifts as they lacked the necessary public benefit element.[12] After the enactment of the 1961 Act, a trust created in favour of religious orders will now take effect as a valid charitable trust "as it will be conclusively presumed that the purpose includes and will occasion public benefit."[13] Also, in former times, the courts when deciding whether a trust or gift for saying masses was a valid charitable trust or gift made a distinction between masses said privately and in public, and if the trust or gift provided for the saying of masses in private only, it was not a valid charitable one.[14] Even though this was approach was later changed by the Irish Court of Appeal in *O'Hanlon v Logue*,[15] s 45(2) of the 1961 Act puts the issue beyond doubt.

5–11 A trust created for an ecclesiastical office holder will be a valid charitable trust if it is created for him (or her), in his (or her) official capacity, though not in his (or her) private capacity.[16] A trust created, for instance, for a parish priest in his private capacity will not be a charitable trust but one created for him in his capacity as parish priest and his successors may be a charitable trust, and this may be so even though the trust includes objects which are not charitable, as under s 49 of the 1961 Act, a trust will continue

---

9 *Re Worth Library* [1994] 1 ILRM 161; *Re Hopkins' Will Trusts* [1964] 3 All ER 46; *Re Delius* [1957] 1 All ER 854; *Re Shaw* [1957] 1 All ER 748; *Re Pinion* [1964] 1 All ER 890.

10 *ibid*; see also *Oppenheim v Tobacco Securities Trust Co Ltd* [1951] AC 297.

11 *Quinn's Supermarket v Attorney General* [1972] IR 1 *per* Walsh J at 23.

12 See *Commissioners of Charitable Donations and Bequests v McCartan* [1917] IR 388; *Gilmour v Coats* [1949] AC 426; *Re Keogh's Estate* [1945] IR 13; *Bank of Ireland Trustee Co. Ltd v Attorney General* [1957] IR 257; *Re Byrne* [1935] IR 782; *Maguire v Attorney General* [1943] IR 238.

13 Charities Act 1961, s 45(1) and (2).

14 *Attorney General v Delaney* (1875) IR 10 CL *per* Palles CB.

15 [1906] 1 IR 247.

16 See *Donnellan v O'Neill* (1870) IR 5 Eq 523; *Reddy v Fitzmaurice* (1952) 86 ILTR 127; *Halpin v Hannon* (1947) 82 ILTR 74.

to be a valid charitable trust even though it includes non-charitable objects. A gift or trust for general religious purposes may also be upheld as a valid charitable gift or trust; for instance, a gift for "foreign missions"[17] or "to Presbyterian missions and orphans."[18] There was a time when a gift or trust which contained a mixture of charitable purposes and non-charitable purposes was not a valid charitable gift or trust.[19] Since s 49 of the 1961 Act, it appears that such a gift or trust may be upheld as charitable insofar as the charitable purposes of the gift or trust are concerned. Gifts in wills for the maintenance of church premises or fittings may also be upheld as valid charitable gifts.

(iv) A Purpose Beneficial to the Community

While charitable trusts created by testators for the relief of poverty, **5–12**
advancement of education and advancement of religion must all contain a public benefit element, subject to the statutory exceptions for certain trusts for the advancement of religion under the 1961 Act, for a trust to be charitable for a purpose beneficial to the community, the public benefit element is of fundamental importance to the existence of the trust.[20] Also, while trusts for the relief of poverty, advancement of education and advancement of religion describe the charitable purpose intended by the testator, it is more difficult to identify charities governed by this category. The public benefit element will be of vital importance to the validity of a charitable trust for a purpose beneficial to the community. It may have a purpose that is obviously beneficial to the community as a whole, for instance, where it benefits a fire brigade or a public park. The following diverse trusts have also been held charitable under this heading: a trust for the sick and aged[21]; a trust to benefit a charitable hospitable will be a charitable trust whether or not the hospital caters for fee-paying patients as well[22]; and also trusts for the general welfare of animals.[23] A trust apparently having a charitable purpose but benefitting a section of the community only may not be deemed a charitable trust; for instance, where the testator intended the trust funds to be used to build a hall for the purpose of promoting temperance in a designated locality. Trusts for political parties are also not valid charitable trusts under this heading. A gift or trust having as its purpose the provision, maintenance or improvement of a tomb, vault or grave, or of a tombstone or any other memorial to a deceased person will be treated as a charitable gift or trust under s 50 of the 1961 Act. However, trusts created for sporting and recreational purposes

---

17 *Dunne v Duignan* [1908] 1 IR 228.

18 *Jackson v Attorney General* [1917] 1 IR 332.

19 *MacLaughlin v Campbell* [1906] 1 IR 588.

20 See *Re Dunlop* [1984] NI 408.

21 *Re McCarthy's Will Trusts* [1958] IR 31; *Re Robinson* [1950] 2 All ER 1148; *Re Lewis* [1954] 3 All ER 257.

22 *Barrington's Hospital v Commissioner of Valuation* [1957] IR 299; see *Re Resch's Will Trusts* [1969] 1 AC 514.

23 *Swifte v Attorney General* [1912] 1 IR 133; *Re Wedgewood* [1915] 1 Ch 113; *Re Grove-Grady* [1929] 1 Ch 557; see *Re Kelly* [1932] IR 255.

cannot be the subject of charitable trusts. In National Tourism Development Authority v Coughlan,[24] Charleton J stated that:

> Sport has never been recognised to be an object of sufficiently wide benefit to the community as to enjoy charitable status. The law has traditionally regarded sport as a form of recreation and, in consequence, trusts for sporting purposes are not recognised as charitable.

The Charities Act 2009

5–13 The Charities Act 2009 (the "2009 Act") introduced major reforms of the law relating to charities. One of its main features is that it provides for the establishment of the Charities Regulatory Authority in place of the Commissioners for Charitable Donations and Bequests and for the registration of charitable organisations by that Authority. Section 25 provides for the transfer of staff from the Office of the Commissioners of Charitable Donations and Bequests when that body is dissolved to the Charities Regulatory Authority. It also contains provisions dealing with the financial regulation and protection of charitable organisations and the regulation of fund-raising by registered charitable organisations. Since the enactment of the 2009 Act, a gift or trust must be for a charitable purpose as defined by s 3 of the Act. Section 89(1) of the Act allows for the remuneration of trustees. Under s 90, the court has the power to grant relief from liability for breach of trust. Section 91 allows for the provision of indemnity insurance in respect of charity trustees.

5–14 Section 3 defines a charitable purpose for the purposes of the 2009 Act. The four *Pemsel* categories are retained with an extended meaning of the charitable purpose for the benefit of the community.

5–15 Section 3 provides that:

> (1) For the purposes of this Act each of the following shall, subject to subsection (2), be a charitable purpose:
> (a) the prevention or relief of poverty or economic hardship;
> (b) the advancement of education;
> (c) the advancement of religion;
> (d) any other purpose that is of benefit to the community.
>
> (2) A purpose shall not be a charitable purpose unless it is of public benefit.
>
> (3) Subject to subsection (4), a gift shall not be of public benefit unless—
> (a) it is intended to benefit the public or a section of the public, and
> (b) in a case where it confers a benefit on a person other than in his or her capacity as a member of the public or a section of the public, any such benefit is reasonable in all of the circumstances, and is ancillary to, and necessary, for the furtherance of the public benefit.
>
> (4) It shall be presumed, unless the contrary is proved, that a gift for the advancement of religion is of public benefit.
>
> (5) The Authority shall not make a determination that a gift for the advancement of religion is not of public benefit without the consent of the Attorney General.

[24] [2009] IEHC 53.

(6) A charitable gift for the purpose of the advancement of religion shall have effect, and the terms upon which it is given shall be construed, in accordance with the laws, canons, ordinances and tenets of the religion concerned.

(7) In determining whether a gift is of public benefit or not, account shall be taken of—

(a) any limitation imposed by the donor of the gift on the class of persons who may benefit from the gift and whether or not such limitation is justified and reasonable, having regard to the nature of the purpose of the gift, and

(b) the amount of any charge payable for any service provided in furtherance of the purpose for which the gift is given and whether it is likely to limit the number of persons or classes of person who will benefit from the gift.

(8) A limitation referred to in subsection (7) shall not be justified and reasonable if all of the intended beneficiaries of the gift or a significant number of them have a personal connection with the donor of the gift.

...

(10) For the purposes of this section, a gift is not a gift for the advancement of religion if it is made to or for the benefit of an organisation or cult—

(a) the principal object of which is the making of profit, or

(b) that employs oppressive psychological manipulation—

(i) of its followers, or

(ii) for the purpose of gaining new followers.

(11) In this section "purpose that is of benefit to the community" includes—

(a) the advancement of community welfare including the relief of those in need by reason of youth, age, ill-health, or disability,

(b) the advancement of community development, including rural or urban regeneration,

(c) the promotion of civic responsibility or voluntary work,

(d) the promotion of health, including the prevention or relief of sickness, disease or human suffering,

(e) the advancement of conflict resolution or reconciliation,

(f) the promotion of religious or racial harmony and harmonious community relations,

(g) the protection of the natural environment,

(h) the advancement of environmental sustainability,

(i) the advancement of the efficient and effective use of the property of charitable organisations,

(j) the prevention or relief of suffering of animals,

(k) the advancement of the arts, culture, heritage or sciences, and

(l) the integration of those who are disadvantaged, and the promotion of their full participation, in society.

Charity Trustees

Section 89(1) of the 2009 Act provides that: **5–16**

(1) A charitable organisation may enter into an agreement (in this section referred to as an "agreement") with a relevant person for the provision by the relevant person of a service to, or on behalf of, the charitable organisation in consideration of the payment to the relevant person out of the property of the charitable organisation of such sum or sums as may be specified in the agreement or as may be determined in accordance with the agreement.

(2) An agreement shall be in writing.

(3) Any sum or sums payable to a relevant person under an agreement shall

not exceed what is reasonable and proportionate having regard to the service provided by the relevant person pursuant to the agreement.

(4) Subject to subsection (5), a charitable organisation shall not enter into an agreement unless the charity trustees of the charitable organisation, other than any charity trustee who—

(a) will provide a service under the agreement,
(b) provides a service under an agreement other than the agreement referred to in paragraph (a),
(c) is in receipt of remuneration out of the property of the charitable organisation other than in accordance with an agreement, or
(d) has a personal connection with a person who—
  (i) will provide a service under the agreement,
  (ii) provides a service under an agreement other than an agreement referred to in paragraph (a) or subparagraph (i), or
  (iii) is in receipt of remuneration out of the property of the charitable organisation other than in accordance with an agreement,

are satisfied that the agreement would be in the best interests of the charitable organisation.

(5) Where, in relation to a charitable organisation, there is only one charity trustee, the charitable organisation shall not enter into an agreement unless—

(a) the charity trustee is satisfied that the agreement would be in the best interests of the charitable organisation, and
(b) the Authority gives its approval to the charitable organisation entering into the agreement.

(6) A charitable organisation shall not enter into an agreement in contravention of the provisions of the constitution of the charitable organisation.

(7) The Authority may give directions or issue guidelines in relation to the making of agreements to which this section applies.

(8) A person to whom a direction under this section applies shall comply with that direction.

(9) A charitable organisation shall, before entering into an agreement, have regard to any guidelines issued by the Authority under this section.

(10) This section shall not apply in relation to—

(a) any remuneration paid to a person in his or her capacity as a charity trustee or under a contract of employment, or
(b) any remuneration to which a person is entitled in accordance with law or a provision of the constitution of a charitable organisation.

(11) Where, in relation to an agreement, there has been a contravention of this section, the agreement shall be null and void.

(12) Subsection (11) shall not operate to prevent a charitable organisation from recovering damages in respect of any loss incurred by it by virtue of an agreement to which that subsection applies.

5–17 The court has the power to grant relief from liability for breach of trust. Section 90 of the 2009 Act provides that:

> If, in any proceedings brought against a charity trustee for breach of trust, it appears to the court hearing the case that the charity trustee is or may be liable in respect of the breach of trust but that he or she acted honestly and reasonably and that having regard to all of the circumstances of the case he or she ought fairly to be excused for the breach of trust, the court may relieve him or her in whole or in part from his or her liability on such terms as the court deems appropriate.

5–18 Section 91 of the 2009 Act provides for indemnity insurance in respect of a charity trustee:

A charitable organisation may enter into an agreement with a charity trustee of the charitable organisation for the payment by the charitable organisation to the insurer under a contract of insurance of such sums as the charity trustee undertakes, in accordance with that contract, to pay to the insurer in consideration of the insurer agreeing to indemnify the charity trustee in respect of any liability of the charity trustee to pay any damages or other sum to a person in respect of any act done or omitted to be done by the charity trustee in good faith and in the performance of his or her functions as charity trustee.

The Application of the *Cy-près* Doctrine

It may happen that the charity the testator intends to benefit by a gift or trust may no longer be in existence at the date of his death. In normal circumstances such a gift or trust would fail by lapse, but because it has a charitable purpose, it may be applied *cy-près* by the court, and the court when applying *cy-près* will adhere as closely as possible to the original charitable intention of the testator. The doctrine of *cy-près* may also be applied to a gift for charitable purposes although the terms prescribed by the testator for its implementation are impracticable or are impossible to carry out. In such cases, the *cy-près* jurisdiction of the court may be invoked and applied.[25] Before *cy-près* may be applied, however, it must first be established that the testator had the requisite charitable intention and this intention may be gathered not only from terms of the gift but also from the will as a whole, and secondly, the charitable purposes are incapable of being carried out in the way prescribed by the gift.[26] **5–19**

The 1961 Act remains the appropriate legislation governing the application of the *cy-près* doctrine. Section 47(1) of the 1961 Act sets out the circumstances under which the original purposes of a charitable gift may be altered to allow the property forming the subject matter of it, or indeed part of it, to be applied *cy-près*. When doing so, the courts will adhere as closely as possible to the original charitable intentions of the testator.[27] Section 47(1) of the 1961 Act provides a comprehensive list of circumstances under which *cy-près* may be applied and they are: **5–20**

(a) where the original purposes, in whole or in part—
  (i) have been as far as may be fulfilled; or
  (ii) cannot be carried out, or cannot be carried out according to the directions given and to the spirit of the gift; or
(b) where the original purposes provide a use for part only of the property available by virtue of the gift; or
(c) where the property available by virtue of the gift and other property applicable for similar purposes can be more effectively used in conjunction, and to that

25 *Re Royal Kilmainham Hospital* [1966] IR 451; *Governors of Erasmus Smith's Schools v Attorney General* (1931) 66 ILTR 57.

26 *Re McGuire* [1941] IR 33; *Re Worth Library* [1994] 1 ILRM 161; *Re Royal Kilmainham Hospital* [1966] IR 451; *Governors of Erasmus Smith's Schools v Attorney General* (1931) 66 ILTR 57.

27 *Re Worth Library* [1994] 1 ILRM 161

end can suitably, regard being had to the spirit of the gift, be made applicable to common purposes; or

(d) where the original purposes were laid down by reference to an area which then was but has since ceased to be a unit for some other purpose, or by reference to a class of persons or to an area which has for any reason since ceased, either to be suitable, regard being had to the spirit of the gift, or to be practical in administering the gift; or

(e) where the original purposes, in whole or in part, have, since they were laid down—
   (i) been adequately provided for by other means; or
   (ii) ceased, as being useless or harmful to the community or for other reasons, to be in law charitable; or
   (iii) ceased in any other way to provide a suitable and effective method of using the property available by virtue of the gift, regard being had to the spirit of the gift.

5–21 Section 47(2) goes on to provide that subs (1) shall not affect the conditions which must be satisfied in order that property given for charitable purposes may be applied *cy-près*, except insofar as those conditions require a failure of the original purposes.

5–22 In *Cheshire Foundation of Ireland v Attorney General*,[28] the Cheshire Foundation applied to the court for an order to frame a scheme *cy-près* of funds held by it in trust for certain only of its homes. The funds consisted of testamentary gifts and monies from fundraising efforts in places where a particular home was situated. However, the Foundation sought general access to these testamentary gifts and monies for the continuance and maintenance of all services provided by the Foundation, otherwise the provision of such services would be put in immediate jeopardy. In her judgment, Laffoy J referred to s 47 and s 51(2) of the 1961 Act, and stated that if the court thought fit it to frame a scheme *cy-près* for the application of property comprised in charitable trusts and gifts, it had the authority to do so. She posed three questions when dealing with the application *cy-près* under s 47 of the 1961 Act:

(i) Whether the restricted funds in the testamentary gifts and monies donated for local purposes were applicable for similar purposes of the Foundation;
(ii) Whether such restricted funds could more effectively be made applicable for the purposes of the Foundation; and
(iii) Whether the restricted funds combined with other assets of the Foundation be consistent with the spirit of the funds so bequeathed and donated for local Homes.

5–23 In relation to question (i), Laffoy J answered that such funds were similarly applicable; in relation to question (ii), she answered that such funds could be more effectively used to further the purposes of the Foundation; in relation to question (iii), she answered that the testamentary gifts and donations were bequeathed and made by the testators and donors with the intention

[28] [2011] IEHC 419.

of ensuring the continuance and maintenance of the services provided by the Foundation.

Laffoy J went on to order that the gifts and monies bequeathed and donated be applied *cy-près* for the purposes of the Foundation. **5–24**

In *Carolan v Jordan*,[29] the deceased testator left a gift of residuary estate to youth clubs in London, and for the purposes of setting up a fund in memory of his deceased son who had been a member of the clubs. The memorial fund, however, was not set up during the lifetime of the testator. The question for the court to decide was whether the residuary estate for the purposes of setting up a memorial fund for the testator's son could be applied *cy-près*. When applying the *cy-près* doctrine to a gift left to a non-existent charitable body, it must first be shown that the testator had a general charitable intention. In the circumstances of the case, White J found that the testator had no such intention, as the residuary gift was created primarily in memory of his son, and could not, therefore, be applied *cy-près*. **5–25**

[29] [2014] IEHC 678.

Chapter 6

POWERS AND WILL TRUSTS

Introduction

A person called the donor may create a power of appointment over property owned by him or her and conferred on and exercisable by a person called the donee in favour of persons called the objects of the power. A power of appointment may be general or special. Where a general power is created by the donor, it may be exercised by the donee in favour of any person, or indeed, in favour of himself or herself. A special power is limited to a specific class of objects and the exercise of the power is confined to that class only. The exercise of a special power is, however, limited to the objects designated in the instrument used by the donor when creating the power. One of the distinguishing features of a power is that the objects of the power cannot, unlike e.g. the beneficiaries of a trust, compel the donee to exercise the power. As trusts are created in the imperative, the beneficiaries may seek the assistance of equity to compel the trustees to administer and distribute the trust estate. Where a will trust purports to exercise a power, it must first, in order to be valid, be executed in compliance with s 78 of the Succession Act 1965 (the "1965 Act").[1] At first glance, powers may appear to be similar to trusts, but they differ from trusts in that the donee's exercise of a power regarding the objects of the power is discretionary, while a trustee is obliged, and may be compelled by the beneficiaries, to carry out the terms of a trust. If a donee does not have this discretion over the exercise of the power regarding the objects or beneficiaries of the power, the courts may decide that the erstwhile power is one in the nature of a trust. Where some doubt exists as to whether the testator intended to create a power of appointment, or one in the nature of a trust, the courts may have to construe and interpret the language used by the donor to ascertain whether he or she intended to create a power, or a power in the nature of a trust. Where the language suggests that the objects of the power are to receive the property, the power may be construed as creating a power in the nature of a trust.[2] One test employed by the courts when determining whether the testator intended to create a power of appointment, or a power in the nature of a trust, is to see whether the power also creates a gift or trust in default of appointment by the donee, and where it does, this is a sufficient indication that the donor intended to create a power, and not a power in the nature of a trust.[3] The test, however, is merely an indication of the existence of a power, and is only 6–01

---

1 See A. Keating, *The Law of Wills* (2nd ed, Clarus Press, Dublin, 2018).

2 *Re Parker* [1966] IR 309.

3 *Re Mills* [1930] 1 Ch 654; *Re Gestetner Settlement* [1953] Ch 672.

that.[4] But where the language suggests that the donor intended the objects of the power to benefit by the property, the court may construe the power as one in the nature of a trust and enforce it accordingly.[5]

6–02 It may be noted that prior to the Land and Conveyancing Law Reform Act 2009 (the "2009 Act"), the rule against perpetuities played a prominent role in the creation and exercise of powers of appointment. The operation of the rule depended on whether the power was a general power or a special power. The rule applied to a general power from the moment of its creation. It applied to a special power from the time of exercising the power. The rule against perpetuities has now been abolished by s 16(d) of the 2009 Act. The exercise of a power may also be subject to formal requirements by the donor specifying the instrument that must be used by the donee when exercising the power, and if the power is exercised by using another instrument, it may be viewed as a defective exercise of the power. The instrument specified by the donor may itself be subject to formal requirements for it to take effect—for example, where a will is the specified instrument, it must be executed in compliance with s 78 of the 1965 Act.

Powers in the Nature of Trusts

6–03 The donor when creating a power of appointment may specify whether he or she intends to create a general or special power of appointment. It is also important that the words used in creating the power are discretionary, and not imperative, in purpose. Where the words used do not afford the donee a degree of discretion in the exercise of the power, they may be construed by the court as creating a power in the nature of a trust. In *Burrough v Philcox*,[6] where the testator left property to his two children for life, and empowered the survivor of them to dispose of the property by will "amongst my nephews and nieces or their children, either all to one of them, or as many of them as my surviving child shall think proper," Lord Cottenham L.C., on holding that a trust, and not a power, was created in favour of the testator's nephews and nieces, went on to state:

> When there appears a general intention in favour of a class, and a particular intention in favour of individuals of a class to be selected by another person, and the particular intention fails, from the selection not being made, the court will carry into effect the general intention in favour of the class.[7]

6–04 Where the court decides that a power in the nature of a trust has been created, it will also apply its maxim that "equality is equity" and will divide the property among the members of the class in equal shares.[8]

---

4 *Re Llewellyn's Settlement* [1921] 2 Ch 281; *Re Weekes' Settlement* [1897] 1 Ch 289; *Re Combe* [1925] Ch 210; *Re Perowne* [1951] Ch 785.
5 *Re Parker* [1966] IR 309.
6 (1840) 5 My & Cr 72.
7 *Burrough v Philcox* (1840) 5 My & Cr 72 at 92.
8 See *Wainright v Howlett* [1947] Ch 131.

As the surviving child in *Burrough v Philcox* had failed to exercise the power, the court ordered that the property be divided equally among the objects or beneficiaries. In relation to the words used by the testator, the court in *Re Parker*[9] had to decide whether they gave the executors a power of a discretionary nature to appoint the income of the fund, or created a power in the nature of an imperative trust, leaving the mode of execution discretionary only. Budd J, having first noted that the residuary bequest was made expressly in trust form, found that the provision regarding the disposal of the income was directory in form. The executors were directed to divide the income among such of the class as they in their discretion thought fit. He stated that:

> It was not a case of the executors being given a discretion to decide whether or not the income is to be divided at all and if so amongst which members of the class, but rather is it a case of a direction as part of the trust to divide amongst such of the class as the executors may think fit.[10]

Accordingly, he held that the power given to the executors was in the nature of an imperative trust. It appears then that where the words used by a testator in creating a power fail to give the donee of the power the discretion essential to a power, such a failure may result in a finding by the court that the testator did not intend to create a pure power, but rather a power in the nature of a trust, and where the beneficiaries are capable of being ascertained, it may enforced as a trust by the court. **6–05**

Where it is contended that a power in the nature of a trust exists, it is essential, as in all trusts, to show that the beneficiaries are capable of being ascertained. Once the beneficiaries are ascertained, they may then enforce the trust. A trust is imperative and the trustees have a duty to carry out the terms of the trust.[11] It is a different matter in the case of a power because of its discretionary nature, and even if all the objects of the power are ascertained or capable of being ascertained, they cannot compel the donee to exercise the power. In *Re Parker*,[12] Budd J found that the testator had created a power in the nature of a trust, and went on to state that: **6–06**

> In cases where the trustees have a duty to distribute the income in question it is essential that they should know, before they perform their duty, who are the potential beneficiaries among whom they have the right of selection, and on the other hand, in the case of a power with a gift over that there is no reason why the trustees, before exercising the power, should have to be able to survey the whole field of objects.[13] The practical result is that a mere power to apply income for the benefit of the members of a class, all of whom cannot be ascertained, with a gift over in default, is valid, and an appointment can validly be made to a person who can properly be said to be a member of the class. But an imperative trust for

[9] [1965] IR 309 at 318.
[10] *Re Parker* [1966] IR 309 at 319.
[11] *Re Ogden* [1933] 1 Ch 678.
[12] [1965] IR 309 at 318.
[13] See *Re Saxone Shoe Co. Ltd's Trust Deed* [1962] 2 All ER 904 at 910.

the division of income between such members of the class as trustees may select is invalid unless the whole class of potential beneficiaries can be ascertained.

The Exercise of Powers of Appointment by Will Trust

6–07 When it comes to exercising the power, not only must the words used by a donee indicate that he or she is exercising a general power of appointment or show a clear intention that he is exercising a special power, but he or she must also use the instrument indicated by the donor when exercising the power. A testator who is a donee of a general power of appointment over property may, when disposing of his own property by will, also exercise the power by creating a trust for the objects he or she intends to benefit. He or she may exercise the power when disposing of the residue of his or her estate as follows:

> I [name of testator/testatrix] of [address] make this as and for my last will and testament and hereby revoke all former wills and testamentary dispositions heretofore made by me.
>
> 1. I appoint AB of [address]
> and CD of [address]
> (hereinafter called "my trustees") to be executors and trustees and appoint them trustees for the purposes of the Land and Conveyancing Law Reform Act 2009 and for the purposes of the Conveyancing Acts and for the purposes of section 57 of the Succession Act 1965.
> 2. I give, devise and bequeath to my trustees the whole of my estate upon trust to sell the same (with power to postpone such sale in whole or in part for such time or times as they shall think fit) and to hold the same or the proceeds of sale thereof on the following trusts:
>   (a) To pay my debts, funeral expenses and testamentary expenses;
>   (b) [Provision for legacies, house and/or contents to, etc., if intended]
>   (c) To hold all the rest, residue and remainder of my property whatsoever and wheresoever situate *including property over which I may have a general power of appointment* I give, devise and bequeath the same unto my trustees upon trust for the benefit of [names of beneficiaries] or any one or more of them exclusive of the others or other of them in such shares and proportions and subject to such trusts, powers, terms, limitations and provisions as my trustees shall from time to time and at any time by deed or deeds revocable or irrevocable or by will appoint and failing such appointment upon trust for [names of beneficiaries] in equal shares. *(emphasis added)*
>
> In addition to all statutory powers that my trustees may have they shall have the following powers:
>
> (i) To exercise the power of appropriation under section 55 of the Succession Act 1965 without serving any of the notices or obtaining any of the required consents.
> (ii) To sell, call in or convert into money at such time or times and in such manner as they shall think fit so much of my estate as shall not be in money form, nevertheless to postpone such sale conversion or calling in indefinitely without being liable for any loss.
> (iii) To sell any asset comprised in my estate at its full open market value to any one or more of my trustees.

(iv) To borrow any amount of money on the security of all or any assets comprised in the estate or without security and generally on such terms as they shall decide without limitation of any kind.
(v) To apply income derived from my estate for the benefit of any beneficiary under the trust hereby created.
(vi) To invest and change investments freely as if they were absolute owners beneficially entitled and to invest in unsecured interest-free loans or other non- income-producing assets including property for occupation or use by any beneficiary.
(vii) To lease, let, mortgage, charge, licence and generally manage and deal with any land which, or the proceeds of sale of which, may for the time being form part of my estate as they were the beneficial owners thereof absolutely entitled.
(viii) To lend money or property to any one or more of the beneficiaries either free of interest or on such terms as to payment of interest and generally as the executors shall in their absolute discretion think fit.
(ix) To trade or take part in any venture in the nature of trade whether solely or jointly with any other person and whether or not by way of partnership and for these purposes to make such arrangements as they shall in their absolute discretion think fit and may delegate any exercise of this power to any one or more of their number or to a company or partnership formed for this purpose.
(x) To insure against any loss or damage from any peril of any property for the time being comprised in my estate for any amount and to pay the premiums out of my estate.
(xi) To appoint a new, additional or substitutional trustee or trustees of this my will.

All income received after my death shall be treated as income of my estate regardless of the period to which it relates and the statutory rules concerning apportionment and the rules in *Howe v Dartmouth* and *Allhusen v Whittell* shall not be applied.

I declare that any of my trustees who is/are engaged in a profession shall be entitled to be paid fees for work done by him/her or his/her firm on the basis that he/she were not one of my trustees but employed to act on behalf of my trustees.

I declare that no trustee of this my will shall be liable for loss not attributable to the trustee's own dishonesty or wilful commission by the trustee of any act known to be a breach of trust.

In witness whereof I have hereunto signed my name the … day of … 20….

SIGNED, PUBLISHED AND DECLARED by the said … as and for his last will and testament in the presence of us who at his request and in his presence and in the presence of each other (all three being present at the same time) have hereunto subscribed our names as witnesses.

Witness 1 [name and address]

Witness 2 [name and address]

Where a power is exercised by an instrument other than by the type of instrument indicated by the instrument creating the power, the exercise may be defective. Where the exercise of a power is defective because an **6–08** instrument other than that indicated was used, the power may be treated as unexercised and entitling the objects to nothing. The donee of the power receives his authority to appoint from the instrument creating the power and should that instrument indicate the form by which the power may be exercised, the exercise must be carried out as indicated by that instrument. If the donee is required to appoint by deed and he appoints by will instead, the power may be treated as unexercised. Even where he or she uses the type of instrument indicated by the power, he must also ensure that the formal requirements for executing the instrument are satisfied. A deed, if that is the instrument indicated, must be properly executed. The same applies to a will where that is the instrument indicated. A will must be executed in compliance with s 78 of the 1965 Act to be valid. Where, however, the instrument creating the power indicates that the instrument to be used in its exercise should observe more than the legal requirements for properly executing that instrument, the extra formality required by the instrument creating the power will not render the instrument exercising the power defective. Where, for instance, a will is to be used in the exercise of the power, but the instrument creating the power requires that the will used to exercise the power must have three witnesses, it will not be a defective exercise of the power if the will is executed in compliance with s 78 that requires only two witnesses.[14] Where the instrument authorised in the exercise of the power is required to be signed, sealed and delivered by two witnesses, the use of a will in the exercise of the power may however not satisfy this requirement.[15]

6–09 Equity may intervene to remedy a defect even though the instrument used in the exercise of a power is other than that indicated by the instrument creating the power, where it is shown that the incorrect instrument was used by accident or by mistake.[16] Equity's intervention in this instance will be confined to remedying the formal defect, but it will not intervene for the purposes of compelling the exercise of a power by using the form indicated by the instrument creating the power. Its intervention may also be dependent on the status or character of the objects to be benefitted, and relief will be granted only where there is a formal defect in favour of a wife, legitimate child, creditor, purchaser or charity.[17] Apparently, it will not remedy a defect in favour of a husband, non-marital child, grandchild or a volunteer.[18] It appears that the list of objects in this instance is exhaustive, and even in the case of children who are included in the list, equity will not grant relief if this would result in depriving other children of equal degree of the property already appointed to them.[19] It must be emphasised that equity will intervene

---

14 *Taylor v Meads* (1865) 4 De GJ & S 597.

15 *Taylor v Meads* (1865) 4 De GJ & S 597.

16 *Garth v Townsend* (1869) LR 7 Eq 220; *Re Huddleston* [1894] 3 Ch 595.

17 *Clifford v Burlington* (1700) 2 Vern 379; *Pollard v Greenvil* (1661) 1 Ch C 10; *Fothergill v Fothergill* (1702) 1 Free Ch 256; *Attorney General v Sibthorpe* (1830) 2 Russ & M 107; *Innes v Sayer* (1851) 3 Mac & G 606.

18 *Moodie v Reid* (1816) 1 Madd 516; *Blake v Blake* (1817) Beat. 575; *Kettle v Townsend* (1700) 1 Salk 187; *Perry v Whitehead* (1801) 6 Ves 522.

19 *Chapman v Gibson* (1791) 3 Bro C C 229 at 230.

only to remedy defects that are of a formal nature. However, a formal defect may affect the substance of a power where a different instrument from that authorised is used in the exercise of the power.[20] Where a power is to be exercised by deed, but it is exercised by a will instead, equity may view this as a formal defect and grant relief accordingly.[21] But where a power is to be exercised by will only, and it is exercised by deed instead, because of the difference in effect between the two types of instrument, the use of a deed instead of a will may affect the substance of the power and debar equity from intervening to remedy the situation. The difference in effect between a deed and a will is that a will is revocable and ambulatory until the death of the testator; a deed, on the other hand, is irrevocable and takes effect upon execution, and likewise the appointment made under it. Because a will may be revoked at any time before death, it allows the donee to revoke the terms of the appointment until his will comes into effect on death, and using a deed instead of a will would not allow a donee to do this.[22]

---

20 *Cockerell v Cholmeley* (1830) 1 Russ & M 418.

21 *Tollet v Tollet* (1728) 2 P Wms 489.

22 *Adney v Field* (1767) Amb 654; *Reid v Shergold* (1805) 10 Ves 370; see *Re Parkin* [1892] 3 Ch 510; *Re Cooke* [1922] 1 Ch 292.

Chapter 7

THE MODIFICATION OF TRUSTS BY EQUITABLE DOCTRINES

Introduction

A trust in a will may be modified by the application of an equitable doctrine. These equitable doctrines are derived from the maxims of equity which act as basic tenets for the courts when exercising their equitable jurisdiction. One of the doctrines is the doctrine of satisfaction, and it is primarily based on the presumed intention of the testator and is derived from the maxim "equity imputes an intention to fulfil an obligation". The doctrine may be applied where legacies are bequeathed in satisfaction of debts, or where legacies are bequeathed in satisfaction of other legacies. The doctrine of conversion becomes applicable where a testator directs his or her executors and trustees to sell his or her real estate, and this direction by the testator to sell may have the effect of converting the real estate into personal estate from the date of his or her death. The maxim employed in this instance is that "equity looks on that as done which ought to have been done"; the real estate will be notionally converted from the date of death of the testator. A power to postpone sale given by a testator to his or her trustees will have the same effect. Such a power will notionally convert the property on the date of the testator's death, and the beneficiaries will thereafter become entitled to the proceeds of the sale. The notional conversion of property by equity may, however, be precluded by the beneficiaries relying on another equitable doctrine, viz. reconversion. Beneficiaries who prefer to receive the property in its unconverted state may rely on this doctrine, and where such is the case, there will be no notional conversion of the property, "as equity, like nature, does nothing in vain." Where, however, an actual conversion takes place by the sale of the property by executors or trustees, the doctrine of reconversion ceases to become operative. According to the rule in *Lassence v Tierney*,[1] where a testator engrafts trusts to an absolute gift "then the absolute gift takes effect so far as the trusts have failed."[2] Where trusts are deemed engrafted onto an absolute gift, the efficacy of the absolute gift will **7–01**

---

[1] (1849) 1 Mac & G 551; see *Hancock v Watson* [1902] AC 14; A. Keating, *The Law of Wills* (2nd ed, Clarus Press, Dublin, 2018); A. Keating, *Probate Motions and Actions Relating to Wills and Intestacies* (Round Hall, Dublin, 2017); A. Keating, *Succession Law in Ireland* (Clarus Press, Dublin, 2015); A. Keating, *Keating on Probate* (5th ed, Round Hall, Dublin, 2015); A. Keating, *Succession Law in Ireland: Principles, Cases and Commentary* (Clarus Press, Dublin, 2016).

[2] *Lassence v Tierney* (1849) 1 Mac & G 551.

depend on the validity of the engrafted trusts.[3] The engrafted trusts may as a result modify the effect of an absolute gift.

The Doctrine of Satisfaction

7–02 The equitable doctrine of satisfaction is based on the presumed intention of the testator, and the maxim "equity imputes an intention to fulfil an obligation". The doctrine of satisfaction may be employed and applied where legacies are left in satisfaction of debts, or legacies are bequeathed in satisfaction of other legacies. A contrary intention appearing from the will may, however, preclude the application of the doctrine.[4] Where a legacy is given in satisfaction of a debt, for the doctrine of satisfaction to work, the legacy must be equal to or greater than the debt owing and due by the testator. Where such is the case, it will be presumed that the legacy was given in satisfaction of the debt.[5] When determining the relative values of the debt and the legacy, any interest accruing on either will not be taken into account.[6] But where the legacy is a residuary legacy, or one that is uncertain or contingent, and as a result not admitting of immediate and finite valuation for the purpose of comparing it with the debt, the doctrine of satisfaction will not be applied.[7] There must be an apparent equality of value between the legacy and the debt for the presumption to arise. The doctrine is also confined in its application to personal property only, and consequently, realty is excluded from the equation.[8]

7–03 The time when a debt was created is also important. A debt, in order to be satisfied by a legacy, must have been due before the testator made his will, and there will be no presumption of satisfaction of a debt contracted subsequent to the making of the will.[9] The payment of a debt by the testator at the time of making the will may have the effect of adeeming the legacy given by him or her in satisfaction of the debt, especially where the debt and legacy are of equal amounts.[10] The underlying tenet at play here is that equity leans against double portions. The doctrine also becomes applicable where two legacies are given to one legatee. Where two legacies of equal amounts are given to one legatee, it will be presumed in the first instance that they are substitutive, and not cumulative.[11] This presumption may be rebutted, however, where the legacies are of unequal amounts,[12] or they are given by

---

3 *Lassence v Tierney* (1849) 1 Mac & G 551.
4 See *Chancey's Case* (1725) 1 P Wms 408; *Bradshaw v Huish* (1889) 43 Ch D 260.
5 *Coates v Coates* [1898] 1 IR 258; *Eastwood v Vinke* (1731) 2 P Wms 613.
6 *Re Rattenberry* [1906] 1 Ch 667; see *Re Horlock* [1895] 1 Ch 516.
7 *Re Keogh's Estate* (1889) 23 LR Ir 257; *Devese v Pontet* (1785) 1 Cox Eq 188; *Crichton v Crichton* [1895] 2 Ch 853; see *Re Van De Burgh W.T.* [1948] 1 All ER 935.
8 *Richardson v Elphinstone* (1794) 2 Ves Jun 463.
9 *Cranmer's Case* (1701) 2 Salk 508; see *Horlock v Wiggins* (1888) 39 Ch D 142.
10 *Re Fletcher, Gillings v Fletcher* (1888) 38 Ch D 373.
11 See *Garth v Meyrick* (1779) 1 Bro CC 30.
12 *Yockney v Hansard* (1844) 3 Hare 620.

different wills,[13] although a second legacy of equal amount in a codicil to the will may not be sufficient to rebut the presumption, unless the testator expresses a motive for giving the two legacies.[14] Even a slight difference in the amounts may be sufficient for the court to render them cumulative, especially where additional admissible extrinsic evidence is supportive of the cumulative nature of the legacy.[15] The onus of proof rests on the party who challenges the cumulative effect of the legacies.[16]

The Doctrine of Election

The doctrine of election is founded on the equitable maxim that equity imputes an intention to fulfil an obligation. The doctrine may be applied to a testamentary gift because there is "an implied condition that he who accepts a benefit under an instrument must adopt the whole of it, conforming to all its provisions and renouncing every right inconsistent with it."[17] The doctrine may be applied to a situation where a testator intends to benefit two beneficiaries, say A and B, by giving each of them a gift in his or her will, but the property in A's gift already belongs to B. As equity will not allow A to go without a gift, it may intervene and apply the doctrine of election by making the gift to B conditional on his transferring the property to A. B must elect between taking the gift left to him in the will and transferring the property to A, and on B's electing not to take the gift, A will become entitled to receive a sum equal in value to the property that B refuses to transfer. The equitable doctrine of election will "impose on him who takes the benefit the obligation of carrying the instrument into full and complete effect."[18] And for this purpose: **7–04**

> Equity fastens on the conscience of the person who is put to his election and refuses to allow him to take the benefit of a disposition contained in the will, the validity of which is not in question, except in certain conditions.[19]

It may also be added that the doctrine is similarly applicable to *inter vivos* gifts by deed.[20] **7–05**

For the doctrine to apply, the testator must first intend to dispose of property that does not belong to him, and secondly, a testamentary gift must be given to the owner of that property.[21] For the beneficiary to make an election, it **7–06**

---

[13] *Foy v Foy* (1785) 1 Cox Eq Cas 163.
[14] *Re Armstrong* (1888) 31 LR Ir 154; see *Bell v Park* [1914] 1 IR 158.
[15] *Hurst v Beach* (1821) 5 Madd 351 at 360–361; *Hall v Hill* (1841) 4 I Eq R 27.
[16] *Quin v Armstrong* (1876) IR 11 Eq 161.
[17] *Codrington v Codrington* (1875) LR 7 HL 854 at 866 *per* Lord Chelmsford.
[18] *Cooper v Cooper* (1874) LR 7 HL 53 at 57 per Lord Hatherley; *Re Sullivan* [1917] 1 IR 38.
[19] *Re Mengel's WT* [1962] Ch 791 at 797 per Buckley J; see *Re Lord Chesham* (1886) 31 Ch D 466 at 473 per Chitty J.
[20] See *Birmingham v Kirwan* (1805) 2 Sch & Lef 444.
[21] *Re Edwards* [1958] Ch 168 at 175 per Jenkins LJ.

must be shown that he or she knew of his or her right of election, and also the relative values of the properties, and the court must be satisfied that he or she intended to exercise a right of election.[22] Once these requisites are present, an election may even be implied from the circumstances of the case.[23] The property that the testator purports to give to a beneficiary must also be alienable property, otherwise no election can be made in relation to it.[24] But where the extent of the beneficiary's ownership in the property is less than was thought to be the case by the testator, a right of election may still be exercised.[25] Where, for instance, a beneficiary's ownership in property amounts to a share in a joint tenancy, but the testator believed that beneficiary was the full owner of it, the disappointed beneficiary's right to compensation will be commensurate only with the value of the share in the joint tenancy.[26] Where no property belonging to the testator can be fixed with the payment of compensation, an election ceases to be a practical proposition.[27] Also, the ownership of the property belonging to a beneficiary, which is given to another as a gift by the testator, must have been created by an instrument other than by the will of the testator: a testator cannot give by one disposition and take away by another in the same will.[28]

The Doctrine of Conversion

7–07 Where a testator directs his or her trustees to sell trust land and convert it into money for the purposes of the trust, the equitable doctrine of conversion will come into play, and the land will be deemed to have been converted into money from the date of death of the testator, unless a contrary intention appears from the provisions of his or her will. Once the obligation to convert the land into money commences, the maxim "equity looks on that as done which ought to be done" becomes applicable. A direction that trust funds are to be employed in the purchase of land will have similar effect from the date of death of the testator. The direction by the testator will empower his or her trustees to convert land into money or money into land, and the new species of property will form the subject matter of the trust.[29] The property will also be deemed converted for the purposes of the devolution of the estate of a deceased testator.[30] Where trustees are directed to convert the property forming the subject matter of the trust, the conversion will occur at the date of death of the testator. The direction to convert itself must be expressed in the imperative mood and must not be merely discretionary.[31]

22 *Sweetman v Sweetman* (1868) IR 2 Eq 141 at 152–153.
23 *Morrison v Bell* (1843) 5 IR 5 Eq 354.
24 *Re Lord Chesham* (1886) 31 Ch D 466.
25 *Re Dicey* [1957] Ch 145.
26 *Re Dicey* [1957] Ch 145.
27 *Re Gordan* [1978] Ch 145; see *Re Saul's Trust* [1951] Ir Jur Rep 34.
28 *Wollaston v King* (1868) LR 8 Eq 165 at 174; *Sweetman v Sweetman* (1868) IR 2 Eq. 141.
29 See *Fletcher v Ashburner* 1 Bro CC 497 at 499.
30 *Chandler v Pocock* (1880) 16 Ch D 491.
31 *McGuire v McGuire* [1900] 1 IR 200 at 203.

A direction, for instance, to sell land with power to postpone the sale will be sufficient. The direction is usually expressed in this way in wills:

> In addition to all statutory powers that my trustees may have they shall have the following powers:
>
> To sell, call in or convert into money at such time or times and in such manner as they shall think fit so much of my estate as shall not be in money form, nevertheless to postpone such sale conversion or calling in indefinitely without being liable for any loss.

A direction may still be considered sufficiently imperative even if a limitation is placed on the amount of money to be spent on the purchase of land, or on the purchase of securities, or on the trustees' discretion regarding the time of purchase.[32] Where, however, a direction to sell is made subject to the assent of another person, who is also empowered to direct the trustees not to sell, it may not be sufficiently imperative to allow a conversion.[33] However, a testator in his or her will may direct that: **7–08**

> In addition to all statutory powers that my trustees may have they shall have the following powers:
>
> To exercise the power of appropriation under section 55 of the Succession Act 1965 without serving any of the notices or obtaining any of the required consents.

Before the trust property is actually sold or trust funds are employed to purchase other property, there will be a notional conversion of the property or funds until the trustees actually exercise the power of sale.[34] Where, however, money is directed to be employed in the purchase of land for the beneficiary of the trust, but he or she dies before the purchase is made, it appears that the beneficiary's estate will be entitled to claim the money, notwithstanding the direction to the trustees to purchase land.[35] While a notional conversion takes place on the death of the testator, it becomes an actual one when the trustees exercise the power of sale. **7–09**

The conversion will take effect at the date of death of the testator unless the will provides otherwise. However, if on that date the beneficiaries of the trust have all predeceased the testator, then not only will the conversion fail to materialise because there is no beneficiary to enforce the sale, but the trust itself will fail by lapse and the trust funds or property will revert to the testator's estate by way of resulting trust.[36] When this takes place, the trust funds or property will form part of the testator's residuary estate, or where the testator does not dispose of his residuary estate, the trust funds or property will be distributed on partial intestacy. **7–10**

---

32 *Earlom v Saunders* (1754) Amb 241.

33 *Re Goodall's Settlement* [1909] 1 Ch 440.

34 *Re Bird* [1892] 1 Ch 279; *Re Dyson* [1910] 1 Ch 750.

35 *Curling v May* (1734) 3 Atk 255; *Re Twopeny's Settlement* [1924] 1 Ch 522.

36 See *Re Lord Grimthorpe* [1908] 2 Ch 675.

7–11 However, a testator's direction to convert may be varied by the beneficiaries of the trust by relying on the sister doctrine of reconversion. While the direction to convert will take effect on the date of death of the testator, the beneficiaries are entitled to insist on receiving the species of property forming the subject matter of the trust by relying on the doctrine of reconversion. Where a beneficiary relies on reconversion, he or she will be entitled to the subject matter of the trust notwithstanding the testator's direction to convert. Indeed, it may be said that the direction to convert itself may be modified by a beneficiary's insistence on receiving the property in its unconverted state; equity does nothing in vain.

Engrafted Trusts

7–12 The rule in *Lassence v Tierney*[37] may apply whether the absolute gift is one of land or is a legacy or bequest, and it is not necessary that the engrafted trusts appear in the same instrument as the absolute gift.[38] While the absolute gift may appear in a will, it may also be governed by engrafted trusts appearing in a subsequent codicil.[39] Nor is it necessary to show how engrafted trusts fail for the absolute gift to take effect.[40] Where, however, the engrafted trusts do not fail, they will have the effect of modifying an absolute gift and may be enforced accordingly.[41] The court may also construe the provisions of a gift as a whole to determine the effect that subsequent trusts may have on a prior absolute gift. In *Re Atkinson*,[42] Gavan Duffy J, when construing the provision "I leave ... my nieces Lucy Pollock and Mabel Olive £3,000 each in trust, at their deaths to their children in equal shares who shall attain the age of 21 years" found that it created an absolute gift, but one that was defeasible in the event of the trusts taking effect. He also found support for his view in *Crozier v Crozier*[43] where a testator gave the residue of his estate to his wife and after her death to his children in equal shares. There were no children, and James LJ held that the widow took absolutely. He also referred to *Monck v Croker*,[44] where a testatrix, after giving the bulk of her estate to her sister B., went on to provide: "I would wish my money to be divided in equal shares after my sister B.'s death between my sister G. and my niece H., should they survive her." It was held that although B. took an absolute interest, it was liable to be divested by the contingent executory gift over, but became indefeasible on her surviving G. and H. Where it is established, however, that the words used by the testator disclosed a motive only for the gift, it will not be treated as a trust, and the beneficiary will take an absolute interest. In *In the Goods of Fitzgibbon*,[45] where the testator bequeathed all

---

[37] (1849) 1 Mac & G 551; see *Hancock v Watson* [1902] AC 14.
[38] *Hancock v Watson* [1902] AC 14 at 22 per Lord Davey.
[39] *Norman v Kynaston* (1861) 3 De G.G. & J 29.
[40] *Watkins v Weston* (1863) 3 De GJ & S 434.
[41] See *Re Atkinson* [1942] IR 268.
[42] *Re Atkinson* [1942] IR 268.
[43] (1843) 3 Dr & War 373.
[44] [1900] 1 IR 56.
[45] (1959) 93 ILTR 56.

the residue of his estate to his second cousin Catherine O'Donoghue "for the benefit of herself and her children Anne, John, and Mary as she in her discretion shall think fit", it was held by Budd J that the words had the effect of vesting an absolute gift in Catherine O'Donoghue unaffected by any trust in favour of her children, as the words used expressed a motive only for the gift and were not intended to create a trust in favour of the children.

CHAPTER 8

THE RULE AGAINST DOUBLE PORTIONS

INTRODUCTION

The equitable doctrine of satisfaction is based on the presumed intention of the testator, and the maxim, "equity leans against double portions". According to that doctrine, where a testator, after making his will, gives a gift to his child, it may be viewed as a portion. A portion arises where a father (not a mother) agrees to give his child, or a testator who agrees to give to a person to whom he stands in loco parentis, a sum of money on marriage or towards setting him or her up in a business or a profession. Since the enactment of the Status of Children Act 1987, it appears that the definition of child for the purposes of the doctrine will also include non-marital children.[1] The application of the doctrine of satisfaction to portions and legacies is confined to the relationship of father and child or a person to whom the testator stands in loco parentis. Where a child or the person to whom the testator stands in loco parentis is subsequently left a legacy it will be presumed that the legacy was given in satisfaction of the agreed portion.[2] The child of the testator or the person to whom the testator stands in loco parentis cannot claim both the sum agreed on foot of the inter vivos agreement to give a portion, and the legacy in the will trust. In the case of satisfaction of a portion by a legacy, the child or the person to whom the testator stands in loco parentis may elect to take either the portion or the legacy.[3] An election between the portion and legacy cannot take place until the will trust comes into effect on the death of the testator. In *Hickey v O'Dwyer*,[4] Laffoy J stated that: **8–01**

> The presumption of satisfaction of a portion by a legacy has traditionally been applied in this jurisdiction where the settlor or testator is the father of, or *in loco*

---

1 See *Hickey v O'Dwyer* [2006] 2 ILRM 81.

2 *Thynne v Earl of Glengall* (1848) 2 HL Cas 131; see *Re Bannon, Callanan v Ryan (No.2)* [1934] IR 701; *Taylor v Taylor* (1875) LR 20 Eq 155; *Re George's W.T.* [1949] Ch 154; A. Keating, "The Effect of Portions and Advancements on Testamentary Gifts to Children, Part One" (2008) 13(2) CPLJ 40; A. Keating, "The Effect of Portions and Advancement on Testamentary Gifts to Children, Part Two" (2008) 13(3) CPLJ 57.

3 See *Hickey v O'Dwyer* [2006] 2 ILRM 81; A. Keating, *The Law of Wills* (2nd ed, Clarus Press, Dublin, 2018); A. Keating, *Probate Motions and Actions Relating to Wills and Intestacies* (Round Hall, Dublin, 2017); A. Keating, *Succession Law in Ireland* (Clarus Press, Dublin, 2015); A. Keating, *Keating on Probate* (5th ed, Round Hall, Dublin, 2015); A. Keating, *Succession Law in Ireland: Principles, Cases and Commentary* (Clarus Press, Dublin, 2016).

4 [2006] 2 ILRM 81.

parentis, to the donee, the first gift is a portion and both gifts are substantially of the same nature and in favour of the same person.

8–02 *Hickey v O'Dwyer* involved a life policy creating a trust effective on death and was viewed as a portion for the purposes of the doctrine of satisfaction, thereby entitling a beneficiary to elect whether to take the portion or the legacy at the date of death of the testator. The property forming the subject matter of the portion and legacy must also be *ejusdem generis*, but if not, a system of valuation may be used for the purposes of comparing the value of the portion with that of the legacy. Where the legacy is less than the portion, it may still be regarded as satisfaction pro tanto of the earlier portion. Where the portion is less than the legacy, the legacy may be regarded as satisfaction *pro tanto* of the later portion, but only for the purposes of determining the balance between the two. It will be remembered that an earlier legacy may be adeemed by a later portion. It appears, however, that there can be no ademption of a legacy where the portion consists of land. The whole question of satisfaction of a portion by a legacy or vice versa is subject to a contrary intention expressed by the testator in his will.

8–03 Portions given or legacies left to a child of a testator may also be taken into account by the court under s 117(1) of the Succession Act 1965 when determining whether the testator has fulfilled his moral duty to make proper provision for the applicant child. Section 117(1) provides that:

> Where, on application by or on behalf of a child of a testator, the court is of opinion that the testator has failed in his moral duty to make proper provision for the child in accordance with his means, whether by his will *or otherwise*, the court may order that such provision shall be made for the child out of the estate as the court thinks just. (emphasis added).

Satisfaction of Portions by Legacies

8–04 The equitable doctrine of satisfaction may come into play when it is alleged that portions were satisfied by legacies or legacies by portions. For the doctrine of satisfaction to apply to portions, the relationship of father and child, or that of a person to whom the testator stands *in loco parentis*, must exist.[5] No other relationship will raise the presumption of satisfaction, not even that of mother and child.[6] Since the enactment of the Status of Children Act 1987, it appears that the relationship of father and a non-marital child will also come within the scope of this presumption.[7] The circumstances of the case will determine whether or not the testator stands *in loco parentis*

[5] *Schofield v Heap* (1858) 27 Beav 93; *Fowkes v Pascoe* (1875) 10 Ch App 343; see *Pym v Lockyer* (1841) 5 My & Cr 29; *Powys v Mansfield* (1837) 3 My & Cr 359.

[6] *Taylor v Taylor* (1875) LR 20 Eq 155.

[7] Status of Children Act 1987, ss 3, 26, 27, 28 and 29; see *Hickey v O'Dwyer* [2006] 2 ILRM 81. It appears that the definition of child and dispositions to children for the purposes of the doctrine of satisfaction also includes illegitimate children. This is in keeping with the definition of relationships in the Status of Children Act 1987.

to another person, and as the expression means "in place of a parent", it seems that the relationship must be tantamount to that which normally exists between father and child.[8] The value of the portion will also be considered, and it must be shown to be substantial enough to carry out the intended purpose, i.e. to make permanent provision for a child or person to whom the testator stands *in loco parentis*.[9] Where, for instance, the sum representing the portion is substantial enough to set a child up in a business, it will be treated as a portion making permanent provision for the child.[10] Personal gifts given during the lifetime of the testator such as birthday presents or commemorating a special event would not normally be viewed as portions.[11]

When determining whether a legacy is in satisfaction of a portion, the court will first look to the intention of the testator, and then proceed to compare the value of the legacy and the portion.[12] There must be parity of value for a legacy to satisfy a portion and this may not be an easy matter to establish, especially, where the legacy and portion are not *ejusdem generis*, i.e. the same kind of property.[13] In all cases where the portion and the legacy are not *ejusdem generis*, some valuation must be given to the portion.[14] A legacy and an agreed portion consisting of the same sum of money lends itself to easy comparison, but if the portion is other than a sum of money, then a valuation will be required.[15] When as a result of a valuation, the differences in value between the portion and the legacy is slight, satisfaction will be presumed.[16] Where however the sum representing the legacy is less than that of the portion, it may still be regarded as *pro tanto* satisfaction.[17] **8–05**

The reason behind the doctrine is that all the children of a testator should be given equal treatment in a distribution of his property, and any *inter vivos* agreement for the giving of a portion to a particular child will be taken into account to ensure that this will occur. Where the doctrine of satisfaction is applied, the child of the testator, or the person to whom the testator is *in loco parentis*, has a choice of either taking the portion agreed between him and the testator or the legacy in the will.[18] As the doctrine only imputes an intention, its application is subject to a contrary intention appearing in the will. **8–06**

---

8 *Fowkes v Pascoe* (1875) 10 Ch App 343; *Powys v Mansfield* (1837) 3 My & Cr 359; *Smyth v Gleeson* [1911] 1 IR 113; see *Re Bannon, Callanan v Ryan* [1934] IR 701.
9 *Taylor v Taylor* (1875) LR 20 Eq 155; *Re Hayward* [1957] Ch 528 at 542.
10 *Lawes v Lawes* (1881) 20 Ch D 81.
11 *Re Tussaud's Estate* (1878) 9 Ch D 363; *Schofield v Heap* (1858) 27 Beav 93.
12 See *Re Battersby's Estate* (1887) 19 LR Ir 359.
13 *Bellasis v Uthwatt* (1737) 1 Atk 426; *Re Jacques* [1903] 1 Ch 267 (CA); *Smyth v Gleeson* [1911] 1 IR 113.
14 *Lawes v Lawes* (1881) 20 Ch D 81; *Re George's W.T.* [1949] Ch 154.
15 *Re George's W.T.* [1949] Ch 154; *Lawes v Lawes* (1881) 20 Ch D 81.
16 *Thynne v Earl of Glengall* (1848) 2 HL Cas 131; see *Re Gleeson* (1878) 9 Ch D 363.
17 *Lord Chicester v Coventry* (1867) LR 2 HL 71; *Warren v Warren* (1783) 1 Bro CC 305; *Hickey v O'Dwyer* [2006] 2 ILRM 81.
18 *Hickey v O'Dwyer* [2006] 2 ILRM 81.

8–07 A life assurance policy creating a trust effective on death may be viewed as a portion for the purposes of the doctrine of satisfaction, and thereby entitle a beneficiary to elect whether to take the portion or the legacy at the date of death of the testator. In *Hickey v O'Dwyer*,[19] Laffoy J considered the application of the doctrine of satisfaction *à propos* the satisfaction of a portion by a legacy. In that case, the testator was the husband of the plaintiff and father of the fourth defendant, who was born on 5 December 1990. The third defendant was the mother of the fourth defendant. The testator and the third defendant were not married. In 1993, the testator took out a life assurance policy and executed a document (the "1993 Trust") consisting of a declaration of trust in a standard form produced by the insurer. It was a special condition of the policy that it was issued pursuant to the 1993 Trust. In the 1993 Trust, the testator declared that the trustees for the time being should hold the policy and the full benefit thereof and all monies which might become payable thereunder upon trust, if the benefit under the policy should become payable in consequence of the death of the testator, for the benefit of all or more of the class of persons named by relationship to the testator—which included spouse and children of the testator—as the testator in his absolute discretion should by deed or deeds revocable or irrevocable appoint. It was expressly provided that no appointment should be made nor any power of revocation exercised after the death of the testator. It was also provided that, in default of and subject to any such appointment, the trust fund should be held for the absolute benefit of the fourth defendant as to 100% of the trust fund. The testator did not exercise the power of appointment over the trust fund conferred on him in the 1993 Trust during his lifetime. Following his death, the proceeds of the policy, IR£223,350, were paid out by the insurers to two trustees of the trust fund on behalf of the fourth defendant.

8–08 The testator made his will on 26 May 1998. He appointed the plaintiff to be his sole executrix and residuary legatee and devisee. There were two dispositive provisions in the will. The provision which gave rise to the issue in the proceedings was clause 4 wherein the testator devised and bequeathed the sum of IR£100,000 to the first, second and third defendants to be held by them in trust as thereinafter set out for his daughter, the fourth defendant, until she should attain the age of 25 years and then to her absolutely. The first, second and third defendants were appointed as trustees of that bequest and the trusts upon which they were to hold the sum of IR£100,000 were set out. The other dispositive provision was the devise and bequest of the residue to the plaintiff for her own use and benefit absolutely. The executrix having renounced her right to probate, letters of administration with the testator's will annexed were granted to the first and second defendants on 15 July 2003. The first and second defendants were party to the proceedings in their capacity as personal representatives of the testator. One of the main issues raised in the special summons concerned the entitlement of the fourth defendant to the proceeds of the policy of life assurance and under the will.

19 [2006] 2 ILRM 81.

The court was asked to determine whether the bequest in the testator's will to set up a trust in favour of the fourth defendant in the amount of IR£100,000 was intended to be in whole or in part satisfaction of the monies held upon trust for her pursuant to the terms of the 1993 trust funds Counsel for the plaintiff submitted that the doctrine of satisfaction was applicable to the circumstances of the case and there was satisfaction of a portion by a legacy. **8–09**

Laffoy J found that **8–10**

> the presumption of satisfaction of a portion by a legacy has traditionally been applied in this jurisdiction where the settlor or testator is the father of, or *in loco parentis*, to the donee, the first gift is a portion and both gifts are substantially of the same nature and in favour of the same person.

She was satisfied that the provision made in 1993 was a portion in the sense of being a gift of a substantial nature relative to the means of the testator and intended to set up the fourth defendant for life. Moreover, she was satisfied that the provision made in the 1993 Trust and the provision made by the testator in his will for the fourth defendant were substantially of the same nature. They were both, essentially, dispositions of money to which the fourth defendant was to be absolutely entitled, although in the case of the bequest in the will, the trustees would have control until she attained 25 years of age. Although the provision in the will was substantially smaller than what the policy yielded, the doctrine of satisfaction admits of a lesser provision in a will being satisfaction *pro tanto* of an earlier portion. Laffoy J thought that the totality of the relevant evidence in relation to the testator's age, marital status and personal circumstances and the state of his assets when he made his will, supported the presumption that the testator did not intend that the fourth defendant should receive both the entirety of the proceeds of the policy and the bequest contained in his will: "[i]n other words, the presumption stands". The consequence of the conclusion that the doctrine of satisfaction applied was that an election had to be made on behalf of the fourth defendant, who was still a minor, between the provision contained in the 1993 Trust and the provision under the will. **8–11**

Satisfaction of Legacies by Portions

In relation to the satisfaction of legacies by portions, Sullivan M.R. in *Curtin v Evans*,[20] stated that **8–12**

> when a parent, or one standing *in loco parentis*, gives by will a sum of money to a child, and afterwards a like or greater sum is secured by settlement in the marriage of that child, the law presumes the legacy to be adeemed.

When explaining the application of the doctrine, Lord Greene MR in *Re Veux*[21] stated that: **8–13**

---

[20] (1872) R 9 Eq 553 at 557.

[21] [1939] Ch 465 at 481; see *Curtin v Evans* (1872) IR 9 Eq 553.

> The conception is that the testator having in his will given to his children that portion of the estate which he decides to give them, when after making his will he confers upon a child a gift of such a nature as to amount to a portion, then he is not to be presumed to have intended that that child should have both, the gift *inter vivos* being taken as being on account of the portion given by the will.

8–14 The equitable doctrine of ademption therefore may also come into play when a portion is given to a child of a testator or the person to whom the testator stands *in loco parentis*, after the making of the will containing the legacy, and as a result, the legacy may be adeemed by the portion. This is because again equity leans against double portions, and it will be presumed that the legacy was given in satisfaction of the portion.[22] In the case of satisfaction of a legacy by a portion, it also appears that no election is possible as the legacy will be adeemed by the portion. It appears that there can be no ademption of a legacy where the portion consists of land: "it is elementary that money is not adeemed unless indeed a money value is put upon the gift."[23] The satisfaction of a legacy by a portion or vice versa is subject to a contrary intention expressed by the testator in his will.

8–15 The legacy may be adeemed by the portion given in the lifetime of the testator by virtue of the equitable doctrine of ademption.[24] Here also equity leans against double portions. The same relationship as in satisfaction of portions by legacies must exist between testator and legatee, namely, the father as testator and his child, or person to whom he stands *in loco parentis*, as legatee.[25] The presumption of ademption of legacies by portions may be rebutted in the case of relationships where it is established that the testator did not stand *in loco parentis* to the legatee. In *Re Bannon, Callanan v Ryan*,[26] the testator left a legacy of £300 to one of his nephews who at an early age came to live with the testator's family. The nephew was later apprenticed to a business in a nearby town, and the testator's mother paid the apprenticeship fee and provided him with pocket money. From that time onwards he ceased to reside with the testator and his family, although he paid occasional visits and spent holidays on the testator's farm. On the nephew's marriage, a business was purchased for him with money provided by his wife and the testator. The amount contributed by the testator was £225. The nephew's own parents were alive during the time he spent with the testator's family, and he also visited them occasionally. On the testator's death, it was claimed by the residuary legatee that when the testator contributed the sum of £225 to the nephew for the purposes of setting him up in business, he stood *in loco parentis* to him, and that legacy of £300 was adeemed accordingly. In the Supreme Court, it was held by Kennedy CJ that as there was no evidence that the testator ever adopted the nephew as his own child, either formally or informally, or made himself responsible for the

22 *Weall v Rice* (1831) 2 Russ & M 251; *Blundell v Blundell* [1906] 2 Ch 222.
23 *Re Wall's Estate* [1922] 1 IR 59 at 61 *per* O'Connor MR.
24 *Re Pollock* (1885) 28 Ch D 552.
25 *Curtin v Evans* (1872) IR 9 Eq 553.
26 [1934] IR 701; see *Smyth v Gleeson* [1911] 1 IR 113.

upbringing of the nephew in any way. The claim that the testator was *in loco parentis* to the nephew failed, and accordingly, the legacy left to him by the testator was not adeemed. Kennedy CJ stated that in such cases the evidence must establish:

> that the testator stood in that relationship to the appellant which is called *in loco parentis*, so that the legacy may be deemed to be the discharge of the testator's obligation, whether legal or moral, to make provision for the legatee *in loco filii*, and the subsequent gift to be an advancement on account of such provision made by will.

It will be presumed: **8–16**

> that both gifts were made to fulfil the same natural or moral obligation of providing for the legatee and consequently that the gift *inter vivos* is either wholly or in part a substitution for or an ademption of the legacy.[27]

The presumption of ademption may be rebutted, however, if the legacy and the portion are not *ejusdem generis*.[28] Similar to the case of satisfaction of a portion by a legacy, where the property comprising the portion and legacy is not the same, and not capable of immediate valuation, the presumption may not be applied, unless the testator provides some system of valuation in his will.[29] Where, however, the portion is less than the value of the legacy, the legacy may be deemed *pro tanto* the value of the portion for the purposes of ascertaining the value of the balance.[30] As in the case of a portion followed by a legacy, the presumption of satisfaction may be rebutted by some form of declaration by a testator in his will that the legacy is given in addition to the agreed portion. A similar declaration may preclude the operation of the doctrine of ademption, and the legatee may become entitled to both portion and legacy. Extrinsic evidence may be adduced to show that the testator intended his child, or person to whom he stands *in loco parentis*, to receive both legacy and portion.[31] **8–17**

---

[27] *Re Pollock* (1885) 28 Ch D 552 at 555.
[28] *Re Jacques* [1903] 1 Ch 267 (CA).
[29] *Holmes v Holmes* (1783) 1 Bro Ch C 555.
[30] *Edgeworth v Johnston* (1877) IR 11 Eq 326; *Pym v Lockyer* (1841) 5 My & Cr 29.
[31] *Weall v Rice* (1831) 2 Russ & M 251.

Chapter 9

EQUITABLE AND STATUTORY ADVANCEMENTS

Introduction

In cases involving the voluntary transfer of property, a resulting trust will be presumed to exist, and the property will revert to the transferor, unless it can be shown that he or she intended to benefit the transferee. Where it is established in evidence that the transferor intended to benefit the transferee, this may be sufficient to rebut the presumption of a resulting trust. Where an express trust fails, the property comprised in it will revert back to the estate by way of a resulting trust. A resulting trust arises by operation of law, or as one judge put it, "automatically".[1] The existence of a resulting trust may also be presumed in cases of voluntary conveyances of land or transfers of personal property. However, where it is established in evidence that the transferor intended to benefit the transferee, this may be sufficient to rebut the presumption of a resulting trust. Where a husband voluntarily transfers property to his wife or child such transfer of property may be presumed to be an equitable advancement. It is the nature of the relationship of husband and wife and father and child that gives rise to the presumption of an equitable advancement, and rebuts the presumption of a resulting trust.[2] It appears that such an advancement made by a mother to her child will not be viewed as an equitable advancement. However, the presumption of advancement may be rebutted by acts or statements by husband or father made before or at the time of making the advancement showing that no advancement was intended.[3] In *RF v MF*,[4] Henchy J treated a wife's subsequent refusal to live with her husband as sufficient grounds for rebutting the presumption of advancement. He stated that: **9–01**

> If the relevant circumstances show that the paper result achieved by the conveyance conceals the real intention of the husband in entering the transaction, so that the benefit contended for by the wife was not intended, the court will hold that the presumption of advancement is rebutted.[5]

Statutory advancements may also be made to children within the meaning of s 63 of the Succession Act 1965 (the "1965 Act"). An advancement under s 63 means making **9–02**

---

1 *Re Vandervell's Trusts (No. 2)* [1974] Ch 269 at 294.
2 *Bennet v Bennet* (1879) 10 Ch D 474; *O'Brien v Sheil* (1873) IR 7 Eq 255.
3 *Shepherd v Cartwright* [1955] AC 431.
4 *R F v M F* [1995] 2 ILRM 572 at 576–577.
5 *RF v MF* [1995] 2 ILRM 572 at 577.

> permanent provision for a child and includes advancement by way of portion or settlement, including any life or lesser interest and including property covenanted to be paid or settled. It also includes an advancement or portion for the purpose of establishing a child in a profession, vocation, trade or business, a marriage portion and payments made for the education of a child to a standard higher than that provided by the deceased for any other or others of his children.[6]

9–03 The definition of child for the purposes of s 63 includes the issue of the child,[7] and also a person to whom the deceased was *in loco parentis*.[8] An advancement made under s 63 will

> be taken as being made in or towards satisfaction of the share of such child in the estate of the deceased or share which such child would have taken if living at the death of the deceased, and as between the children shall be brought into account in distributing the estate.[9]

9–04 The making of an advancement under s 63 is subject to a contrary intention "expressed or appearing from the circumstances of the case."[10] Unlike equitable advancements, it appears that an advancement made by a mother to her child will also be taken into account for the purposes of s 63. An advancement under the equitable doctrine for a purpose not falling under s 63 may not be taken into account when deciding the value of a child's testamentary gift or share on intestacy.

9–05 Advancements made to a child of a testator may also be taken into account by the court under s 117(1) of the 1965 Act when determining whether the testator has fulfilled his moral duty to make proper provision for the applicant child. Section 117(1) provides that:

> Where, on application by or on behalf of a child of a testator, the court is of opinion that the testator has failed in his moral duty to make proper provision for the child in accordance with his means, whether by his will *or otherwise*, the court may order that such provision shall be made for the child out of the estate as the court thinks just. (emphasis added).

The Presumption of Resulting Trusts

9–06 Equitable property rights may be acquired by resulting trusts, and such trusts will be presumed to exist in cases of voluntary conveyances of land or transfers of personal property. However, where it is established in evidence that the transferor intended to benefit the transferee, this may be sufficient to rebut the presumption of a resulting trust. In *Stanley v Kieran*,[11] the appellant supplied the purchase money for the purchase of a property which was later

---

6 Succession Act 1965, s 63(6).
7 Succession Act 1965, s 63(3) and (4).
8 Succession Act 1965, s 63(10).
9 Succession Act 1965, s 63(1).
10 Succession Act 1965, s 63(1).
11 [2011] IESC 19.

transferred to a company. The share capital of the company was registered in the respondent's name. The appellant and respondent were cohabitants. A dispute arose concerning the beneficial ownership of the property, and whether a resulting trust existed in favour of the appellant in the property and share capital in the company. Denham CJ, having stated that there is a presumption that a person who provides the purchase money for the purchase of property is the beneficial owner of the property, referred to Delany's *Equity and the Law of Trusts in Ireland*,[12] for the statement that:

> Where a person provides the purchase money for property, whether real or personal, which is conveyed or transferred to another person or to himself and the other person jointly, it is presumed that the latter holds the property on a resulting trust for the person who provided the purchase money.

Such a presumption may, however, be rebutted by evidence showing a contrary intention to the creation of a resulting trust. There was no such evidence adduced, and accordingly, Denham CJ found that a resulting trust existed in favour of the appellant against the respondent and company. **9–07**

The Presumption of Advancement and Spouses

The presumption of a resulting trust may also be rebutted by reliance on the equitable doctrine of advancement. Where a testator during his lifetime transfers property to his wife the property so transferred may be viewed as an equitable advancement, and as such the property forming part of the advancement will not form part of a testator's estate. It is essentially the nature of the relationship between the transferor and transferee that gives rise to the presumption of advancement. It must be emphasised, however, that it is a wife or child who may rely on the presumption; no such presumption will be made where a wife transfers property to her husband. The presumption of advancement may be rebutted by proof of a contrary intention. The doctrine of advancement raises a presumption only, and it is one that may be rebutted by acts or statements made before or at the time of making the advancement showing that no advancement was intended.[13] In such cases the onus is on the husband or father to show "by reference to acts or statements before or around the transaction, that a beneficial interest was not intended to be conveyed in the circumstances relied on."[14] Acts done or statements made after the making of the advancement will not, however, be admitted in evidence to support a rebuttal of the presumption.[15] In *RF v MF*,[16] Henchy J treated a wife's subsequent refusal to live with her husband as sufficient grounds for rebutting the presumption of advancement. He stated that: **9–08**

> If the relevant circumstances show that the paper result achieved by the

---

[12] (4th ed, Thomson Round Hall, Dublin, 2007), p 161.
[13] *Shepherd v Cartwright* [1955] AC 431.
[14] *RF v M F* [1995] 2 ILRM 572 at 576–577.
[15] *RF v MF* [1995] 2 ILRM 572 at 576–577.
[16] *RF v MF* [1995] 2 ILRM 572 at 576–577.

> conveyance conceals the real intention of the husband in entering the transaction, so that the benefit contended for by the wife was not intended, the court will hold that the presumption of advancement is rebutted.[17]

9–09 The courts will be slow to rebut the presumption, and will only do so where there is evidence of acts or statements that go towards showing that no advancement was intended, or that the circumstances of the case show, as in *RF v MF*, the existence of an arrangement between husband and wife and her subsequent breach of that arrangement.[18] Where it is discovered that the husband made the advancement for an illegal purpose, evidence of the illegal purpose cannot be adduced for the purposes of rebutting the presumption.[19] The equitable doctrine of advancement may also be relied on by a child where there is a voluntary transfer of property that would normally give rise to a resulting trust but for the fact that the transferor is the father (not the mother) of the child. In such a case, it is the nature of the relationship between father and child that gives rise to the presumption of advancement. The presumption of advancement to a child may of course be rebutted by proof of a contrary intention. In *O'Meara v Bank of Scotland*,[20] which concerned a dispute involving the presumption of advancement and a joint deposit bank account of a husband and wife, Laffoy J in the course of her judgment referred to the following passage in the judgment of Keane J in *JH v JHC*[21]:

> Where property is taken in the joint names of two or more persons, but the purchase money is advanced by one of them alone, the law presumes a resulting trust in favour of the person who advanced the purchase money. This presumption may however be rebutted; and in particular the circumstances of the person in whose name the property is conveyed being the wife of the person advancing money may be sufficient to rebut the presumption under the doctrine of advancement.

9–10 Evidence may be adduced rebutting the presumption of advancement, but where no such evidence is adduced, the presumption will continue to be applied, as in *O'Meara v Bank of Scotland*, where Laffoy J found that the conduct of the defendant was wholly consistent with the monies being jointly owned by the deceased and the plaintiff.

The Presumptions of Advancement and Children

9–11 A voluntary transfer of property, which would normally give rise to a resulting trust, may be viewed as an equitable advancement where the transferor is the father of the child. In such a case, it is the nature of the relationship between father and child that gives rise to the presumption

[17] *RF v MF* [1995] 2 ILRM 572 at 577.
[18] See *Malone v McQuaid*, unreported, High Court, O'Sullivan J, 28 May 1998.
[19] *Parker v Parker* [1980] ILRM 137.
[20] [2011] IEHC 402.
[21] Unreported, High Court, Keane J, 4 August 1982.

of advancement.[22] As regards the relationship of father and child and the presumption of advancement, it was stated by Jessel MR in *Bennet v Bennet*[23] that a father "is under that obligation from the mere fact of his being the father, and therefore no evidence is necessary to show the obligation to provide for his child." He went on to say that in the case of a father, "you have only to prove that he is the father," and when that is done the obligation at once arises. It is the nature of the relationship that gives rise to the presumption of advancement and rebuts the presumption of a resulting trust. The intention of a father, or person *in loco parentis*, to make an advancement may be gathered from:

> contemporaneous acts, and even contemporaneous declarations of the parent, may amount to such evidence … Subsequent acts and declarations of the parent are not evidence to support the trust, although subsequent acts and declarations of the child may be so; but generally speaking we are to look to what was said and done at the time.[24]

Apparently, a gift made by a mother to her child will not be an advancement for the purposes of the equitable doctrine.[25] The presumption of advancement may however be rebutted where a contrary intention is evident.[26] Therefore, for advancement to be presumed, there must be a voluntary transfer of property, and the transferor is a father and the transferee is his child or a child to whom he is *in loco parentis*. **9–12**

Such equitable advancements to children may also be taken into account by the court under s 117(1) of the 1965 Act when determining whether the testator has fulfilled his moral duty to make proper provision for the applicant child. Section 117(1) provides that: **9–13**

> Where, on application by or on behalf of a child of a testator, the court is of opinion that the testator has failed in his moral duty to make proper provision for the child in accordance with his means, whether by his will *or otherwise*, the court may order that such provision shall be made for the child out of the estate as the court thinks just. (emphasis added)

Statutory Advancements to Children

An advancement coming within the meaning of s 63 of the 1965 Act may be taken into account when computing the value of a child's testate or intestate share in the estate of a deceased person. Section 63(1) provides that any advancement made to the child of a deceased person during his **9–14**

---

22 *Bennet v Bennet* (1879) 10 Ch D 474; *O'Brien v Sheil* (1873) IR 7 Eq 255.

23 (1879) 10 Ch D 474at 476.

24 *Sidmouth v Sidmouth* (1840) 2 Beav. 447, at 455 *per* Lord Langdale; see *O'Brien v Sheil* (1873) IR 7 Eq 255.

25 *Bennet v Bennet* (1879) 10 Ch D 474.

26 See *O'Brien v Sheil* (1873) IR 7 Eq 255; *Shephard v Cartwright* [1955] AC 431; *Marshall v Crutwell* (1875) LR 20 Eq 328; *RF v MF* [1995] 2 ILRM 572.

lifetime, the issue of the child, or a person to whom the deceased was *in loco parentis*, will

> be taken as being made in or towards satisfaction of the share of such child in the estate of the deceased or share which such child would have taken if living at the death of the deceased, and as between the children shall be brought into account in distributing the estate.[27]

9–15 But for such advancement to be taken into account, it must be for one of the purposes set out in s 63 of the 1965 Act. An advancement for the purposes of s 63 means a gift intended for establishing a child in a profession, vocation, trade or in a business, or for the education of a child to a standard higher than that provided by the transferor for any other of his children or intended to make permanent provision for a child, and this includes an advancement by way of portion or settlement, including any life or lesser interest and including property covenanted to be paid or settled, and will not be taken into account where the child is left a gift in the father's or mother's will or his share on intestacy. Where an advancement of real or personal property is made for any of the purposes in s 63, it will be taken as being made in satisfaction of a gift in a will, or share on intestacy, and will be brought into account in distributing the estate.[28] Such advancement will be reckoned as part of the estate and its value will be reckoned as at the date of advancement.[29] If the advancement coming within the provisions of s 63 is equal to or greater than the share which a child is entitled to receive under the will or intestacy, the child, or indeed, issue of the child, will be excluded from taking his testate or intestate share in the estate.[30] Where, however, the advancement is less than the legacy or share on intestacy, the child will be entitled to receive in satisfaction of the legacy or share so much only of the estate as, when added to the advancement, is sufficient, as nearly as can be estimated, to make up the full amount of the share.[31] The onus of proving that an advancement was given to a child rests upon the person so asserting, unless the advancement has been expressed in writing by the deceased.[32] The provisions under s 63 will not, however, be applicable where a contrary intention is expressed or appears from the circumstances of the case.[33]

9–16 Although s 63(9) provides that the section will not affect any rule of law as to the satisfaction of portion debts by legacies, portions and advancements share certain characteristics.[34] While the purposes for giving an advancement

---

27 Succession Act 1965, s 63(1).
28 Succession Act 1965, s 63(1).
29 Succession Act 1965, s 63(2).
30 Succession Act 1965, s 63(3).
31 Succession Act 1965, s 63(4).
32 Succession Act 1965, s 63(5).
33 Succession Act 1965, s 63(1).
34 See A. Keating, "The Effect of Portions and Advancements on Testamentary Gifts to Children, Part One" (2008) 13(2) CPLJ 40; A. Keating, "The Effect of Portions and Advancement on Testamentary Gifts to Children, Part Two" (2008) 13(3) CPLJ 57.

under s 63 and that of a portion are similar, the prerequisites regarding relationships are different. For a portion, the relationship must be between father and child, including a person to whom the deceased was *in loco parentis*, but for the purposes of an advancement under s 63, the relationship may be the father or mother of a child or issue of a child, or a person to whom the deceased was *in loco parentis*. Since the introduction of the Status of Children Act 1987, the definition of children also includes non-marital children, and the relationship of father and child also includes a non-marital child for the purposes of advancements.[35] Similar to an advancement, the value of the portion must be shown to be substantial enough to carry out the intended purpose, i.e. to make permanent provision for a child or person to whom the testator stands *in loco parentis*.[36] It is also expressly provided in s 63(8) of the 1965 Act that nothing in the section shall prevent a child retaining the advancement and abandoning his right to a share under the will or on intestacy, and so like satisfaction of a legacy by a portion, a child under s 63(8) may elect between the advancement and a gift in the will or a share on intestacy.

However, after the trusts provisions for children in will trusts, testators may declare that no advancement under s 63 may be taken into account when distributing the trust estate. A testator in his or her will trust may provide as follows: **9–17**

> I give, devise and bequeath to my trustees the whole of my estate upon trust to sell the same (with power to postpone such sale in whole or in part for such time or times as they shall think fit) and to hold the same or the proceeds of sale thereof on the following trusts:
> (a) To pay my debts, funeral expenses and testamentary expenses;
> (b) [Provision for legacies, house and/or contents to, etc., if intended]
> (c) To hold the residue (hereinafter called "my Residuary Estate") in trust for my son/daughter until he/she attains the age of 21 years [or 18 years] BUT if my son/daughter should die before me or before attaining a vested interest leaving a child or children, then such child or children shall on reaching the age of 21 years [or 18 years] take the share my son/daughter would otherwise have taken, and if more than one, in equal shares absolutely AND I DECLARE that no advancement within the meaning of section 63 of the Succession Act 1965 shall be brought into account in the distribution of my estate.

Advancements to children of a testator may be taken into account by the court under s 117(1) of the 1965 Act when determining whether the testator has fulfilled his moral duty to make proper provision for the applicant child. Even where an advancement within the meaning of s 63 is expressly excluded by a clause in a will, the value of it may still be taken into account by the court when determining whether a testator has fulfilled his moral duty to make proper provision for his children by will or otherwise under s 117(1). Section 117(1) provides that: **9–18**

---

35 Status of Children Act 1987, ss 3, 26, 27, 28 and 29; see *Hickey v O'Dwyer* [2006] 2 ILRM 81.

36 *Taylor v Taylor* (1875) LR 20 Eq 155; *Re Hayward* [1957] Ch 528 at 542.

> Where, on application by or on behalf of a child of a testator, the court is of opinion that the testator has failed in his moral duty to make proper provision for the child in accordance with his means, whether by his will *or otherwise*, the court may order that such provision shall be made for the child out of the estate as the court thinks just. (emphasis added)

9–19 Although an advancement may be taken into account by the court under s 117(1), a child of the testator may still succeed in having his share in the estate re-computed to his advantage, especially where the other beneficiaries are not children of the testator. It may also be mentioned here that advancements made by a father to his child under the equitable doctrine of advancement may be taken into account in an application under s 117(1) in the same way as portions, legacies and advancements covered by s 63.

Part Two

EXECUTORS AND TRUSTEES OF WILL TRUSTS

Chapter 10

EXECUTORS AND TRUSTEES OF WILL TRUSTS

Introduction

The words: 10–01

> I hereby appoint AB and XY *(hereinafter called "my trustees")* to be the executors and trustees of this my will for the purposes of the Land and Conveyancing Law Reform Act 2009 and for the purposes of the Conveyancing Acts and for the purposes of s 57 of the Succession Act 1965. (Emphasis added)

will be sufficient to appoint trustees of will trusts. Thus, where executors and trustees are appointed for the purposes of the will trust, and "hereinafter called my trustees", their functions as executors and trustees will merge for the purposes of administering and distributing the estate of the deceased testator. Where the testator appoints his or her executors to act as his or her trustees, once a grant of probate has issued to the executors the dual role of performing their duties and exercising their powers of executorship and trusteeship will commence simultaneously. The testator may appoint persons to act as executors only and appoint other persons to act as trustees only of his or her will trust, and where such is the case, the executors may administer the whole estate, other than the trust estate. Once the executors have applied for, and obtained, a grant of probate, they may commence to administer and distribute the estate as a whole, but may have to assent to the vesting of the trust estate in the trustees where the executors and trustees are not the same persons, and once such assent is given, the trustees may then commence the administration and distribution of the trust estate. However, on the death of the testator, and in the event of the executors not wishing to act as such, they may renounce their entitlement to apply for a grant of probate of the will trust. Further, in the event of trustees not wishing to act as such, they may also disclaim their trusteeship. Where the executors apply for and obtain a grant of probate, the right to renounce their executorship will no longer be available to them; if the trustees, after the issuing of the grant of probate to the executors, commence the performance of their functions as trustees of the trust estate, their right to disclaim their trusteeship will no longer be open to them, although they retire as trustees at a later stage.

Where the executors and trustees are the same persons, their powers and duties to the whole estate become operative once the grant of probate has issued. Where the executors and trustees are not the same persons, the persons who are appointed executors may perform their duties and exercise their powers once a grant of probate has issued to them, and thereafter the 10–02 persons who are appointed trustees may perform their duties and exercise their powers in relation to the trust estate, once the executors have vested the trust estate in them. While the duties and powers of executors and trustees are similar in nature, in the case of executors, their powers and duties relate to the whole estate of the deceased; the duties and powers of trustees relate to the trust estate only.

10–03 On the death of a testator, his or her estate will devolve on and vest in his or her executors. Section 10(1) of the Succession Act 1965 (the "1965 Act") provides that the estate of the deceased "shall on his death, notwithstanding any testamentary disposition, devolve and become vested in his personal representative." The executors under s 10(2) "are deemed in law his heirs and assigns within the meaning of all trusts and powers." Under s 10(3), the executors "shall be the representatives of the deceased in regard to his real and personal estate and shall hold the estate as trustees for the persons entitled thereto." The whole of the estate vests in the executors, who nevertheless do not hold the estate on their own behalf, but "as a trustee for the persons in law who are entitled to it, and he must act accordingly." The beneficiaries also "have an immediate beneficial equitable interest in the estate by way of trust," subject to rights of the executors.[1]

10–04 For the purposes of the Land and Conveyancing Law Reform Act 2009 (the "2009 Act"), the general rule on "overreaching" is that a purchaser from the trustee or legal owner gets a good title to the land.[2] Section 21(1) of the 2009 Act provides that a conveyance to a purchaser of a legal estate or legal interest in land by the person or persons specified in s 21(2) overreaches any equitable interest in the land so that it ceases to affect that estate or interest, whether or not the purchaser has notice of the equitable interest. Section 21(1) expresses the general rule on "overreaching": that a purchaser from the trustee or legal owner gets a good title to the land for the purposes of the 2009 Act. Section 21(2) provides that for the purposes of s 21(1) the "person or persons specified" shall be at least two trustees or a trust corporation where the trust land comprises a strict settlement, or a trust, including a trust for sale, of land held for persons by way of succession, or land vested in or held on trust for a minor, or may be a single trustee or owner of the legal estate or interest in the case of any other trust of land.

Trustees of Will Trusts of Land

10–05 Section 19(1) of the 2009 Act identifies the persons who may become trustees of will trusts of land, and they include executors named in will trusts of land. Section 19(1)(a) provides that the following persons in the case of a strict settlement are the trustees of a trust of land:

---

1 *O'Hagan v Grogan* [2012] IESC 8; A. Keating, *The Law and Practice of Personal Representatives* (2nd ed, Round Hall, Dublin, 2017).

2 Land and Conveyancing Law Reform Act 2009, s 21(1).

(i) where the settlement existed at the commencement of the 2009 Act, the tenant for life within the meaning of the Settled Land Act 1882 together with any trustees of the settlement for the purposes of that Act, and
(ii) where created after the commencement of the 2009 Act, the persons who would fall within s 19(1)(b) if the instrument creating it were deemed to be an instrument creating a trust of land.

Section 19(1)(b) provides that in the case of a trust of land created expressly: **10–06**

(i) any trustee nominated by the trust instrument, but, if there is no such person, then,
(ii) any person on whom the trust instrument confers a present or future power of sale of the land, or power of consent to or approval of the exercise of such a power of sale, but, if there is no such person, then,
(iii) any person who, under either the trust instrument or the general law of trusts, has power to appoint a trustee of the land, but, if there is no such person, then,
(iv) the settlor or, in the case of a trust created by will, the testator's personal representative or representatives.

Section 19(1)(c) provides that in the case of land vested in a minor before the commencement of the 2009 Act or purporting so to vest after such commencement, the persons who would fall within s 19(1)(b) will be deemed the trustees. Section 19(1)(d) provides that in the case of land the subject of an implied, resulting, constructive or bare trust, the person in whom the legal title to the land is vested will be deemed the trustee. However, s 19(3) provides that nothing in s 19 affects the right of any person to obtain an order of the court appointing a trustee of land or vesting land in a person as trustee. **10–07**

Trustees may also be appointed for the purposes of s 57 of the 1965 Act. Section 57(1) provides that: **10–08**

> Where an infant is entitled to any share in the estate of a deceased person and there are no trustees of such share able and willing to act, the personal representatives of the deceased may appoint a trust corporation or any two or more persons (who may include the personal representatives or any of them or a trust corporation) to be trustees of such share for the infant and may execute such assurance or take such other action as may be necessary for vesting the share in the trustee so appointed. In default of appointment the personal representatives shall be trustees for the purposes of this section.

Section 57(2) of the Succession Act 1965 provides that: **10–09**

> On such appointment the personal representatives, as such, shall be discharged from all further liability in respect of the property vested in the trustees so appointed.

Application for Probate by Executors

The executor or executors named by the testator in his or her will may apply for a grant of probate. An application for a grant of probate may be made to **10–10** the Probate Office (Seat Office) under Ord 79, r 3 of the Rules of the Superior Courts (the "RSC"). The Probate Office now accepts applications for grants by post, and where the post is used, such applications must be accompanied by the relevant and completed postal application form (PAS1). Under Ord 80, r 2 and r 3 of the RSC, applications for grants of probate may be made to a District Probate Registry where the deceased testator at the date of death was resident within the area of that District Probate Registry. Before the application for a grant of probate, an Inland Revenue Affidavit must be prepared by the executor setting out the particulars and assets of the estate of the deceased testator.[3] The Inland Revenue Affidavit may be lodged or sent to the Probate Office (or a District Probate Registry) together with the other necessary proofs. Once the grant of probate has issued, a copy of the Inland Revenue Affidavit must be forwarded to the Revenue Commissioners with a copy of the will.[4]

10–11 The following are the essential proofs when applying for a grant of probate[5]:

Checklist of Proofs

10–12 The Original Will (and Codicils, if any)

Certified copy of will

Oath of executor

Copy oath of executor

Inland Revenue Affidavit (CA24 (2010 edition) for deaths after 5 December 2001 and CA24 (2000 edition) where the deceased died before 5 December 2001)

Death certificate of the testator

Form PAS1 must be submitted where the application for the grant is made by post (Probate Office Update 2012)

Charitable Bequest Form PAS3 is required for charitable bequests in wills, including money bequeathed for masses, and the precise wording making the bequest must be replicated in Form PAS3[6]

Court Orders (if any) (an official copy of the court order must be exhibited in the oath of executor)[7]

Additional proofs, where necessary, e.g. Affidavit of Due Execution of the Will or Affidavit of Testamentary Capacity of the Testator.

---

3 See Finance Act 2010, s 147.

4 See Finance Act 2010, s 147.

5 See A. Keating, *Irish Probate Precedents Service* (Round Hall, Dublin, 2009); A. Keating, *The Law and Practice of Personal Representatives* (2nd ed, Round Hall, Dublin, 2017).

6 See Probate Office Update 2012.

7 See Probate Office Update 2012.

Oath of Executor

THE HIGH COURT
PROBATE

The Probate Office/The District Probate Registry at …

In the estate of [name of testator] late of [address], deceased.

I, [name of executor] of [address] aged eighteen years and upwards, make oath and say, that I believe the paper writing hereto annexed, and marked by me, to contain the true and original last will [or last will with … codicils] of [name of testator] late of [address and description], deceased; that same was made by the said … after attaining the age of eighteen years, and that he did not intermarry with any person after the making of same; that I am the [state relationship; if not a blood relation, insert "stranger in blood"] of the said [name of testator] and the sole executor named in the said will; that I will faithfully administer the estate of the said testator, by paying his just debts and the legacies bequeathed by his said will [or will and codicils], so far as the same shall thereto extend and the law bind me; that I will exhibit a true inventory of the said estate, and render a true account thereof, whenever required by law so to do; that the testator died at … on the … day of … [where application is made in District Probate Registry add: and that the testator has at the time of his death a fixed place of abode at … within the district of …] and that the whole of the estate which devolves on and vests in his legal personal representative amounts in value to [the gross assets, without any deductions for debts] and no more, to the best of my knowledge, information and belief.

Sworn, &c.

Renunciation of Probate by Executors

An executor may accept the office by applying for a grant of probate, but where he or she renounces, he or she must do so in writing, and the renunciation must be exhibited by a remaining executor in the oath of executor and included among the proofs submitted for a grant of probate. Where a sole executor renounces, the person next entitled by virtue of Ord 9, r 5(6) of the Rules of the Superior Courts may apply for a grant of letters of administration with the will annexed, but not probate. The renunciation must be exhibited in the oath of administrator with the will annexed and included among the proofs submitted for the grant. Where there is no executor named in the will, and the person entitled to apply for a grant of letters of administration with the will annexed renounces, the person next entitled may apply for a grant, and when doing so, the renunciation by the person with prior title to the grant must be exhibited in the oath of administrator with the will annexed. Where the deceased died intestate, and the person entitled to apply for a grant of letters of administration intestate under Ord 79, r 5(1) renounces, the person next entitled may apply for a grant, and the renunciation by the person with prior title must be exhibited in the oath of administrator intestate. **10–13**

10–14 The following are the essential proofs when applying for a grant of letters of administration with the will annexed on renunciation by the executor[8]:

Checklist of Proofs

10–15 The original will (and codicils, if any)

Copy of will

Oath of administrator

Copy oath of administrator

Administration bond

Inland Revenue Affidavit (Form CA24 (2010 edition))

Death certificate of the testator

Affidavit of Market Value or Certificate of Market Value

Renunciation of probate

Form S1 must be submitted where the application for the grant is made by post.

Charitable Bequest Form PAS3 is required for charitable bequests in wills, including money bequeathed for masses, and the precise wording making the bequest must be replicated in Form PAS3.

Court Orders (if any).

OATH OF ADMINISTRATOR WITH THE WILL

THE HIGH COURT
PROBATE

The Probate Office/The District Probate Registry at …

In the estate of [name of deceased] late of [address], deceased.

I, [name of applicant] of [address] aged eighteen years and upwards, make oath and say, that I believe the paper writing hereunto annexed, and marked by me, to contain the true and original last will [or last will with … codicils] of … late of [address and description], deceased, and that same was made by the said after attaining the age of years, and that he did not intermarry with any person after the making of same, and that he did therein name AB sole executor and that the said AB duly renounced his rights upon which renunciation dated the day of 20…. I have signed my name and marked with the letter 'A' prior to the swearing hereof and that I am the residuary legatee and devisee named in the said will and that I will well and faithfully administer the estate of the said testator, by paying his just debts and the legacies bequeathed by his said will [or will and codicils] and distributing the residue of his estate according to law; and that I will exhibit

[8] See A. Keating, *Irish Probate Precedents Service* (Round Hall, Dublin, 2009); A. Keating, *The Law and Practice of Personal Representatives* (2nd ed, Round Hall, Dublin 2017).

a true and perfect inventory of the said estate, and render a true account thereof whenever required by law so to do; and that the testator died at … on the … day of … [where application is made in a District Probate Registry, add "and had at the time of his death a fixed place of abode at … within the district of …"] and that the whole of the personal estate of the said testator amounts in value to the sum of [the gross personal estate, without any deductions for debts] and that the whole of the real estate of the said testator which devolves on and vests in his legal personal representative is of the market value of [the amount shown in the affidavit of market value] and no more to the best of my knowledge, information and belief.

Sworn, &c.

RENUNCIATION OF PROBATE

THE HIGH COURT
PROBATE

In the estate of [name of deceased] late of [address] deceased.	Whereas [name of deceased] late of [address] deceased, died on the … day of 20…, at …

[where application is made in a District Probate Registry, add "having at the time of his death a fixed place of abode at … within the district of …"] and whereas he made and duly executed his last will [or will and … codicils] bearing date the … day of … 20…, and thereof named AB … sole executor.

Now I, the said AB … aged eighteen years and upwards, do declare that I have not intermeddled with the estate of the said deceased, and will not hereafter intermeddle therein, with the intent to defraud creditors, and I do hereby expressly renounce my right to probate of the said will and of the estate of the said deceased.

Dated

(Signed)

Witness

THE RETIREMENT OF TRUSTEES

The will trust itself may also contain provisions dealing with the retirement of trustees, but in the absence of such provisions, the provisions of the Trustees Act 1893 (the "1893 Act") may then become relevant. Under s 10 of the 1893 Act, where a trustee wishes to retire, a new trustee may be appointed in his or her stead. All of the beneficiaries of the trust who have attained the age of majority may consent to the retirement of a trustee. However, the appointment of a new trustee may not be necessary where there are two remaining trustees.[9] Under s 25 of the 1893 Act, the court may appoint a **10–16**

---

9 See Trustees Act 1893, ss 10 and 11.

new trustee. The provisions of the trust may also provide circumstances for the removal of a trustee. In the absence of such provisions, s 10 of the 1893 Act provides that a trustee may be removed for incompetence, or if he is unfit to act, or is incapable of acting as a trustee.

Disclaimer by Trustees

10–17 Where the person appointed trustee has indicated acceptance of the office, the right to disclaim may be lost. In the case of an executor who is also appointed trustee, the official act of taking out a grant of probate may be a sufficient indication of his acceptance of the office of trustee.[10] Contrariwise, a renunciation by an executor who is also a trustee may not be viewed as a disclaimer of the office of trustee.[11] While circumstances may render it impossible or too late for a trustee to disclaim, he or she may, however, be allowed to retire by relying on the provisions of the trust dealing with the retirement of trustees, or where the beneficiaries of the trust estate, having attained the age of majority, consent to his retirement. Alternatively, a trustee may rely on the provisions of the Trustee Act 1893 to retire. Under s 11 of the Trustee Act, where a trustee expresses his intention to retire by deed, and there are at least two continuing trustees, he or she may be allowed to retire once the continuing trustees consent to his or her retirement; or he or she may apply to the court under s 25 of the 1893 Act to have a new trustee appointed in his or her stead.

Duties and Powers of Executors and Trustees

10–18 Where the executors of a will trust are also its trustees, once a grant has issued to executors, they may commence the administration and distribution of the estate as a whole. Where the executors and trustees of a will trust are not the same persons, once a grant has issued to the executors, they may commence to administer and distribute the estate as a whole, and may then vest the trust estate in the trustees allowing them to administer and distribute the trust estate. Where the executors and trustees are the same persons, their duties and powers will merge and relate to the whole estate of the deceased testator. Where the executors and trustees are not the same persons, the duties and powers of executors will extend to the whole estate, and the duties and powers of the trustees will be confined to the trust estate only.

(i) Administrative Duties of Executors

10–19 The first duty of executors is to gather in the estate of the deceased "in a timely fashion." In *In the Estate of White*,[12] Charleton J stated that:

[10] *Mucklow v Fuller* (1821) Jac 198.
[11] See *Re Gordon* (1877) 6 Ch D 531.
[12] [2015] IESC 84; Succession Act 1965, s 45(1).

> The bounden duty of an executor is to commence the process of the identification, gathering in, accounting for taxation purposes and proper distribution of the estate. This must be done in a timely fashion.

He also stated that: **10–20**

> The duties of executors are solemn and require the pursuit of such reasonable avenues of enquiry as may uncover property to the benefit of the estate.

The second duty of executors is to discharge funeral expenses, testamentary expenses and debts owing by the estate.[13] As regards funeral expenses, the executors may pay the funeral expenses out of the estate, although in practice, it is the family of the deceased who take possession of the remains for funeral arrangements and burial or cremation. The third duty of executors is to discharge all debts due and owing by the estate and seek the payment of debts owing to the estate. The executors also have a duty to distribute the estate among the beneficiaries. It was stated by Uthwatt J in *Re Tankard*[14] that: **10–21**

> The duty is owed, not only to creditors, but also to beneficiaries, for the ultimate object of administration of an estate is to place the beneficiaries in possession of their interest, and that cannot be fully achieved unless all debts are satisfied.

(ii) Distributive Duties of Executors

As the estate vests in the executors they will have to give their assent to the transmission and vesting of testamentary gifts or shares on intestacy in the beneficiaries. Where devises of land are involved, whether or not they are specific or residuary, the personal representatives may give their assent in writing in order to vest title in the devisees, and the form of assent will depend on whether the land is registered or unregistered. They may also assent to the transmission and vesting of legacies and bequests. In *Dolan v Reynolds*,[15] Abbott J, when considering the law relating to assents by personal representatives to the vesting of land in beneficiaries, referred to s 52 of the 1965 Act which provides that personal representatives, may at any time after the death of the deceased, execute an assent vesting land in the person entitled to it. He also referred to *Re King's Will Trusts*[16] for the definition of an assent as "the instrument or act whereby a personal representative effectuates a testamentary disposition by transferring the subject-matter of the disposition to the person entitled to it". **10–22**

(iii) Powers of Executors

The executors may exercise the statutory powers bestowed on them during **10–23**

---

13 Succession Act 1965, s 45(1).

14 [1942] 2 All ER 458 at 463.

15 [2011] IEHC 334; see A. Keating, "Probate and Succession Law" in *Annual Review of Irish Law 2011* (R. Byrne and W. Binchy eds, Round Hall, Dublin, 2012).

16 [1964] Ch 542 at 547.

the administration and distribution of the estate. These powers are found in the 1965 Act. A testator may also give the personal representatives additional powers. The main statutory power of executors is that they may sell the whole or any part of the estate, not only for the payment of debts to creditors, but also for the purpose of distributing the estate among the beneficiaries, although in relation to the latter, their wishes "so far as practicable" may be taken into account.[17] The personal representatives and trustees may also lease land and premises as may be reasonably necessary for the due administration of the estate or the trust.[18] Personal representatives have powers of appropriation over the whole estate, and the trustees may be given similar powers in relation to the trust estate. Under s 55 of the 1965 Act, the personal representatives may, for instance, appropriate any part of the estate in or towards the satisfaction of any share in the estate. Section 56 of the 1965 Act provides that a surviving spouse or civil partner may require the personal representatives to appropriate the dwelling and household chattels in or towards the satisfaction of that spouse's share in the estate.

(iv) Duties of Trustees

10–24 Before trustees carry out their duties, they should first acquaint themselves with the nature of the trust and its provisions in the will trust. The basic duty of trustees is to fulfil the objects of the trust.[19] As well as this basic duty:

(i) Trustees must act honestly and in good faith.[20]
(ii) Trustees must avoid conflicts of interest, especially where trustees are also beneficiaries.
(iii) Trustees' duties to avoid conflicts of interest are not confined to cases where trustees are also beneficiaries, as the fiduciary obligations of trustees have a broader base.
(iv) Decisions by trustees "which are properly to be characterised as being ones that no reasonable of trustees could have made may in law be condemned."[21]
(v) Once a consideration is relevant, it is for the trustees to determine how much weight should be accorded to that particular factor, and how relevant factors should be balanced overall.
(vi) Where the trustees' decision "is identified as one which no reasonable body of trustees properly informed and considering the decision could have made, the court should not decide that too much or too little weight has been given to a particular factor unless this is, firstly, based on tenable evidence and not mere speculation and, secondly, the measure of appreciation inherent in the decision that brings the decision outside those parameters."[22]
(vii) It is appropriate for the court not to interfere "save for decisions which are plainly unreasonable, it must remain within the ambit of the powers of trustees to weigh one factor more heavily and another less. To otherwise analyse a decision of trustees would be for the court to substitute its own judgment."[23]

---

[17] Succession Act 1965, s 50(1).
[18] Succession Act 1965, s 60(1)(a).
[19] See *In the Estate of Stanley* [2016] IEHC 8.
[20] See *Greene v Coady* [2014] IEHC 38.
[21] See *Greene v Coady* [2014] IEHC 38 at para 3.1.
[22] See *Greene v Coady* [2014] IEHC 38 at para 4.0.
[23] See *Greene v Coady* [2014] IEHC 38 at para 4.1.

(viii) Trustees must not place themselves in a position which may entail a conflict of interest with the duty they owe to the beneficiaries of the trust.
(ix) Decisions of trustees that are guided by an "improper motive" would always be a breach of trust.
(x) An allegation of a conflict of interest between duty and interest must be proved as a fact.
(xi) "Conflicts of duty are to be equated to conflicts of interest as the duty does not arise without the interest and the genesis of the rule in the frailty of human nature requires that both are equally treated."[24]
(xii) Where it is implicit in the nature of the trust that a particular decision involving trust business will affect the trustees personally, there is an exception to the rule that trustees cannot act in a situation where a conflict of interest arises, and the exception does not apply beyond the scope of what is inherently contemplated by the trust.[25]
(xiii) The Rules of the Superior Courts require that the interests of the trust should be represented in the face of any challenge to the validity or operation of that trust.[26]
(xiv) Where a summons is taken out by the trustees, the named defendants should be, "at least in the first instance, one or more of those persons claiming an interest in the trust as beneficiary."[27]
(xv) It would be improper to issue proceedings impugning the validity of a trust in a non-trustee capacity without joining the trustees of the trust estate.
(xvi) In order for the court to properly exercise its supervisory jurisdiction, the trustees must appraise the court of the steps that the trustees have taken both to become acquainted with the nature of the trust and to carry out the testator's wishes.[28]

(v) Powers of Trustees

A testator, when making an express a will trust, is also free to extend the statutory powers of his or her executors and trustees when dealing with trust property, and may empower them to do the following: **10–25**

(i) To exercise the power of appropriation under section 55 of the Succession Act 1965 without serving any of the notices or obtaining any of the required consents.
(ii) To sell, call in or convert into money at such time or times and in such manner as they shall think fit so much of my estate as shall not be in money-form, nevertheless to postpone such sale conversion or calling in indefinitely without being liable for any loss.
(iii) To sell any asset comprised in my estate at its full open market value to any one or more of my trustees.
(iv) To borrow any amount of money on the security of all or any assets comprised in the estate or without security and generally on such terms as they shall decide without limitation of any kind.
(v) To apply income derived from my estate for the benefit of any beneficiary under the trust hereby created.
(vi) To invest and change investments freely as if they were absolute owners beneficially entitled and to invest in unsecured interest-free loans or other

24 See *Greene v Coady* [2014] IEHC 38 at para 5.8.
25 See *Greene v Coady* [2014] IEHC 38.
26 See *In the Estate of Stanley* [2016] IEHC 8.
27 See *In the Estate of Stanley* [2016] IEHC 8.
28 See *In the Estate of Stanley* [2016] IEHC 8.

non-income-producing assets including property for occupation or use by any beneficiary.

(vii) To lease, let, mortgage, charge, licence and generally manage and deal with any land which, or the proceeds of sale of which, may for the time being form part of my estate as though they were the beneficial owners thereof absolutely entitled.

(viii) To lend money or property to any one or more of the beneficiaries either free of interest or on such terms as to payment of interest and generally as the executors shall in their absolute discretion think fit.

(ix) To trade or take part in any venture in the nature of trade whether solely or jointly with any other person and whether or not by way of partnership and for these purposes to make such arrangements as they shall in their absolute discretion think fit and delegate any exercise of this power to any one or more of their number or to a company or partnership formed for this purpose.

(x) To insure against any loss or damage from any peril of any property for the time being comprised in my estate for any amount and to pay the premiums out of the estate.

(xi) To appoint a new, additional or substitutional trustee or trustees of this my will.

10–26 Section 20 of the 2009 Act, which deals with powers of trustees of land, provides in subs (1) that subject to (a) the duties of a trustee, and (b) any restriction imposed by statute (including the 2009 Act) or general law of trusts or by any instrument or court order relating to the land, a trustee of land has the full power of an owner to convey or otherwise deal with it. Under s 20(2), the power of a trustee under s 20(1) includes the power to

(a) permit a beneficiary to occupy or otherwise use the land on such terms as the trustee thinks fit

and

(b) sell the land and to re-invest the proceeds, in whole or in part, in the purchase of land, whether or not situated in the State, for such occupation or use.

The Concept of Overreaching

10–27 The Settled Land Acts 1882–1890 gave the tenant for life wide powers of dealing with the settled land. Under the Acts, the tenant for life had the power to sell the fee simple in the land, so that the purchaser obtained the fee simple freed and discharged from the estates and interests attaching to the land under the settlement. After sale, those estates and interests attached to the capital money arising from the sale and were handed over to the trustees of the settlement for them to invest it, and not to the tenant for life or any other individual interested in the settlement. In *Irish Land Law*,[29] Wylie stated that the process by which land was sold free of all encumbrances created by the settlement, which thereupon was transferred to the capital money, came to be known as overreaching. In *Land Law in Ireland*, it is stated:

[29] J.C.W. Wylie, *Irish Land Law* (2nd ed, Professional Books Ltd, Abingdon, 1986), pp 431–432, at para 8.04.

> The Settled Land Acts provided for the interests of those entitled beneficially under the settlement to be overreached on the sale of the fee simple, i.e. their interests (legal or equitable) would be cleared off the legal title to the land and they would have corresponding interests in the capital money held by the trustees of the settlement.[30]

The Settled Land Acts 1882–1890 have now been repealed and replaced by the Land and Conveyancing Law Reform Act 2009. **10–28**

For the purposes of the 2009 Act, the general rule on "overreaching" is that a purchaser from the trustee or legal owner gets a good title to the land.[31] Section 21(1) of the 2009 Act provides that a conveyance to a purchaser of a legal estate or legal interest in land by the person or persons specified in s 21(2) overreaches any equitable interest in the land so that it ceases to affect that estate or interest, whether or not the purchaser has notice of the equitable interest. Section 21(1) expresses the general rule on "overreaching": a purchaser from the trustee or legal owner gets a good title to the land for the purposes of the 2009 Act. Section 21(2) provides that for the purposes of s 21(1) the "person or persons specified" shall be at least two trustees or a trust corporation where the trust land comprises a strict settlement, or a trust, including a trust for sale, of land held for persons by way of succession, or land vested in or held on trust for a minor, or may be a single trustee or owner of the legal estate or interest in the case of any other trust of land. Section 21(3) provides that s 21(1) does not apply to: **10–29**

> (a) any conveyance made for fraudulent purposes of which the purchaser has actual knowledge at the date of the conveyance or to which the purchaser is a party, or
> (b) any equitable interest—
> (i) to which the conveyance is expressly made subject, or
> (ii) protected by deposit of documents of title relating to the legal estate or legal interest, or
> (iii) in the case of a trust coming within subsection (2)(b), protected by registration prior to the date of the conveyance or taking effect as a burden coming within section 72(1)(j) of the Act of 1964 (or, in the case of unregistered land, which would take effect as such a burden if the land were registered land).

Section 21(4) provides that for the purposes of s 21(3)(b)(iii), "registration" means registration in the Registry of Deeds or the Land Registry. Section 21(5) provides that where an equitable interest is overreached under s 21, it attaches to the proceeds arising from the conveyance. Section 21(6), the final provision on overreaching, provides that nothing in s 21 affects the operation of the Family Home Protection Act 1976. This final safeguard against overreaching applies where the land is a family home under the Family Home Protection Act 1976. Under that Act, a conveyance by the "owning" spouse (who has the legal title) must have the consent of the **10–30**

---

30 A. Lyall with A. Power, *Land Law in Ireland* (3rd ed, Round Hall, Dublin, 2010), p 388.

31 Land and Conveyancing Law Reform Act 2009, s 21(1).

"non-owning" spouse (whether or not he or she has an equitable interest). Section 21(6) preserves that position.

10–31 Section 22(1) provides that any person having an interest in a trust of land, or a person acting on behalf of such a person, may apply to the court in a summary manner for an order to resolve a dispute; for instance, between the trustees, beneficiaries, or trustees and beneficiaries, or other operation of the trust. Under s 22(4), a "person having an interest" includes a mortgagee or other secured creditor, a judgment mortgagee or a trustee. The court may make whatever order and direct whatever inquiries it thinks fit in the circumstances of the case. In considering an application, the court shall have regard to the interests of the beneficiaries as a whole and,

> (3) … subject to these, to—
> (a) the purposes which the trust of land is intended to achieve,
> (b) the interests of any minor or other beneficiary subject to any incapacity,
> (c) the interests of any secured creditor of any beneficiary,
> (d) any other matter which the court considers relevant.

CHAPTER 11

BENEFICIARIES OF WILL TRUSTS

INTRODUCTION

Since the Status of Children Act 1987, where the word "issue" is used in creating a trust in a will, it will mean marital, non-marital and adopted children, unless a contrary intention appears from the provisions of the will trust. Under s 3(2) of the Succession Act 1965 (the "1965 Act"), **11–01**

> descendants and relatives of a deceased person begotten before his death but born alive thereafter shall, for the purposes of this Act, be regarded as having been born in the lifetime of the deceased and as having survived him.[1]

Where the words "die without issue" or "die without leaving issue" are used in a devise or trust of land—for instance, to X, but if he dies without issue then to B—two things must occur before the contingency takes effect. First, the death of the testator will give effect to the devise or trust containing the contingency. Secondly, the death of the devisee or beneficiary will give effect to the contingency in the devise or trust, i.e. X must have issue either during his lifetime or at the date of his death, subject, however, to a contrary intention appearing from the provisions of the devise or trust in the will. A trust in a will may also be created for the purpose of benefitting members of a designated group of persons, and where such is the case, the class-closing rules may be applied to determine the identity of the beneficiaries entitled to a share in the trust.[2] **11–02**

The application of the doctrine of lapse may become applicable where a beneficiary pre-deceases the testator, and as a result the property forming part of lapsed trust will forms part of the testator's residuary estate, unless a contrary intention appears from the will.[3] The nature of the relationship between testator and beneficiary may, however, determine whether or not the doctrine of lapse is to apply to the trust. Where a child of the testator predeceases him or her, any trust created in favour of that child may be saved from lapse provided that he or she leaves issue living at the date of death of the testator. Section 98 of the 1965 Act provides that where the predeceased beneficiary is a child or other issue of the testator who leaves issue of his or her own surviving at the date of death of the testator, the **11–03**

---

1 See *Gregory v McCarthy* [2015] IEHC 311; A. Keating, *The Law of Wills* (2nd ed, Clarus Press, Dublin, 2018).

2 See A. Keating, *The Law of Wills* (2nd ed, Clarus Press, Dublin, 2018).

3 See Succession Act 1965, s 91.

doctrine of lapse will not apply, and the gift will take effect as if the death of that child or other issue had happened immediately after the death of the testator, unless a contrary intention appears from the will. As a trust or gift under s 98 of the 1965 Act is saved from lapse because of the existence of living issue of the predeceased child at the date of death of the testator, a new interpretative construction of s 98 may conclude that the trust or gift takes effect as a trust or gift to the living issue of a predeceased child at the date of death of the testator.

Beneficiaries of Trusts in Wills

11–04 Beneficiaries of trust in wills include marital, non-marital and adopted children, unless a contrary intention is indicated. In *Gregory v McCarthy*,[4] Hunt J, when interpreting s 3(2) of the 1965 Act, stated that "the policy set out therein should also govern the construction of relevant words or terms in wills." He went on to state:

> In the absence of binding authority, as a matter of principle the term "issue" encompasses children conceived but not yet born at the date of death of the testator, unless a contrary intention appears from other language used in the will, or from admissible extrinsic evidence.

11–05 Where the contingency of a beneficiary's death is coupled with that of his or her leaving issue, not only must the beneficiary survive the testator, but he or she must also have issue during his lifetime or at the date of his death, to prevent either lapse or a gift over in default. In the former instance, the operative date is that of the testator's death; in the latter instance, while the date of death of the testator will give effect to a gift, the time for deciding whether or not the contingency has been satisfied is the date of the beneficiary's death. Thus, if a beneficiary has issue during his lifetime or leaves issue at the date of his death, he will be deemed to have satisfied the contingency, and the gift will take absolute effect at the date of the testator's death in the event of his having issue at that time.

11–06 The contingency dying without issue is invariably, though not always, antecedent to a gift over to another beneficiary, and the matter may further be complicated by the contingency attaching to a series of gifts over, and perhaps, not being satisfied by any beneficiary leaving issue surviving. The question may then be asked whether, in such an event, the final beneficiary's estate will become entitled to the gift or whether intestacy ensues. This question was considered in *Mulhern v Brennan*.[5] In that case, the court was asked to determine the meaning of "dying without issue" in the context of

---

4 [2015] IEHC 311.

5 *Mulhern v Brennan*, unreported, High Court, McCracken J, 26 May 1998; see *Re Hall* [1944] IR 54; *Woodroofe v Woodroofe* [1894] 1 IR 299; *Re Richardson's Trust* (1896) 1 Ch D 295 at 300.

the residuary clause. Did the phrase "dying without issue" which appeared in the residuary clause mean:

(i) dying during the lifetime of the deceased to the effect, in the events which have happened, that each of the sons took absolutely a quarter share of the residue of the estate,
(ii) dying at any time to the effect that on the death without issue of each son his share passed to the then surviving brother, or brothers, and ultimately, without issue that an intestacy arose, or
(iii) dying at any time but to the effect that the defeasance provision in the clause only applied for so long as there was a surviving brother.

It happened that the testator's four sons all survived him, but ultimately all **11–07** four of them died without issue. In his judgment, McCracken J, having stated that the primary rule was to discover the intention of the testator from the words used by him in his will, went on to consider whether the phrase "dying without issue" referred to the death of a beneficiary during the lifetime of the testator only, or whether it referred to his death without issue at any time. He remarked that if it was intended to limit the contingency to the death of any of the testator's sons during his lifetime, it would have been easy for him to have said so in his will. In relation to the expression contained in the will before him, he found that, on a true construction, the gifts took effect on the death of any of the testator's sons without issue at any time, either before or after the death of the testator. He then turned to the question of what happens when the contingency "dying without issue" takes effect in relation to a series of beneficiaries. He found that in the light of events, the entire estate became vested in the last surviving son of the testator, as the stated contingency had occurred in relation to the other three sons. He also thought that the provision was open to two constructions: one, that the testator totally failed to make any provision for the event which happened, in which case there would an intestacy, and two, that there was a further contingency in the will which provided that there must be a surviving brother or brothers to take the share and, as that contingency had not occurred, the last surviving brother took the estate absolutely. He reiterated the approach of the court that, when construing a will, it will presume that the testator did not intend to die intestate as to any part of his estate, for otherwise he would not have made a will. He referred to the judgment of Lord Esher MR in *Re Harrison*[6] for the statement that:

> There is one rule of construction, which to my mind is a golden rule, viz., that when a testator has executed a will in solemn form you must assume that he did not intend to make it a solemn farce— that he did not intend to die intestate when he has gone through the form of making a will. You ought, if possible, to read the will so as to lead to a testacy, not an intestacy. This is the golden rule. I do not deny that this will may be read in two ways, or that it requires a blank should be filled up. But it may be read in such a way as not to amount to a solemn farce.

6 (1885) 30 Ch D 390 at 393.

Beneficiaries of Class Trusts in Wills

11–08 A will may also create a class gift or trust for beneficiaries who are members of a particular class of persons. A class gift or trust is one where a testator leaves his or her estate to a designated group of beneficiaries, for instance, to the children of X. Where such a trust or gift is created by will, it may also be subject to class-closing rules. The basic rule is that the date of distribution of such a trust or gift is the date when the first member of the class becomes entitled to an interest in possession, and thereafter the class closes. The gift will be confined to the children of X born before the death of the testator, and any children born after the death of the testator will be excluded as beneficiaries, unless a contrary intention appears from the will.[7] The class will close at the date of death of the testator. Where, however, there are no children of the designated class in existence at the date of the testator's death, then all children born after that date will be entitled to a share.[8] A class member may also be a person who becomes a member of a class by statutory definition; for instance, a class gift created for the children of X may include a non-marital child of X by virtue of the Status of Children Act 1987. Prior to the 2009 Act, the rule against perpetuities had also to be observed, and while children of the designated class may be in existence at the date of the testator's death, a gift that infringed the rule against perpetuities was deemed invalid. The 2009 Act abolished the rule against perpetuities.

11–09 The creation of a class trust or gift for children may also be made subject to a contingency—for instance, a testator may specify a particular age to be attained by the children before they become entitled under the trust or gift—and where there is a contingency of this nature, the rule is that once a child of the designated class attains the specified age before the testator's death, the class closes. A child born after the testator's death will be excluded even though he or she may eventually attain the specified age. This rule, like the other class-closing rules, is subject to a contrary intention appearing from the will creating the trust or gift. While the class-closing rules may seem unfair to children born subsequent to the testator's death, the rules at least allow the beneficiaries entitled under the gift to ascertain the minimum value of their shares in the estate, and such rules may also facilitate an early administration and distribution of the testator's estate that might otherwise be postponed indefinitely.

11–10 A class trust or gift may also not take immediate effect on the testator's death owing to the existence of a prior or intermediate life estate, and where such is the case, children who are born after the testator's death may become entitled to a share in the estate, if they are born during the lifetime of the life tenant. Moreover, the share of a child who predeceases the life tenant may form part of that child's estate. If no children are born into the class at

7 *Re Poe* [1942] IR 535 at 537.
8 *Harris v Lloyd* (1823)1 T & R 310; *Weld v Bradbury* (1715) 2 Ver 705; *Re Chartres* [1927] 1 Ch 466.

the time of death of the testator or life tenant, the class will remain open to let in children who are born before the death of the person whose children form the objects of the gift.[9] Where there is not only a delayed vesting due to the existence of an intermediate life estate, but where also the gift or trust is subject to the contingency of attaining a specified age, the class will remain open to include children who attain that age at the date of death of the life tenant.[10] In the event of no child attaining the specified age at the date of death of the life tenant, the first child who subsequently attains that age will have the effect of closing the class. The share of any child who attains the requisite age and subsequently dies will form part of his estate. Where, however, the vesting of the class gift is accelerated owing to the life tenant predeceasing the testator, the relevant time for ascertaining the members of the class will again be the date of death of the testator. A vesting may also be accelerated by a life tenant's own act—for instance, by disclaimer—and as a result a question may arise in relation to the date of entitlement to a share in a class gift.[11]

The class-closing rules may not, however, become applicable if the objects of the gifts are designated by name.[12] The rules may also not be applicable where the testator intends to benefit children of a class once born alive as each child will become entitled to a share in the gift or trust at birth.[13] Where the designated class includes the testator's own children, and where one of the children dies before the testator leaving issue of his own, his or her share in the gift will not lapse, but will go to his surviving issue, unless a contrary intention appears from the will.[14] **11–11**

Lapse of Trusts

Under the doctrine of lapse, where a beneficiary predeceases the testator, the gift or trust to that beneficiary will lapse or fail to take effect, and, as a result the subject matter of the gift will form part of the testator's residuary estate.[15] The doctrine of lapse may be said to derive from, or is a consequence of, the ambulatory nature of a will, i.e. a will has no effect until the death of the testator, and where a beneficiary predeceases the testator, the gift left to him or her will lapse at the date of the testator's death. The nature of the gift may, however, save it from lapse. Where a gift is comprised of a joint tenancy and where one of the joint tenants predeceases the testator, the gift will not lapse but will pass by right of survivorship to the joint tenants who survive the testator. Where the gift creates a tenancy in common by which **11–12**

9 *Re Chartres* [1927] 1 Ch 466.
10 See *Re Paul's S.T.* [1920] 1 Ch 99.
11 See *Re Davies* [1957] 1 WLR 922; *Re Harker's Will Trust* [1969] 1 WLR 1124.
12 *Re Ramadge* [1969] NI 71; *Re Harker's Will Trust* [1969] 1 WLR 1124.
13 See *Gregory v McCarthy* [2015] IEHC 311; *Re Edmondson Will Trust* [1972] 1 WLR 183; *Re Ransome* [1957] Ch 348; *Re Tom's Settlement* [1987] Ch 63.
14 See Succession Act 1965, s 98.
15 Succession Act 1965, s 91; see A. Keating, "The Doctrine of Lapse and Section 98 of the Succession Act" (2013) 31 ILT 181.

beneficiaries are given equal shares and where one of the beneficiaries predeceases the testator, the equal share of that beneficiary will lapse, and unlike a joint tenancy, the share of the beneficiary will not pass to the surviving tenants-in-common.

11–13 An exception to the doctrine of lapse is found in s 98 of the 1965 Act. Section 98 provides that where the predeceased beneficiary is a child or other issue of the testator who leaves issue of his own surviving at the date of death of the testator, the doctrine of lapse will not apply, and the gift will take effect as if the death of that child or other issue had happened immediately after the death of the testator, unless a contrary intention appears from the will. Section 33 of the Wills Act 1837 (the "1837 Act") formerly dealt with matters similar to those set out in s 98 of the 1965 Act, but the entirety of the 1837 Act was repealed by the 1965 Act, including (of course) s 33 of the 1837 Act. Section 33 of the 1837 Act was amended by s 19 of the UK Administration of Justice Act 1982 and by art 22 of the Wills and Administration Proceedings (Northern Ireland) Order 1994 (SI 1994/1899), to allow a gift to a predeceased child to take effect as a gift to the issue living at the testator's death.

11–14 The traditional interpretation given to s 33 of the 1837 Act, which was replaced by s 98 of the 1965 Act, kept a will of a predeceased child "alive", regardless of whether or not it benefitted the issue of that child who were living at the death of the testator, and whose very existence at that time saved the gift to the predeceased child from lapse. But s 98 of the 1965 Act, as the existing and prevailing legislation on the matter in Ireland, is capable of an interpretation that allows a gift to a predeceased child to take effect as a gift to issue living at the time of the testator's death. Section 98 provides that where the predeceased beneficiary is a child or other issue of the testator who leaves issue of his own surviving at the date of death of the testator, the doctrine of lapse will not apply, and the gift will take effect as if the death of that child or other issue had happened immediately after the death of the testator, unless a contrary intention appears from the will.

11–15 Where a beneficiary predeceases the testator, the gift or trust to him or her will lapse and it will fall into the testator's residuary estate, unless a contrary intention appears from the will. Section 91 of the 1965 Act provides that:

> Unless a contrary intention appears from the will, any estate or intended to be comprised in any devise or bequest contain in the will which fails or is void by reason of the fact that the devisee or legatee did not survive the testator, or by reason of the devise or bequest being contrary to law or otherwise incapable of taking effect, shall be included in any residuary devise or bequest, as the case may be in the will.

11–16 Section 33 of the Wills Act 1837 (the "1837 Act") formerly dealt with matters similar to those set out in s 98 of the 1965 Act, but the entirety of the 1837 Act was repealed by the 1965 Act including of course s 33 of the 1837 Act. Section 33 of the 1837 Act was amended by s 19 of the UK

Administration of Justice Act 1982 and by art 22 of the Northern Ireland Wills and Administration Proceedings (NI) Order 1994, to allow a gift to a predeceased child to take effect as a gift to the issue living at the testator's death. The question may then be asked: is s 98 of the 1965 Act, as the existing and prevailing legislation on the matter in Ireland, capable of an interpretation that allows a gift to a predeceased child to take effect as a gift to issue living at the testator's death, as opposed to continuing the interpretation of the repealed s 33 of 1837 Act, which kept a will of a predeceased child "alive" regardless of whether or not it benefitted the issue of that child who were living at the time of the death of the testator, and whose very existence at that time saved the gift to the predeceased child from lapse.

Section 98 of 1965 Act deals with matters formerly governed by s 33 of the 1837 Act, but s 98, besides replacing s 33, also contains marginal notes which states that it deals with "gifts to children or other issue who leave issue living at the testator's death", and this helpful pointer appears to suggest that s 98 is capable of a new interpretation, and one that may differ from the interpretation given to the former s 33 of the 1837 Act. The statement in the margin of s 98, i.e. "gifts to children or other issue who leave issue living at the testator's death" can only be taken to mean that the provisions of s 98 relate to such gifts only. If the intent of s 98 was to save a gift from lapse for the purpose of benefiting a predeceased child's estate, why was it necessary to make it conditional on the existence of living issue of the predeceased at the date of the testator's death? The only logical conclusion is that s 98 saves a gift to a predeceased child from lapse, not for the purpose of benefitting all those in his will, but for the benefit of his issue living at the testator's death, unless a contrary intention appears from the will. Section 98 also saves from lapse any property given through the exercise by will of any power of appointment, whether as a gift to that person as an individual or as a member of a class, and which will pass to the issue. Section 98 may then be interpreted to allow a gift by the testator to a predeceased child to take effect as a gift to his or her issue living at the date of death of the testator, unless a contrary intention appears from the will. The marginal notes which state that s 98 deals with "gifts to children or other issue who leave issue living at the testator's death" points to such a conclusion and thereby obviates the need for amending legislation similar to s 19 of the UK's Administration of Justice Act 1982 and art 22 of the Wills and Administration Proceedings (Northern Ireland) Order 1994 (SI 1994/1899). **11–17**

It is the nature of the relationship between testator and beneficiary that determines whether or not the doctrine of lapse is to apply to a gift. Where a child of the testator predeceases him or her, any gift to that child may be saved from lapse provided that he or she leaves issue living at the date of death of the testator. Under s 33 of the 1837 Act, in the absence of a contrary intention appearing from the will, a devise or bequest to a predeceased child of the testator not determinable at or before the death did not lapse if the predeceased child had issue of his own living at the date of death of the testator, and the devise or bequest took effect as if the predeceased child **11–18** or other issue had died immediately after the testator, and the devise or bequest became disposable under the will of the predeceased child. Once the provisions of s 33 were satisfied, the devise or bequest was saved from lapse, and it passed to those beneficially entitled under the predeceased child's will. A contrary intention may appear from the will by the testator providing that in the event of his child predeceasing him that the gift should then go to the issue of that child. But where no such provision was made by the testator, the predeceased child's issue living at the testator's death had no right to share in the gift, though their existence was vital for saving the gift from lapse, and for the purpose of rendering a will of the predeceased child effective.

Chapter 12

THE REMOVAL OF EXECUTORS AND TRUSTEES

Introduction

While there is no escaping the sepulchral tone of words like "removal" and "passing over" used to describe the possible consequences of serious misconduct by executors and/or trustees, such words aptly describe what in fact occurs to executors and/or trustees who are guilty of conflict of interests or inordinate delay while administering the estate, or who, for similar reasons, may be passed over and removed, after, of course, the removal of the testator to his or her final resting place. Where the executors and trustees of a will trust are the same persons, and are called "hereinafter my trustees", their functions, duties and powers will merge, and they may therefore be removed as executors or trustees on similar grounds. Where the executors and trustees of a will trust are not the same persons, the functions of executors and trustees will not merge, and in such cases, the executors of a will trust may be removed and replaced only on grounds for the removal and replacement of executors, and the trustees may be removed only on grounds which relate to the removal of trustees, although the grounds for the removal of either executors or trustees are similar. **12–01**

Section 26(2) of the Succession Act 1965 (the "1965 Act") provides that the High Court "shall have power to revoke, cancel or recall any grant of probate." Under s 27(2) of the 1965 Act, a personal representative who is an administrator may be removed by the court revoking the grant of letters of administration with will annexed made to him or her in accordance with the Rules of the Superior Courts (the "RSC"). Section 27(2) of the 1965 Act provides that the High Court "shall have power to revoke, cancel or recall any grant of administration." Where an executor or administrator is removed under s 26(2) or s 27(2), he or she may be replaced by the applicant for a grant, or by his or her nominee, under s 27(4) of the 1965 Act. The onus of proof is on the applicant to establish to the satisfaction of the court that the executor or administrator is guilty of serious misconduct and/or that there are serious special circumstances requiring his or her removal and replacement under s 26(2) and s 27(4).[1] A similar onus rests on an applicant where he or she seeks the passing over of a nominated executor or person entitled to apply for a grant of letters of administration with the will annexed or intestate under the Rules of the Superior Courts, and the appointment of administrator under s 27(4) to apply for a grant. **12–02**

---

1 See *Scally v Rhatigan* [2012] IEHC 140.

12–03 The guiding criteria for removal and replacement of an executor were formulated by Lynch J in *Dunne v Heffernan*.[2] He stated that:

> An order removing the appellant as executrix (which would be made by virtue of s 26(2) and not s 27(4) of the Succession Act 1965) and appointing some other person as administrator with the will annexed by virtue of s 27(4) is a very serious step to take.

12–04 He went on to state that:

> It would require serious misconduct and/or serious special circumstances on the part of the executrix to justify such a drastic step.

12–05 Therefore, for the court to remove and replace a personal representative under s 26(2) or 27(2) and s 27(4) of the 1965 Act, the applicant must show to the satisfaction of the court that the executor or administrator was guilty of serious misconduct in the administration of the estate, and/or, that the "serious special circumstances" of the case require his or her removal, and that it is necessary or expedient to remove and replace him or her.[3] Instances of serious special circumstances which may justify the removal of an executor or administrator include a conflict of interest, a "pronounced" delay by a personal representative in the administration of an estate, or a failure by a personal representative "to discharge the fundamental duty to collect and get in the estate and administer it according to law."[4] It appears also that a personal representative who is an administrator may be replaced more readily than one who is an executor.[5]

12–06 The overriding principle to which the courts must have regard in exercising its power to remove trustees is the welfare of the beneficiaries.[6] In *Spencer v Kinsella*,[7] Barron J, when referring to conflicts of interest by trustees, stated that:

> The welfare of the beneficiaries is being affected by the present situation. There is a conflict of interest which I have identified and it would be difficult to reorganise

---

2 [1997] 3 IR 431; see also *Flood v Flood* [1999] 2 IR 234; *Dunne v Dunne* [2016] IECA 269; *Muckian v Hoey* [2016] IEHC 688; *Davies v Hutchinson* [2017] IEHC 693; A. Keating, *The Law and Practice of Personal Representatives* (Round Hall, Dublin, 2017); A. Keating, "The Removal, Passing Over and Replacement of Personal Representatives" (2017) 22(1) CPLJ 2.

3 See *Dunne v Heffernan* [1997] 3 IR 431; *Flood v Flood* [1999] 2 IR 234; *In the Estate of O'Callaghan* [2016] IEHC 668; *Muckian v Hoey* [2016] IEHC 688; *Davies v Hutchinson* [2017] IEHC 693.

4 See *Flood v Flood* [1999] 2 IR 234; *Dunne v Dunne* [2016] IECA 269; *Muckian v Hoey* [2016] IEHC 688; *Scally v Rhatigan* [2012] IEHC 140; *Davies v Hutchinson* [2017] IEHC 693.

5 *Muckian v Hoey* [2016] IEHC 688.

6 See *Spencer v Kinsella* [1996] 2 ILRM 401 at 409; *Scally v Rhatigan* [2012] IEHC 140; *Davies v Hutchinson* [2017] IEHC 693.

7 [1996] 2 ILRM 401 at 409; see *Scally v Rhatigan* [2012] IEHC 140; *Davies v Hutchinson* [2017] IEHC 693.

> with such conflict on the part of some of the trustees continuing to exist. It is accordingly appropriate that such persons should step down.

Barron J, having commented that no trustee should allow his interests to conflict with his duty, went on to state: **12–07**

> A trust is set up for the welfare of its beneficiaries. In my view, therefore before determining whether or not any trustee should be removed from his or her office it is necessary to determine whether his or her continuation in that office will be detrimental to such welfare.

A trustee may also be removed under express provisions in the will trust to do so, or under s 23 of the Trustee Act 1893. The court may replace a trustee whose conduct is shown to interfere with the effective implementation of the provisions of a will trust.[8] **12–08**

Grounds for Removal of Executors

An executor may be removed for: **12–09**

(i) Serious Misconduct

An executor may be removed by the court for serious misconduct and/or serious special circumstances on the part of the executor or administrator in the administration and distribution of the deceased's estate. The criteria for the removal of an executor under s 26(2), and his or her replacement by an administrator by virtue of s 27(4), were first formulated by Lynch J in his judgment for the Supreme Court in *Dunne v Heffernan* as follows: **12–10**

> An order removing the appellant as executrix (which would be made by virtue of s.26(2) and not s.27(4) of the Succession Act 1965) and appointing some other person as administrator with the will annexed by virtue of s.27(4) is a very serious step to take. It is not justified because one of the beneficiaries appears to have felt frustrated and excluded from what he considered his legitimate concerns. It would require serious misconduct and/or serious special circumstances on the part of the executrix to justify such a drastic step.[9]

In that case, the defendant, who was the sole surviving executrix of the testatrix, was issued with a grant of probate. The plaintiff, who was a beneficiary, sought an order revoking and cancelling the grant of probate which had issued to the defendant. The dispute between the plaintiff and the defendant centred on the fact that the defendant had valued preference shares in Dunnes Holding Company, which passed under the will of the testatrix, at IR£265 on the Inland Revenue affidavit furnished to the Revenue Commissioners, which the plaintiff, who had been a preference shareholder of that company, contended was a gross undervalue and exposed him to **12–11**

8 See *Arnott v Arnott* (1924) 58 ILTR 185.

9 See *Dunne v Heffernan* [1997] 3 IR 431 at 442–443; *Davies v Hutchinson* [2017] IEHC 693.

capital gains tax liability in relation to the sale of his preference shares in the company for several million pounds, which sale had occurred prior to the death of the testatrix. Lynch J found that the appellant had done nothing wrong in her capacity as executrix, and that the alleged conflict of interest was "flimsy in the extreme." There were no grounds which justified the removal of the appellant as executrix under s 26(2) of the 1965 Act or her replacement under s 27(4).

12–12 In *Flood v Flood*,[10] the executor was removed and replaced because he had refused to pay back monies borrowed from the deceased during his lifetime by claiming that the money was given to him as a gift. Macken J, applying the criteria set down by Lynch J in *Dunne v Heffernan* for the removal and replacement of an executor, found that a "very serious matter" arose in the administration of the estate, "and the only way in which that can be dealt with is to remove the defendant as executor" and appoint another person as administrator with the will annexed pursuant to s 27(4) of the 1965 Act. However, she also stated that:

> A court should not remove an executor from his role, unless it is satisfied that it is necessary to do so. It is clear from the decision in *Dunne v Heffernan* [1997] 3 I.R. 431 that the Supreme Court considers this should only occur where the court is satisfied it must be done and that Court made it clear that it is a very serious step to take. It is not justified because one of the beneficiaries appears to have felt frustrated and excluded, but requires serious misconduct and/or serious special circumstances on the part of the executor to justify such a drastic step.[11]

12–13 The criteria formulated by Lynch J in *Dunne v Heffernan*[12] for the removal and replacement of an executor appear to be similarly applicable to cases where an administrator is sought to be removed and replaced on the grounds of conflict of interest. In *Dunne v Dunne*,[13] the plaintiffs sought the removal and replacement of the defendant as administrator of their late father's estate on the grounds of a conflict of interest in his role as administrator of the estate and his claim to possessory title of it. In that case, the plaintiffs and the defendant were siblings, and together comprised 10 of the 14 children of the late Cecil Dunne who died intestate on 29 March 1994 and the late Eileen Dunne, his widow, who survived him and died testate on 20 October 2010. Following the death of Cecil Dunne, letters of administration intestate issued to his widow Eileen Dunne. On the death intestate of her husband, she became entitled to two-thirds of his estate, and the remaining one-third was divisible equally between each of 14 children of the marriage. The litigation arose because prior to her death Eileen Dunne had not completed the administration of her late husband's estate, and in particular had not vested in each child the share to which he or she was entitled in c.62 acres of farm lands. In her will she named her son, William Dunne, the defendant in the case, as her sole executor, as well as her sole residuary devisee and

10 [1999] 2 IR 234.
11 *Flood v Flood* [1999] 2 IR 234 at 244.
12 [1997] 3 IR 431 at 442–443.
13 [2016] IECA 269.

legatee. On 31 August 2011, the defendant took out a grant of letters of administration intestate *de bonis non* to the estate of his late father which would enable him to complete the administration of that estate. On 12 October 2011, he extracted a grant of probate in the estate of the late Eileen Dunne. The plaintiffs claimed that the defendant in his capacity as legal personal representative of their late mother's estate had failed to properly account for her administration of their late father's estate prior to her death. The defendant, however, claimed that he had acquired the bulk of the assets of the estate by virtue of adverse possession, and therefore had acquired a possessory title which defeated the interests of the plaintiff.

In *Davies v Hutchinson*,[14] the plaintiffs instituted an administration action by special summons and sought four substantial reliefs against the defendant in respect of the administration of the estate of the deceased. The reliefs included an order under s 26 (2) of the 1965 Act revoking or cancelling the grant of probate which issued to the defendant on 13 December 2005, thereby removing her as executrix in the estate of the deceased, together with an ancillary order under s 27(1) of the 1965 Act granting administration to a third party. The plaintiff also sought the relief of a direction to the defendant to render within a specified time a true and perfect inventory and account of the estate, and in the alternative, an order compelling the defendant within a specified time to complete the administration and distribution of the estate. The contention between the parties in the matter that came before the court on 6 November 2017 related to the removal of the defendant under s 26(2) of the 1965 Act. The plaintiffs asserted that the defendants' misconduct arose because of gross delay, the failure to render accounts, excessive fee, non-accounting for interest since 2008 and the withholding of monies contingent on a waiver of all claims. However, O'Regan J, when applying the principles formulated in *Dunne v Heffernan*,[15] *Flood v Flood*,[16] *Scally v Rhatigan*,[17] and *Dunne v Dunne*[18] to the circumstances of the case and the evidence adduced by the parties, concluded that: **12–14**

> I am not satisfied that the plaintiffs have achieved the high threshold required to remove an executrix at this time, however the delays in completing the administration of the estate are most unsatisfactory and at a minimum there remains outstanding a query in respect of accumulated interest from 2008 to July 2017.

A trustee may be removed by the court exercising its inherent jurisdiction on the same grounds, and a new trustee may be appointed in his or her stead, and indeed, may be replaced, on the grounds of convenience, by the person appointed as administrator by the court under s 27(4) of the 1965 Act. **12–15**

---

14 [2017] IEHC 693; see A. Keating, *The Law and Practice of Personal Representatives* (Round Hall, Dublin, 2017).

15 [1997] 3 IR 431.

16 [1999] 2 IR 234.

17 [2012] IEHC 140.

18 [2016] IECA 269.

(ii) Conflict of Interests

12–16 An executor may be removed by the court and replaced by an administrator appointed under s 27(4) of the 1965 Act where the special circumstances of the case warrant his or her replacement, and further, that it is necessary or expedient to do so, where a serious conflict of interest exists between that of the executor or administrator and his or her administration and distribution of the estate of the deceased. In the High Court, Cregan J stated that he had to decide whether the defendant's claim to possessory title of the estate gave rise to a conflict of interest necessitating his removal as administrator of the estate. In his judgment, Cregan J referred to *Dunne v Heffernan*,[19] *Flood v Flood*,[20] and *Scally v Rhatigan*[21] as providing the relevant legal criteria in an application to remove an administrator, and stated that:

> Mr Dunne's claim for adverse possession may be a good, or a bad claim, that is not the point in this application. Again, as I stated above, that is a matter for the trial judge. The issue here, is whether he is in a conflict of interest situation and in my view, he is. The fact that this is so is also confirmed by the fact that both counsel confirmed, that in the event that Mr Dunne was replaced as personal representative, what would happen, is that a new personal representative would be appointed, that he or she would review the file and that he or she may decide not to plead the statute. However, it would then fall on William Dunne to hand back land to which he has claimed possessory title and if he did not do so, then it would result either in the new personal representative issuing proceedings against Mr Dunne, or, Mr Dunne issuing proceedings against the personal representative, seeking declaratory orders in relation to his alleged possessory title.

12–17 As a result, he found that "Mr Dunne was in a serious, obvious and indefensible conflict of interest situation in his role as personal representative" and that this amounted to "a serious special circumstance to justify his removal within the terms of the Supreme Court decision in *Dunne v Heffernan*."

12–18 The defendant appealed the decision of Cregan J to the Court of Appeal.[22] In his judgment for the Court of Appeal, Peart J when arriving at his decision referred to the decision and remarks of Macken J regarding the removal of an executor in *Flood v Flood*,[23] and found that they were applicable "to the present case even though in *Flood* the target of the application was an executor and not an administrator." He concluded that the conflict of interest or the potential conflict of interest was not "one which has the capacity to hinder or prevent the proper and fair determination of the issue that had arisen". The issue involving the statute of limitations and adverse possession was one between the personal representative and the plaintiff, and not one between the personal representative and the estate. He described it as an "operative conflict", capable of resolution in a suitable application to the

---

19 [1997] 3 IR 431.
20 [1999] 2 IR 234.
21 [2012] IEHC 140; see also *Hilton v Barker Booth* [2005] 1 All ER 651; *Moody v Cox* [1917] 2 Ch 71.
22 *Dunne v Dunne* [2016] IECA 269.
23 [1999] 2 IR 234 at 244.

court in proceedings between the parties or under Ord 3, r 2 of the Rules of the Superior Courts, and refused to remove and replace the administrator under s 27(4) of the 1965 Act.

Peart J stated that: **12–19**

> In my view the trial judge took too narrow a view of the question of conflict of interest, and failed to give sufficient weight to the question of necessity. In my view, the replacement of the defendant as legal personal representative is not necessitated in the circumstances of this case, and I would allow the appeal, including the appeal against the order for costs of the motion made against the defendant personally. Such an order for costs would in my view require a finding of some misconduct or other culpable behaviour on the part of the defendant, and there was none.

However, it appears that an administrator may be removed and replaced more readily than an executor. In *Dunne v Heffernan*,[24] Lynch J stated: **12–20**

> Where the person nominated to be executor renounces, or where no executor is appointed, or on an intestacy, the right to administration is determined by the Rules of the Superior Courts in O.79, r. 5. In such a case, the person entitled to the grant of administration may be passed over more readily and someone else appointed pursuant to s 27, sub-s. 4 than where an executor is appointed and accepts the appointment by proving the will when weighty reasons must be established before the grant of probate would be revoked and cancelled pursuant to s 26, sub-s. 2 and the testator's chosen representative thereby removed, and someone else not chosen by the testator appointed pursuant to s 27, sub-s. 4 of the Act of 1965.

(iii) Inordinate Delay in Administering Estates

A personal representative who is an executor or administrator may be removed and replaced by another administrator appointed under s 27(4) where the special circumstances of the case warrants his or her replacement, and further, that it is necessary or expedient to do so, where there is a pronounced delay on the part of a personal representative in the administration of an estate, and/or a failure by a personal representative **12–21**

> to discharge the fundamental duty to collect and get in the estate and administer it according to law can, depending on the gravity or extent of that failure, whether alone or in combination with other factors, amount to a special circumstance warranting the removal and replacement of that person.[25]

In *Muckian v Hoey*,[26] Keane J, referring to the judgment and criteria formulated by Lynch J in *Dunne v Heffernan*, concluded that: **12–22**

> (a) A pronounced delay on the part of a personal representative in the administration of an estate could, alone or in combination with other factors,

[24] [1997] 3 IR 431 at 444; see also *Muckian v Hoey* [2016] IEHC 688.

[25] See *Muckian v Hoey* [2016] IEHC 688.

[26] [2016] IEHC 688; A. Keating, *The Law and Practice of Personal Representatives* (Round Hall, Dublin, 2017).

amount to a special circumstance warranting the removal and replacement of that person.

(b) A failure by a personal representative to discharge the fundamental duty to collect and get in the estate and administer it according to law can, depending on the gravity or extent of that failure, whether alone or in combination with other factors, amount to a special circumstance warranting the removal and replacement of that person.

(c) An administrator (or administratrix) may be replaced more readily in such circumstances than an executor.

(d) The factors identified at (a) and (b) above are both applicable in the circumstances of the present case and each demonstrates a want of proper capacity on the part of the first respondent to execute the duties of administratrix, amounting to a special circumstance.

(e) Considering those factors individually in this case, I am satisfied that it is appropriate, indeed necessary, by reference to each to replace the first respondent as administrator of the deceased's estate. It is certainly necessary to do so on considering them in combination.

In exercise of the power conferred on the Court by s. 27, sub-s. 2 of the Succession Act 1965, I will therefore revoke the grant of administration to the first respondent and, in the special circumstances arising, I will order, pursuant to s. 27, sub-s. 4 of that Act, that administration of the deceased's estate be granted to Cleaver, Fulton and Rankin Trustees Limited.

12–23 In his judgment, Keane J also noted that the applicants had issued proceedings in Northern Ireland in relation to estate of the deceased situated there seeking an order under art 35 of the Wills and Administration Proceedings (Northern Ireland) Order 1994 (SI 1994/1899), removing the first respondent as adminstratrix of the estate, and referred to the *ex tempore* judgment of Deeny J of the Northern Ireland High Court acceding to the application and appointing a firm of professional trustees, Cleaver, Fulton and Rankin Trustees Ltd, as administrator of the estate in place of the first respondent.

12–24 An executor removed for inordinate delay in applying for a grant of probate, who is also a trustee, may be replaced as trustee by the person appointed by the court to apply for a grant under s 27(4) of the 1965 Act.

12–25 Where no grant of probate has issued to the executor named in the deceased's will, he or she may be passed over, and the court may appoint another person to apply for a grant of letters of administration with the will annexed under s 27(4), where the special circumstances of the case warrant it, and when it is necessary or expedient to do so. In *Scally v Rhatigan*,[27] Laffoy J, referring to *Dunne v Heffernan*,[28] stated that the onus of establishing "serious special circumstances" on the part of the nominated executor rests on the person seeking his or her passing over. When considering whether the plaintiff should be precluded from acting as executrix of the will, Laffoy J found that:

[27] [2012] IEHC 140; see A. Keating, *The Law and Practice of Personal Representatives* (Round Hall, Dublin, 2017); A. Keating, "The Removal, Passing Over and Replacement of Personal Representatives" (2017) 22(1) CPLJ 2.

[28] [1997] 3 IR 431.

> It is her past professional involvement as solicitor for the Testator and for the multiplicity of corporate vehicles in which the assets of the Golden Promise Trust were vested which gives rise to the professional conflict, coupled with the justified opposition of the defendant, as a major beneficiary of the estate assets, which, in my view, precludes the plaintiff from acting as executor of the Will. That involvement goes way beyond the three examples I have addressed in detail in this judgment. While one can understand that the plaintiff would like to fulfil the task which the Testator reposed in her, I am of the view that it would be impossible for her to steer a non-conflicted passage between the beneficiaries of the estate assets, on the one hand, and the interest of the beneficiaries of the non-estate assets, on the other hand, so as to take all of the steps in the administration, including the protection of the assets, of the estate of the Testator and of the trusts created by the Will that require to be taken by the personal representative.

Laffoy J concluded that: **12–26**

> In the circumstances, I consider that it would be inappropriate to grant probate of the Will to the plaintiff. Therefore, it will be necessary for the court, pursuant to its power under s.27(4), to appoint some person other than the plaintiff to administer the estate of the Testator.

It appears that the person entitled to apply for a grant of letters of administration with the will annexed or intestate under the Rules of the Superior Courts may also be passed over where existing special circumstances so warrant, and an administrator may be appointed by the court pursuant to s 27(4) to apply for a grant of letters of administration with the will annexed or intestate. It also appears that the person entitled to apply for a grant under the Rules of the Superior Court may be passed over more readily than an executor.[29] **12–27**

Grounds for Removal of Trustees

The primary purpose of entering into the office of trustee "is to fulfil the objects of the trust and this cannot happen if there is a conflict between duty and interest."[30] Therefore, trustees must not place themselves in a position which may entail a conflict of interest with the duty they owe to the beneficiaries of the trust, or they may be removed. The court has an inherent jurisdiction to remove trustees, and may, when considering whether or not to remove a trustee, take into account the following matters: **12–28**

- (i) A trust is set up for the welfare of its beneficiaries. Therefore, before determining whether or not any trustee should be removed from his or her office, it is necessary to determine whether his or her continuation in that office will be detrimental to such welfare.[31]
- (ii) "Conflicts of duty are to be equated to conflicts of interest as the duty does

---

[29] See *Dunne v Heffernan* [1997] 3 IR 431 at 444; see also *Muckian v Hoey* [2016] IEHC 688.

[30] See *Greene v Coady* [2014] IEHC 38.

[31] See *Spencer v Kinsella* [1996] 2 ILRM 401 at 409.

not arise without the interest and the genesis of the rule in the frailty of human nature requires that both are equally to be treated."[32]

(iii) Where it is implicit in the nature of the trust that particular decisions involving trust business will affect the trustees personally, there is an exception to the rule that trustees cannot act in a situation where a conflict of interest arises, and the exception does not apply beyond the scope of what is inherently contemplated by the trust.[33]

(iv) An allegation of a conflict of interest between duty and interest must be proved as a fact.[34]

12–29 In *Spencer v Kinsella*,[35] an application was made to remove, as a body, the trustees of land in the town of Gorey used as showgrounds, which were the subject of trusts pursuant to a scheme made under the Irish Land Act 1903, as amended, on the grounds that they had persistently refused to act when called upon to do so. In his judgment, Barron J, having commented that, in all cases of trust, it is a truism to say that no trustee should allow his interests to conflict with his duty, he stated that:

> In the present case the main problem lies in the failure of the trustees to execute agreements with the users of the trust. There is also the further problem that some of the trustees are too closely identified with the interests of some of those users to be regarded as being capable of being truly impartial in any decision-making process involving the trustees. None of these faults have resulted from any deliberate or conscious conduct or misconduct on the part of the trustees. Nevertheless where a conflict of interest arises it is doubtful that a continuation by such persons in office could be remedied.[36]

12–30 He further stated:

> The welfare of the beneficiaries is being affected by the present situation. There is a conflict of interest which I have identified and it would be difficult to reorganise with such conflict on the part of some of the trustees continuing to exist. It is accordingly appropriate that such persons should step down. It will however serve no purpose if they step down, but at the same time no other reorganisation takes place.

12–31 Having stated that what was needed was the appointment of trustees who would be, so far as possible, impartial as between the users of the grounds, Barron J stated that he did not propose to exercise the powers of the court at that point in time. As he saw it, it was essentially a matter for the people of Gorey and the Department of Agriculture, Forestry and Food to reorganise the administration of the trust, and accordingly, he adjourned the matter for six months to enable the administration of the trust to be placed on a proper footing.

---

[32] See *Greene v Coady* [2014] IEHC 38 at para 5.8.
[33] See *Greene v Coady* [2014] IEHC 38 at paras 5.11–5.12.
[34] See *Greene v Coady* [2014] IEHC 38 at para 5.6.
[35] [1996] 2 ILRM 401 at 409; see *Scally v Rhatigan* [2012] IEHC 140; *Davies v Hutchinson* [2017] IEHC 693.
[36] See *Spencer v Kinsella* [1996] 2 ILRM 401 at 409.

CHAPTER 13

THE LIABILITY OF EXECUTORS, TRUSTEES AND SOLICITORS

INTRODUCTION

As in the case of removal of executors and trustees of will trusts, where the executors and trustees of a will trust are the same persons, and are called "hereinafter my trustees", their functions, duties and powers will merge, and they may therefore be rendered liable as executors and trustees on similar grounds. Where the executors and trustees of a will trust are not the same persons, the functions of executors and trustees will not merge, and in such cases, the executors of a will trust may be rendered liable on grounds relating to the liability of executors only, and the trustees may be rendered liable on grounds relating to the liability of trustees only, although, it may be added, the grounds of liability of executors and trustees are similar. Executors and trustees must act diligently and prudently when distributing the estate among the beneficiaries, bearing in mind that "the ultimate object of administration of an estate is to place the beneficiaries in possession of their interest". While executors and trustees are required to act diligently so as to save the estate unnecessary expenditure, they must also act prudently to ensure that the beneficiaries receive their share in the estate, and where, owing to "carelessness", a beneficiary does not receive the share to which he or she is entitled, executors and trustees may be liable accordingly.[1] Where it is shown that executors or trustees have failed to act prudently and diligently when dealing with the deceased's property, and loss is caused to a beneficiary's interest in the estate by a "*devastavit*", they may be found personally liable to the beneficiary in the tort of negligence for any loss incurred to his or her interest in the estate.[2] A *devastavit* occurs where the assets of the deceased's estate are reduced in value owing to an executor's non-performance of the duties of prudence and diligence when administering the estate. The personal representatives when administering and distributing the estate, and trustees the trust estate, are obliged to act not only diligently[3] **13–01**

---

1 *Re Gunning* [1918] 1 IR 221 at 226.

2 *Re Gunning* [1918] 1 IR 221; *Shaughnessy v Shaughnessy* [2016] IEHC 303; A. Keating, *The Law and Practice of Personal Representatives* (Round Hall, Dublin, 2017).

3 *Re Tankard* [1942] 2 All ER 458; see A. Keating, "Personal Liability of Nominated Executors" (2017) 22(2) CPLJ 26; A. Keating, *The Law and Practice of Personal Representatives* (Round Hall, Dublin, 2017).

but also prudently.[4] The duty to act diligently[5] and prudently[6] endures until the completion of the administration and distribution of the estate.[7]

13–02 A solicitor owes a duty to exercise "considerable" care and skill in drafting and executing a will and may be liable in damages to intended beneficiaries for loss of legacies where he has failed to exercise such care and skill, and for any other attendant loss flowing naturally from the solicitor's lack of care.[8] In *Condon v Law Society of Ireland*,[9] Kearns P, when considering the question of the accountability of solicitors who are also executors to beneficiaries, stated that a solicitor who is appointed as executor may also be rendered accountable to beneficiaries as clients. In *Rojack v Taylor and Buchalter*,[10] it was held that a solicitor does not owe a duty to inform the children of a testator of their right to make an application under s 117 of the Succession Act 1965.

Breach of Duties of Diligence and Prudence

13–03 Executors and trustees who are "hereinafter my trustees" owe a duty of diligence and prudence when administering an estate and discharging the debts owing by the estate. In *Re Tankard*,[11] Uthwatt J stated that:

> Due diligence may, indeed, require that payment should be made before the expiration of the executor's year, and the circumstances affecting the estate and the assets comprised in it may justify non-payment outside the year, but, if debts are not paid with the year, the onus is thrown upon the executors to justify the delay.[12]

13–04 In *Re Tankard*,[13] Uthwatt J also stated that the duty of diligence is owed to beneficiaries, because the ultimate object of administration of an estate is to place the beneficiaries in possession of their interest. While personal representatives are required to act diligently, and save the estate from all unnecessary expenditure, they must also act prudently to ensure that the beneficiaries receive their share in the estate, and if as a result of their "carelessness" a beneficiary does not receive his share they may be liable

4 *Re Gunning* [1918] 1 IR 221; *Job v Job* (1877) 6 Ch D 562; *Hayward v Kinsey* (1701) 12 Mod Rep 568.

5 *Re Tankard* [1942] 2 All ER 458; see A. Keating, "Personal Liability of Nominated Executors" (2017) 22(2) CPLJ 26.

6 *Re Gunning* [1918] 1 IR 221; *Job v Job* (1877) 6 Ch D 562; *Hayward v Kinsey* (1701) 12 Mod. Rep. 568.

7 *Marsden v Regan* [1954] 1 WLR 423; *Re Tankard*, above, n.3; *Re Rowson* (1885) 29 Ch D 358; *Hilliard v Fulford* (1876) 4 Ch D 389.

8 *Ross v Caunters* [1980] Ch 297; *Wall v Hegarty and Callanan* [1980] ILRM 124.

9 [2010] IEHC 52.

10 Unreported, High Court, Quirke J, 10 February 2005.

11 [1942] 2 All ER 458; see A. Keating, *The Law and Practice of Personal Representatives* (Round Hall, Dublin, 2017).

12 [1942] 2 All ER 458.

13 [1942] 2 All ER 458 at 463.

accordingly.[14] In *Re Gunning*,[15] Ross J stated that the executors must be proved to have acted without ordinary prudence. The standard of ordinary prudence is "that the executor in managing the trust must take all precautions which an ordinary prudent man in business would take in managing similar affairs of his own." In that case, the testatrix left a legacy of £150 to "J.G. of Vancouver, B.C." J.G.'s sister informed the executors that his address was at "Portland, Oregon, U.S.A." The executors sent a banker's draft to that address without making further inquiries. The wrong person received the draft. Ross J found that the loss of a banker's draft was the natural result of the executors' carelessness. The loss was the natural and probable result of their failure to take precautions:

> The executor when he assumes the duty must know that if he is not careful to act up to the court's standard of prudence, he will be obliged to bear the loss himself.[16]

Ross J, when referring to an executor's standard of care when dealing with the property of the deceased's estate, stated that: **13–05**

> There must be one standard for all ... and the standard is this: that the executor in managing the trust must take all those precautions which an ordinary prudent man in business would take in managing similar affairs of his own. It is allowed to him to employ proper agents. He is not bound to scrutinize with suspicion each step taken by such agents or to deal with them as if they were dishonest; but he must not expose the trust funds to unreasonable or unnecessary risks. An ignorant, uneducated trustee cannot escape from liability by reason of his shortcomings. On the other hand, a highly educated man is not to be held to stricter accountability by reason of his superior training. Each must act up to the Court's standard of prudence. No more is required, and no less can be accepted. These are the well-settled principles applicable to the matter in question.

He also stated that: **13–06**

> Executors cannot be charged with the loss of the testator's assets without wilful default. Gross negligence may amount to wilful default.[17]

As a result of *Re Tankard* and *Re Gunning*, personal representatives when administering and distributing an estate must act not only diligently, but also prudently. **13–07**

In *Shaughnessy v Shaughnessy*,[18] Gilligan J stated that: **13–08**

> The important aspect is that the personal representatives in whom the whole estate vests must perform their duties diligently (*Re Tankard* [1942] Ch. 69; *Re Gunning* [1918] 1 IR 221) and if they fail to do so the beneficiaries may bring an action against them (*Re Hayes WT* [1971] 2 All E.R. 341).

---

14 *Re Gunning* [1918] 1 IR 221 at 226.
15 *Re Gunning* [1918] 1 IR 221 at 226.
16 *Re Gunning* [1918] 1 IR 221 at 226.
17 *Re Gunning* [1918] 1 IR 221 at 224.
18 [2016] IEHC 303.

Personal Liability of Executors and Trustees

13–09 Executors and trusts who are called "hereinafter my trustees" may be rendered personally liable to the estate and/or beneficiaries. In *Shaughnessy v Shaughnessy*,[19] Gilligan J, when considering the duties of an executor and his or her liability to beneficiaries stated that:

> If it appears to the Court that the executor acted with due diligence in carrying out their duties then they shall be absolved of their liabilities. However, if the Court finds that the executor simply sat on his hands, out of idleness or for personal gain, as the value of assets bequeathed under the will fall, to the detriment of the beneficiaries, then the Court may form a view that the executor is liable for any losses incurred. Of course, the normal rules of reasonable foreseeability of loss shall apply. The circumstances of this case must impress upon executors of an estate the onus that lies upon them to carry out their legal duties in accordance with the will, in a reasonable and prudent manner and in a reasonable period of time.

13–10 In *Shaughnessy v Shaughnessy*, the plaintiff and defendant were sister and brother, and beneficiaries in their mother's will who died on 7 September 2007. Following the deceased's death, the defendant proceeded to attend to the administration of the deceased's estate, and gathered details of the assets and liabilities for the purpose of preparing an Inland Revenue affidavit prior to applying for probate of the will of his deceased mother. The Inland Revenue affidavit was prepared and approved by the Revenue Commissioners on 4 November 2008. However, the defendant did not apply for a grant for a grant of probate, despite being repeatedly called upon by the plaintiff to do so, especially in the light of economic exigencies which arose from 2007 onwards when the value of property began to fall drastically. In this regard, the plaintiff submitted valuations of the residence bequeathed to her and her two sisters in their mother's will. In September 2007, the property was valued at €300,000.00. One year later, the market value of the property in question dropped to €270,000.00. In July 2012, the value of the property was estimated at €125,000.00. In July 2014, the value remained at €125,000.00. This marked a loss of €175,000.00 between the date of the plaintiff's mother's death and July 2014. A half-acre building site was also left to the plaintiff and a valuation put the open market value of it at €70,000.00 in September 2008. In October 2012, the site was valued at €25,000.00, showing a loss of €45,000.00.

13–11 Gilligan J, when considering the question of the defendant's duty of care to the estate and beneficiaries, and his personal liability to beneficiaries for negligence in dealing with the property of the deceased's estate, stated that:

> I am satisfied that the defendant in his capacity as the nominated executor of his mother's estate failed in the duty of care which he owed to the estate and to the plaintiff as a beneficiary thereof. The reality of the situation is that it was a straightforward situation to pay the funeral and testamentary expenses, pay

[19] [2016] IEHC 303; see A. Keating, *The Law and Practice of Personal Representatives* (Round Hall, Dublin, 2017); A. Keating, "Personal Liability of Nominated Executors" (2017) 22(2) CPLJ 26.

> out the amounts that were due to each of his three sisters in accordance with his mother's will, transfer the title to his mother's house to his three sisters and agree a site of ½ acre each with them and transfer the lands to them and finalise matters relating to his own bequest but clearly he prevaricated and wanted to obtain advice in respect of the will and in effect as of September, 2009, he still had not advanced the situation. He should have renounced as executor so as to enable his three sisters as beneficiaries and devisees under the will to have taken his place and administered the estate and he did not do so. Accordingly, in my view, in his capacity as executor he was guilty of negligence and breach of duty"

He assessed the loss incurred by the plaintiff as follows: **13–12**

> At the date of death in 2007 the site was valued at €90,000.00. As of September, 2008, the value was €70,000.00, and by June, 2009, the site was valued at €50,000.00. As of October, 2012, the value was €25,000.00. Allowing time for a sale and some leeway for the exigencies of the market I take the view that if a sale could have been effected within a reasonable period of time after the death of the deceased the plaintiff would have obtained a price in the region of 50 – 60,000.00 Euro and in October, 2012, a price of €25,000.00, and thus the plaintiff's loss can be ascertained at €30,000.00.

Therefore, where it is shown that the nominated executor or trustee has **13–13** failed to act prudently and diligently when dealing with the property of the deceased's estate, and where owing to his or her negligence loss is incurred by the beneficiaries, for instance, loss caused by a *devastavit* or wasting of assets of the estate, he or she may be personally liable to the beneficiaries in action for damages in negligence for the loss incurred by them.[20]

The property of a deceased testator's estate vests in his or her nominated **13–14** executor at the date of the death of the testator.[21] A nominated executor is also empowered, from the date of the testator's death, to deal with the property of the estate.[22] When dealing with the property of the deceased's estate, a nominated executor must perform his or her duties prudently and diligently, and if he or she fails to do so, and loss is sustained by the beneficiaries, they may bring an action in negligence for damages against him or her to recover their loss, for instance, where loss is caused to the beneficiaries and the estate by a *devastavit* or wasting of assets of the estate, the executor may be personally liable in damages to the beneficiaries for any loss so caused.[23]

Professional Liability of Solicitors

(i) A Solicitor's Duty of Care to Beneficiaries of Will Trusts

A solicitor owes a duty to exercise "considerable" care and skill in drafting **13–15**

[20] *Re Gunning* [1918] 1 IR 221 at 226; *Shaughnessy v Shaughnessy* [2016] IEHC 303; *Re Tankard* [1942] Ch 69; see also *Doyle v White* [2017] IEHC 44; A. Keating, *The Law and Practice of Personal Representatives* (Round Hall, Dublin, 2017).

[21] Succession Act 1965, s 10(1).

[22] See *O'Hagan v Grogan* [2012] IESC 8.

[23] *Re Gunning* [1918] 1 IR 221; *Shaughnessy v Shaughnessy* [2016] IEHC 303.

and executing a will and may be liable in damages to intended beneficiaries for loss of legacies where he has failed to exercise such care and skill, and for any other attendant loss flowing naturally from the solicitor's lack of care.[24] Sir Robert Megarry, when considering the issue of professional liability in *Ross v Caunters*[25] stated that a solicitor must know that if he fails in his professional duty to draft and execute a will properly, a beneficiary will suffer loss. He formulated the extent of a solicitor's duty of care towards beneficiaries as follows:

> (i) A solicitor may be liable both to his client and to others in the tort of negligence;
> (ii) The basis of the solicitor's liability to others is either an extension of the *Hedley Byrne* principle, or more probably, a direct application of the principle of *Donoghue v Stevenson*;
> (iii) A solicitor who is instructed by his client to carry out a transaction that will confer a benefit on an identified third party owes a duty of care towards that third party in carrying out that transaction;
> (iv) The mere fact that the loss to such a third party caused by the negligence is purely financial, and is no way a physical injury to person or property, is no bar to the claim against the solicitor; and
> (v) In such circumstances there are "no considerations which suffer to negative or limit the scope of the solicitor's duty to the beneficiary."

13–16 In *Wall v Hegarty and Callanan*,[26] Barrington J, when referring with approval to the *dicta* of Sir Robert Megarry in *Ross v Caunters*, stated that a solicitor owes a duty to exercise "considerable" care and skill in drafting and executing a will, and may be liable in damages to intended beneficiaries for loss of legacies where he or she has failed to exercise such care and skill, and for any other attendant loss flowing naturally from his or her lack of care. He also added that a solicitor who drafts a will in which an executor is named must foresee that that executor will eventually seek the admission of the will to probate, and therefore it followed that the costs incurred by the plaintiff as executor in having the will admitted to probate flowed naturally from the solicitor's lack of care and were recoverable by him. He also recognised the plaintiff's entitlement to recover damages for loss of interest on his legacy.

(ii) The Accountability of Solicitors as Executors of Will Trusts

13–17 As a result of the decision of Kearns P in *Condon v Law Society of Ireland*,[27] a solicitor who accepts the office of executor by applying for a grant of probate not only owes a duty to beneficiaries to duly administer the estate but he is also accountable to them as clients under s 2 of the Solicitors (Amendment) Act 1994, and the beneficiaries as clients will be afforded all of the protections under that Act which any other client of a solicitor would be entitled to, including the making of complaints regarding the provision

---

[24] *Ross v Caunters* [1980] Ch 297; *Wall v Hegarty and Callanan* [1980] ILRM 124.
[25] [1980] Ch 297.
[26] [1980] ILRM 124.
[27] [2010] IEHC 52.

of inadequate professional services under s 8(1) of the Act.[28] Where the Law Society's Complaints and Client Relations Committee in the exercise of its powers under s 8(1) of the 1994 Act directs a solicitor to hand over a file relating to the estate of which he is executor, it will sever the relationship of solicitor and client between him and the beneficiaries, but it will not, or indeed, cannot, remove him as executor, as that is a matter for the courts to decide.[29] But the effect of such a determination may so reduce an executor's participation in administering the estate, or may so curtail the exercise of his powers as executor, that he may end up an executor in all but name. This, however, it may be said, is much more preferable than instituting expensive proceedings seeking the removal of an executor.

(iii) A Solicitor's Duty of Care to Personal Representatives

Solicitors who accept instructions to administer an estate owe a duty to undertake the administration in a professional manner, and they may be liable in damages for breach of duty. As the whole estate of a deceased person vests in the personal representatives, they are appropriate persons to bring actions for loss sustained by the estate through the negligence of a solicitor.[30] Where, for instance, an estate is comprised of income-bearing assets but due to a solicitor's delay in applying for a grant of probate, the assets remain unutilised and produce no income as a result, he or she may be liable for loss of income.[31] In *Chappell v Somers & Blake*,[32] the testatrix died in December 1995 and left her residuary estate to a sole beneficiary. The residuary estate included two properties, neither of which had been let at the time of the testatrix's death. In January 1996, the executrix instructed the defendant solicitors to act on her behalf in the administration of the estate. Over the following five years the solicitors did nothing at all to progress the administration of the estate. The executrix terminated the solicitors' retainer in April 2001 and instructed other solicitors to apply for a grant of probate. The two properties that formed part of the residuary remained unlet until after they were transferred to the beneficiary. The executrix brought an action against her former solicitors in her capacity as personal representative for breach of contractual and tortious duties owed by them to her. She claimed that if the solicitors had acted in accordance with their duty, the two properties would have been assented to the beneficiary five years earlier, and that income would have been earned from them during that period either by renting or by selling them and enjoying the interest on the proceeds of sale, and that the loss of income for that period was caused by the solicitors' breach of duty by their failure to advise her properly or at **13–18**

[28] *Condon v The Law Society of Ireland* [2010] IEHC 52; A. Keating, *The Law and Practice of Personal Representatives* (Round Hall, Dublin, 2017).

[29] *Condon v Law Society of Ireland* [2010] IEHC 52.

[30] See *Re Tankard* [1942] 2 All ER 458 at 72–74; *Re Gunning* [1918] 1 IR 221; A. Keating, *The Law and Practice of Personal Representatives* (Round Hall, Dublin, 2017).

[31] See *Chappell v Somers & Blake* [2003] 3 All ER 1076.

[32] *Chappell v Somers & Blake* [2003] 3 All ER 1076.

all. Neuberger J in the course of his judgment stated that it was appropriate to treat the executrix as representing the interest of the owner of the property and she was therefore entitled to recover damages from the solicitors on behalf of the estate.[33]

(iv) A Solicitor's Duty to Personal Representatives and Potential s 117 Applicants

13–19 A solicitor's primary duty is to advise personal representatives in the administration and distribution of the deceased's estate. There is no duty imposed on them to give advice to a beneficiary as to the existence of a potential claim under s 117 of the Succession Act 1965, or to inform him or her to seek separate and independent legal advice on the matter.[34] In *Rojack v Taylor and Buchalter*,[35] the plaintiff, who was a beneficiary and executrix of her mother's will, claimed that she suffered financial loss and damage as a result of the defendant solicitors' failure to advise her of the existence of a potential claim against the estate under s 117 of the Succession Act 1965, and of the necessity to seek separate and independent legal advice on the matter within the time allowed by s 117. The time allowed for making an application under s 117 had elapsed. The defendants argued that they agreed only to act as solicitors for the purpose of administering the estate and advising the plaintiff in her capacity as executrix of the estate, but not in her capacity as beneficiary. They also rejected the contention that the plaintiff had a probable cause of action against the estate under s 117. It was held by Quirke J that the defendants were retained only to advise the plaintiff in her capacity as personal representative of the testatrix, and accordingly, the duty imposed on them was that imposed on any solicitor retained to advise a personal representative in the administration of an estate. There was no duty imposed on them to give advice to the plaintiff in her capacity as beneficiary as to the existence of a potential claim under s 117 of the Succession Act or indeed to seek separate and independent legal advice on the matter. Although a solicitor advising a personal representative who receives an enquiry from a child of the testator in relation to a potential claim under s 117 "has a duty to the estate and possibly to the child to advise the child to seek independent legal advice upon the matter", where no enquiry is received, no such duty exists.

[33] See *Marshall (Inspector of Taxes) v Kerr* [1994] 3 All ER 106.
[34] *Rojack v Taylor and Buchalter*, Unreported, High Court, Quirke J, 10 February 2005.
[35] Unreported, High Court, Quirke J, 10 February 2005.

Part Three

EQUITABLE PROPERTY RIGHTS

Chapter 14

SNELL'S PRINCIPLES

Introduction

Snell's principles have frequently been referred to and adopted by the courts when considering questions relating to the existence of an estoppel over property. In *Haughan v Rutledge*,[1] Blaney J, and in *McDonagh v Denton*,[2] O'Sullivan J adopted Snell's principles and conditions for establishing a proprietary estoppel against an owner of land. Blayney J stated that Snell provided "a correct statement of the law and that if these four conditions are satisfied then an equity will arise which can be enforced against the owner of the land." In *Revenue Commissioners v Moroney*,[3] Kenny J adopted the definition of a promissory estoppel provided by the 26th edition of *Snell's Principles of Equity* as follows: **14–01**

> Where by his words or conduct one party to a transaction makes the other a promise or assurance which is intended to affect the legal relations between them, and the other party acts upon it, altering his position to his detriment, the party making the promise or assurance will not be permitted to act inconsistently with it.[4]

In *National Asset Loan Management Ltd v Downes*,[5] Charleton J referred to the 32nd edition of *Snell's Principles of Equity*, for a modern statement of the doctrine of promissory estoppel, as follows: **14–02**

> Where by his words or conduct one party to a transaction freely makes to the other a clear and unequivocal promise or assurance which is intended to affect the legal relations between them (whether contractual or otherwise) or was reasonably understood by the other party to have that effect, and, before it is withdrawn, the other party acts upon it, altering his or her position so that it would be inequitable to permit the first party to withdraw the promise, the party making the promise or assurance will not be permitted to act inconsistently with it.[6]

He added that estoppel "is based either on representation or situations of behaviour that, reasonably construed, clearly withdraw or alter the strictures of legal obligations in such a way that it would be unfair to later enforce these." **14–03**

A proprietary estoppel may be used not only as a shield (defence to an **14–04**

---

1 [1988] IR 295 at 300; see *Snell's Principles of Equity* (28th edn, Sweet & Maxwell, London, 1982); A. Keating, *The Law of Wills* (2nd ed, Clarus Press, Dublin, 2018).

2 Unreported, High Court, 15 April 2005.

3 [1972] IR 372 at 381.

4 *Snell's Principles of Equity* (26th ed, Sweet & Maxwell, London, 1966).

5 [2014] IEHC 71.

6 (Sweet & Maxwell, London, 2010), para 12-009.

action), but also as a sword (instituting an action), while the sister concept of promissory estoppel can be used only as defence or shield, and not as a sword.[7] It was stated by Hoffmann LJ in *Walton v Walton*[8] that proprietary estoppel in contrast to promissory estoppel:

> ... does not look forward into the future and guess at what might happen. It looks backwards from the moment when the promise falls due to be performed and asks whether, in the circumstances which have actually happened, it would be unconscionable for the promise not to be kept.[9]

14–05 In *Thorner v Major*,[10] Walker LJ, when distinguishing between the doctrines of promissory estoppel and proprietary estoppel, added that:

> The former must be based on an existing legal *relationship* (usually a contract, but not necessarily a contract relating to land). The latter need not be based on an existing legal relationship, but it must relate to *identified property* (usually land) owned (or, perhaps, about to be owned) by the defendant. It is the relation to identified land of the defendant that has enabled proprietary estoppel to develop as a sword, and not merely a shield: see Lord Denning MR in *Crabb v Arun DC* [1976] Ch 179, 187.

14–06 Another form of estoppel is estoppel by convention. In *National Asset Loan Management Ltd v Downes*,[11] Charleton J described estoppel by convention as follows:

> Estoppel by convention may arise where both parties to a transaction 'act on an assumed state of fact or law, the assumption being either shared by both or made by one and acquiesced in by the other'. The parties are then precluded from denying the truth of that assumption, if it would be unjust or 'unconscionable' to allow them (or one of them) to go back on it. Such an estoppel differs from estoppel by representation and from promissory estoppel in that it does not depend on any 'clear and unequivocal' representation or promise. It can arise where the assumption was based on a mistake spontaneously made by the party relying on it, and acquiesced in by the other party, though the common assumption of the parties, objectively assessed, must itself be 'unambiguous and unequivocal'.

14–07 A claimant who successfully establishes rights to property under the doctrine of proprietary estoppel or promissory estoppel, or indeed, estoppel by convention, may acquire equitable rights to the property, and be recognised as such by equity.

Snell's Principles of Proprietary Estoppel

14–08 The Irish courts have consistently referred to various editions of *Snell's Principles of Equity* for definitions of the doctrine of doctrine of proprietary

---

7 See *Combe v Combe* [1951] 2 KB 215.

8 Unreported, Court of Appeal, 14 April 1994.

9 Cited with approval by Lord Walker and Lord Neuberger in *Thorner v Major* [2009] UKHL 18.

10 [2009] UKHL 18.

11 [2014] IEHC 71 at para 20.

estoppel. The conditions set out in *Snell's Principles of Equity*[12] for establishing a proprietary estoppel were adopted by Blayney J in *Haughan v Rutledge*[13] and by O'Sullivan J in *McDonagh v Denton*[14] when deciding on the existence of a proprietary estoppel. In *Snell's Principles of Equity*, four conditions must be satisfied for a proprietary estoppel to arise:

> *1. Detriment*
> The person claiming must have incurred expenditure or otherwise have prejudiced himself or acted to his detriment.
>
> *2. Expectation or Belief*
> The person relying on the doctrine must have acted as though he already owned a sufficient interest in the property to justify the expenditure or that he would obtain such an interest.
>
> *3. Encouragement*
> The person relying on the concept must have been encouraged by the other person's agent or predecessor in title.
>
> *4. No Bar to the Equity*
> No equity will arise if to enforce the right the claim would contravene some statute, or prevent the exercise of a statutory discretion or prevent or excuse the performance of a statutory duty.

In *Haughan v Rutledge*, Blayney J thought that *Snell's Principles of Equity* provided "a correct statement of the law and that if these four conditions are satisfied then an equity will arise which can be enforced against the owner of the land." In *McDonagh v Denton*, O'Sullivan J also referred to *Greasley v Cooke*,[15] where it was said by Lord Denning MR, when dealing with the question of detriment, that "in many cases of proprietary estoppel there has been a money expenditure. But that is not a necessary element." It will be **14–09**

> sufficient if the party, to whom the assurance is given, acts on the faith of it, in such circumstances that it would be unjust and inequitable for the party making the assurance to go back on it: see *Moorgate Mercantiile Company Limited v Twitchings* [1976] 1 Q.B. 225 and *Crabb v Arun District Council* [1976] 1 Ch. 179, 188.

This view was echoed, though *obiter*, by Murphy J in *McCarron v McCarron*[16] when he said: **14–10**

> In principle I see no reason why the doctrine should be confined to the expenditure of money or the erection of premises on the land of another. In a suitable case it may well be argued that a plaintiff suffers as severe a loss or detriment by providing his own labours or services in relation to the lands of another and accordingly should equally qualify for recognition in equity.

---

12 *Snell's Principles of Equity* (28th edn, Sweet & Maxwell, London, 1982).
13 [1988] IR 295 at 300.
14 Unreported, High Court, 15 April 2005.
15 [1980] 1 WLR 1306.
16 Unreported, Supreme Court, 13 February 1997.

14–11 Applying the Snell conditions to the facts in *Haughan v Rutledge*, Blayney J found that the second and third conditions (expectation and encouragement) had not been satisfied because the plaintiffs spent money on the construction of a racetrack:

> ... in the hope and expectation that the defendant would continue to make lettings of the track to them, but as that hope and expectation was not created or encouraged by the defendant, the plaintiffs have no claim which can be enforced by law or equity.[17]

14–12 In *McDonagh v Denton*, O'Sullivan J found that all four of the Snell conditions were satisfied because (1) the plaintiff had prejudiced himself or acted to his detriment in the sense indicated in contracting to sell the disputed plot of ground and thereby exposing himself to specific performance proceedings; (2) he acted in the belief that he already owned a clear and transferable title in the property conveyed to him; (3) he was encouraged in this belief by the silence of the defendants' solicitor when confronted with an assertion of the plaintiff's title; (4) there was no bar to the equity. As it would be unjust and inequitable if the defendants were able to assert their prior registered title to the disputed plot of ground as against the plaintiff, O'Sullivan J restrained the defendants from interfering with the plaintiff's beneficial ownership. It may be noted that the decisions in *Haughan v Rutledge* and *McDonagh v Denton* involved *inter vivos* transactions and were not inheritance-related.

Snell's Principles of Promissory Estoppel

14–13 The Irish courts have also referred to various editions of *Snell's Principles of Equity* for definitions of the doctrine of doctrine of promissory estoppel. In *Revenue Commissioners v Moroney*,[18] Kenny J stated that:

> In my view there is no reason why the principle of promissory estoppel should be confined to cases where the representation related to existing contractual rights. It includes cases where there is a representation by one person to another that rights which will come into existence under a contract to be entered into will not be enforced. This is the way in which the principle is stated at p. 627 of *Snell's Principles of Equity* 26th ed. (London: Sweet & Maxwell, 1966):
>
> > 'Where by his words or conduct one party to a transaction makes the other a promise or assurance which is intended to affect the legal relations between them, and the other party acts upon it, altering his position to his detriment, the party making the promise or assurance will not be permitted to act inconsistently with it.'
>
> Or in other words, a person who makes to another a clear and unambiguous representation of fact intending that other to act on it, if the representation turns out to be untrue, and if that other does act upon it to his prejudice, the representor is prevented or estopped from denying its truth.

---

[17] [1988] IR 295 at 303; see also *Ramsden v Dyson* (1866) LR 1 HL129.

[18] [1972] IR 372 at 381.

In *Doran v Thompson*,[19] Griffin J stated the doctrine of promissory estoppel to mean: **14–14**

> Where one party has, by his words or conduct, made to the other a clear and unambiguous promise or assurance which was intended to affect the legal relations between them and to be acted on accordingly, and the other party has acted on it by altering his position to his detriment, it is well settled that the one who gave the promise or assurance cannot afterwards be allowed to revert to their previous legal relations as if no such promise or assurance had been made by him, and that he may be restrained in equity from acting inconsistently with such promise or assurance.

In the same case, Kenny J cited as being correct the statement of the law on promissory estoppel in *Snell's Principles of Equity*,[20] as follows: **14–15**

> Where by his words or conduct one party to a transaction makes to the other an unambiguous promise or assurance which is intended to affect the legal relations between them (contractual or otherwise) and the other party acts upon it, altering his position to his detriment, the party making the promise or assurance will not be permitted to act inconsistently with it.[21]

In *Central London Property Trust Ltd v High Trees House Ltd*,[22] Denning J stated that where a contract exists between parties and a promise made by one party and intended to be binding and acted upon, and in fact acted upon by the other party, the promise is binding insofar as its terms properly apply. In *Combe v Combe*,[23] the court held that the doctrine can only be used as a defence and not as a cause of action; to allow a plaintiff to sue upon such a promise is simply to ignore the necessity of consideration. In the same case, Birkett LJ used the celebrated metaphor that the doctrine may be "used as a shield and not a sword." In *Kenny v Kelly*,[24] Barron J, when referring to the doctrine of promissory estoppel, stated that: **14–16**

> In *Central London Property Trust Ltd v High Trees House Ltd*, the essence of promissory estoppel was said to be a promise intended to be binding, intended to be acted upon and in fact acted upon. In my view, the facts of the present case come within these principles. Each of the elements necessary to establish the estoppel is present.

In *Re J.R. (A Ward of Court)*,[25] Costello J, referring to *Snell's Principles of Equity*[26] stated that: **14–17**

> A promissory estoppel will arise here if one party has, by his words or conduct, made an unambiguous representation as to his future conduct, intending that the representation will be relied on, and to affect the legal relations between the parties

19 [1978] IR 222 at 230.
20 See *Snell's Principles of Equity* (27th ed, Sweet & Maxwell, London, 1973), p 563.
21 [1978] IR 222 at 233.
22 [1947] KB 130.
23 [1951] 1 All ER 767.
24 Unreported, High Court, Barron J, 27 July 1988.
25 [1993] ILRM 657.
26 *Snell's Principles of Equity* (27th ed, Sweet & Maxwell, London, 1973), p 556.

> and the representee acts on it or alters his or her position to his or her detriment the representor will not be permitted to act inconsistently with it.

14–18 In *Daly v Minister for the Marine*,[27] Fennelly J stated that the Supreme Court in *Doran v Thompson*[28] explained the doctrine of promissory estoppel very clearly and cited the above passages from the judgments of Griffin J and Kenny J, but emphasised that a party must alter his or her position to his or her detriment to rely on the doctrine.

14–19 In *Chartered Trust Ireland Ltd v Healy*,[29] the plaintiff contended that it is entitled to sue on foot of a hire-purchase agreement since the defendant is estopped from denying its validity. Barron J stated that it has been said many times that a promissory estoppel does not operate as a sword but only as a shield, and accordingly, there was no agreement upon which the plaintiff was entitled to sue and that its claim failed. However, Barron J went on to state that:

> This rule as to the effect of an estoppel does not prevent the plaintiff from relying upon an estoppel as a defence to the defendant's counterclaim.

14–20 In *National Asset Loan Management Ltd v Downes* the plaintiff argued that estoppel here was being used as a sword and not a shield. However, Charleton J referred to a passage in the judgment of Brandon LJ in *Amalgamated Property Co v Texas Bank*[30] which stated:

> In my view much of the language used in connection with these concepts is no more than a matter of semantics. Let me consider the present case and suppose that the bank had brought an action against the plaintiffs before they went into liquidation to recover moneys owed by A.N.P.P. to Portsoken. In the statement of claim in such an action the bank would have pleaded the contract of loan incorporating the guarantee, and averred that, on the true construction of the guarantee, the plaintiffs were bound to discharge the debt owed by A.N.P.P. to Portsoken. By their defence the plaintiffs would have pleaded that, on the true construction of the guarantee, the plaintiffs were only bound to discharge debts owed by A.N.P.P. to the bank, and not debts owed by A.N.P.P. to Portsoken. Then in their reply the bank would have pleaded that by reason of an estoppel arising from the matters discussed above, the plaintiffs were precluded from questioning the interpretation of the guarantee which both parties had, for the purpose of the transactions between them, assumed to be true.
>
> In this way the bank, while still in form using the estoppel as a shield, would in substance be founding a cause of action on it. This illustrates what I would regard as the true proposition of law, that, while a party cannot in terms found a cause of action on an estoppel, he may, as a result of being able to rely on an estoppel, succeed on a cause of action in which, without being able to rely on that estoppel, he would necessarily have failed. That, in my view, is, in substance, the situation of the bank in the present case.

---

[27] [2001] 3 IR 513.
[28] [1978] IR 222 at 230.
[29] Unreported, High Court, Barron J, 10 December 1985.
[30] [1982] 1 QB 84 at 131–132.

Charleton J, when referring with apparent approval to *Amalgamated Property Co v Texas Bank*,[31] added that: **14–21**

> As I have illustrated earlier in this judgment that is exactly the position which pertains in this case.

Estoppel by Convention

In *National Asset Loan Management Ltd v Downes*,[32] Charleton J, when referring to the doctrine of estoppel by convention, stated that: **14–22**

> Estoppel by convention may arise where both parties to a transaction 'act on an assumed state of fact or law, the assumption being either shared by both or made by one and acquiesced in by the other'.

He went on to state that: **14–23**

> Such an estoppel differs from estoppel by representation and from promissory estoppel in that it does not depend on any 'clear and unequivocal' representation or promise. It can arise where the assumption was based on a mistake spontaneously made by the party relying on it, and acquiesced in by the other party, though the common assumption of the parties, objectively assessed, must itself be 'unambiguous and unequivocal'.

And also that: **14–24**

> Estoppel is not based on bare assumption. Estoppel is based either on representations or on situations of behaviour that, reasonably construed, clearly withdraw or alter the strictures of legal obligations in such a way that it would be unfair to later enforce these. Where the matter is one of representation, it should be easy to identify the legal term supposedly altered and the representation directed in this regard. Where it is a matter of both parties proceeding on the basis of a common understanding, the mutual convention of the parties may suffice as a foundation for estoppel. If it is so, it is because of that common understanding.

He continued: **14–25**

> In this particular case, both parties knew that the contract was lawfully rescinded and both parties accepted that that was to remain the position subject only to the proviso that both would act on the artificial assumption that the contract was still alive and enforceable if the sale was completed on a particular date and time.[33]

He referred to *Courtney v McCarthy*[34] and the decision of Brandon LJ **14–26**

---

31 [1982] 1 QB 84 at 131–132.

32 [2014] IEHC 71; see *Courtney v McCarthy* [2008] 2 IR 376; *Amalgamated Property Co. v Texas Bank* [1982] 1 QB 84.

33 [2014] IEHC 71 at para 21; see *Courtney v McCarthy* [2008] 2 IR 376; *Amalgamated Property Co. v Texas Bank* [1982] 1 QB 84.

34 [2008] 2 IR 376.

in *Amalgamated Property Co v Texas Bank*,[35] where Brandon LJ, when describing estoppel by convention, stated that:

> This form of estoppel is founded, not on a representation of fact made by a representor and believed by a representee, but on an agreed statement of facts the truth of which has been assumed, by the convention of the parties, as the basis of a transaction into which they are about to enter. When the parties have acted in their transaction upon the agreed assumption that a given state of facts is to be accepted between them as true, then as regards that transaction each assumed.

[35] [1982] 1 QB 84.

Chapter 15

THE ACQUISITION OF EQUITABLE PROPERTY RIGHTS BY RE-FORMULATED PROPRIETARY AND PROMISSORY ESTOPPEL

Introduction

While the Snell principles for establishing proprietary estoppel and promissory estoppel seem to have been accepted with approval by the courts for claims relating to present interests in land, some recent decisions of seem to make a distinction between claims based on present interests in land and those based on future interests; for instance, such future interests as may arise on the death testate or intestate of the owner of the land. In relation to future interests, say, occurring on the death of the owner of the land, the courts have re-formulated the doctrine of proprietary estoppel, especially regarding the nature of the detriment suffered by the claimant.[1] The same may be said where a claim to land is based on a promissory estoppel.[2] The Irish courts also seem to have assimilated the doctrines of proprietary and promissory estoppel regarding future claims to interests in land. Therefore, it appears that both doctrines may be used as a "sword" and a "shield" in relation to claims to future interests in land, and assimilated accordingly where such interests are involved. It may be added that promissory estoppel was traditionally viewed as a defensive mechanism or one that may be used as a "shield" only and proprietary estoppel as both "sword" and "shield", but, it appears that where land is concerned, promissory estoppel, like its sister doctrine of proprietary estoppel, may now also be used as a "sword".[3] 15–01

As a result of the re-formulation of the doctrine of proprietary estoppel by the House of Lords in *Thorner v Major*,[4] a proprietary estoppel may be established once it is shown by the claimant that the representation or assurance was made to him or her by the owner of land, that he or she relied on the representation or assurance, and suffered a detriment in consequence of a reasonable reliance on it.[5] Further, the detriment occasioned by the 15–02

1 See *Thorner v Major* [2009] UKHL 18; A. Keating, *The Law of Wills* (2nd ed, Clarus Press, Dublin, 2018).
2 See *Naylor v Maher* [2012] IEHC 408.
3 See *Naylor v Maher* [2012] IEHC 408.
4 [2009] UKHL 18.
5 See *Thorner v Major* [2009] UKHL 18; A. Keating, "The Primacy of a Proprietary

claimant need not now take the form of a money expenditure on the land, as it is "sufficient if the party, to whom the assurance is given, acts on the faith of it, in such circumstances that it would be unjust and inequitable for the party making the assurance to go back on it."[6] In *McCarron v McCarron*,[7] Murphy J, when commenting on the nature of detriment, stated, albeit *obiter*, that in "a suitable case it may well be argued that a plaintiff suffers as severe a loss or detriment by providing his own labours or services in relation to the lands of another and accordingly should equally qualify for recognition in equity." In *Coyle v Finnegan*,[8] Laffoy J referred to the judgment of Murphy J in *McCarron v McCarron*, and stated that "the plaintiff suffered a loss or detriment by providing his own labours and services to assist the deceased in running the farm without any remuneration for his endeavours." The onus of proof rests on the claimant to show that all of the elements necessary for establishing a proprietary estoppel have been satisfied. It now appears that the re-formulated elements that constitute a proprietary estoppel by the foregoing decisions of the courts must be shown to exist for the purposes of establishing an equitable right to land. In *Naylor v Maher*,[9] O'Keeffe J referred with approval to the conditions necessary for establishing the re-formulated proprietary estoppel in *Thorner v Major*,[10] and to the judgment of Murphy J in *McCarron v McCarron*,[11] regarding the nature of the detriment suffered by the claimant. He also appears to have applied the very same conditions in *Thorner* for establishing a proprietary estoppel over land, for the purposes of establishing a promissory estoppel over land, and by so doing, assimilated the conditions necessary for establishing both a proprietary estoppel and a promissory estoppel over land. Where a claimant successfully establishes a proprietary estoppel or promissory estoppel over land, he or she, as a result, may acquire equitable property rights to the land in question.

Re-Formulated Proprietary Estoppel

15–03 In *Thorner v Major*,[12] Walker LJ, when considering whether the appellant acquired a proprietary estoppel in the deceased's estate, stated that the concept of proprietary estoppel is based on three main elements:

(i) a representation or assurance made to the claimant by the owner of land;
(ii) the claimant relied on the representation or assurance made or given by the owner in relation to the land; and

Estoppel or Remedial Constructive Trust" (2013) 18(1) CPLJ 9; A. Keating, "The Recognition of Services as a Detriment for Proprietary Estoppel" (2014) 19(1) CPLJ 2.

6 *Thorner v Major* [2009] UKHL 18.
7 Unreported, Supreme Court, 13 February 1997.
8 [2013] IEHC 463.
9 [2012] IEHC 408.
10 [2009] UKHL 18.
11 Unreported, Supreme Court, 13 February 1997.
12 [2009] UKHL 18.

(iii) the claimant suffered a detriment in consequence of his or her reasonable reliance on the representation or assurance made or given by the owner.

In *Thorner v Major*, the appellant David Thorner did substantial work without pay on the farm of his father's cousin Peter Thorner for nearly thirty years. The evidence showed that from 1990 until his death in 2005, Peter encouraged David to believe that he would inherit the farm, and that David acted in reliance on this assurance. Peter died without having made a will. David claimed that by reason of the assurances made by Peter, and his reliance on them, Peter's estate was estopped from denying that he has acquired the beneficial interest in the farm. Hoffmann LJ, when dealing with the date when an assurance became unequivocal, said: **15–04**

> I do not think that the judge was trying to pinpoint the date at which the assurance became unequivocal and I think it would be unrealistic in a case like this to try to do so. There was a close and ongoing daily relationship between the parties. Past events provide context and background for the interpretation of subsequent events and subsequent events throw retrospective light upon the meaning of past events. The owl of Minerva spreads its wings only with the falling of the dusk. The finding was that David reasonably relied upon the assurance from 1990, even if it required later events to confirm that it was reasonable for him to have done so.

While changes in the character or extent of the property in question are relevant to the relief which equity will provide, such changes will not exclude a remedy in proprietary estoppel, once the property forming the subject matter of the proprietary estoppel can be identified. In relation to this matter, Walker LJ stated that **15–05**

> changes in the character or extent of the property in question are relevant to the relief which equity will provide but do not exclude such a remedy where there is still an identifiable property. In the present case, I see no reason to question the judge's decision that David was entitled to the beneficial interest in the farm and the farming business as they were at Peter's death.

Neuberger LJ thought that: **15–06**

> It would represent a regrettable and substantial emasculation of the beneficial principle of proprietary estoppel if it were artificially fettered so as to require the precise extent of the property the subject of the alleged estoppel to be strictly defined in every case.

Furthermore, the nature of the detriment incurred by the claimant need not be in the form of a money expenditure on land to qualify for recognition in equity. A claimant may suffer "as severe a loss or detriment by providing his own labours or services in relation to the lands of another and accordingly should equally qualify for recognition in equity." **15–07**

In *Coyle v Finnegan*,[13] Laffoy J when referring to the three re-formulated **15–08**

[13] [2013] IEHC 463.

elements which constitute a proprietary estoppel, and applying them to the facts of the case before her, stated that:

> (a) In this case, unlike many cases, there was an express representation or assurance by the Deceased to the plaintiff that, if the plaintiff assisted the Deceased in running the farm, the Deceased would leave the farm to the plaintiff in his will. Not only that, but, in accordance with that representation, the Deceased made the August 1991 Will to fulfil that assurance and he told the plaintiff that he had made it. Further, he told the plaintiff that, if he were to change his mind, he would tell the plaintiff. It was reasonable for the plaintiff to assume that, if the Deceased did change his mind, he would recognise that the plaintiff should be rewarded for the assistance given by him to the Deceased up to that time. Indeed, in view of the provision in the amount of €5,000 made by the Deceased for the plaintiff in the August 2003 Will, it is reasonable to assume that the Deceased considered that it was fair and just that the plaintiff should be rewarded for the services he had rendered post-1991.
>
> (b) Between 1991 and 2000 the plaintiff acted in reliance on the assurances given to him by the Deceased both before and after August 1991, in particular, the assurance he gave him on the day following the making of the August 1991 Will and the confirmation on the way home from the seminar on early retirement schemes.
>
> (c) The plaintiff did suffer a detriment in consequence of his reasonable reliance on the Deceased's assurances and such detriment was of the type envisaged by Murphy J in *McCarron v McCarron*, in that the plaintiff suffered a loss or detriment by providing his own labours and services to assist the Deceased in running the farm without any remuneration for his endeavours. As Murphy J pointed out, that type of detriment should qualify for recognition in equity and, in my view, in this case it does.

15–09 She went on to state that "it would be unconscionable if the plaintiff was not recompensed for the labours and services he provided to the Deceased over the period from 1991 to 2000", and that equity required that "the plaintiff be reasonably remunerated for the labours and services which he gave the deceased". She also agreed with the comment made by Murphy J in his judgment in *McCarron v McCarron*[14]:

> that a charge or lien on the lands for a sum equivalent to reasonable remuneration for services rendered might constitute adequate compensation, in my view, is particularly suitable to the situation here and meets the equity of this case. I propose adopting that course here. It remains to determine the measure of reasonable remuneration.

15–10 While changes in the character or extent of the property in question are relevant to the relief which equity will provide, they will not exclude such a remedy once the property forming the subject matter of the proprietary estoppel can be identified. The appeal in *Thorner v Major* raised two issues. The first and main issue concerned the character or quality of the representation or assurance made to the claimant. The other, which was a subsidiary part of the main issue, was whether, if the other elements for proprietary estoppel were established, the claimant must fail if the land to which the assurance related had been inadequately identified, or had

---

[14] Unreported, Supreme Court, 13 February 1997.

undergone a change (in its situation or extent) during the period between the giving of the assurance and its eventual repudiation. In the course of his speech Walker LJ stated that:

> In my opinion it is a necessary element of proprietary estoppel that the assurances given to the claimant (expressly or impliedly, or, in standing-by cases, tacitly) should relate to identified property owned (or, perhaps, about to be owned) by the defendant.

It must relate: **15–11**

> to *identified property* (usually land) owned (or, perhaps, about to be owned) by the defendant. It is the relation to identified land of the defendant that has enabled proprietary estoppel to develop as a sword, and not merely a shield: see Lord Denning MR in *Crabb v Arun DC* [1976] Ch 179, 187.

The applicable principles of proprietary estoppel may be stated as follows: **15–12**

> 1. The representations or assurances regarding future interests in land acted upon by the claimant are unconditional.
> 2. The detriment suffered by the claimant may:
>   (a) take the form of a money expenditure on foot of representations or assurances made or given by the owner of the land, or
>   (b) consist of the provision of free labour on the land on foot of representations or assurances made or given by the owner of land.

Re-Formulated Promissory Estoppel

In *Naylor v Maher*,[15] O'Keeffe J referred with approval to the House of Lords decision in *Thorner v Major*, especially the judgments of Walker, Hoffman and Neuberger LJJ dealing with the conditions necessary for establishing a proprietary estoppel over land. When dealing with the issue of detriment he accepted the dicta of Murphy J in *McCarron v McCarron*,[16] who stated that in "a suitable case it may well be argued that a plaintiff suffers as severe a loss or detriment by providing his own labours or services in relation to the lands of another and accordingly should equally qualify for recognition in equity." In *Naylor*, the plaintiff worked on the deceased's lands for minimal remuneration for over a period of thirty years. The deceased during his lifetime promised the plaintiff that he would devise his lands to him. In fact, the deceased made a will in 2005 under which he devised the lands to the plaintiff. However, he made another will in 2006 by which he devised the lands to the defendant and made a bequest of the sum of €150,000 to the plaintiff. The plaintiff submitted that the defendant was estopped from denying that the plaintiff had an interest in the lands. In his judgment, O'Keeffe J stated that: **15–13**

> Promises were made by the deceased in the context of low income being paid

[15] [2012] IEHC 408.
[16] Unreported, Supreme Court, 13 February 1997.

> by him to the plaintiff and the deceased being anxious to secure reliable long term assistance in the management of the farm. Such a long term aspiration of the deceased would be totally consistent with the lifelong farmer (the deceased) endeavouring to secure within the extended family, a permanent and trusted labour supply to assist in the management and working of the farm. This promise or commitment by the deceased becomes more understandable against the background of the plaintiff being acknowledged by the deceased as his stepson and even more so with the plaintiff now acknowledged as the natural child of the deceased, a fact now known to the surviving members of the family.

15–14 O'Keeffe J also accepted "the evidence of the witnesses called on behalf of the plaintiff who recalled promises, utterances or statements made by the deceased that the land would be the plaintiffs; by virtue of the plaintiff's contribution to the deceased's farming activities." He found that the plaintiff's claim to the lands was established by the application of the doctrine of promissory estoppel.

15–15 Therefore, it appears that conditions necessary for establishing either a promissory estoppel or a proprietary estoppel relating to future interests in land are the same. The property forming the subject matter of a promissory estoppel or proprietary estoppel must be identifiable, and while changes in the character or extent of the property in question are relevant to the relief, they will not exclude a remedy based on a promissory estoppel or proprietary estoppel. The detriment suffered by the claimant need not take the form of a monetary expenditure on the land, as it "is not a necessary element" and it will be "sufficient if the party, to whom the assurance is given, acts on the faith of it, in such circumstances that it would be unjust and inequitable for the party making the assurance to go back on it." As was stated in *McCarron v McCarron* by Murphy J, a plaintiff who suffers as severe a loss or detriment by providing his own labours or services in relation to the lands of another should equally qualify for recognition in equity. O'Keeffe J in *Naylor v Maher* and Laffoy J in *Coyle v Finnegan and Finnegan* accepted the re-formulated conditions for establishing a proprietary estoppel in *Thorner v Major*, and also adopted the extended meaning given to the necessary condition of detriment by Murphy J in *McCarron v McCarron*.

15–16 In *Naylor v Maher*,[17] Peart J, in his judgment for the Court of Appeal, stated that the focus of the appeal is the trial judge's conclusion that the plaintiff was entitled to the lands on the basis of promises made to him, and his acting in reliance upon them – in other words on the basis of a promissory estoppel.

15–17 Peart J stated that:

> 15. In addition, it is important also to state that the representations made to the plaintiff by the deceased that he would get these lands, and the reliance which the plaintiff placed upon them, in truth amount to a contract which ought to be fulfilled. The deceased should be kept to his contract - *'pacta sunt servanda'*.

[17] [2018] IECA 32.

> The satisfaction of the plaintiff's equity by receiving a transfer of the lands will attend to this, and does not offend good conscience.

As regards the detriment suffered by the claimant, Peart J stated that: **15–18**

> The detriment to him is not confined to a reduction of income or other purely monetary loss. He altered the course of his life. One cannot forecast how his life might have evolved had he remained working in Dublin or, indeed, in any other urban environment, but it is reasonable to presume that he would not have spent his life as a farmer. But there will be other cases where the circumstances presented may indicate that it is just that the particular equity found to exist would be justly satisfied by a pecuniary award.

When referring to the bequest of €150,000, Peart J stated: **15–19**

> 18. While I have expressed my respectful agreement with the trial judge's conclusions in relation to the plaintiff's entitlement to have the lands transferred to him, I differ from him in relation to the bequest to the plaintiff of €150,000 under the 2006 Will which was upheld. The trial judge stated that he did not think that there was any basis for excluding the plaintiff from the benefit of this bequest. I disagree. In my view the equitable jurisdiction of the court is sufficient to provide a just result in accordance with equitable principles if the Court is satisfied that it would not be a fair and just result if the plaintiff received not only the lands as promised by the deceased, but also the bequest of €150,000 under the 2006 which was clearly intended by the deceased to be in substitution for the lands. The promises by the deceased amounted to a contract whereby the plaintiff would receive the lands. It was never part of that contract that the plaintiff would receive an additional €150,000. On the facts as found by the trial judge, it is clear that when he executed the 2006 Will the deceased's intention was to replace the devise of the lands in the earlier Will with the bequest of €150,000.

The applicable principles of promissory estoppel may be stated as follows: **15–20**

1. The representations or assurances regarding future interests in land arise out of a contract between the claimant and owner of land.
2. The detriment suffered by the claimant may:
   (a) take the form of a money expenditure on foot of representations or assurances made or given by the owner of the land, or
   (b) consist of the provision of free labour on the land on foot of representations or assurances made or given by the owner of land.

Assimilation of Proprietary and Promissory Estoppel

Therefore, it appears from the foregoing decisions, that the conditions necessary for establishing a promissory estoppel are the same as those necessary for establishing a proprietary estoppel with regard to the acquisition of equitable property rights to future interests in land. The only remaining distinction between the two type of claims in relation to the acquisition of equitable property rights to land at some future time is that a claim based on promissory estoppel arises out of a pre-existent contract between the claimant and the owner of the land. It also appears **15–21** that promissory estoppel may be used not only as a "shield" but also as a "sword" in claims of equitable property rights and future interests in land.

Chapter 16

THE CONCEPT OF REMEDIAL CONSTRUCTIVE TRUST

Introduction

The re-formulated principles of proprietary and promissory estoppel provide that the representations or assurances regarding future interests in land—for example, interests arising on the death of the owner of land—were acted upon by the claimant in an unconditional fashion, and that he or she incurred money expenditures on the land, or that he or she provided free labour on the land on foot of representations or assurances made or given to him or her by the owner of land.[1] It also appears that the conditions or prerequisites for establishing both estoppels insofar as they apply to future interests in land are similar, and are thus, assimilated.[2] The circumstances giving rise to a proprietary estoppel, or indeed a promissory estoppel, may also be properly "regarded as giving rise to a species of constructive trust, which is the concept employed by a court of equity to prevent a person from relying on his legal rights where it would be unconscionable for him to do so."[3] In cases involving unconscionable behaviour which has future effect, it appears that the imposition of a constructive trust may be the more appropriate remedy, rather than a proprietary estoppel which is primarily designed to afford immediate effect to a right to property. In *Thorner v Major*,[4] Scott LJ stated that he: **16–01**

> would prefer to keep proprietary estoppel and constructive trust as distinct and separate remedies, to confine proprietary estoppel to cases where the representation, whether express or implied, on which the claimant has acted is unconditional and to address the cases where the representations are of future benefits, and subject to qualification on account of unforeseen future events, via the principles of remedial constructive trusts.

In *Finnegan v Hand*,[5] White J also appears to have adopted the approach mentioned by Scott LJ in *Thorner v Major* regarding the distinction made between proprietary estoppel and remedial constructive trusts, and imposed a remedial constructive trust rather than a proprietary estoppel as the more appropriate remedy in the circumstances of the case. Where a claimant **16–02**

---

1 [2009] UKHL 18; see A. Keating, *The Law of Wills* (2nd ed, Clarus Press, Dublin, 2018).

2 See Chapter 15: The Acquisition of Equitable Property Rights by Re-Formulated Proprietary and Promissory Estoppel.

3 *Finnegan v Hand* [2016] IEHC 255.

4 [2009] UKHL 18.

5 [2016] IEHC 255.

successfully establishes the existence of a remedial constructive trust over property forming part of a deceased person's estate, he or she may acquire equitable rights to that property.

16–03 Remedial constructive trusts may also be claimed by children of testators as an alternative to making applications for provision to be made for them out of the estate of a deceased testator under s 117(1) of the Succession Act 1965 (the "1965 Act"). Under s 117(1) of the 1965 Act, the court, where it is of the opinion that a testator has failed in his moral duty to make proper provision for a child in accordance with his means whether by will or otherwise, may order that such provision be made out of the estate as it thinks just. The special circumstances giving rise to the moral duty "arise if a child is induced to believe that by, for example, working a farm he will ultimately become the owner of it thereby causing him to shape his upbringing, training and life accordingly." These special circumstances giving rise to the moral duty are remarkably similar to those giving rise to a remedial constructive trust, and may be relied on as an alternative to making an application under s 117(1) of the 1965 Act.

The Concept of Remedial Constructive Trust

16–04 In *Thorner v Major*,[6] Scott LJ distinguished between a proprietary estoppel founded on present and future interests in land. He identified a present interest as arising during the lifetime of the owner of land against whom the claim of proprietary estoppel is made, and a future interest in land as arising on the death of the owner and against whose estate the claim is made. The latter may arise out of representations and assurances made or given to the claimant, who relied on them, that he or she would be left land by the owner in his or her will if he or she would work on the land for no or reduced wages, but on the death of the owner, it is discovered that the owner had left the land by will to another person. In such circumstances, Scott LJ was of the view that a claim should be based on a remedial constructive trust rather than proprietary estoppel. In that case, the appellant David Thorner did substantial work without pay on the farm of his father's cousin Peter Thorner for nearly thirty years. The evidence showed that from 1990 until his death in 2005, Peter encouraged David to believe that he would inherit the farm and that David acted in reliance on this assurance. Peter died without making a will. David claimed that by reason of the assurances made by Peter and his reliance on them, Peter's estate was estopped from denying that he has acquired the beneficial interest in the farm. In his judgment, Scott LJ thought that proprietary estoppel was the more appropriate remedy in claims involving immediate interests in property, and a remedial constructive trust was more appropriate in inheritance cases involving unconscionable behaviour regarding assurances which had future effect. In relation to claims based on proprietary estoppel, he stated that:

---

6 [2009] UKHL 18.

> There are many cases in which the representations relied on relate to the acquisition by the representee of an immediate, or more or less immediate, interest in the property in question. In these cases, a proprietary estoppel is the obvious remedy. The representor is estopped from denying that the representee has the proprietary interest that was promised by the representation in question.

He referred to past decisions of the courts where proprietary estoppel was shown to be the more appropriate remedy in such cases. In *Crabb v Arun District Council*,[7] the Council had represented to the plaintiff that he would be entitled to have access to the private road at gateway B and had confirmed that representation by erecting gateposts and a gate across the gateway. Once the plaintiff, in reliance on that representation, had acted to his detriment in selling off a portion of his land so that his only means of access to and egress from his retained land was via gateway B, it was too late for the Council to change its mind. The Council was estopped from denying that Mr Crabb had the necessary access rights. Scott LJ also cited *Ramsden v Dyson*,[8] and commented that: **16–05**

> In cases where the owner of land stands by and allows a neighbour to build over the mutual boundary, representing either expressly or impliedly that the building owner is entitled to do so, the owner may be estopped from subsequently asserting his title to the encroached upon land. This, too, seems to me straightforward proprietary estoppel. There are many other examples of decided cases where representations acted on by the representee have led to the representor being estopped from denying that the representee had the proprietary interest in the representor's land that the representation had suggested. Constructive trust, in my opinion, has nothing to offer to cases of this sort.

But in cases where the representation or assurance is made in relation to inheritance prospects, Scott LJ found it difficult "to square with the principles of proprietary estoppel established by the *Ramsden v Dyson* and *Crabb v Arun District Council* line of cases and, for my part, I find them made easier to understand as constructive trust cases." He preferred: **16–06**

> to keep proprietary estoppel and constructive trust as distinct and separate remedies, to confine proprietary estoppel to cases where the representation, whether express or implied, on which the claimant has acted is unconditional and to address the cases where the representations are of future benefits, and subject to qualification on account of unforeseen future events, via the principles of remedial constructive trusts.

He was of the view that the facts in *Thorner v Major* justified relief by a remedial constructive trust. He went on to refer to former decisions of the courts where the remedial constructive trust was held to be the more appropriate remedy, and stated that: **16–07**

> The possibility of a remedial constructive trust over property, created by the common intention or understanding of the parties regarding the property on the

---

7 [1975] 3 All ER 865.
8 (1866) LR 1 HL 129.

> basis of which the claimant has acted to his detriment, has been recognised at least since *Gissing v Gissing* [1971] AC 886 (see particularly Lord Diplock, at p 905).[9]

16–08 Scott LJ concluded that the imposition of a remedial constructive trust is more appropriate in inheritance cases involving unconscionable behaviour regarding assurances which have future effect rather than a proprietary estoppel which is more suitable for dealing with immediate circumstances.

16–09 In *Finnegan v Hand*,[10] White J referred with apparent approval to the decision in *Thorner v Major*,[11] where the court found that "a constructive remedial trust arose, notwithstanding that representations were never made expressly but were a matter of implication and inference from indirect statements and conduct." In *Finnegan*, the plaintiff based his claim on the existence of a proprietary estoppel, or in the alternative, a remedial constructive trust. The facts were that the plaintiff worked on the deceased's farm for 38 years, put in long hours, and was "substantially underpaid". On different occasions, the deceased both "directly and obliquely" led the plaintiff to believe that he would, at least, name the plaintiff as a beneficiary in his will. The deceased died without making a will. White J found that:

> Because of the behaviour of the deceased in holding out to the plaintiff that he would be rewarded in the future with an interest in the farm which led to the plaintiff devoting a very substantial part of his adult life to work on the farm and also suffering the inadequate facilities of a substandard home for fourteen years, it would be unconscionable that the estate would accrue in its entirety to the blood relations of the deceased. While the court can hold that proprietary estoppel arises, because of the uncertain nature of the promises made as to the future intentions of the deceased, the court is of the opinion that a constructive remedial trust arises.[12]

16–10 As a result:

> 71. The court has discretion on the remedy to be provided to the plaintiff. The plaintiff should obtain a share in the farm, stock and machinery. As it is an equitable relief, I am not bound to transfer all the estate to the plaintiff as requested by him. That would be an injustice to the next of kin of the defendant.
>
> 72. The appropriate remedy is that the plaintiff be awarded half that portion of the estate which includes the farmlands comprised in all the Folios, half the value of the stock and machinery and miscellaneous items sold. Any money that was resting in bank accounts at the date of death should go to the next of kin rather than the plaintiff. The plaintiff should give credit to the defendant for the gift of the site which is valued at €10,000.

16–11 Thus, a remedial constructive trust, as defined by Lord Scott in *Thorner v Major*,[13] and accepted by White J in *Finnegan v Hand*,[14] may be imposed by the courts in place of a proprietary estoppel concerning future interests in

---

9 See also *Gillett v Holt* [2001] Ch 210, *In re Basham* [1986] 1 WLR 1498.
10 [2016] IEHC 255.
11 [2009] UKHL 18.
12 [2016] IEHC 255 at para 70.
13 [2009] UKHL 18.
14 [2016] IEHC 255.

land, and result in the acquisition of equitable property rights to the land. The conditions for establishing a remedial constructive trust and the acquisition of equitable property rights include the necessary condition of detriment, and it must be shown that the claimant "suffers as severe a loss or detriment by providing his own labours or services in relation to the lands of another and accordingly should equally qualify for recognition in equity." The detriment may take the form identified in *McCarron v McCarron*[15] by Murphy J, that in "a suitable case it may well be argued that a plaintiff suffers as severe a loss or detriment by providing his own labours or services in relation to the lands of another and accordingly should equally qualify for recognition in equity." In *Coyle v Finnegan*,[16] Laffoy J, when considering the nature of the detriment, also stated that the plaintiff:

> did suffer a detriment in consequence of his reasonable reliance on the deceased's assurances and such detriment was of the type envisaged by Murphy J in *McCarron v McCarron*, in that the plaintiff suffered a loss or detriment by providing his own labours and services to assist the deceased in running the farm without any remuneration for his endeavours.

It may also be argued that the concept of remedial trust may be extended to include claims to equitable property rights to land, and in particular dwellings, where the owner of the dwelling makes representations or gives assurances to the claimant that in return for caring and looking after the owner during sickness and/or old age for no wage, and also maintaining the dwelling at his or her own cost, that he or she would be left the dwelling by will, and in the event of the owner failing to do so, that the services and maintenance so provided may be viewed as constituting a sufficient detriment suffered by the claimant for the purposes of establishing a remedial constructive trust. This is especially so where the claimant's own predicament is worsened by his or her old age and illness, and also by having to face the daunting prospect of being rendered homeless. **16–12**

Claims of Remedial Constructive Trusts as an Alternative to Applications under Section 117

A remedial constructive trust may be imposed by the courts in place of a proprietary estoppel concerning future interests in land, and result in the acquisition of equitable property rights to the land.[17] The conditions for establishing a remedial constructive trust and the acquisition of equitable property rights include the necessary condition of detriment, and it must be shown that the claimant "suffers as severe a loss or detriment by providing his own labours or services in relation to the lands of another and accordingly should equally qualify for recognition in equity."[18] A remedial constructive **16–13**

[15] Unreported, Supreme Court, 13 February 1997; see *Coyle v Finnegan* [2013] IEHC 463; *Naylor v Maher* [2012] IEHC 408.
[16] [2013] IEHC 463.
[17] See *Finnegan v Hand* [2016] IEHC 255.
[18] See *Thorner v Major* [2009] UKHL 18.

trust may, perhaps, also be relied on by a child of a testator instead of making an application to the courts under s 117(1) of the 1965 Act alleging breach of a testator's moral duty to make proper provision for him or her. Under s 117(1), where the court is of the opinion that a testator has failed in his moral duty to make proper provision for a child in accordance with his means whether by will or otherwise, it may order that such provision be made out of the estate as it thinks just. It may be argued that a testator may fail in his or her moral duty to make proper provision for his or her child if a child is induced by the testator to believe that by, for example, "working a farm he will ultimately become the owner of it thereby causing him to shape his upbringing, training and life accordingly."[19] Such representations and assurances are remarkably similar to those that give rise to a remedial constructive trust, and the child of the testator may pursue an alternative claim in remedial constructive trust arising out of such representatives and assurances made or given by the testator. The same perhaps may be said in relation to such representations and assurance made or given to a child of the testator in relation to a family business owned by the testator. Or, indeed, in a case where a child takes on the role of permanent carer of a sole surviving parent as a result of an inducement that that child will ultimately become owner of the family home.

16–14 It is arguable that the special circumstances that give rise to a moral duty as identified by Kearns J in *In the Estate of ABC* may equally give rise to a remedial constructive trust.[20] Where such special circumstances exist, the child of a testator may have a choice of either pursuing a claim under s 117, or calling upon equity to intervene for the purposes of enforcing a remedial constructive trust. The advantage of pursuing a claim in remedial constructive trusts is that the property forming the subject matter of the trust does not form part of the estate, and may not therefore be available for other computations; for instance, when computing the value of the legal right of a surviving spouse or civil partner, or indeed, when reckoning the value of proper provision for other children of the testator who also make claims under s 117. On the other hand, a child who is successful in establishing a remedial constructive trust over the estate belonging to the testator, and makes a subsequent application to the court under s 117, he or she may be deemed to have been properly provided for out of the estate in a way otherwise than by will.

16–15 The limitation period for bringing applications under s 117(6) of the 1965 Act, as amended by the s 46 of the Family Law (Divorce) Act 1996, is six months from the first taking out of representation.[21] This is a very brief time period for making applications by children of testators under s 117(1) of the 1965 Act. The time limits for grounding claims of remedial constructive

[19] See *In the Estate of ABC* [2003] 2 IR 250.

[20] *In the Estate of ABC* [2003] 2 IR 250.

[21] See A. Keating, "A Constructive Interpretation of Section 117(6) of the Succession Act 1965" (2014) 19(2) CPLJ 33.

trusts against estates of deceased persons are found in s 9(2) of the Civil Liability Act 1961. Under s 9(2), no proceedings will be maintainable in respect of any cause of action whatsoever which has survived against the estate of a deceased person, such as one based on the existence of a remedial constructive trust, unless either (a) proceedings against him in respect of that cause of action were commenced within the relevant period prescribed by the Statute of Limitations 1957 and were pending at the date of death; or (b) proceedings were commenced in respect of that action within the relevant period prescribed by the Statute of Limitations 1957, or within the period of two years after his death, "whichever period first expires."[22] Where the brief time limit has run out for the making applications by children of testators under s 117(6) of the 1965 Act, a claim based on the existence of a remedial constructive trust and acquisition of equitable property rights may, perhaps, be the only alternative available to them. However, as stated, there are also time limits for basing claims of remedial constructive trusts against estates of deceased persons under s 9(2) of the Civil Liability Act 1961, and once such time limits have expired, any such claims may be deemed statute-barred.

---

[22] See *Cavey v Cavey* [2014] IESC 16.

CHAPTER 17

THE ACQUISITION OF EQUITABLE PROPERTY RIGHTS BY CONSTRUCTIVE TRUSTS

INTRODUCTION

The intervention of equity may result in the imposition of a constructive trust in claims involving unjust enrichment and restitution, and such intervention may also result in the acquisition of equitable rights to property by the claimant. Such a trust was described by Lord Denning MR in *Hussey v Palmer*[1] as a trust "imposed by law whenever justice and good conscience require it" and as "a liberal process, founded on large principles of equity, to be applied in cases where the defendant cannot conscientiously keep the property for himself alone, but ought to allow another to have the property or a share in it." He also stated that such a trust provided "an equitable remedy by which the court can enable an aggrieved party to obtain restitution." Such a trust subsequently became known as a new model constructive trust. Equity may also intervene in claims involving pre-testamentary agreements entered into by testators to make mutual wills benefitting one another and where one such testator dies, and the surviving testator refuses to comply with the terms of such agreement, equity may compel him or her to do so by the imposition of a constructive trust which may also lead to the acquisition of equitable property rights by the claimant. Where such pre-testamentary agreements are entered by spouses or civil partners with the knowledge that the survivor may be compelled in equity to comply with the terms of such wills, it may be argued that such agreements voluntarily entered into by spouses and civil partners, may also be viewed as a form of renunciation of the legal right for the purposes of s 113 of the Succession Act 1965 (the "1965 Act"). Section 113 provides that the legal right of a surviving spouse or civil partner may be renounced in writing in an ante-nuptial contract or pre-civil partnership contract made between parties to an intended marriage or civil partnership, or where such contracts are entered into during the lifetime of such parties. **17–01**

NEW MODEL CONSTRUCTIVE TRUSTS

Equity may intervene in an appropriate case and impose a new model **17–02**

[1] [1972] 3 All ER 744 at 747; see also *Binions v Evans* [1972] 2 All ER 70; *Eves v Eves* [1975] 3 All ER 768; see A. Keating, *The Law of Wills* (2nd ed, Clarus Press, Dublin, 2018).

constructive trust as a remedy whenever justice and good conscience require it. This type of constructive trust was identified and described by Lord Denning MR in *Hussey v Palmer*.[2] In that case, the plaintiff sold her house and was invited to live with her daughter and son-in-law, the latter being defendant in the case. As the defendant's house was too small for all three of them, he arranged for the building of an extension to the house to be used as a bedroom by the plaintiff. The plaintiff paid the costs of the extension to the builder. There was no arrangement between the plaintiff and the defendant for the repayment of the costs of the extension. Owing to differences later arising between the plaintiff and her daughter and the defendant, she went to live elsewhere. She needed money, and asked the defendant for financial assistance but he refused. She then asked the repayment of the money spent by her on the extension, but this request was refused also. She sued the defendant for the repayment of her money alleging that there was a resulting trust. The case finally came before the Court of Appeal. Lord Denning MR, allowing the appeal, held that the trust in the case was more in the nature of a constructive trust and one that "is imposed by law whenever justice and good conscience require it." He described it as a liberal process "founded on large principles of equity, to be applied in cases where the defendant cannot conscientiously keep the property for himself alone, but ought to allow another to have the property or a share in it. The trust may arise at the outset when the property is acquired, or later on, as the circumstances may require." In *N.A.D. v T.D.*,[3] Barron J stated that the imposition of the trust "is dependent upon the conduct of the person upon whom the trust is imposed and prevents him from acting in breach of good faith." In *HKN Invest OY v Incotrade PVT Ltd*,[4] Costello J referring to *Hussey v Palmer* stated that the principle "is that where a person who holds property in circumstances which in equity and good conscience should be held and enjoyed by another he will be compelled to hold the property in trust for another."

17–03 In *Murray v Murray*,[5] the plaintiff was the defendant's nephew. The plaintiff and his mother lived in a property belonging to the defendant. The plaintiff's mother paid the mortgage repayments owing on the property and most of the outgoings. When the plaintiff's mother died, he claimed that as her nearest next-of-kin, he was entitled to a beneficial interest in the property. He argued that it would be unconscionable for the defendant to rely on his legal title to the property so as to deny him of his beneficial interest it. Barron J stated *Hussey v Palmer* was an authority for the proposition that, where equity required it, "a debt could be secured by the device of a constructive trust on the property created by the money involved." The absence of any evidence to show that the plaintiff's mother intended to create a beneficial interest precluded Barron J from holding that a resulting trust arose, and so he therefore made use of the more flexible constructive

---

2 [1972] 3 All ER 744.
3 [1985] ILRM 153 at 160.
4 [1993] 3 IR 152 at 162.
5 [1996] 3 IR 25.

trust to provide a remedy. He stated that it is "quite clear that the law will impose a constructive trust in all circumstances where it would be unjust and unconscionable not to do so."

In *Re Cahill*,[6] the testator devised all of his property to his wife and brother as joint tenants for life, with the remainder to trustees in trust for his nephew. He died without revoking his will. His brother died two years later. Two years before his death, the testator attended his solicitor, and informed him that he no longer wished to benefit his nephew, and wished instead to leave all of his property to his wife absolutely without any remainder provision. However, instead of altering his will, a deed of transfer was prepared which transferred the testator's registered lands from his sole ownership to that of himself and his wife. Certain of the registered lands, however, were excluded by mistake in the transfer deed. As the testator had not revoked his will, a question arose as to whether the registered lands excluded from the deed of transfer passed under the terms of the will, or whether, in the circumstances, the nephew named as remainderman in the will held the lands as a constructive trustee for the testator's widow. Barr J found that the net issue to be addressed was whether the inadvertence of the testator's solicitor resulted in a failure to carry out the testator's intentions by not including all of his registered lands in the transfer deed, and whether a constructive trust arose comprising the lands which were not transferred in the way intended by the testator. **17–04**

In his judgment, Barr J referred to the concept of the new model constructive trust as explained by Ronan Keane (the former Chief Justice) in his book *Equity and the Law of Trusts in the Republic of Ireland*,[7] and as described by Lord Denning MR in *Hussey v Palmer*, but he preferred and adopted Keane's description of a new model constructive trust. In relation to such trusts, Keane wrote that **17–05**

> the principle of unjust enrichment requires the restoration by the defendant to the plaintiff of a benefit which it would be unjust for him to retain. Sometimes this can be done by a simple award of money, e.g., the refund of money paid under a mistake of fact. But sometimes the restoration of the benefit can only be achieved by giving the plaintiff an interest in property. Thus, the constructive trust is imposed by the court as an equitable remedy intended to restore to the plaintiff the benefit of which he has been deprived.

Following on this, Barr J found that the "kernel of the question" he had to determine was whether the evidence established "a clear, positive intention on the part of the testator that his wife should inherit all of his property on his death," and thought that the "essential element" was that the testator changed his mind regarding the disposition of his estate after his death, and he took appropriate steps to give effect to his intention. That intention having **17–06**

---

6 Unreported, High Court, Barr J, 18 January 2001.

7 *Equity and the Law of Trusts in the Republic of Ireland*, First Edition, Ronan Keane, (London: Butterworths, 1988) at pp 186–187.

been established to the satisfaction of the court, it followed that "justice and good conscience" required that the nephew should not be allowed to inherit any part of the testator's property, and that his interest in remainder under the will should be deemed a constructive trust in favour of the testator's widow. Barr J was of the opinion that "a 'new model' constructive trust of that nature the purpose of which is to prevent unjust enrichment is an equitable concept which deserves recognition in Irish law."

Constructive Trusts Enforcing Pre-Testamentary Agreements to Make Mutual Wills

17–07 Where testators make mutual wills in furtherance of a pre-testamentary agreement, equity may intervene and impose a constructive trust to prevent a surviving testator from revoking the will. The prevention of fraud is also one of the reasons why equity intervenes for the purposes of imposing a constructive trust in the case of agreements by testators to make mutual wills.[8] A mutual will, like all other wills, is ambulatory and revocable during the lifetime of the testators who make such a will on foot of an agreement to do so, but unlike other wills, it may cease to be revocable by a surviving testator through the intervention of equity, especially where the surviving testator also receives a benefit under the deceased testator's will. In other words, a mutual will may become irrevocable on the death of one of the testators. Equity may intervene because:

> [H]e, that dies first, does by his death carry the agreement on his part into execution. If the other refuses, he is guilty of fraud, can never unbind himself, and become a trustee of course. For no man shall deceive another to his prejudice. By engaging to do something that is in his power, he is made a trustee for the performance, and transmit that trust to those that claim under him.[9]

17–08 The death of one of the testators activates the constructive trust founded on the pre-testamentary agreement, and equity may enforce it.

17–09 The surviving testator is not precluded from making a new will *simpliciter*, but he or she may be precluded from making a new will which revokes the terms of the earlier mutual will made by him or her and the deceased testator. The mutual will continues to be irrevocable. Even should a surviving testator disclaim a beneficial interest under the mutual will, he or she may, nevertheless, continue to be bound by the constructive trust created by the pre-testamentary agreement, and which becomes operative on the death of the first testator. In *Re Hagger*,[10] Clauson J stated that:

> *Dufour v Pereira* (1769) 1 Dick. 419; 21 E.R. 332 decides that where there is a joint will such as this, on the death of the testator who first dies the position as

---

[8] *Dufour v Pereira* (1789) 1 Dick 419; *Birmingham v Renfrew* (1937) 57 CLR 666; see also *Re Hagger* [1972] 3 All ER 620.

[9] *Dufour v Pereira* (1789) 1 Dick 419.

[10] [1972] 3 All ER 620.

> regards that part of the property which belongs to the survivor is that the survivor will be treated in this court as holding the property on trust to apply it so as to carry into effect the provisions of the joint will.

In *Re Hagger*, a husband and wife made a joint will where they both agreed that neither of them would revoke the will without the consent of the other. The wife was the first to die. One of the remaindermen named in the will died during the husband's lifetime. A question arose as to whether the deceased remainderman became entitled to a vested interest on the death of the wife. Clauson J felt that he was bound to hold that: **17–10**

> [F]rom the death of the wife the husband held the property, according to the tenor of the will, subject to the trusts thereby imposed upon it, at all events if he took advantage of the provisions of the will.[11]

So far as the husband's interest in the property was concerned, the will operated as a trust from the date of the wife's death. Accordingly, there was no lapse by reason of the remainderman's death during the husband's lifetime. **17–11**

The sole fact that testators make contemporaneous and similar wills does not render them mutual wills. An essential prerequisite for the concept of mutual wills to apply is the irrevocability of the mutual intentions, and this must be made clear by the agreement entered into by the testators not to change their intentions on the death of the first of them.[12] Evidence may have to be adduced from the surrounding circumstances to show that they intended their wills to be irrevocable, but once this is established, a constructive trust may be found to exist by operation of law.[13] But there must be evidence of the agreement between the testators not to change their intentions, and although the making of mutual wills by testators may be a relevant factor to be taken into account when deciding on the question of intention, that factor alone will not be sufficient for the concept to apply.[14] **17–12**

In the event of the surviving testator marrying again, or entering into a new civil partnership, the mutual will made by him or her will be subject to s 85(1) of the 1965 Act which provides that a subsequent marriage or civil partnership will automatically revoke any pre-existing will by a testator, unless that will was made in contemplation of marriage or civil partnership which includes mutual wills. However, while a will may be revoked under s 85(1), it appears that the terms of the pre-existing testamentary agreement by testators to make mutual wills continues to subsist and be enforceable by equity by the imposition of a constructive trust by the executors of the deceased testator. It also appears that even should the surviving testator divorce his or her new **17–13**

---

[11] [1972] 3 All ER 620 at 622.

[12] *Re Goodchild* [1996] 1 WLR 1216.

[13] *Re Oldham* [1925] Ch 75; *Re Cleaver* [1986] 1 WLR 939; *Re Goodchild* [1996] 1 WLR 1216.

[14] *Re Cleaver* [1986] 1 WLR 939; see *Gray v Perpetual Trustee Co Ltd* [1928] AC 391.

spouse or civil partner, and then go on to remarry again or enter into a new civil partnership, the original pre-testamentary agreement to make mutual wills with his or her deceased spouse or civil partner will continue to subsist, and remain binding and enforceable by equity imposing a constructive trust. The same might be said where the surviving testator purports to revoke his or her mutual will by any of the other methods of revocation under s 85(2) of the 1965 Act. It is the continued binding effect of the original pre-testamentary agreement between testators that makes mutual wills different from other wills, and further, by the intervention of equity imposing an overriding constructive trust on a surviving testator to comply with the terms of the pre-existing testamentary agreement to make mutual wills.

Declarations of Pre-Testamentary Agreements to Make Mutual Wills

17–14 It may happen that testators may make contemporaneous wills containing similar provisions, but that does not necessarily mean that such wills are mutual wills, unless they are made in furtherance of a pre-testamentary agreement to do so. It is usual for spouses and civil partners with children to make contemporaneous wills mainly on the grounds of convenience containing survival clauses of thirty days and trust provisions for their children, but such wills may not be mutual wills unless, of course, they enter into a formal pre-testamentary agreement to do so. The pre-testamentary agreement between testators appears to be what converts their wills into mutual wills and is enforceable by equity by the imposition of a constructive trust. Where the surviving testator purports to contravene the terms of the pre-testamentary agreement, he or she will have acted in breach of contract, and may be sued by the executors of the estate of the deceased testator for such breach, and equity may intervene to impose a constructive trust on the surviving testator compelling him or her to comply with the terms of the pre-testamentary agreement. It appears that the onus of proof rests on the party alleging the existence of such agreement, and sufficient evidence must be adduced by him or her establishing the existence of such agreement for the courts to impose a constructive trust on the surviving testator. Such onus may be discharged where it is shown that the testators have declared in their wills that they were made in furtherance of a pre-testamentary agreement to make mutual wills.

17–15 Testators who are spouses or civil partners may declare the existence of a pre-testamentary agreement to make mutual wills in their individual wills in words similar to the following:

> I declare that this my will is made on foot of a pre-testamentary agreement dated the … day of … 20… entered into between me and my spouse/civil partner to make mutual wills.

Testators who are neither spouses nor civil partners may use words similar to the following: **17–16**

> I declare that this my will is made on foot of a pre-testamentary agreement dated the … day … of 20… entered into between me and [name of other testator] to make mutual wills.

Section 113 of the 1965 Act provides that the legal right may be renounced in writing in an ante-nuptial contract or pre-civil partnership contract made between the parties to the intended marriage or civil partnership or after the marriage or civil partnership, and during the lifetime of the testator. It may be argued that a declaration of the existence of a pre-testamentary agreement between spouses or civil partners to make mutual wills similar to the foregoing may also be construed as a renunciation of the legal right of a surviving spouse or civil partner. **17–17**

Chapter 18

THE CREATION OF EQUITABLE PROPERTY RIGHTS BY SECRET AND HALF-SECRET TRUSTS

Introduction

The secret or half-secret trust is another equitable device by which equitable property rights may be created. A secret trust may be created where the testator communicates his or her wish to a devisee or legatee in his or her will to leave the subject matter of the devise or legacy in trust for another named individual, and the devisee or legatee agrees to do so either expressly or by his or her conduct, or simply acquiesces to the trust. A half-secret trust may be created where the testator nominates a devisee or legatee in his or her will to act as trustee of a trust for a named individual, and the devisee or legatee accepts such a role. Or as Wylie succinctly puts it: a secret trust is created **18–01**

> whenever a testator leaves property in his will to a legatee or devisee and no trust appears on the face of the will;[1] a half-secret trust is created "when the legatee or devisee of property is designated as trustee of the property given to him by will, but the objects of the trust are communicated independently.[2]

The trustee of such trusts is under an obligation to carry out the terms of the trusts as communicated to him or her by the testator.[3] In the case of a secret trust, the court will take the view that the testator relied on the express or implied promise of the devisee or legatee to fulfil his or her wishes after his or her death and will deal with his or her property accordingly.[4] Where it is established that before or at the time of the execution of the will, the testator communicated to the legatee that the legacy was given in trust for another, and the legatee consents to this, equity will compel the execution of the trust so communicated as a secret trust. But where there is a mention of a trust in the devise or legacy, though not the way by which it is to be executed, then such a trust will be a half-secret trust.[5] **18–02**

---

1 J.C.W. Wylie, *Irish Land Law* (2nd ed, Professional Books Ltd, Abingdon, 1986), p 475; see *Blackwell v Blackwell* [1929] AC 318 at 334; A. Keating, *The Law of Wills* (2nd ed, Clarus Press, Dublin, 2018).

2 J.C.W. Wylie, *Irish Land Law* (2nd ed, Professional Books Ltd, Abingdon, 1986), p 478; see also *Blackwell v Blackwell* [1929] AC 318 at 334; A. Keating, *The Law of Wills* (2nd ed, Clarus Press, Dublin, 2018).

3 *Blackwell v Blackwell* [1929] AC 318 at 334; see A. Keating, *The Law of Wills* (2nd ed, Clarus Press, Dublin, 2018).

4 *French v French* [1902] 1 IR 172 at 230.

5 *Re Prendiville* [1995] 2 ILRM 578.

18–03 In *Re Prendiville*,[6] Barron J stated that the principles of law applicable to secret trusts and half-secret trusts were essentially the same, and went on to say that the only difference between a half-secret trust and a secret trust "was that the person named in the will is an express trustee in the first case and a beneficiary in the latter." Once the terms of the trust have been communicated, the "person who had on his own behalf agreed to hold an apparently beneficial gift on trust could not in conscience refuse to carry out such trust. That is the position in the case of a secret trust." Equity will not allow a will to be used as a vehicle of fraud, and where the beneficiary of a gift in the will consents to the terms of a secret trust communicated to him or her by the testator, he or she will be bound by it, and such a trust will be enforceable in equity.

18–04 The creation of secret and half-secret trusts may also impinge on provisions of the Succession Act 1965, especially the provisions in s 115(1), which deal with the right of a surviving spouse or civil partner right to elect between a devise or bequest in a will and a legal right, and the provisions, in s 117(1), which deal with applications to the courts by children of the deceased testator alleging that he or she failed to fulfil his or her moral duty to make proper provision for them by his or her will.

The Conditions Necessary for the Creation of Secret and Half-Secret Trusts

18–05 The conditions necessary for creating secret trusts are as follows:

(i) The testator must communicate his or her wishes to the devisee or legatee that the property left to him or her is to be held in trust for a named individual or individuals.

(ii) The devisee or legatee agrees to hold the subject matter of the devise or legacy for the named individual or individuals, or on a construction of the evidence by the courts of equity that the devisee or legatee is deemed to have agreed to do so by his or her conduct, or has acquiesced to same.

18–06 In *Re Browne*,[7] the testator by a will dated 17 October 1935 gave his executor "all my real and personal property of what nature or kind soever. I relying on his carrying out the wishes that I expressed to him and/or may do so hereafter." The wishes of the testator were set down in written instructions which, though dated 23 November 1939, were not given to the person named in the will until 25 February 1942 which also happened to be the date of the testator's death. It was made clear to the testator that his wishes would be carried out. The executor accepted that he was not entitled as a beneficiary, but sought the opinion of the court as to whether the instructions were binding. Overend J held that on a proper construction of the clause in the will the executor was entitled as a beneficiary, and not as trustee, but by

[6] [1995] 2 ILRM 578.
[7] [1944] IR 90.

accepting the trust the elements of a fully secret trust had been established. He cited with approval the judgment of Monroe J in *Re King's Estate*[8] and *Blackwell v Blackwell*.[9]

The conditions necessary for creating half-secret trusts are as follows: **18–07**

(i) The testator communicated his or her intentions to create such a trust and nominated the devisee or legatee as trustee of same.
(ii) The devisee or legatee agrees to hold the subject matter of the devise or legacy as trustee for the named individual or individuals, or on a construction of the evidence by the courts of equity that the devisee or legatee is deemed to have agreed to do so by his or her conduct, or has acquiesced to same.

In *Blackwell v Blackwell*,[10] the question to be determined was whether or not a half-secret trust had been properly communicated. For a valid half-secret trust to exist the testator must communicate his intention to create such a trust to the person named as the beneficiary in the will, and the beneficiary must communicate his acceptance of the terms of the trust. Lord Sumner in the course of his speech expressed the principle as follows: **18–08**

> It is communication of the purpose to the legatee, coupled with acquiescence or promise on his part, that removes the matter from the provision of the Wills Act and brings it within the law of trusts, as applied in this instance to trustees, who happen also to be legatees.[11]

Warrington LJ stated that: **18–09**

> It is the fact of the acceptance of the personal obligation which is the essential feature, and the rest of the evidence is merely for the purpose of ascertaining the nature of that obligation.[12]

In *Re Prendiville*,[13] Barron J, having referred to *Re Browne*,[14] *Re King's Estate*,[15] *Blackwell v Blackwell*[16] and *Re Bateman's Will Trusts*,[17] decided that the rules to be applied were those set out by Monroe J in *Re King's Estate*. As a result, he concluded that the principles of law applicable to secret trusts and half-secret trusts were essentially the same, and went on to say that the only difference between a half-secret trust and a secret trust "was that the person named in the will is an express trustee in the first case and a beneficiary in the latter." Once the terms of the trust have been communicated the "person who had on his own behalf agreed to hold an **18–10**

8 (1888) 21 LR Ir 273 at 277.
9 [1929] AC 318.
10 [1929] AC 318.
11 [1929] AC 318 at 339.
12 [1929] AC 318 at 342.
13 [1995] 2 ILRM 578.
14 [1944] IR 90.
15 (1888) 21 LR Ir 273.
16 [1929] AC 318.
17 [1970] 3 All ER 817.

apparently beneficial gift on trust could not in conscience refuse to carry out such trust. That is the position in the case of a secret trust."

18–11 He went on to state that:

> Should it be the same in the case of a half-secret trust where the beneficiary has not made any such promise to the testator? The answer is yes and for the reasons set out in the passages from the judgment of *Blackwell v Blackwell* to which I have referred.[18]

18–12 Applying the principles to the circumstances of the case, Barron J concluded that there was a trust on the face of the will; the terms of it were communicated to the testator's wife and accepted by her during his lifetime; and the assent by her was sufficient to validate the half-secret trust.

A Construct of the Circumstances and Evidence for the Creation of Secret and Half-Secret Trusts

18–13 The following will illustrate the type of circumstances and evidence that may create a secret trust:

18–14 In *O'Brien v Condon*,[19] the testator in his will declared that:

> I do hereby will and bequeath any money I shall die possessed of to the Rev. William O'Brien C.C. Doneraile, to be distributed as he thinks fit.

18–15 There was no executor named in the will. One of the testator's next-of-kin was a witness to the will, and who was also one of the persons whom the testator intended to benefit under a secret trust. The next-of-kin was also one of the witnesses to the will, and a question arose as to whether she lost all benefit under the secret trust by witnessing the testator's will. In that case, the Master of the Rolls stated that:

> The law is fixed, and that it does not make any matter whether the trust is disclosed before the making of the will or at the time it was made, or even afterwards, if the legatee, knowing the testator's wishes, has given him to understand that he will carry out his intentions. The statement of the testator in the present case appears to have been a contemporaneous transaction with will, and constitutes a secret trust within the meaning of the doctrine of the court, and the legatee takes subject to this trust which is fastened on his conscience and will be enforced.[20]

18–16 The Master of the Rolls went on to state:

---

18 *Re Prendiville* [1995] 2 ILRM 578 at 585.

19 [1905] 1 IR 51.

20 [1905] 1 IR 51 at 56–57; see *Moss v Cooper* (1861) 1 J & H 352 at 366; *Johnson v Ball* (1851) 5 De G & Sm 85; *Re Fleetwood* (1880) 15 Ch D 594.

> What she takes under the trust is something not under the will, but solely by virtue of the secret trust, not disclosed on the will.[21]

He commented that this benefit "provided Mrs. Condon is not, in my opinion, a legacy given by will; nor is it an interest or benefit given by will, but rather something claimed and obtained against the will."[22] He concluded that "Bridget Condon does not lose her interest under the trust by reason of her being a witness to the will."[23] **18–17**

The following will illustrate the type of circumstances and evidence that may create a half-secret trust: **18–18**

The testator made a will dated 13 October 1961 and died on 21 June 1964. The testator left all his property to his wife but however "to be used by her according to my wishes—as she has been advised." Prior to his death, the testator informed his son Brendan that he had written out his wishes regarding the disposal of his estate after his wife's death. He showed Brendan a handwritten document dated 7 May 1961 which contained his wishes. The document included the following provision: **18–19**

> Monies to be divided after my wife's death. My wife Mary is to get all my monies, property and debts due, during her lifetime. Billy to get preference of Cluincorrig house on a reasonable valuation—if he lives or intends to live in Killorglin.

Billy was also one of the testator's sons. On the reverse side of the document, there was a valuation of the testator's and that of his wife's estates. A value of £6,000 was put on the testator's residence. The testator's widow made a statutory declaration on 6 June 1967 acknowledging the acceptance of the terms of her husband's wishes. She made a will on 29 September 1970 leaving her late husband's estate in accordance with his written wishes. She died on 3 January 1986 without having fully administered her husband's estate. Brendan instituted proceedings claiming that there was an enforceable fully secret or half-secret trust under which he had an option to purchase the residence and land of Cluincorrig house at a reasonable valuation. **18–20**

It was found that there was a trust on the face of the will; the terms of it were communicated to the testator's wife and accepted by her during his lifetime; the assent by her was sufficient to validate the half-secret trust.[24] **18–21**

The Enforcement of Secret and Half-Secret Trusts

For such trusts to be enforceable by equity, it must be shown that before or **18–22**

[21] [1905] 1 IR 51 at 56–57; see *Moss v Cooper* (1861) 1 J & H 352 at 366; *Johnson v Ball* (1851) 5 De G & Sm 85; *Re Fleetwood* (1880) 15 Ch D 594.

[22] [1905] 1 IR 51 at 59.

[23] [1905] 1 IR 51 at 58–59; see *Moss v Cooper* (1861) 1 J & H 352 at 366; *Johnson v Ball* (1851) 5 De G & Sm 85; *Re Fleetwood* (1880) 15 Ch D 594.

[24] *Re Prendiville* [1995] 2 ILRM 578.

at the time of the execution of the will, the testator communicated the terms of the trust to the devisee or legatee, and that he or she agreed to hold the subject matter of the devise or legacy in trust for persons mentioned by the testator, and where such is established, equity will compel the execution of the trust so communicated as a secret trust. Where there is mention of a trust in the devise or legacy, though not the way by which it is to be executed, such a trust will be recognised as a half-secret trust. A secret or half-secret trust may be created before or at the time of the execution of a will by the testator informing the person

> to whom he proposes to give a legacy that the legacy is given upon trust to be applied in a particular way, and if the legatee expressly or tacitly consents to take the legacy on these terms, the Court of Chancery will not permit him to be guilty of a fraud, but will compel the execution of the trust so communicated.[25]

18–23 It is essential to the creation of such a trust that the communication of it is made to the devisee or legatee and that he or she does not object to the execution of the trust.[26] The communication by the testator may be done orally or in writing. The terms on which the trust is expressed must also not be vague or uncertain.[27] The testator must have died, "leaving the property in his will in a particular manner on the faith and in the reliance upon an express or implied promise by the legatee to fulfil his wishes."[28] If there are two or more devisees or legatees, a valid trust will be created if the communication is made to one of them—for instance, one of three joint tenants, though not apparent tenants-in-common, who have to receive separate communications of the creation of the trust, before or at the time of the execution of the will.[29] Where the communication is made after the execution of the will, it must be made to all the legatees and devisees against whom the trust is enforced.[30] The beneficiary under a secret trust derives his or her title to the property solely by virtue of the secret trust, and not under the will,[31] and therefore he or she will not lose his or her benefit even if he or she witnesses the will,[32] or predeceases the testator.[33]

18–24 The trustee of secret and half-secret trusts is under an equitable obligation to carry out the terms of the trusts.[34] As the testator has placed reliance on the express or implied promise of the devisee or legatee to fulfil his or her wishes after his or her death, the devisee or legatee will be obliged by equity

---

25 *Re King's Estate* (1888) 21 LR Ir 273 at 277.
26 *Re King's Estate* (1888) 21 LR Ir 273.
27 *Re King's Estate* (1888) 21 LR Ir 273 at 277; *Re Boyes* (1884) 26 Ch D 531; see *Moss v Cooper* (1861) 1 J & H 352.
28 *French v French* [1902] 1 IR 172.
29 *Re King's Estate* (1888) 21 LR Ir 273.
30 See *Re King's Estate* (1888) 21 LR Ir 273; see also *Re Stead* [1900] 1 Ch 237 at 241.
31 *Cullen v Attorney-General for Ireland* (1866) LR 1 HL 190.
32 *O'Brien v Condon* [1905] 1 IR 51; *Re Young* [1951] Ch 344.
33 *Re Gardiner* [1923] 2 Ch 344.
34 *French v French* [1902] 1 IR 172 at 230; *Blackwell v Blackwell* [1929] AC 318 at 334.

to hold the property as trustee for the beneficiaries of the trust.[35] Where the existence of the secret or half-secret trust is established, equity may compel the execution of its terms. As the property forming part of a devise or legacy will thereafter form the subject matter of the secret or half-secret trust, the devise or legacy will effectively be adeemed under the doctrine of ademption, and the erstwhile beneficiary of the devise or legacy may instead become the trustee of the property forming part of the devise or legacy for the named objects or beneficiaries of the secret or half-secret trust.

The Effect of Secret and Half-Secret Trusts on Provisions of the Succession Act

It may be argued that where a secret or half-secret trust is created in favour of a child of a testator, the property forming the subject matter of such a trust may be viewed as fulfilling the testator's moral duty to make proper provision for that child in the event of that child making an application to the court under s 117(1) of the Succession Act 1965. Section 117(1) provides that where on application to the court by or on behalf of a child of a testator, the court is of opinion that the testator has failed in his or her moral duty to make proper provision for the child in accordance with his or her means, whether by his or her will or otherwise, the court may order that such provision shall be made for the child out of the estate as the court thinks fit. The creation of a secret or half-secret trust by a testator for the benefit of his or her child may be viewed by the court as fulfilling his or her moral duty towards the child otherwise than by will, in the event of the child making application under s 117(1). The creation of a valid secret or half-secret trust over property in a devise or legacy may also impact on the value of the legal right of a spouse or civil partner, as the property will no longer be part of the deceased testator's estate, and indeed, a surviving spouse or civil partner may be the trustee of such trusts upon acceptance of the terms of such trusts established by the testator. **18–25**

The creation of valid secret or half-secret trusts may also limit the right of election of surviving spouses or civil partners under s 115(1) of the Succession Act 1965, which provides at s 115(1)(a), that where under the will of the deceased person who dies wholly testate, there is a devise or bequest to a spouse or civil partner, the spouse or civil partner may elect to take either that devise or bequest or the share to which he or she is entitled as a legal right, and at s 115(1)(b), in default of election, the spouse or civil partner will not be entitled to take any share as a legal right. It may be argued that where a surviving spouse or civil partner agreed the creation of and to be a trustee of a secret or half-secret trust over the devise or bequest left to him or her, that the right to elect may be limited or confined to taking the **18–26**

[35] *French v French* [1902] 1 IR 172 at 230; *Blackwell v Blackwell* [1929] AC 318 at 334.

legal right only, as the devise or bequest may be adeemed by the property forming the subject matter of the secret or half-secret trust.

18–27 Section 13 of the Succession Act 1965 provides that the legal right of a spouse or civil partner may be renounced in an ante-nuptial contract made in writing between parties to an intended marriage or between civil partners, or may be renounced by the spouse or civil partner after the marriage or civil partnership and during the lifetime of the testator. The acceptance of the role of trustee of a secret or half-secret trust by a spouse or civil partner, especially in writing, may also be viewed as a limited renunciation of the legal right regarding the property of which he or she agreed to be trustee in writing for the purposes of a secret or half-secret trust.

Chapter 19

THE CREATION OF PROPERTY RIGHTS BY *DONATIONES MORTIS CAUSA*

Introduction

Property rights may be created by a *donatio mortis causa*. A *donatio mortis causa* was once described as a gift "of an amphibious nature, being a gift which is neither entirely *inter vivos* nor testamentary".[1] Whatever its nature, a *donatio mortis causa* is an exception to the equitable principle that equity will not perfect a voluntary gift, and it may create property rights.[2] A primary feature of *donatio mortis causa* is that it must be made in contemplation of death. The subject matter of the *donatio*, which is normally personal property, must be delivered by the donor to the donee with the intention of transferring dominion over the property to him or her. In England, as a result of the Court of Appeal decision in *Sen v Headley*,[3] land may also form the subject matter of a *donatio mortis causa*, and dominion over the land may be effected by the handing over of the title deeds of the land by the donor to the donee. The delivery may be carried out by the donor him or herself, or he or she may appoint an agent to act on his or her behalf.[4] The donee may also appoint an agent to accept delivery on his or her behalf.[5] The mode of delivery may depend on the nature of the property to be transferred, for instance, light goods may be delivered by simply handing them over to the donee.[6] They must, however, be handed over with the intention of transferring dominion over the goods, and not just for safekeeping.[7] Delivery may also be deemed a constructive delivery where, for instance, the donor gives the donee the only key to unlock a safety deposit box containing the subject matter of the *donatio*.[8] The delivery will be completed once the necessary intention of transferring dominion over property to the donee exists, and property is in fact delivered either physically or constructively **19–01**

---

1 *Re Beaumont* [1902] 1 Ch 889 at 892; A. Keating, *The Law of Wills* (2nd ed, Clarus Press, Dublin, 2018).

2 See A. Keating, *Succession Law in Ireland* (Clarus Press, Dublin, 2015).

3 [1991] Ch 425; see A. Lyall, *Land Law in Ireland* (3rd ed, Round Hall, Dublin, 2010), pp 1086–1094 for a discussion of the Court of Appeal decision in *Sen v Headley* concerning the transfer of dominion over land forming the subject matter of a *donatio mortis causa*.

4 See *Re Weston* [1902] 1 Ch 680.

5 *Moore v Darton* (1851) 4 De G & Sm 517; *Re Thompson* [1928] IR 606; *Murphy v Quirke* (1909) 43 ILTR 225.

6 *Birch v Treasury Solicitor* [1951] Ch 298.

7 *Birch v Treasury Solicitor* [1951] Ch 298.

8 See *Jones v Selby* (1710) Prec Ch 300.

to the donee. But where documents are required to be signed to complete a transfer of the property forming the subject matter of the *donatio*, they must first be signed before a delivery can take place—for instance, where the *donatio* consists of shares in a company, the necessary transfer forms must first be signed by the donor before the donee can claim title to them.[9] On the death of the donor, his personal representatives may be compelled by the courts to sign all the documentation required to complete the transfer of the *donatio* to the donee.[10]

19–02 The onus of proof rests on the party claiming the *donatio* to satisfy the court on the balance of probabilities that all the prerequisites for the creation of a valid *donatio mortis causa* have been met.[11] Where, however, the property forming the subject matter of a *donatio mortis causa* is also disposed of by will, the donee may have the added onus placed on him of showing that the donor when making the *donatio mortis causa* had a "positive intention" of altering the way by which he disposed of his property. The evidence adduced by the donee grounding the prerequisites for making a *donatio mortis causa* will also be closely examined by the courts when deciding on the existence and validity of the *donatio mortis causa.*

19–03 Under s 121(1), (2) and (10) of the Succession Act 1965 (the "1965 Act"), where a *donatio mortis causa* is made by the donor for the purposes of defeating or substantially diminishing the share of a surviving spouse or civil partner as a legal right, or leaving children insufficiently provided for, it may be viewed as a disinheriting disposition, and should it be set aside, the court may further order that the *donatio mortis causa* form part of the donor's estate as though it were a devise or legacy or bequest.

A Construct of Circumstances and Evidence for Determining the Validity of *Donationes Mortis Causa*

19–04 The circumstances of the case, and sufficient supportive evidence satisfying the conditions necessary for the creation of a *donatio mortis causa*, and adduced by the donee, will determine the existence of a valid *donatio mortis causa*, such as in the following set of circumstances:

19–05 The donor, three weeks prior to his death, delivered a parcel containing £658 in currency notes, various coins and a number of share certificates to the second defendant. When delivering the parcel, he asked the second defendant to deliver it to the plaintiff saying, "If anything should happen to me while I am away, will you give this to my brother". The donor was

[9] *Mills v Shields and Kelly* [1948] IR 367; *Delgoffe v Fader* [1939] Ch 922; see *Re Weston* [1902] 1 Ch 680.
[10] See *Birch v Treasury Solicitor* [1951] Ch 298.
[11] *Bentham v Potterton*, Unreported, High Court, Barr J, 28 May 1998.

seriously ill at the time. Three weeks later, he planned to go to Dublin for medical treatment. However, he left the train *en route* to Dublin and committed suicide. The plaintiff sought a declaration of the court that the parcel was delivered to him as a gift and constituted a *donatio mortis causa.* The donee had established a valid *donatio mortis causa.*[12]

Where the circumstances and evidence fail to satisfy the necessary conditions, the *donatio* may be deemed invalid. This may be illustrated by the following two sets of circumstances: **19–06**

First Set

The donor lived with his brother for a number of years. Four days before his death and when very ill in bed, he called his brother to his bedside and asked him to bring him a cash-box. He then asked to be given his waistcoat and took the key of the cash-box out of one of the pockets and unlocked the box. He took out a deposit receipt for £650, and two cheques, one for £104 2s. 9d. and the other for £33 10s. He then said: "Here, Jamsie, is all belonging to me; I am sorry I have not more to give you. You were very good to me. You will do the same for me as you did for Kitty and Tom." The deposit receipt and cheques were then returned to the cash-box, and the key was returned to the donor's waistcoat pocket. A question arose as to whether the words spoken and acts done by the donor constituted a *donatio mortis causa* in favour of his brother. The court decided that the evidence did not establish a good *donatio mortis causa.*[13] If, however, the donee had asked to be allowed to put the documents back into the box for safe custody, and the deceased had assented to this, this would not have destroyed the effect of the *donatio*. But the replacing of the documents in the box immediately afterwards showed that the deceased never intended to part with the actual possession of the documents in such a way as to lose dominion and control over them during his life.[14] **19–07**

Second Set

The deceased shortly before her death sent her grandniece to her house to collect four bank books from a suitcase in her bedroom. She then told her grandniece to place them in a safe owned by the grandniece. The deceased knew about the safe as she had seen it at an earlier time when visiting the grandniece. The grandniece found four bank books under some clothes in the suitcase. She then put the four bank books in her safe as requested by the deceased. She returned to the hospital on the following day and the deceased asked her: "Mary, did you do that for me? Did you put the bank books in a safe place?" The deceased went on to say that if anything was **19–08**

---

12 *Mills v Shields and Kelly* [1948] IR 367; see also *Delgoffe v Fader* [1939] Ch 922; see *Re Weston* [1902] 1 Ch 680.

13 *In Re Mulroy* [1924] 1 IR 98.

14 [1924] 1 IR 98 at 104–105.

to happen to her, the grandniece was to keep the contents of the books and "give Sarah a few bob out of it." Some weeks after the death of the deceased, the grandniece handed over the bank books to the deceased's solicitor. The deceased was eighty-six years of age when she died and had made a will three years before her death. This gave rise to the question as to whether the transaction between the deceased and her grandniece in relation to the bank books constituted a *donatio mortis causa.* The court decided that "the surrounding facts raise substantial doubt in that regard and in the circumstances I am obliged to hold that the plaintiffs have not established the validity of the alleged gift on the balance of probabilities."[15]

Prerequisites for Establishing Valid *Donationes Mortis Causa*

(i) The *Donatio* Must be Made in Contemplation of Death

19–09 The *donatio* must be made in contemplation of death, and it appears that a *donatio* given by a donor who is suffering from a terminal illness, and later commits suicide may still be deemed to have satisfied this prerequisite. It is immaterial to the case whether or not the donor made the *donatio* under the apprehension of being visited with an irresistible impulse to commit suicide. In *Mills v Shields and Kelly*,[16] Gavan Duffy P, when deciding that the plaintiff had established a valid *donatio mortis causa*, went on to say that:

> The substance of the direction that accompanied his *donatio* was that the gift was to become effective if he should die when he went away for treatment; and on a fair view of the evidence I think that is what happened, for I think this was the journey in contemplation. I follow the decision of Lord Tomlin in *Wilkes v Allington* [1931] 2 Ch. 104 in holding that the *donatio* is not defeated by the fact that the donor, having set out for Dublin, did not die, as he had feared, from treatment in a nursing home, but from another cause.

19–10 In *Agnew v The Belfast Banking Company*,[17] a question arose as to whether the donor's sister was entitled to a sum of £200.00 in a deposit account on the basis that it was given as a valid *donatio mortis causa*. The donor of the deposit account book gave it to her sister saying at the same time, "Maria that is yours; if anything should happen to me, that is yours in God's name." She committed suicide shortly afterwards by taking poison. Walker LC in his judgment stated that although there was a subject matter capable of being the subject of a *donatio mortis causa*, and also that there was sufficient evidence to establish a gift and a delivery of it, the fact remained that the donor was found to have committed suicide by the jury.[18]

---

[15] *Bentham v Potterton*, Unreported, High Court, Barr J, 28 May 1998.

[16] [1948] IR 367; see also *Delgoffe v Fader* [1939] Ch 922; see *Re Weston* [1902] 1 Ch 680.

[17] [1896] 2 IR 204.

[18] [1896] 2 IR 204 at 212.

He went on to say that: **19–11**

> This entire incompleteness of the donee's title till the event happens makes immaterial the knowledge or ignorance of the donee, and I may here say that it is in my opinion very difficult to apply the definition given by Justinian, which is stated out of several to be the correct one, to a contemplation of suicide or death by suicide at all. The words '*quae propter mortis fit suspicionem*' seem inapplicable to one who does not apprehend death, but voluntarily seeks it; and the words '*si quid humanitus ei contigisset*' seem to mean 'should anything happen to him human and mortal as we are.'[19]

He concluded that a *donatio* was void as against public policy which was **19–12** to take effect "on and not until the commission of a felony by the giver, and that felony of the highest form: for we know the terrible consequences which English Law imposed on a *felo de se*."[20] He dismissed the appeal accordingly.

In Re Mulroy,[21] Molony CJ, when deciding that the evidence did not establish **19–13** a good *donatio mortis causa*, stated that:

> In order to establish an effective *donatio mortis causa* three things must combine, as was laid down in *Cain v Moon* [1896] 2 Q.B. 283 *per* Lord Russell C.J., p. 286: 'First, the gift or donation must have been made in contemplation, though not necessarily in expectation, of death; secondly, there must have been delivery to the donee of the subject-matter of the gift; and thirdly, the gift must be made under such circumstances as show that the thing is to revert to the donor in case he should recover.' As regards delivery, it was enunciated in the *Union of London and Smith's Bank Ltd. v Wasserberg* [1915] 1 Ch. 195 that 'an inchoate or imperfect delivery of chattels may be sufficient for effectuating a *donatio mortis causa*.'[22]

(ii) Delivery of the Subject Matter of the *Donatio*

The second prerequisite is that the subject matter of the *donatio* must be **19–14** delivered with the intention of transferring dominion over it to the donee. The kind of delivery involved will of course depend on the nature of the property to be transferred. Personal property, for instance, taking the form of goods or money may present no difficulty as a handing over of the property by the donor to the donee with the intention of making a *donatio* will be a sufficient delivery. The handing over of personal property by the donor to the donee for safekeeping only will not however be treated as a delivery for the purpose of creating a *donatio*. The subject matter of the *donatio* must also be capable of delivery in a physical sense, and personal property consisting of goods and choses in action may simply be handed over to the donee at the time of making the *donatio*; for instance, jewellery, furniture or paintings present no problems in this respect. However, while the donor may intend to create a *donatio mortis causa*, there can be no delivery in cases of choses

19 [1896] 2 IR 204 at 213.
20 [1896] 2 IR 204 at 214.
21 [1924] 1 IR 98.
22 [1924] 1 IR 98 at 103–104.

in action until the transfer is completed by using the correct documentation. Once delivery can be made, it is unnecessary for the donor himself to make the delivery; an agent acting under his authority will suffice. Similarly, an agent of the donee may accept delivery on his or her behalf. Delivery may also be constructive—for instance, where the only existing key to unlock a safety deposit box that contains the subject matter of the *donatio* is handed over by the donor to the donee. Where a donor resumes dominion over the subject matter, the *donatio* will be revoked and will not be perfected by the death of the donor. Where, however, a *donatio* is not revoked it will be perfected by the death of the donor and will take effect from that date.

19–15 It appears that the Irish courts are insistent that where any procedural steps are required to complete a transfer of a chose in action and pass ownership, these must be completed by the donor before an effective delivery can take place. In *Re M'Wey*,[23] the donor was in hospital suffering from a disease that was subsequently to cause his death. In response to a request by the donor, the defendant visited him in hospital. During the course of the visit, he handed her two receipts, one for the payment of the purchase money on the transfer of a shareholding of £300, and the other for the payment of the purchase money on the transfer of a shareholding of £400. On the handing over of the receipts he said: "Sell these through M'Cann & Son, the Stockbrokers. You can call on them and they will give you all the information you want. These are for yourself. Do not say anything about it to anybody except your brother Charlie, and do not sell them until after my death." The defendant claimed that she was entitled to two shareholdings on the ground that she had receipts for the stock and that they were delivered to her by the deceased shortly before his death as a *donatio mortis causa*. In his judgment, Meredith J first made the observation that the receipts were not, strictly speaking, receipts for the stock, but only receipts for the consideration paid for the stock.[24] He had no doubt that the deceased gave the receipts intending to create a *donatio mortis causa*. The question accordingly was whether or not that intention alone was sufficient, notwithstanding the nature of the property—in each case a share or interest in certain stock made transferable in a specified Bank—and notwithstanding the nature of the actual thing delivered, which was in each case a mere memorandum. He stated that:

> To hold that it is sufficient would, in my opinion, be to hold that the case of *Ward v Turner* 2 Ves. Sen. 431 is no longer good law. But the authority of that case was recognised by the House of Lords in *Duffield v Elwes* 1 Bli. (n.s.) 497 at 536 and was followed in *Moore v. Moore* L.R. 18 Eq. 474, 483 and, as was held in the last-mentioned case, so I hold in this, that the receipts in question here do not differ substantially from the receipts for the South Sea Annuities, which were the subject matter in *Ward v Turner* 2 Ves. Sen. 431.[25]

19–16 In *Sen v Headley*,[26] the Court of Appeal in England held that land may also

[23] [1927] IR 486.
[24] [1927] IR 486 at 491.
[25] [1927] IR 486 at 492.
[26] [1991] Ch 425; see A. Lyall, *Land Law in Ireland* (3rd ed, Round Hall, Dublin, 2010),

form the subject matter of a *donatio mortis causa*, and dominion over the land may be effected by the handing over of the title deeds of the land by the donor to the donee. The delivery may be carried out by the donor him or herself, or he or she may appoint an agent to act on his or her behalf.[27]

(iii) The Onus of Proof Rests on the Donee

19–17 The onus of proof rests on the donee to show on the balance of probabilities that the prerequisites necessary for establishing the existence of a *donatio mortis causa* have been satisfied. It also appears that where a will exists, the donee may have the added task of showing that the donor at the time of making the *donatio mortis causa* had a positive intention of altering the way by which he disposed of his property. The evidence adduced will be of vital importance to the existence of a *donatio mortis causa*. The case law on the matter demonstrates that the court will examine the evidence very closely when determining whether the conditions for a *donatio mortis causa* have been satisfied. Where the donee has adduced sufficient evidence to the satisfaction of the court, he or she will acquire a right to the property forming the subject matter of the *donatio mortis causa*. In *Bentham v Potterton*,[28] Barr J stated that the onus of proof rested on the party claiming the *donatio* to satisfy the court that all the conditions for establishing a *donatio mortis causa* had been met. He then turned to the facts of the case, and asked the question: "Was the gift made by the donor in contemplation of her death? It seems to me that the facts fall short of establishing that proposition on the balance of probabilities." The donor had already made a will three years before her death, and Barr J was

> not satisfied that the deceased positively intended to make a radical change in the disposition of her property in contemplation of her death. Although that may have been her intention, the surrounding facts raise substantial doubt in that regard and in the circumstances I am obliged to hold that the plaintiffs have not established the validity of the alleged gift on the balance of probabilities.

Section 121 of the Succession Act 1965 and *Donationes Mortis Causa*

19–18 Under s 121(2) of the 1965 Act, where the court is satisfied that a disposition was made for the purpose of defeating or substantially diminishing the share of his spouse, whether as a legal right or on intestacy, or the intestate share of any of his or her children, or of leaving any of his or her children insufficiently provided for, the disposition may be deemed in whole or in part "to be a devise or bequest made by him by will and to form part of his estate, and to have had no other effect." Section 121 was amended by the

pp 1086–1094 for a discussion of the Court of Appeal decision in *Sen v Headley* concerning the transfer of dominion over land forming the subject matter of a *donatio mortis causa*.

[27] See *Re Weston* [1902] 1 Ch 680.

[28] Unreported, High Court, Barr J, 28 May 1998.

Status of Children Act 1987 to include non-marital children and the Civil Partnership and Certain Rights and Obligations of Cohabitants Act 2010 to include civil partners. Section 121(10) of the 1965 Act that a disposition for the purposes of s 121 includes a *donatio mortis causa*. In *LC (a minor) v HS*,[29] Clark J stated that a "disposition" for the purposes of s 121 of the 1965 Act does not include an acquisition or purchase: "an acquisition of property by purchase/gift/inheritance cannot equate to the divesting of the beneficial ownership of property which involves the sale/transfer/gift by will or a *donatio mortis causa*."

[29] [2014] IEHC 32.

CHAPTER 20

THE CREATION OF CONTRACTUAL AND EQUITABLE RIGHTS BY JOINT BANK ACCOUNTS

INTRODUCTION

In *Owens v Greene*,[1] the Supreme Court viewed joint bank accounts as creating resulting trusts in favour of the deceased depositor's estate, except where the survivor was the wife or child of the depositor or a person to whom the depositor stood *in loco parentis*.[2] The Supreme Court in *Lynch v Burke*,[3] however, found that opening such an account created a contract between the joint account-holders and the bank, with the survivor having rights to the monies on deposit either based on contract, or by way of a gift which was contingent on the death of the depositor, and the court went on to overrule the decision in *Owens v Greene*.[4] In *Lynch v Burke*,[5] O'Flaherty J stated that this interpretation relating to survivors of joint bank accounts "restores equity to the high ground which it should properly occupy to ameliorate the harshness of common law rules on occasion rather than itself be an instrument of injustice." In *O'Meara v Bank of Scotland PLC*,[6] Laffoy J, affirming *Lynch v Burke*, stated that the legal effect of opening a joint bank account was that the bank became contractually bound to both account-holders and, as a matter of contract, between the surviving account-holder and the bank, and the surviving account-holder became entitled to the balance in the account on the death of the deceased account-holder. A right of set-off may also be exercised by a bank against a joint account on the death of the other account-holder who had a loan account with the bank, and where the right is exercised, a surviving joint account-holder's entitlement to the monies in the joint account may become subject to that right. But where a right of set-off is claimed after the negotiations and agreement for the opening of a joint account have been concluded, it will not be enforced by the courts. In *O'Meara v Bank of Scotland PLC*,[7] Laffoy J stated that as the date of the set-off claimed by the defendant bank post-dated the negotiations and agreement for the opening of the joint account between the **20–01**

1 [1932] IR 225.
2 [1932] IR 225 at 240.
3 [1996] ILRM 114.
4 [1932] IR 225.
5 [1996] ILRM 114.
6 [2011] IEHC 402.
7 [2011] IEHC 402.

defendant bank and the plaintiff's deceased husband and herself, the claim by the defendant to a set-off was invalid, and the plaintiff became entitled to the monies in the joint account on the date of death of her husband by way of survivorship.

A Construct of Circumstances that Creates Contractual and Equitable Rights to Monies in Joint Bank Accounts

20–02 As regards contractual and equitable property rights created by joint bank accounts, it is mainly the circumstances and evidence that will determine their existence. The following will illustrate the type of circumstances that may create contractual rights by joint bank accounts:

20–03 A widow by her will left all her property to her sister, the plaintiff, as well as appointing her sole executrix. The defendant was her niece. The niece went to Glasgow in 1971 when she was 17. She married in 1975, and in 1976, her marriage ended. Her husband ceased to make maintenance payments a short time afterwards and, in times of want, the deceased sent her money. In September 1983, the deceased visited her niece in Glasgow, and told her that she wanted to add her name to a joint bank account. On 28 September 1983, a deposit account was opened in the joint names of the deceased and her niece. A sum of £29,401.72 was lodged into the account by the deceased, and there were further intermittent lodgements made after that date. At the date of trial there was £53,364 in the joint account and around £65,000, including accumulated interest, when the appeal was heard by the Supreme Court. The account was endorsed as payable to the deceased only or survivor. The word "only" was underlined. The defendant's address in Glasgow was inserted beneath the deceased's name.

20–04 The court found that

> the niece had a legal interest in the monies on deposit either by reason of the contractual relationship of the parties or, in the alternative, as a gift which admittedly was not a completed gift in the conventional sense but is nonetheless one that should be upheld as being a gift subject to a contingency *viz.* that of the death of the donor which contingency does not disqualify it as being a proper gift.[8]

The Effect of Opening Joint Bank Accounts

20–05 Prior to the Supreme Court decision in *Lynch v Burke*,[9] joint bank accounts were viewed, as a result of a decision by the Supreme Court in *Owens v Greene*,[10] as creating resulting trusts in favour of the deceased depositor's

[8] *Lynch v Burke* [1996] ILRM 114 at 121.
[9] [1996] ILRM 114.
[10] [1932] IR 225.

estate, except where the survivor was the wife or child of the depositor or a person to whom the depositor stood *in loco parentis*.[11] In the absence of any evidence rebutting the presumption of a resulting trust, the joint account was treated as forming part of the deceased depositor's estate.[12] In *Owens*, the Supreme Court held that the effect of opening joint bank accounts was to give rise to a presumption of a resulting trust for the benefit of the deceased depositor's estate and, unless the presumption was rebutted, a surviving joint account-holder was not entitled to claim the monies in the account, and the monies on account reverted to the deceased depositor's estate.[13] The presumption of a resulting trust was, however, capable of rebuttal by proof of circumstances which gave rise to an overriding presumption of advancement. The presumption of advancement still exists as an equitable concept, but is confined in its application to cases where a husband and wife, or a father and son or daughter, were joint account-holders. It is the relationship between husband and wife, and father and son or daughter that gives rise to the presumption of advancement, though it is capable of rebuttal by proof of the existence of a contrary intention to benefit.[14] But as there were no such relationships in *Owens v Greene*, the presumption of a resulting trust prevailed, and the surviving account-holder was not entitled to the monies in the account.

In *Lynch v Burke*,[15] the effect of opening a joint bank account was considered afresh by the Supreme Court. In his judgment, O'Flaherty J first considered the legal effect of opening a joint bank account. He was of the view that opening such an account gave rise to a contract between the joint account-holders and the bank. The survivor had therefore a legal interest in the monies on deposit either based on contract, or indeed, by way of a gift which was made subject to the contingency of the death of the depositor. He stated: **20–06**

> I believe that at law the niece had a legal interest in the monies on deposit either by reason of the contractual relationship of the parties or, in the alternative, as a gift which admittedly was not a completed gift in the conventional sense but is nonetheless one that should be upheld as being a gift subject to a contingency *viz.* that of the death of the donor which contingency does not disqualify it as being a proper gift.[16]

He went on to overrule *Owens v Greene*, and found that the concept of the resulting trust was devised primarily to defeat the misappropriation of property as a consequence of potentially fraudulent or improvident transactions, and was not to be used to defeat the clear intention of the **20–07**

---

[11] [1932] IR 225 at 240.

[12] See *Owens v Greene* [1932] IR 225 at 240; *McCabe v Ulster Bank Ltd* [1939] IR 1; *Re Walsh* [1942] IR 403; *McDonnell v McNeilly* [1917] 1 IR 117; *Doyle v Byrne* (1922) 56 ILTR 125.

[13] See *McCabe v Ulster Bank Ltd* [1939] IR 1; *Re Walsh* [1942] IR 403; *McDonnell v McNeilly* [1917] 1 IR 117; *Doyle v Byrne* (1922) 56 ILTR 125.

[14] *RF v MF* [1995] 2 ILRM 572.

[15] [1996] ILRM 114.

[16] [1996] ILRM 114 at 121.

depositor to benefit the surviving account-holder on death. He concluded by saying that his decision "restores equity to the high ground which it should properly occupy to ameliorate the harshness of common law rules on occasion rather than itself be an instrument of injustice."

20–08 Since the decision in *Lynch v Burke*, the opening of a joint bank account no longer gives rise to a presumption of a resulting trust, but instead to a contract between the joint account-holders and the bank, giving a survivor a legal interest in the monies on deposit arising out of the contract. Further, as the relationship between the joint account-holders is not an essential component of the contract entered into with the bank and of a surviving account-holder's entitlement to the monies in the account, the presumption of advancement would now appear to be a redundant concept in its application to such accounts. Therefore, on the death of one joint account-holder, the survivor becomes the sole owner of the account.

20–09 In *O'Meara v Bank of Scotland PLC*,[17] Laffoy J stated that, as a result of *Lynch v Burke*, the legal effect of opening a joint bank account was that the bank became contractually bound to both account-holders and, as a matter of contract between the surviving account-holder and the bank, the surviving account-holder became entitled to the balance in the account on the death of the deceased account-holder. The balance in the account accrued to the surviving account-holder by the right of survivorship. A surviving account-holder was entitled to withdraw the balance in the account on demand.

The Presumption of Advancement and Joint Bank Accounts

20–10 Where a husband transfers property to his wife, the presumption of advancement will become applicable and will override any presumption of a resulting trust, as a result of which the property will become the property of the wife. It is basically the relationship of husband and wife that gives rise to the presumption of advancement in circumstances where a husband transfers property to his wife; it appears that no such presumption will arise where a wife transfers property to her husband. It was stated by Keane J in *JC v JHC*[18] that the presumption of a resulting trust

> may however be rebutted; and in particular the circumstances in whose name the property is conveyed being the wife of the person advancing the money may be sufficient to rebut the presumption under the doctrine of advancement.

20–11 The presumption of advancement is applicable to all forms of property,

[17] [2011] IEHC 402; see A. Keating, "The Devolution of Joint Bank Accounts" (2012) 17(2) CPLJ 29.

[18] Unreported, High Court, 4 August 1982.

including joint bank accounts.[19] In *O'Meara v Bank of Scotland PLC*,[20] Laffoy J commented that it was reasonable to infer that by opening the joint account the plaintiff's deceased husband intended to make provision for her should she predecease her. The doctrine of advancement may also be relied on by a child where there is a voluntary transfer of property that would normally give rise to a presumption of a resulting trust but for the fact that the transferor is the father (not the mother) of the child. It was stated by O'Sullivan MR in *O'Brien v Sheil*[21] that:

> a lodgment by a father in the joint names of himself and his child is as powerful and strong an indication of advancement as a lodgment in the name of the child alone. Now, what is the effect of that doctrine of advancement attaching on a sum lodged in the joint names of father and child (the latter surviving), or in the name of the child alone, unexplained by any evidence? It is a gift of the property to the child in the one case immediately, and in the other if the child survives.

The presumption of advancement may be rebutted by proof of a contrary intention. The doctrine of advancement raises a presumption only and it is one that may be rebutted by acts or statements made before or at the time of making the advancement showing that no advancement was intended.[22] In such cases, the onus is on the husband or father to show "by reference to acts or statements before or around the transaction, that a beneficial interest was not intended to be conveyed in the circumstances relied on."[23] Acts done or statements made after the making of the advancement will not, however, be admitted in evidence to support a rebuttal of the presumption.[24] In *RF v MF*,[25] Henchy J treated a wife's subsequent refusal to live with her husband as sufficient grounds for rebutting the presumption of advancement. He stated that: **20–12**

> If the relevant circumstances show that the paper result achieved by the conveyance conceals the real intention of the husband in entering the transaction, so that the benefit contended for by the wife was not intended, the court will hold that the presumption of advancement is rebutted.[26]

The courts, however, will be slow to rebut the presumption, and will only do so where there is evidence of acts or statements that go towards showing that no advancement was intended, or that the circumstances of the case show, as in *RF v MF*, the existence of an arrangement between husband and wife and of her subsequent breach of the arrangement.[27] Where it is discovered, however, that the husband made the advancement for an illegal **20–13**

---

19 See *O'Meara v Bank of Scotland PLC* [2011] IEHC 402.

20 [2011] IEHC 402; see A. Keating, "Probate and Succession Law" in *Annual Review of Irish Law 2011* (R. Byrne and W. Binchy eds, Round Hall, Dublin, 2012).

21 (1873) IR 7 Eq 255.

22 *Shepherd v Cartwright* [1955] AC 431.

23 *RF v MF* [1995] 2 ILRM 572 at 576–577.

24 *RF v MF* [1995] 2 ILRM 572.

25 [1995] 2 ILRM 572.

26 *RF v MF* [1995] 2 ILRM 572 at 577.

27 See *Malone v McQuaid*, Unreported, High Court, O'Sullivan J, 28 May 1998.

purpose, evidence of the illegal purpose cannot be adduced for the purposes of rebutting the presumption.[28]

Rights of Set-Off

20–14 It may happen that the depositing account-holder may also have a loan account with the bank, and it may be agreed between joint holders and the bank when negotiating the opening of the joint account that the bank has a right of set-off against the joint account for any monies owing on the loan, and where such agreement, exists the surviving account-holder's entitlement to the monies in the joint account may become subject to the bank's right of set-off. But for a claim of set-off to succeed, the right to it must exist at the time of opening the joint bank account. Any claim to a right of set-off at a later date against the joint account will not be enforced by the courts.[29] Furthermore, any claims to set-offs by a bank against the joint account in relation to loans of a deceased joint account-holder must be mutually agreed between the account-holders and the bank during the negotiations for the setting up of such an account before the courts will entertain such claims. In the absence of such agreement regarding set-offs, the surviving account-holder will become entitled to the balance in the account free of set-off.

20–15 In *O'Meara v Bank of Scotland PLC*,[30] the proceedings related to the ownership of monies in two deposit accounts in the joint names of the plaintiff's deceased husband and herself. The primary relief sought by the plaintiff was a declaration that all monies standing in both accounts on the date of death of her husband belonged to her by way of survivorship. The defendant denied such ownership and further claimed a right of set-off on foot of a loan account in her deceased husband's sole name against the monies standing to the credit of the joint accounts. Laffoy J stated that if the defendant had a valid right of set-off against the joint accounts, that right was exercisable notwithstanding the death of the plaintiff's husband, and the plaintiff's entitlement by way of survivorship would have been subject to it. But as the date of the set-off post-dated the negotiations and agreement for the opening of the joint account between the defendant and the plaintiff's deceased husband and herself, the claim by the defendant to a set-off was invalid. When considering the validity of the defendant's claim to a set-off against the joint account, it was held by Laffoy J that the defendant was not entitled to a set-off claimed after the negotiations and agreement for the opening of a joint bank account between it and the plaintiff's deceased husband and plaintiff had taken place. In relation to the ownership of the joint bank account and the bank's right of set-off, Laffoy J stated that:

> As regards joint deposit account No. 101, I have come to the conclusion that

---

28 *Parker v Parker* [1980] ILRM 137.

29 *O'Meara v Bank of Scotland PLC* [2011] IEHC 402.

30 [2011] IEHC 402; see A. Keating, "Probate and Succession Law" in *Annual Review of Irish Law 2011* (R. Byrne and W. Binchy eds, Round Hall, Dublin, 2012).

> the monies in that account were jointly beneficially owned by Mr. O'Meara and the plaintiff and that they passed to the plaintiff by right of survivorship on the death of Mr. O'Meara. I have further concluded that the defendant was not entitled to set-off the monies due on loan account No. 128 against those monies, as it purported to do in January 2010. Accordingly, the plaintiff is entitled to a declaration that all the monies which were standing to the credit of that account on 28th November, 2009 are the property of the plaintiff.

A right of set-off may, therefore, be exercised by a bank against a joint account on the death of an account-holder who has a loan account with the bank, and where the right is exercised, a surviving joint account-holder's entitlement to the monies in the joint account may become subject to the right of set-off. But where a right of set-off is claimed after the negotiations and agreement for the opening of a joint account have been concluded, it will not be enforced by the courts. **20–16**

Part Four

ACTIONS INVOLVING WILL TRUSTS AND EQUITABLE PROPERTY RIGHTS

Chapter 21

ACTIONS INVOLVING TRUSTS AND WILLS

Introduction

Trusts created by will must clearly identify the subject matter or objects of the trust, otherwise they may be deemed ineffective and invalid.[1] The words used by testators must be expressed in the imperative mood when creating trusts in wills, and must be sufficient to identify the property as the subject matter of the trust and beneficiaries as objects of the trust.[2] Actions involving trusts in wills may be instituted to determine the validity of trusts in wills where the identity of the subject matter or objects of the trust are unclear, and such actions may also involve the application of the doctrines of ademption or lapse of trusts. Trusts in wills may also be deemed to have failed where the subject matter is no longer in existence, and where such is the case, the trusts may be adeemed under the doctrine of ademption. Trusts in wills may be deemed to have lapsed where the objects or beneficiaries of the trust have predeceased the testator under the doctrine of lapse. A probate action may be instituted for the purposes of putting the validity of a will creating a trust beyond doubt by seeking a grant of the court in solemn form of law. A probate action may also be instituted for the purposes of challenging a will for non-compliance with the statutory rules of execution, or that the testator lacked testamentary capacity, or that the testator was coerced into making a will by undue influence being exerted on him or her. In probate actions, the court may order that the costs be paid out of a deceased testator's estate, and this includes the costs of an unsuccessful litigant party, who may be allowed costs out of the estate, if it is established that there were reasonable grounds for instituting the litigation and that the proceedings were conducted in a bona fide manner.[3] **21–01**

The costs of actions involving trusts are governed by Ord 99, r 1 of the Rules of the Superior Courts 1986 (the "1986 RSC") which provides that the costs of, and incidental to, every proceeding in the Superior Courts shall be at the discretion of those courts and r 1A of the Rules of the Superior Courts 2008 **21–02**

---

1 See A. Keating, *Probate Motions and Actions Relating to Wills and Intestacies* (Round Hall, Dublin, 2017); A. Keating, *The Law of Wills* (2nd ed, Clarus Press, Dublin, 2018); A. Keating, *Succession Law in Ireland* (Clarus Press, Dublin, 2015); A. Keating, *Keating on Probate*, (5th ed, Round Hall, Dublin, 2015); A. Keating, *Succession Law in Ireland: Principles, Cases and Commentary* (Clarus Press, Dublin, 2016); A. Keating, "Ademption of Testamentary Gifts" (2012) 30 ILT 69.

2 See A. Keating, *The Construction of Wills* (2nd ed, Clarus Press, Dublin, 2017).

3 See *Vella v Morelli* [1968] IR 11; see A. Keating "Costs in Probate Actions" CPLJ (2014) 19(4) 94.

(the "2008 RSC") inserted immediately following r 1 of Ord 99 of the 1986 RSC. In probate actions, the court may order that the costs be paid out of a deceased testator's estate, and this includes the costs of an unsuccessful litigant party, who may be allowed costs out of the estate, if it is established that there were reasonable grounds for instituting the litigation and that the proceedings were conducted in a bona fide manner.[4]

21–03 Actions involving trusts are also subject to the time periods prescribed by the Statute of Limitations 1957 (the "1957 Act") for instituting such actions. A trustee for the purposes of the 1957 Act does not include a person "whose fiduciary relationship arises by construction or implication of law and whose fiduciary relationship is not deemed to be that of an express trustee."[5] The definition of trustee for the purposes of the 1957 Act is therefore confined to express trustees only. Section 25(1) of the 1957 Act provides that the provisions of the 1957 Act shall apply to equitable estates in land in a like manner as they apply to legal estates in land.

21–04 The Land and Conveyancing Law Reform Act 2009 (the "2009 Act") introduced new provisions dealing with the resolution of disputes of land, and applications to the courts relating to such disputes may be instituted by special summons. Under s 22(1) of the 2009 Act, any person having an interest in a trust of land, or a person acting on behalf of such a person, may apply to the court in a "summary manner" for an order to resolve a dispute, and such applicants may include trustees and/or beneficiaries.

Proceedings Involving Trusts in Wills

21–05 The validity of trust created by will may be challenged on the following grounds:

1. That the subject matter of the trust, i.e. the property, is not clearly specified.[6]
2. That the objects of the trust, i.e. the beneficiaries, are not clearly identified.[7]
3. That the subject matter of the trust was disposed of by the testator during his or her lifetime, resulting in the failure of the trust under the doctrine of ademption.
4. That the objects of the trust predeceased the testator, resulting in the failure of the trust under the doctrine of lapse.
5. That the property of the lapsed trust forms part of the testator's residuary estate.[8]
6. That the object or beneficiary of the trust is a predeceased child of the testator

[4] See *Vella v Morelli* [1968] IR 11; see A. Keating "Costs in Probate Actions" CPLJ (2014) 19(4) 94.

[5] Statute of Limitations 1957, s 2(2)(a).

[6] *Chambers v Fahy* [1931] IR 17 at 21 *per* O'Byrne J; see A. Keating, *The Law of Wills* (2nd ed, Clarus Press, Dublin, 2018).

[7] *Chambers v Fahy* [1931] IR 17 at 21 *per* O'Byrne J; see A. Keating, *The Law of Wills* (2nd ed, Clarus Press, Dublin, 2018).

[8] See Succession Act 1965, s 91.

who leaves issue him or her surviving and therefore the trust is not subject to the doctrine of lapse.[9]

7. The words used by the testator fail to show that the testator intended "to create an obligation," or manifest an intention to create a trust.[10]
8. That the words used by the testator in creating the trust do not clearly state that the person appointed as trustee holds the property in trust for the named beneficiaries.[11]
9. That the words creating the trust merely request something to be done, or are "precatory".[12]
10. That the words used by the testator in creating the trust are not sufficiently mandatory, and are in fact discretionary.[13]

Instituting Trust Proceedings

Actions involving trusts in wills may be instituted by the issuing of a plenary summons out of the Central Office.[14] Under Ord 5, r 13 of the RSC, the issue of a summons in equitable proceedings must be preceded by the filing of an affidavit made by the plaintiff or one of the plaintiffs in verification of the indorsement on the summons. The indorsement in the summons must show whether the plaintiff claims as trustee, executor, administrator, residuary legatee, legatee, next-of-kin, heir-at-law, devisee, or in any other capacity.[15] Order 9, r 3 of the RSC provides that personal service shall be effected by delivering a copy of the summons to the defendant in person, and showing him the original or duplicate original, and Ord 9, r 12 provides that the person serving a summons shall, within three days at most after service, indorse on the summons the day and date of the service thereof, and every affidavit of service of such summons shall mention the date on which such indorsement was made. Order 10, r 1 of the RSC provides that if it be made to appear to the court that the plaintiff is from any cause unable to effect prompt personal service, or such other service as is prescribed by the RSC, the court may make an order for substituted or other service, or for the substitution for service of notice by advertisement or otherwise. The defendant must deliver his defence and counterclaim within twenty-eight days from the date of delivery of the statement of claim.[16] Where a counterclaim is filed, a reply to it will be governed by the same rules applicable to a defence.[17] Order 15, r 13 of the RSC also provides that the court may, at any stage of the proceedings, **21–06**

> either upon or without the application of either party, and on such terms as may appear to the court to be just, order that the names of any parties improperly

---

[9] See Succession Act 1965, s 98.

[10] *Chambers v Fahy* [1931] IR 17 at 21 *per* O'Byrne J; *Re Keyford* [1975] 1 All ER 604.

[11] *Re Humphrey's Estate* [1916] 1 IR 21; *Re Sweeney* [1976–77] ILRM 88.

[12] See *Re Blackwood* [1953] NI 23; *Re Coulson* 87 ILTR 93.

[13] See A. Keating, *The Construction of Wills* (2nd ed, Clarus Press, Dublin, 2017).

[14] Ord 1, r 2; Ord 5, r 1.

[15] Ord 4, r 10.

[16] Ord 21, r 1(b).

[17] Ord 23, r 5.

joined, whether as plaintiffs or as defendants, be struck out and that the names of any parties, whether as plaintiffs or defendants, who ought to have been joined, or whose presence before the court may be necessary in order to enable the court effectually and completely adjudicate upon and settle all the questions involved in the cause or matter, be added.

21–07 Plenary Summons

PLENARY SUMMONS
THE HIGH COURT

… 20… No. …
Between A. B., Plaintiff,
and C.D., Defendant.

To the defendant …
of … in the County of …
This plenary summons is to require that within eight days after the service thereof upon you (exclusive of the day of such service) you in person or by solicitor do enter an appearance in the Central Office, Four Courts, Dublin, in the above action; and TAKE NOTICE that, in default of your so doing, the plaintiff may proceed therein, and judgment may be given in your absence.

BY ORDER,
Chief Justice of Ireland,
the day of two thousand and eighteen

N.B.—This summons is to be served within twelve calendar months from the date hereof, and, if renewed within six calendar months from the date of the last renewal, including the day of such date, and not afterwards.

The defendant may appear hereto by entering an appearance either personally or by solicitor at the Central Office, Four Courts, Dublin.

GENERAL INDORSEMENT OF CLAIM

The plaintiff's claim is
(Signed)
This summons was issued by the plaintiff who resides at …
[state address accurately] and
is, and whose address for
service is …
or,
This summons was issued by …, whose registered place of
business is …,
solicitor for the plaintiff, who resides at …
and is ….
This summons was served by me at …
on the defendant …
on the … day of … 20…
Indorsed the … day of … 20…
(Signed)
(Address)

INDORSEMENT OF CHARACTER OF PARTIES.

For instance: The plaintiff's claim is as executor and trustee of C.D., deceased, for, &c.

MEMORANDUM OF APPEARANCE IN GENERAL

THE HIGH COURT

… 20 No. …
Between A.B., Plaintiff,
and C.D., Defendant.

Enter an appearance for C.D., the defendant in this action. Dated …
(Signed)
E.F.,
solicitor for the defendant.
The registered place of business of E.F. is …
[or C.D., the defendant in person.
The place of residence of C.D. is
His address for service is …].
To the Registrar of the Central Office.
Take notice, that I have this day entered an appearance at the Central Office, Four Courts, Dublin,
for to the originating summons in this action.
[If statement of claim is required, add] The said
requires delivery of a statement of claim

Dated
(Signed)

To
(Signed)

STATEMENT OF CLAIM

Heading of Statement of Claim
THE HIGH COURT

… 20… No. …
Between A.B., Plaintiff,
and C.D., Defendant.

Statement of claim
Delivered on the … day of …, 20…, by E.F., of [registered place of business], solicitor for the plaintiff [or as the case may be].

DEFENCE

Heading of defence
THE HIGH COURT

... 20... No. ...

Between A.B., Plaintiff,
and C.D., Defendant.

Defence.
Delivered on the ... day of ..., 20..., by G.H. of [registered place of business], solicitor for the defendant.

REPLY

Heading of reply
THE HIGH COURT

... 20... No. ...
Between A.B., Plaintiff,
and C.D., Defendant.

REPLY.
Delivered on the day of by E.F., of [registered place of business], solicitor for the plaintiff.
1. The plaintiff joins issue with the defendant on his defence save and in so far as the same contains admissions.
2. [as may be necessary].

NOTICE OF COUNTERCLAIM

[Title of action]

To the within-named X.Y.
Take notice that if you do not appear to the within counter-claim of the within-named C.D. within ten days from the service of this defence and counter-claim upon you, you will be liable to have judgment given against you in your absence. Appearance is to be entered [&c., as in Form No. 1].

NOTICE OF TRIAL (ORDINARY FORM)

[Title of action].

Take notice of trial of this [or of the issues in this ordered to be tried] [or as the case may be] for the ... day of ... 20... at ...
Dated

(Signed)

Cost Issues in Trust Proceedings

Order 99, r 1 of the Rules of the Superior Courts provides that the costs of and incidental to every proceeding in the Superior Courts shall be at the discretion of those courts. The 2008 RSC inserts r 1A(1) immediately following Ord 99, r 1 of the 1986 RSC. Rule 1A(1) provides that notwithstanding r 1(3) and r 1(4): **21–08**

(a) The Supreme Court, in considering the awarding of the costs of any appeal or any application in respect of an appeal, may, where it considers it just, have regard to the terms of any offer in writing sent by any party to any other party or parties offering to satisfy the whole or part of that other party's (or those other parties') claim or counterclaim the subject of the appeal, or application.

(b) The High Court, in considering the awarding of the costs of any action (other than an action in respect of a claim or counterclaim concerning which a lodgment or tender offer in lieu of lodgment may be made in accordance with Order 22) or any application in such an action, may, where it considers it just, have regard to the terms of any offer in writing sent by any party to any other party or parties offering to satisfy the whole or part of that other party's (or those other parties') claim, counterclaim or application.

Order 99, r 1A(2) of the 1986 RSC provides that "an offer in writing" includes any offer made without prejudice save as to the issue of costs. Order 99, r 1(2) provides that no party will be entitled to recover any costs of, or incidental to, any proceeding from any other party to such proceeding, except under an order or as provided by the RSC. Order 99, r 1(3) provides that, subject to sub-rule (4A) of the 2008 RSC, the costs of an action will follow the event, unless the court otherwise directs. The 2008 RSC amended Ord 99, r 1(3) of the 1986 RSC by providing that: "Subject to sub-rule (4A), the costs of an action, question or issue tried by a jury shall follow the event unless the court, for special cause, to be mentioned in the order, shall otherwise direct." The 2008 RSC also amended Ord 99, r 1(4) of the 1986 RSC by providing that: "Subject to sub-rule (4A), the costs of every issue of fact or law raised upon a claim or counterclaim shall, unless otherwise ordered, follow the event." As a result of the amendment of the 1986 RSC by the 2008 RSC, Ord 99, r 1(4A) of the 1986 RSC, now provides that: "The High Court or the Supreme Court, upon determining any interlocutory application, shall make an award of costs save where it is not possible justly to adjudicate upon liability for costs on the basis of the interlocutory application." Order 99, r 1(5) provides that where in any proceeding in the High Court or Supreme Court, the costs of any party are ordered to be paid by another party, or by a fund or estate, those costs shall, if the High Court or the Supreme Court respectively so directs, include, in addition to the costs allowed on taxation as between party and party, all or any other costs, charges and expenses reasonably incurred for the purposes of the proceedings. The principles regarding costs may also be garnered and derived from former decisions of the courts. Such principles may also be reformulated by the courts. **21–09**

Time Limits for Instituting Proceedings

21–10 Section 25(2) of the 1957 Act provides that where any land is held upon trust, the trustees will continue to have title to the land on behalf of the beneficiaries until all of them have been statute-barred in succession. Once a beneficiary with a limited interest remains in possession of the land, the limitation period will not commence to run against either the trustees or other beneficiaries. Where, however, a beneficiary is statute-barred, the trustees' title to recover the land will continue for other beneficiaries who have not been statute-barred. Therefore, the trustees may recover the land for remaindermen, even though the beneficiary with the life interest has been statute-barred by the person in adverse possession of the land. Where the beneficiary with the life interest has also a future interest in the trust estate, the future interest will also be statute-barred under s 25(5) of the 1957 Act, unless the trustees or a beneficiary with an intermediate interest recover possession of the trust estate from the person in adverse possession.

Section 71 of the 1957 Act postpones the date of the accrual of the cause of action in cases involving fraud to the date when the fraud was, or could with reasonable diligence have been, discovered. The 1957 Act provides that where the action is either "based on" or "concealed by" the fraud of the defendant, the limitation period does not begin to run until the plaintiff either discovered the fraud or could, with reasonable diligence, have discovered it. In *Moore v Moore*,[18] Murphy J referred to the judgment of Lord Evershed MR in *Kitchen v Royal Air Force Association*[19] for the "classic statement" on the meaning of fraud, when considering the provisions of s 26(b) of the UK Limitation Act 1939, and said that the meaning of fraud was by no means limited to common law fraud or deceit. He stated that:

> It is now clear, however, that the word 'fraud' in s 26(b) of the Limitation Act 1939, is by no means limited to common law fraud or deceit. Equally it is clear, having regard to the decision in *Beaman v ARTS Ltd* [1949] 1 All E.R. 465, that no degree of moral turpitude is necessary to establish fraud within the section. What is covered by equitable fraud is a matter which Lord Hardwicke did not attempt to define two hundred years ago, and I certainly shall not attempt to do so now, but it is, I think clear that the phrase covers conduct which having regard to some special relationship between the two parties concerned, is an unconscionable thing for the one to do towards the other

21–11 Section 72(1) of the 1957 Act provides that:

> Where, in the case of any action for which a period of limitation is fixed by this Act, the action is for relief from the consequences of mistake, the period of limitation shall not begin to run until the plaintiff has discovered the mistake or could with reasonable diligence have discovered it.

21–12 Section 72(2) provides that:

---

18 [2010] IEHC 462.
19 [1958] 1 WLR 563 at 572–573.

> Nothing in subsection (1) of this section shall enable any action to be brought to recover, or enforce any charge against, or set aside any transaction affecting, any property which has been purchased for valuable consideration, subsequently to the transaction in which the mistake was made, by a person who did not know or have reason to believe that the mistake was made.

In *Moore v Moore*,[20] Murphy J referred to Wylie,[21] for his comments on s 72 of the 1957 Act as follows: **21–13**

> ... the general rule is that mistake does not stop time running (*Re Jones's Estate* [1914] 1 I.R. 188) and squatter's rights are often acquired by such means, e.g., where neighbouring landowners make a mistake as to where the boundary lies between their adjoining lands. However, where the action in question is for relief from the consequences of mistake, time does not run until the plaintiff discovers the mistake, or could have done so with reasonable diligence. (Statute of Limitations 1957, s 72(1)). In the case of land, relief for mistake usually involves an application for *equitable relief*, i.e., rescission or rectification, and as such is not subject to the statute of limitations anyway. Like all *equitable relief*, on the other hand, it is subject to the doctrine of laches.

He also referred to Brady & Kerr[22] for the statement that: **21–14**

> Time does not begin to run until the plaintiff has discovered his mistake or could have discovered it with reasonable diligence. The language of s 72(1) is narrower in scope than that in s 71(1) and it is the fact of a mistake and not its concealment which gives rise to the equitable relief. Case law suggests that the mistake must be an essential ingredient to the cause of action.

Murphy J commented that: "While Brady and Kerr refer to the *plaintiff's* mistake, nothing in the provision would suggest that it is restricted to a mistake on the part of the plaintiff."[23] **21–15**

He stated that: **21–16**

> As a result of the receipt and use of the incorrect death certificate, the Folio was changed and the property sold after the Grant of Letters of Administration was obtained. This prevented the plaintiff asserting her rights (s.72(2) also supports this), because of the right of the third defendant and that of her bank. A consequence of the first and second defendants' mistake was that the plaintiff was not located and contacted on her late husband's death. The first and second named defendants acknowledge in the Inland Revenue Affidavit (sworn on the 12th March 2001) that the plaintiff was his spouse. However in pleadings they refer to her 'alleged widowhood' and state that they do not admit that she was his widow and that they require proof of same. If those defendants had not made the mistake in relation to the death certificate, and had located the plaintiff, she would have been able to attempt to assert her rights at that stage.

---

20 [2010] IEHC 462.

21 *Irish Land Law* (4th edn, Bloomsbury Publishing, Haywards' Heath, 2010) at para 23.25.

22 *The Limitation of Action* (2nd edn, Law Society of Ireland, Dublin, 1994) at pp 196–198

23 See *Phillips-Higgins v Harper* [1954] 1 QB 411.

21–17 He went on to say that:

> There were two consequences of the mistake: the Folio was amended, and the plaintiff was not told about her estranged husband's death. The plaintiff would have been the party to take out the grant of letters of administration, or alternatively to renounce her right to do so. There is no indication in the papers before the court as to what the personal representatives (the first and second defendants) swore in the Oath of Administration Intestate, which is the document setting out the correct history of entitlement of the applicant to extract the Grant.

21–18 Therefore, the defendants' mistake resulted in the plaintiff not being able to take out the grant of letters of administration and asserting her right to a share in her late husband's estate. For this reason, Murphy J stated that the plaintiff was entitled to damages and costs against the first- and second-named defendants.

Proceedings Involving the Validity of Wills

21–19 The following are grounds for challenging the validity of wills creating trusts:

1. That the testator lacked testamentary capacity.[24]
2. That a severe form of physical illness affected the testator's mental powers when he or she executed his or her will.[25]
3. That medical evidence fails to show the testamentary capacity of the testator at the time he executed his or her will.[26]
4. That, having regard to all of the evidence and by applying the evidential standard of the balance of probabilities, the testator was not of sound disposing mind "when the testamentary document which is being propounded was executed."[27]
5. That the testator was subject to undue influence when he or she made his or her will.
6. That, in the event of a finding of undue influence, to set aside "any undue gift and to allow the same to fall into the residuary estate".[28]
7. That the existence of undue influence in prior dealings with the same person is sufficient to show that such influence was also exerted on the testator when he or she made his or her will.[29]
8. That the onus of proof rests on the party who alleges the existence of undue influence.[30]
9. That the will was procured by a beneficiary.
10. That the will was prepared and executed in suspicious circumstances.[31]
11. That, where a will was prepared in suspicious circumstances, the onus of proof rests on the propounding party who prepared the will to satisfy the

---

24 Succession Act 1965, s 77; see A. Keating, *The Law of Wills* (2nd ed, Clarus Press, Dublin, 2018); A. Keating, "Testamentary Capacity" (2011) 16(3) CPLJ 46.
25 *Laaser v Earls* [2016] IECA 63.
26 *Laaser v Earls* [2016] IECA 63.
27 *Scally v Rhatigan* [2010] IEHC 475; *Laaser v Earls* [2016] IECA 63.
28 *Lambert v Lyons* [2010] IEHC 29.
29 *Boyse v Rossborough* (1857) 6 HLC 2 at 48; *Baudins v Richardson* [1906] AC 169; *Craig v Lamourex* [1920] AC 349.
30 *Lambert v Lyons* [2010] IEHC 29.
31 See *Re Begley* [1939] IR 479 at 490; *Tyrell v Painton* [1894] P 151.

court that the will was executed by a testator who was not only "free" to make his or her will, but was "competent" also.[32]

12. That the question of the righteousness of the transaction arises "when it is a question of knowledge and approval of the contents of a will the circumstances which are held to excite the suspicions of the court must be circumstances attending, or at least relevant to, the preparation and execution of the will itself."[33]
13. That the will was not duly executed in compliance with s 78 of the Succession Act 1965.[34]

Instituting Probate Actions

A probate action may be instituted by the issuing of a plenary summons out of the Central Office.[35] Under Ord 5, r 13 of the RSC, the issue of a summons in probate proceedings must be preceded by the filing of an affidavit made by the plaintiff, or one of the plaintiffs, in verification of the indorsement on the summons. Rule 13 also provides that, on the issue of a summons, the plaintiff must, if he or she has not already done so, enter a *caveat* in the Probate Office entitled in the name of the deceased person. The summons must be headed with the name of the deceased as well as the names of the parties to the action. The indorsement in the summons must show whether the plaintiff claims as executor, administrator, residuary legatee, legatee, next-of-kin, heir-at-law, devisee, or in any other capacity.[36] In probate actions, the plaintiff on issuing the summons must, if he or she has not already done so, enter a *caveat* in the Probate Office.[37] The summons must be served in the same way as in all other actions commenced by plenary summons.[38] Order 9, r 3 of the RSC provides that personal service shall be effected by delivering a copy of the summons to the defendant in person, and showing him the original or duplicate original, and Ord 9, r 12 provides that the person serving a summons shall, within three days at most after service, indorse on the summons the day and date of the service thereof, and every affidavit of service of such summons shall mention the date on which such indorsement was made. Order 10, r 1 of the RSC provides that if it be made to appear to the court that the plaintiff is from any cause unable to effect prompt personal service, or such other service as is prescribed by the RSC, the court may make an order for substituted or other service, or for the substitution for service of notice by advertisement or otherwise. In probate actions, however, any person not named in the summons may intervene and **21–20**

[32] *Barry v Butlin* (1838) 2 Moo PC 480; *Fulton v Andrew* (1875) LR 7 HL 448; *In the Goods of Corboy* [1969] IR 148; A. Keating, "A Plea of Want of Knowledge and Approval as an Alternative to Undue Influence" (2008) 13(1) CPLJ 10; A. Keating, "Principles of Knowledge and Approval of Contents of Wills by Testators" (2017) 22(4) CPLJ 66.

[33] *Re R deceased* [1951] P 10 at 17.

[34] See A. Keating, *The Law of Wills* (2nd ed, Clarus Press, Dublin, 2018).

[35] Ord 1, r 2; Ord5, r 1.

[36] Ord 4, r 10.

[37] Ord 4, r 10.

[38] Ord 9.

appear in the action by filing an affidavit in the Central Office showing his interest in the estate of the deceased.[39]

21–21 Order 12, r 27 of the RSC provides that in probate actions, the plaintiff and defendant, within eight days of the entry of appearance on the part of the defendant, are respectively to file their affidavits as to scripts in the Central Office, whether they have or have not any script in their possession. Such affidavit shall be in the Form No 22 in Appendix C. Under Ord 12, r 28 every script which has at any time been made by, or under the direction of, the testator, whether will, codicil, draft of a will or codicil, or written instructions for the same, of which the deponent has any knowledge, information, or belief, is to be specified in his affidavit of scripts, and every script in the custody or under the control of the party making the affidavit is to be annexed thereto, and deposited therewith in the Central Office. Order 12, r 29 provides that no party to the proceeding, nor his solicitor, shall be at liberty, except by leave of the court, to inspect the affidavit as to scripts, or the scripts annexed thereto, filed by any party to the cause, until his own affidavit as to scripts shall have been filed.

21–22 The plaintiff and defendant must within eight days of the entry of appearance file affidavits as to scripts in the Central Office whether or not they have any scripts relating to the estate of the deceased in their possession.[40] The affidavit as to scripts must exhibit all testamentary papers within the possession of a party to a probate action. In *Prendergast v McLoughlin*,[41] Clarke J provided a very instructive note on the function of the affidavit of scripts in testamentary proceedings. In probate actions the plaintiff and defendant must file an affidavit of scripts or affidavits as to scripts. This makes it incumbent on the plaintiff and defendant to disclose by affidavit all testamentary scripts of the deceased, executed or unexecuted, which have at any time come into the possession or knowledge of the parties. The affidavit concerned must describe every testamentary script of the deceased whose estate is the subject of the action of which the deponent has any knowledge, or if it be the case, that the deponent knows of no such script. The term "scripts", in that context, denotes any papers made or written by or under the direction of the deceased, being or purporting to be a will, codicil, draft or copy of a will or codicil, or of any part of a will or codicil, or written instructions for a will or codicil, or having the form or effect of a will or codicil, or other testamentary disposition of the deceased. Clarke J. stated that procedural rules on affidavits as to scripts clearly envisage that such an affidavit should disclose all written documents that are in the possession or knowledge of the deponent. The definition of scripts does not seem to cover any oral instructions. He said it was clear that the categories of discovery in the case before him were very closely based on the definition of "scripts" as specified in the Rules of the Superior Courts. Therefore, in probate actions

---

39 Order 12, r 14.
40 Order 12, rr 27 and 28.
41 [2008] IEHC 296.

it would not be open to either party to decline to disclose the contents of any such documents on the grounds of privilege.

Under Ord 21, r 17 of the RSC, in probate actions the party opposing a will may, with his defence, give notice to the party setting up the will that he merely insists upon the will being proved in solemn form of law, and only intends to cross-examine the witnesses produced in support of the will, and he shall thereupon be at liberty to do so, and shall not, in any event, be liable to pay the costs of the other side unless the court shall be of opinion that there was no reasonable ground for opposing the will. Order 27, r 7 provides that in probate actions, if any defendant makes default in delivering a defence, the action may proceed, notwithstanding such default. The defendant must deliver his defence and counterclaim within 28 days from the date of delivery of the statement of claim.[42] The defendant may, however, limit his costs by serving notice with his defence that he intends only to cross-examine the witnesses supporting the will. Where a counterclaim is filed a reply to it will be governed by the same rules applicable to a defence.[43] The will propounded by the plaintiff in the statement of claim may be counterclaimed by the defendant propounding a later will.[44] **21–23**

Plenary Summons **21–24**

PLENARY SUMMONS.
THE HIGH COURT.

... 20... No.
Between A. B., Plaintiff,
and C.D., Defendant.

To the defendant ...
of ... in the County of ...
This plenary summons is to require that within eight days after the service thereof upon you (exclusive of the day of such service) you in person or by solicitor do enter an appearance in the Central Office, Four Courts, Dublin, in the above action; and TAKE NOTICE that, in default of your so doing, the plaintiff may proceed therein, and judgment may be given in your absence.

BY ORDER,
Chief Justice of Ireland,
the day of two thousand and eighteen

N.B.—This summons is to be served within twelve calendar months from the date hereof, and, if renewed within six calendar months from the date of the last renewal, including the day of such date, and not afterwards.

The defendant may appear hereto by entering an appearance either personally or by solicitor at the Central Office, Four Courts, Dublin.

---

42 Ord 21, r 1(b).
43 Ord 23, r 5.
44 *Craig v Kennedy* (1896) 30 ILTR 23.

GENERAL INDORSEMENT OF CLAIM

The plaintiff's claim is

(Signed)
This summons was issued by the plaintiff who resides at ...
[state address accurately] and
is, and whose address for
service is ...
or,
This summons was issued by ..., whose registered place of
business is ...,
solicitor for the plaintiff, who resides at ...
and is ....
This summons was served by me at ...
on the defendant ...
on the ... day of ... 20...
Indorsed the ... day of ... 20...
(Signed)
(Address)

INDORSEMENT OF CHARACTER OF PARTIES

For instance: The plaintiff's claim is as executor [or administrator] of C.D., deceased, for, &c.

Or, The plaintiff's claim is against the defendant A.B., as executor [or, &c.] of C.D., deceased, for &c.

Or, The plaintiff's claim is against the defendant A.B., as executor of X.Y., deceased, for &c., and against the defendant C.D., in his personal capacity, for, &c.

SAMPLE GENERAL INDORSEMENT OF CLAIM

Probate propounding will in solemn form:
The plaintiff's claim is as executor of the last will, dated the ... day of ... 20..., of C.D., late of ... deceased, who died on the ... day of ... 20... to have the said will established. This summons is issued against you as one of the next-of-kin of ... the said deceased [or as the case may be].

Revocation of probate:
The plaintiff's claim is as executor of the last will dated the ... day of ... 20..., of C.D., late of ... , deceased, who died on the ... day of ... 20..., to have the probate of a pretended will of the said deceased, dated the ... day of ... 20..., revoked. This summons is issued against you as the executor of the said pretended will [or as the case may be].

Revocation of letters of administration:
The plaintiff's claim is as executor of the last will dated the ... day of ... 20... of C.D., late of ..., deceased, who died on the ... day of ... 20..., to have the said will established and to have the grant of administration of the estate of the said deceased obtained by the defendant revoked.

By a person claiming a grant of administration as next-of-kin of the deceased, but where next-of-kin is disputed:
The plaintiff's claim is as the lawful brother and sole next-of-kin of C.D. late of …, deceased, who died on the … day of … 20…, intestate, to have a grant of administration to the estate of the said intestate. This summons is issued against you because you have entered a caveat, and have alleged that you are the sole next-of-kin of the deceased [or as the case may be].

MEMORANDUM OF APPEARANCE IN GENERAL

THE HIGH COURT

… 20… No. …
Between A.B., Plaintiff,
and C.D., Defendant.

Enter an appearance for C.D., the defendant in this action.

Dated
(Signed)
E.F.,
solicitor for the defendant.
The registered place of business of E.F. is …
[or C.D., the defendant in person.
The place of residence of C.D. is …
His address for service is …].
To the Registrar of the Central Office.
Take notice, that I have this day entered an appearance at the Central Office, Four Courts, Dublin,
for to the originating summons in this action.
[If statement of claim is required, add] The said …
requires delivery of a statement of claim

Dated

(Signed)

To

(Signed)

AFFIDAVIT OF SCRIPTS

[Title of action]

I, A.B., of [place of abode and description] the plaintiff [or C.D., of (place of abode and description), the defendant] in this action, make oath and say as follows:—

1. No paper or parchment writing at any time made or written by or under the direction of late of [place of abode and description] deceased, the deceased in this cause, being or purporting to be a will, codicil, draft or copy of a will or codicil, or of any part of a will or codicil, or written instructions for a will or codicil, or

for any part of a will or codicil, or having the form or effect of a will or codicil, or of part of a will, codicil, or other testamentary disposition of the said ..., has at any time, either before or since his death, come to the hands, possession, or knowledge, or under the control of me, this deponent, save and except the true and original last will [and one codicil or codicils, or draft copies, or as the case may be] of said deceased hereunto annexed, the said will, bearing date the day of ... , 20 [and the said codicil (or as the case may be) bearing date, &c.], and also save and except [here add the dates and particulars of any other testamentary papers of which the deponent has any knowledge, information or belief; and state the person or persons in whose possession same are, and the address of such person or persons), and also save and except the next hereinafter mentioned papers (here describe the papers, with dates, &c.], which I verily believe are in the possession or under the control of ... and I say that I have not, nor has any person for me, or by my consent or desire, or at all to my knowledge or belief, cancelled, suppressed, or destroyed, or caused to be cancelled, suppressed, or destroyed, any paper or parchment writing, being or purporting to be a will, codicil, or pan of a will or codicil, draft or copy of a will or codicil, or of any part of a will or codicil, or written instruction for a will or codicil, or for any part thereof, or having the form or effect of a will or codicil, or other testamentary disposition, or any part of a will or codicil or other testamentary disposition of the said deceased.
Sworn, &c.

This affidavit is filed on behalf of

STATEMENT OF CLAIM

Heading of Statement of Claim

THE HIGH COURT
... 20... No. ...
Between A.B., Plaintiff,
and C.D., Defendant.

Statement of claim
Delivered on the ... day of ..., 20... , by E.F., of [registered place of business], solicitor for the plaintiff [or as the case may be].

DEFENCE

Heading of defence
THE HIGH COURT
... 20... No. ...
Between A.B., Plaintiff,
and C.D., Defendant.
Defence.
Delivered on the ... day of ... , 20..., by G.H. of [registered place of business], solicitor for the defendant.

REPLY

Heading of reply
THE HIGH COURT
... 20... No. ...
Between A.B., Plaintiff,
and C.D., Defendant.
REPLY
Delivered on the day of by E.F., of [registered place of business], solicitor for the plaintiff.
1. The plaintiff joins issue with the defendant on his defence save and in so far as the same contains admissions.
2. [as may be necessary].

Cost Issues in Probate Actions

The court, when awarding costs in probate actions will first be guided by the principles set out in Ord 99 of the Rules of the Superior Courts (the "RSC"). In probate actions, the court may order that the costs be paid out of a deceased testator's estate, and this includes the costs of an unsuccessful litigant party, who may be allowed costs out of the estate, if it is established that there were reasonable grounds for instituting the litigation and that the proceedings were conducted in a bona fide manner. In *Vella v Morelli*,[45] Budd J traced the Irish practice of awarding costs in probate actions back to the time of the Prerogative Court and in particular the judgment of Dr Radcliff in *Fairtlough v Fairtlough.*[46] Budd J found the old Irish practice "a very fair and reasonable one" and one that also resulted in allaying the reasonable fears of persons as regards costs when faced with the decision of whether or not to litigate. He then went on to reaffirm the Irish practice, but stressed that before the practice can operate in any particular case, two questions must be answered, viz. (a) was there reasonable ground for litigation? (b) was it conducted bona fide? In *Elliot v Stamp*,[47] the Supreme Court had to consider an appeal regarding the award of costs in a probate action. During the course of his judgment, Kearns J stated that: **21–25**

> Thus, while it may be reasonable to commence and bring proceedings, and bring them *bona fide*, a point may arrive where, as a result of a disclosure made by the defence, the further maintenance of the claim can no longer be reasonable. In such circumstances, it seems to me a trial judge should not be fettered in the exercise of his discretion as to costs and should be free both to decline costs from the estate to an unsuccessful or even to award costs against such a litigant from the time of disclosure.

In *Elliot v Stamp*, Kearns J seems to have introduced a new factor to be considered by the court when deciding on the issue of costs in a probate **21–26**

---

[45] [1968] IR 11; see A. Keating "Costs in Probate Actions" (2014) 19(4) CPLJ 94.
[46] (1839) 1 Milw 36 at 39; see *Kavanagh v Fegan* [1932] IR 566; *Murphy v Finlen* [1931] LJ Ir 50; *Mulligan v McKeown* [1955] IR 112.
[47] [2008] IESC 10; see A. Keating, "Probate and Succession Law" in *Annual Review of Irish Law 2008* (R. Byrne and W. Binchy eds, Round Hall, Dublin, 2009).

action when he said that certain disclosures by the defence may make further maintenance of the claim no longer reasonable.

21–27 **Derived Principles**

(i) In *Vella v Morelli*,[48] Budd J stated that in probate actions the costs of an unsuccessful party may be awarded out of the estate of a deceased testator, where it is shown that there were reasonable grounds for the proceedings, and the proceedings were conducted in a bona fide manner

(ii) In *Elliot v Stamp*,[49] Kearns J stated that while it may be reasonable to commence and bring proceedings, and bring them bona fide, a point may arrive where, as a result of a disclosure made by the defence, the further maintenance of the claim can no longer be reasonable, and as a consequence "a trial judge should not be fettered in the exercise of his discretion as to costs and should be free both to decline costs from the estate to an unsuccessful litigant or even to award costs against such a litigant from the time of disclosure."

21–28 This special rule or practice regarding the award of costs in probate actions is not applicable to administration actions. The principles in *Vella v Morelli* and *Elliott v Stamp* regarding the issue of costs in probate actions will not be extended to issues of costs in administration actions. The principles have no application to the question of costs in administration actions involving disputes between beneficiaries in a will or intestacy, or *lites inter partes* between beneficiaries under the will or intestacy.[50]

Probate Motions

21–29 A probate motion may be an ex parte motion or notice of motion. The ex parte motion procedure may be used where the applicant is not required to put another party on notice when applying to the court for a ruling. Such applications must be made in accordance with the special rules for motion papers in Ord 79, r 87 of the Rules of the Superior Courts.

21–30 Under Ord 79, r 87:

1. The motion paper must contain a brief statement of the main facts on which the application is grounded and conclude with the terms on which the application is to be made.
2. The grounding affidavit or affidavits must contain all the facts of the case that require the attention of the court.
3. The statement in the motion paper must contain no facts which are unsupported by the grounding affidavit or affidavits or official documents, and any ruling made by the probate officer on the subject-matter of the application must be mentioned in the motion paper.

---

48 [1968] IR 11; see A. Keating "Costs in Probate Actions" (2014) 19(4) CPLJ 94.

49 [2008] IESC 10; see A. Keating, "Probate and Succession Law" in *Annual Review of Irish Law 2008* (R. Byrne and W. Binchy eds, Round Hall, Dublin, 2009).

50 See *Rennick v Rennick* [2012] IEHC 559; *O'Connor v Markey* [2007] 2 IR 194; *Scally v Rhatigan* [2012] IEHC 387; *Cawley v Lillis* [2012] IEHC 70.

4. The motion paper must be lodged in the Rules Office section of the Probate Office two clear days before it is intended to move the application.

According to a Probate Office Update of 14 August 2012, the following proofs must be lodged in the Rules Office: **21–31**

(i) original ex parte motion paper and copy of same;
(ii) original affidavits and copies of same;
(iii) an indexed and paginated booklet of copies of (i) and (ii) including copy exhibits.

The court, for instance, when making an order giving leave to apply for a grant of the lost will may limit it to the terms of the copy pending the discovery of the original will. The necessary proofs may then be prepared for lodgement in the Seat Office or a relevant District Probate Registry. Where the application is for a grant of probate, the order of the court must be exhibited in the oath of executor. Where the application is for a grant of letters of administration with the will annexed, the order of the court must be exhibited in the oath of administrator with the will annexed. **21–32**

Under Ord 79, r 88: **21–33**

1. The motion paper must contain the names and descriptions of the parties to the motion, the style and object of the cause or proceeding before the court, and must state any proceedings already heard in the cause mentioned in the motion paper. It must also contain the prayer of the party on whose behalf the motion is made and a brief mention of the circumstances on which it is founded.
2. If the motion paper is deficient in relation to any of the matters mentioned in 1 above, it will not be accepted without the permission of the Probate Officer.
3. The motion paper must be deposited in the Probate Office together with the grounding affidavit or affidavits and copies of any testamentary papers referred to as exhibits. The Probate Officer may require any original documents referred to in the grounding affidavit or affidavits and to be used at the hearing of the motion to be lodged in the Probate Office. However, as already stated, it is not the policy of the Rules Office to retain original exhibits either before, or indeed after, the hearing.
4. Any affidavits or documents already filed or deposited in the Probate Office will be sent with the motion to the court.

According to a Probate Office Update dated 14 August 2012: **21–34**

When issuing an application for the probate list the following documents must be presented:

(i) Original notice of motion and copy of same,
(ii) Original affidavits and copies of same, and
(iii) An indexed, bound and paginated booklet of copies of all the foregoing documentation including copy exhibits. Original exhibits must not be submitted to the Probate Office.

The grounding affidavit plays an essential role in ex parte and notice of motion procedure, and accordingly, special attention should be paid to **21–35** the assemblage of the supportive evidence mentioned in it, and references to exhibits by it. While the probate cause or matter to be determined by the court will be stated in the motion paper, the evidence contained in the grounding affidavit must be sufficient and supportive of the cause or matter mentioned in the motion paper. There is also a whole host of procedural rules that must be complied with in the preparation of grounding affidavits. Order 79, r 39 provides that all affidavits filed or used in the Probate Office must comply with the general provisions of Ord 40, as amended by the Rules of the Superior Courts (Affidavits) 2009 (SI No 95 of 2009). The court may also order the attendance for cross-examination of the person making an affidavit on the application of either party to the motion.

21–36 The following are suggested determinant factors for deciding on the type of motion procedure to be adopted in applications to the court, viz. ex parte motion or motion on notice:

1. A motion is a form of procedure for application to the court.

1.1 A motion as a form of procedure for application to the court may be an ex parte motion or motion on notice.

2. The probate issue may determine the nature of the motion application, i.e. by ex parte motion or by motion on notice.

2.1 The probate issue must be set out on the face of a motion ex parte or motion on notice supported by a grounding affidavit or affidavits.

3. An ex parte motion is an application to the court by one party only.

3.1 A motion on notice is an application to the court by one party who serves notice of the motion on another party or a number of parties.

4. The probate issue in an ex parte application involves one party only.

4.1 The probate issue in a motion on notice may involve one or more parties.

5. The determination of the court regarding the probate issue in an ex parte application will affect the applicant only.

5.1 The determination of the court regarding the probate issue in a motion on notice application will affect the applicant and may affect other involved parties.

6. The determination by the court of the effect of the probate issue (a) will affect the applicant in an ex parte motion and (b) will affect the applicant in the motion on notice and may affect other involved parties.

7. Therefore, the appropriate procedure by ex parte motion or motion on notice may be determinable by the nature of the probate issue for determination by the court, the number of the parties joined in the motion relative to their interests in the probate issue, and the likely effect of a determination by the court of the probate issue may have on their interests.

21–37 The following are the determinant formulae of factors for deciding on the appropriate motion procedure:

(i) Determinant Formula Ex Parte Motion – Factors – Probate Issue @ 1.1 + 2, Motion Procedure @ 3, Ex Parte Motion @ 4, Determination of the Court @ 5 + 6(a), conclude, @ 7.

(ii) Determinant Formula Notice of Motion – Factors – Probate Issue @ 1.1 + 2 + 2.1, Motion Procedure @ 3.1 + 4.1, Notice of Motion @ 4.1, Determination of the Court @ 5.1 + 6(b), conclude @ 7.

21–38 Probate issues include seeking the admission of lost wills in terms of copies to probate, presuming the death of a testator or intestate, setting aside caveats, and the removal and replacement of personal representatives.[51] Where, however, the probate issue involved is one that touches upon the validity of a will or the revocation of grant of probate or letters of administration already made, the motion procedure is not the appropriate procedure for application to the court. Probate issues involving the validity of a will or the revocation of grants are the substance of probate actions which are instituted by plenary summons, and such issues will not be entertained by the court by motion procedure.[52] Where an application is made to the court by probate motion, no issues touching upon the validity of a will may be raised, as such issues can only be determined only by a probate action.

The Resolution of Disputes Relating to Trusts of Land

Prior to the enactment of the 2009 Act, the Settled Land Acts 1882–1890 Acts governed all settlements and trusts of land created by testators.[53] The Settled Land Acts 1882–1890 have now been repealed and replaced by the 2009 Act, and the various kinds of settlements and trusts relating to land will now comprise a "trust of land" for the purposes of s 18 of the 2009 Act. A trust of land covers every kind of settlement (whether or not the instrument creating it creates an express trust), holding trusts and trusts for sale whereby land is to be held for persons in succession to each other, and any other situation where land is subject to a trust, including a constructive or resulting trust declared by a court. Section 18(3) of the 2009 Act provides that a trust of land is governed by the general law of trusts. The general law comprises the body of law built up by the courts over the centuries relating to, for example, trustees' duties owed to beneficiaries (based on the principle that they must act always in the interests of the beneficiaries and not seek personal gain) and statute law, such as the provisions of the Trustee Act 1893 dealing with administration of trusts and trustees' powers. Section 22 of the 2009 Act deals with the resolution of disputes concerning trusts of land. Under the section, any person having an interest in a trust of land may apply to the court in a "summary manner" to resolve a dispute involving the trust. For the purposes of s 22, a person having an interest in a trust of land includes a mortgagee, secured creditor, judgment mortgagee, or a trustee of the trust. The court, when considering an application under s 22 of the 2009 Act will have regard to the interests of the beneficiaries as a whole and the purposes which the trust of land is intended to achieve. Sections 23 and 24 of the 2009 Act deal with applications to vary trusts **21–39**

[51] See A. Keating, *Probate Motions and Actions Relating to Wills and Intestacies* (Round Hall, Dublin, 2017).

[52] See A. Keating, *Probate Motions and Actions Relating to Wills and Intestacies* (Round Hall, Dublin, 2017).

[53] See A. Keating, *The Law of Wills* (2nd ed, Clarus Press, Dublin, 2018); A. Keating, "The Effect of the Land and Conveyancing Law Reform Act 2009 on Wills Precedents Referring to the Settled Land Acts and Conveyancing Acts (2010) 28 ILT 252.

and the jurisdiction of the courts to hear such applications. The Rules of the Superior Courts (Land and Conveyancing Law Reform Act 2009) 2010 (SI No 149 of 2010), amended the Rules of the Superior Courts 1986 to take account of ss 22, 23 and 24 of the 2009 Act.

> 2. (1) Proceedings for the following reliefs under the Act shall be commenced by special summons in accordance with Order 3:
> (a) An order to resolve a dispute mentioned in section 22;
> (b) An order to approve an arrangement specified in an application under section 24.

(i) Parties to Trust of Land Disputes

21–40 Section 22(1) of the 2009 Act provides that:

> Any person having an interest in a trust of land, or a person acting on behalf of such a person, may apply to the court in a summary manner for an order to resolve a dispute between the—
> (a) trustees themselves, or
> (b) beneficiaries themselves, or
> (c) trustees and beneficiaries, or
> (d) trustees or beneficiaries and other persons interested,
> in relation to any matter concerning the—
> (i) performance of their functions by the trustees, or
> (ii) nature or extent of any beneficial or other interest in the land, or
> (iii) other operation of the trust.

(ii) Applications to the Court under Section 22

21–41 Section 22(2) provides that:

> (2) Subject to subsection (3), in determining an application under subsection (1) the court may make whatever order and direct whatever inquiries it thinks fit in the circumstances of the case.
> (3) In considering an application under subsection (1)(i) and (iii) the court shall have regard to the interests of the beneficiaries as a whole and, subject to these, to—
> (a) the purposes which the trust of land is intended to achieve,
> (b) the interests of any minor or other beneficiary subject to any incapacity,
> (c) the interests of any secured creditor of any beneficiary,
> (d) any other matter which the court considers relevant.
> (4) In subsection (1), "person having an interest" includes a mortgagee or other secured creditor, a judgment mortgagee or a trustee.
> (5) Nothing in this section affects the jurisdiction of the court under section 36 of the Act of 1995.

(iii) Rules of the Superior Courts (Land and Conveyancing Law Reform Act 2009) 2010

21–42 These Rules shall be construed together with the Rules of the Superior Courts 1986 to 2010 and may be cited as the Rules of the Superior Courts (Land and Conveyancing Law Reform Act 2010. These Rules came into operation on 10 May 2010.

Special Summons 21–43

SPECIAL SUMMONS
THE HIGH COURT

In the matter of … 20… No. …
Between A. B., Plaintiff,
and C.D., Defendant.
(or if not *inter partes*)
On the application of A.B.
To
Of … in the County of …
This special summons is to require you to attend before the Master at the Four Courts, Dublin, on the day of … at … o'clock in the forenoon at the hearing of this summons issued on the day of … , and if you do not attend in person or by solicitor at the time and place aforesaid, such order will be made, and proceedings taken as the Court may think just and expedient; and TAKE NOTICE that if you wish to attend and to be heard, you should first enter an appearance.
BY ORDER,
Chief Justice of Ireland,
The … day of … two
thousand and …
N.B.—This summons is required to be served not less than four days before the return day mentioned therein (exclusive of the day of service).

SPECIAL INDORSEMENT OF CLAIM

The plaintiff's claim is
(Signed)
Schedule of affidavit or affidavits intended to be used by the plaintiff (or applicant) on the hearing of the summons.
This summons was issued by the plaintiff (or applicant) who resides at [state address accurately] and is …
or,
This summons was issued by …, whose registered place of …
business is …,
solicitor for the plaintiff, who resides at …
and is ….
This summons was served by me at …
on the defendant on … day the …
day of 20…
Indorsed the … day of 20…
(Signed)
(Address)

SAMPLE SPECIAL INDORSEMENT OF CLAIM

For instance: The plaintiff's claim is as one of the next-of-kin of the above named X.Y., deceased, who died on [date] intestate for an order for the administration of the estate of the said deceased with all necessary and proper accounts, inquiries and directions.
(Indorsement of character in which defendant is sued.)
(Signed)

Or: The plaintiff's claim is as the executor and trustee of the said will mentioned in the title hereof of X. Y., deceased, for the determination of the following questions arising (in the administration of the estate, and) upon the construction of the said will of the said testator, and in the events that have happened, viz.:- [Set out questions in form which will enable them as far as possible to be answered "yes" or "no"] and that the cost of the proceedings may be provided for.

The defendant is sued as [state nature of his interest, or capacity in which he is sued].
(Signed)

DEFENCE

Heading of defence

THE HIGH COURT
... 20... No. ...
Between A.B., Plaintiff,
and C.D., Defendant.
Defence
Delivered on the ... day of ... , 20..., by G.H. of [registered place of business], solicitor for the defendant.

REPLY

Heading of reply
THE HIGH COURT
...20... No. ...
Between A.B., Plaintiff,
and C.D., Defendant.
REPLY
Delivered on the day of by E.F., of (registered place of business), solicitor for the plaintiff.
1. The plaintiff joins issue with the defendant on his defence save and in so far as the same contains admissions.
2. [as may be necessary].

NOTICE OF COUNTERCLAIM

[Title of action]

To the within-named X.Y.
Take notice that if you do not appear to the within counter-claim of the within-named C.D. within ten days from the service of this defence and counter-claim upon you, you will be liable to have judgment given against you in your absence. Appearance is to be entered [&c., as in Form No. 1].

NOTICE OF TRIAL (ORDINARY FORM)

[Title of action]

Take notice of trial of this [or of the issues in this ordered to be tried] [or as the case may be] for the … day of … 20… at
Dated
(Signed)

CHAPTER 22

THE CONSTRUCTION OF WILL TRUSTS

INTRODUCTION

The words used by the testator in creating a trust in a will must be expressed in a mandatory fashion, "so as to show that the testator intended to create an obligation."[1] Although there is no set formula of words for creating a trust, the words employed by the testator must be sufficient to manifest an intention to create a trust.[2] The testator's words must clearly state that the person appointed as trustee holds the property in trust for the named beneficiaries.[3] Words that merely request something to be done, or words that are "precatory", will not create a trust.[4] The following words (in italics) are sufficient to create a trust in a will: **22–01**

> "I appoint AB of (address)
>
> and CD of (address)
>
> (hereinafter called "my Trustees") to be executors and trustees and appoint them trustees for the purposes of the Land and Conveyancing Law Reform Act 2009 and for the purposes of the Conveyancing Acts and for the purposes of s 57 of the Succession Act 1965.
>
> *I give, devise and bequeath to my Trustees the whole of my real and personal estate upon trust to sell the same (with power to postpone such sale in whole or in part for such time or times as they shall think fit) and to hold the same or the proceeds of sale thereof on the following trust:*
>
> (a) To pay my debts, funeral expenses and testamentary expenses;
> (b) [Provision for legacies, house and/or contents to, etc., if intended]
> *(c) To divide the residue (hereinafter called "my residuary estate") among such of my children as shall survive me and reach the age of 18 [or 21] years and, if more than one, in equal shares absolutely BUT if any child of mine dies before me or before attaining a vested interest leaving a child or children, then such child or children shall on reaching the age of 18 years take* per stirpes *the share his/her or their parent would otherwise have taken, and if more than one, in equal shares absolutely.*"

---

1 *Chambers v Fahy* [1931] IR 17 at 21 *per* O'Byrne J; see A. Keating *The Construction of Wills* (2nd ed, Clarus Press, Dublin, 2017); A. Keating, *Probate Motions and Actions Relating to Wills and Intestacies* (Round Hall, Dublin, 2017); A. Keating, *The Law of Wills* (2nd ed, Clarus Press, Dublin, 2018).

2 *Re Keyford* [1975] 1 All ER 604.

3 *Re Humphrey's Estate* [1916] 1 IR 21; *Re Sweeney* [1976–'77] ILRM 88.

4 See *Re Blackwood* [1953] NI 23; *Re Coulson* (1953) 87 ILTR 93.

22–02 While the words used by the testator are sufficient to create a trust, but where there remains some doubt regarding the property forming the subject matter of the trust, or the identity of the beneficiaries, a construction suit may become necessary to determine the issue.[5] In a construction suit involving wills, the court may apply principles and rules of construction, and may admit extrinsic evidence in an attempt to ascertain and give effect to the intention of the testator regarding the disposition of the trust property or the beneficiaries of the trust, and where such evidence assists in showing the intention of the testator. The principles of constructive interpretation formulated by Lowry LCJ (the Lowry Principles) in *Heron v Ulster Bank Ltd*[6] may be applied by the courts when ascertaining the intention of a testator in cases involving wills trusts. Section 90 of Succession Act 1965 (the "1965 Act") permits the courts to adduce extrinsic evidence "to show the intention of the testator and to assist in the construction of, or to explain any contradiction in a will." In *Rowe v Law*[7] and *O'Connell v Bank of Ireland*,[8] the Supreme Court, when undertaking an interpretative construction of s 90 of the 1965 Act, held that extrinsic evidence will only be admitted where it shows the testator's intention *and* assists the court in the construction of a will. Where a gift is capable of more than one interpretation, s 99 of the 1965 Act provides that "if the purport of a devise or legacy admits of more than one interpretation, then, in case of doubt, the interpretation according to which the devise or bequest will be operative will be preferred." Where words of limitation are legally required to be used in the creation of estates in will trusts, such formula of words have to be used, otherwise the trust may be deemed invalid.[9]

Principles of Constructive Interpretation

22–03 The words must sufficiently identify the property as the subject matter of the trust and the beneficiaries as objects of the trust, otherwise a construction suit may ensue for the purposes of ascertaining the intention of the testator by applying principles of constructive interpretation. The following principles of constructive interpretation may be applied by courts when asked to ascertain and give effect to the intention of a testator regarding the disposition of trust property or the identity of the beneficiaries in will trusts.

(i) The Intention of the Testator

22–04 When attempting to ascertain the testator's intention, the court will construe

---

[5] See *Curtin v O'Mahony* [1991] 2 IR 562 at 573; *Corrigan v Corrigan* [2007] IEHC 367; *Corrigan v Corrigan* [2016] IESC 56.

[6] [1974] NI 44 at 52–53; see also, *Howell v Howell* [1992] IR 290; A. Keating, *The Construction of Wills* (2nd ed, Clarus Press, Dublin, 2017).

[7] [1978] IR 55.

[8] [1998] 2 IR 596.

[9] See *Corrigan v Corrigan* [2007] IEHC 367.

the words used by him or her in his or her will.[10] If, having read the will as a whole, it becomes clear that a literal meaning would defeat the intention, the court may even go so far as "to do violence" to the language in order to give effect to the testator's intention.[11] In *Dunlop v Greer*,[12] Porter MR stated that the court "is competent not only to *fix* the sense of *ambiguous* words, but to *control* the sense even of *clear* words, and to *supply* the place of *express* words, in cases of difficulty and ambiguity". In *Curtin v O'Mahony*,[13] O'Flaherty J, approving of the approach adopted by Porter MR in *Greer v Dunlop*, went on to say that it was the first duty of a court in construing a will to give effect to the intention of the testator. He warned, however, that a judge:

> is to tread cautiously so as not to offend against the judicial inheritance which is that one is entitled to construe a will but not to make one. However, two injunctions are on collision course in this case: one is that a court is not entitled to make a will for a testator but on the other hand there is the requirement that effect should be given to the intention of the testator, if at all possible. If the will is given a literal meaning then the intention of the testator is clearly defeated and an absurd result is produced.[14]

(ii) The Lowry Principles

In *Heron v Ulster Bank Ltd*,[15] Lowry LCJ set down the following principles of construction: **22–05**

1. Read the immediate relevant portion of the will as a piece of English and decide, if possible, what it means.
2. Look at the other material parts of the will and see whether they tend to confirm the apparently plain meaning of the immediately relevant portion or whether they suggest the need for modification in order to make harmonious sense of the whole or, alternatively, whether an ambiguity in the immediately relevant portion can be resolved.
3. If ambiguity persists, have regard to the scheme of the will and consider what the testator was trying to do.
4. One at this stage must have resort to rules of construction, where applicable, and aids, such as the presumption of early vesting and the presumptions against intestacy and in favour of equality.
5. Then see whether any rule of law prevents a particular interpretation from being adopted.
6. Finally, and, I suggest, not until the disputed passage has been exhaustively studied, one may get help from the opinions of other courts and judges on similar words, rarely as binding precedents, since it has been well said that 'no will has a twin brother' (per Werner J in *Matter of King* 200 N.Y. 189, 192 (1910), but more often as examples (sometimes of the highest authority)

---

10 *Curtin v O'Mahony* [1991] 2 IR 562 at 573; see *Williams and O'Donnell v Shuel and Barham*, Unreported, High Court, Morris P, 6 May 1997; A. Keating, *The Construction of Wills* (2nd ed, Clarus Press, Dublin, 2017).

11 *Dunlop v Greer* [1899] 1 IR 324.

12 [1899] 1 IR 324.

13 [1991] 2 IR 562.

14 *Curtin v O'Mahony* [1991] 2 IR 562.

15 [1974] NI 44 at 52–53; see also *Howell v Howell* [1992] IR 290.

> of how judicial minds nurtured in the same discipline have interpreted words in similar contexts.

22–06 He also went on to make a distinction between a rule of law and a rule of construction.

> Any rule the application of which is independent of the intention of the testator, and one which may operate against or to defeat that intention, is generally known as a rule of law. Any rule adopted by the court for ascertaining or effectuating the intention of the testator as declared in the will, and dependent, for its application to any will, upon whether it is consonant with or contrary to the whole will, is generally called a rule of construction.

22–07 Thus, where words of limitation are required by law to be used in creating estates, and where incorrect words are used by the testator in doing so, the trust may fail whether or not it defeats the testator's intention.

(iii) The Presumption Against Intestacy

22–08 The court when attempting to uphold a will may also rely on the general presumption against intestacy, but in doing so, it cannot redraft the will. The court will lean against intestacy, and will attempt to save the devise, bequest or trust.

(iv) Extrinsic Evidence

22–09 Extrinsic evidence may also be adduced and admitted by s 90 of the 1965 Act "to show the intention of the testator and to assist in the construction of, or to explain any contradiction in, the will." In *Rowe v Law*,[16] Henchy J when interpreting s 90 of the 1965 Act stated that extrinsic evidence may be adduced if it met the double requirement of "(a) showing the intention of the testator *and* (b) assisting in the construction of, or explaining any contradiction in, a will."

(v) Section 99 of the 1965 Act

22–10 Section 99 of the 1965 Act provides that where a devise or bequest or trust is capable of more than one interpretation, the interpretation that renders the devise or bequest or trust operative will be the preferred interpretation. However, s 99 requires a devise, bequest or trust to be capable of more than one interpretation before the statutory principle becomes applicable. Where only one interpretation is possible as a result of the uncertainty of the gift, intestacy may ensue. Section 99 may be applied to irreconcilable trusts where they are capable of more than one interpretation, and in such cases, the section requires that the interpretation that renders such trusts operative

---

16 [1978] IR 55; see also *O'Connell v Bank of Ireland* [1998] 2 IR 596; *Corrigan v Corrigan* [2007] IEHC 367; *McGuinness v Sherry & Anor* [2008] IEHC 134; A. Keating, *The Construction of Wills* (2nd ed, Clarus Press, Dublin, 2017).

is to be preferred, especially where the alternative is intestacy. But as already stated, where a trust is capable only of a single interpretation, and it is one that leaves a trust void for uncertainty, then the trust will fall into residue, and where the residue is not disposed of, it will be distributed on partial intestacy. It may be said that the principle in s 99 is a principle of last resort and one that brings the court to the very limits of its powers to save a trust.

Words of Limitation

In *Heron v Ulster Bank Ltd*,[17] Lowry LCJ also made a distinction between a rule of law and a rule of construction. He stated that: **22–11**

> Any rule the application of which is independent of the intention of the testator, and one which may operate against or to defeat that intention, is generally known as a rule of law.

The words of limitation for the creation of interests in land must be complied with, and where a trust in a will creates such an interest but without using the correct words of limitation, the trust may fail as a result, no matter what the intention of the testator. In *Corrigan v Corrigan*,[18] the plaintiff as executor sought a construction of a provision in the deceased's will. The relevant provision stated as follows: **22–12**

> 1. I have 21 acres of land in Folio 13658 Co. Westmeath and I have been advised that said land or part thereof is rezoned for residential and/or industrial development. I direct my executors to hold the said lands upon the following trusts:
>
> (a) To allow my son Sean to hold and enjoy the profits of the land for his own benefit until there is acquisition of my lands for the purposes mentioned above. In such event the net proceeds of the sale of my land shall be divided equally amongst all my children and any section of the farm not so acquired shall become the absolute property of my son Sean.

At the time of the execution of the will the land referred to in the bequest was zoned for agricultural use only. Later, however, certain parts of the land were rezoned for use as a special district for business and enterprise development. **22–13**

McGovern J thought that the bequest only made sense in the light of the first part of the clause and seemed predicated on it. He said: **22–14**

> This can clearly be seen from the words '... until there is acquisition of my lands for the *purposes mentioned above*' (my highlights). On the face of it, it appears that the intention of the testator was that the first named defendant should hold and enjoy the profits of the lands until they were acquired for the development purposes which are stated to be residential and/or industrial. This would appear from the use of the words 'to *allow* my son Sean to hold and enjoy the profits of

[17] [1974] NI 44 at 52–53; see also *Howell v Howell* [1992] IR 290; A. Keating, *The Construction of Wills* (2nd ed, Clarus Press, Dublin, 2017).

[18] [2007] IEHC 367.

> the lands for his own benefit *until* …' (my highlights). In other words the testator expected the lands or part of them to be acquired for a value that would reflect the fact that they were zoned for residential and/or industrial development in that event the proceeds of sale would be divided equally among his children and the first named defendant would hold any part of the lands not so acquired.

22–15 It was clear from the evidence that the testator acted under a mistake of fact when he declared that "the said land or parts thereof is zoned for residential and/or industrial development." He went on to state that he "may well have been advised that that was the case but the advice was wrong and he was therefore acting under a mistake of fact."

22–16 He stated that when interpreting a will the court may have regard to s 90 of the 1965 Act. Section 90 provides that "extrinsic evidence shall be admissible to show the intention of the testator and to assist in the construction of, or to explain any contradiction in, a will." He went on to refer to *Rowe v Law*[19] and *O'Connell v Bank of Ireland*[20] where the Supreme Court held that s 90 must be strictly interpreted. In *Rowe v Law*, Henchy J stated: "I read s 90 as allowing extrinsic evidence to be received if it meets the double requirement of (a) showing the intention of the testator, and (b) assisting in the construction of, or explaining any contradiction in, a will." Henchy J further stated that:

> s.90 allows extrinsic evidence of the testator's intention to be used by a court of construction only where there is a legitimate dispute as to the meaning or effect of the language used in the will. In such a case … it allows the extrinsic evidence to be drawn on so as to give the unclear or contradictory words in the will a meaning which accords with the testator's intention as thus ascertained. The section does not empower the court to rewrite the will in whole or in part.

22–17 He found that, owing to the lack of clarity and ambiguity of clause 1 of the bequest, the extrinsic evidence found in the notes taken by the testator's solicitor on taking instructions for the drafting of the will was admissible.

22–18 By applying the Lowry principles of constructive interpretation, McGovern J had to decide whether the provision in clause 1 of the bequest was a declaration of the testator's belief, or whether it constituted a condition attaching to the bequest. He went on to hypothesise that if it was a condition, it had to be a condition subsequent. There was a presumption of early vesting and it was clear that, if the words at the beginning of the bequest constituted a condition, that the first-named defendant was to hold and enjoy the profits of the lands until such time as the condition was fulfilled, namely, the lands were acquired for the purposes of residential and/or industrial development. He referred to the authorities for the proposition that where a condition is attached to a bequest the court should approach the condition prima facie

[19] [1978] IR 55; A. Keating, *The Construction of Wills* (2nd ed, Clarus Press, Dublin, 2017).

[20] [1998] 2 IR 596.

as a condition subsequent unless its construction as a condition precedent was unavoidable.[21] He went on to say that:

> If a condition subsequent is found to be void the beneficiary takes the bequest freed from the condition. So in this case if the clause 1 of the bequest is a condition subsequent and is found to be void for uncertainty or incapable of taking effect, the first named defendant would take the bequest free from the condition. (See judgment of Laffoy J in *McGowan v Kelly* [2007] IEHC 228 and judgment of Gavan Duffy P. in *Burke and O'Reilly v Burke and Quayle* [1951] I.R. 216 at 223).

However, McGovern J, in the concluding part of his judgment, found that the bequest to the first named defendant in clause 1 did not contain a condition. **22–19**

As regards the effect of a factual error in the belief of the testator, he found that a gift made upon a mistake of fact cannot be cut down or altered to suit the supposed facts. Correction of mistakes by the court can only arise where the words used do not accurately reflect what the testator intended. A court can only supply or omit words in exceptional circumstances and with the greatest caution. If the gift to the first-named defendant was made by a mistake of fact, then the entire bequest would have failed and the bequest would have fallen into the residuary estate by virtue of s 91 of the 1965 Act. **22–20**

The plaintiff and the first-named defendant both raised the possibility that the estate intended to be created by the bequest to the first-named defendant could be regarded as a conditional or determinable freehold. It was argued that where the word "until" was used in the grant of a fee simple, the general rule of construction prescribed that it might be construed as giving rise to a determinable fee simple.[22] McGovern J was of the view that: "If it is a determinable fee simple then it gives rise to a 'possibility of a reverter' in the grant or settlor, in this case, the estate of the deceased." The rule against perpetuities also did not apply to the possibility of a reverter in such a situation.[23] As a result, if the bequest to the first-named defendant was a determinable fee simple, then it followed that if the determining events were void for uncertainty, or otherwise, the entire limitation failed. He turned to Lyall's *Land Law in Ireland*, for the statement: **22–21**

> At common law, if the determining event occurs, the land reverts automatically to the grantor. The grantor has the possibility of a reverter. Indeed, this is the only interest that can exist after the determinable fee simple at common law. At common law the grantor cannot, in the same deed create a determinable fee and then provide that if the event occurs, the land is to pass to someone else. The grantor cannot create a gift over to a third party after a determinable fee.[24]

---

21 See *McGowan v Kelly* [2007] IEHC 228; *Mackessy v Fitzgibbon* [1993] 1 IR 520 and *Re Porter* [1995] NI 157; A. Keating, *The Construction of Wills* (2nd ed, Clarus Press, Dublin, 2017).

22 See Lyall, *Land Law in Ireland* (2nd ed, Round Hall, Dublin, 2000), p 179; see also A. Lyall with A. Power, *Land Law in Ireland* (3rd edn, Round Hall, Dublin, 2010), pp 201–202.

23 See *Attorney General v Cummins* [1906] IR 406.

24 Lyall, *Land Law in Ireland* (2nd ed, Round Hall, Dublin, 2000), p 180.

22–22 In the concluding parts of his judgment McGovern J found that the use of the words "allow" and "until" caused him to take the view that the bequest to the first-named defendant was in the nature of a determinable fee simple. He was satisfied that at common law:

> the testator cannot, in his will, create a determinable fee simple to the first named defendant and then provide that, in the event that a determining event occurs, the land is to pass to someone else. A testator cannot create a gift over to third parties after a determinable fee. On that ground, the entire limitation and entire bequest fails.

22–23 He was also satisfied that the determining event specified in clause 1 of the bequest was void for uncertainty and it followed therefore that, on this basis, the entire limitation failed. It followed that the subject matter of the bequest in clause 1 fell into the residuary estate of the testator.

Instituting Construction Suits Involving Will Trusts

22–24 A construction suit involving a will trust may be instituted by the issuing of a special summons. A beneficiary, personal representative or trustee may commence a construction suit for the purposes of determining his or her rights or interests arising out of a will trust.[25] Under Ord 3, r 7 of the Rules of Superior Courts (the "RSC") a special summons may be used for the determination of any question of construction arising under any deed, will, or other written instrument, and a declaration of the rights of the persons interested. The personal representatives or trustees may institute proceedings by way of special summons for the determination of a question of construction arising out of the will trust, or for a declaration of the rights of the persons interested in the estate.[26] Order 15, r.8 of the RSC provides that:

> Trustees, executors, and administrators may sue and be sued on behalf of or as representing the property or estate of which they are trustees or representatives, without joining any of the persons beneficially interested in the trust or estate, and shall be considered as representing such persons ... .

22–25 Order 54, r.1 of the RSC provides that:

> [T]he executors or administrators of a deceased person or any of them, and the trustees under any deed or instrument or any of them, and any person claiming to be interested in the relief sought as creditor, devisee, legatee, next-of-kin, or heir-at-law of a deceased person, *cestui que trust* under the trust of any deed or instrument ... may take out, a special summons for relief of the nature or kind specified in Order 3(1) to (7) inclusive.[27]

22–26 The persons to be named as defendants in any summons under Ord 54, r 1

[25] Ord 3, r 7; Ord 54, rr 1 and 2.
[26] Ord 3, r 7.
[27] See *In the Estate of Stanley* [2016] IEHC 8; *O'Byrne v Davoren* [1994] 3 IR 373.

"where the summons is taken out by executors, administrators or trustees or any of them" may include a creditor, devisee, legatee, next-of-kin or *cestui que trust*.[28] Under Ord 54, r 2(2) where the summons is taken out "by any person other than executors, administrators or trustees: the said executors, administrators or trustees" may be named as defendants. The court may also direct other persons to be served with the special summons as it thinks fit.[29] Where, however, there is some difficulty in ascertaining a beneficiary, or class of beneficiaries, or next-of-kin, the court may, in order to save expense or for some other reason, determine the question of construction before such beneficiaries or next-of-kin who have been ascertained by means of inquiry or otherwise, and for this purpose, it may appoint one or more persons to represent the beneficiaries or next-of-kin.[30] The court may also require the application to be supported by such evidence as it thinks fit, and it may not determine the question of construction if it is of the opinion that the procedure by special summons in the matter is inappropriate.[31] It may also be added that, as an administrator derives his title from a grant of letters of administration, he or she will not be entitled to institute proceedings on behalf of the estate, or indeed, defend proceedings, before a grant of administration is issued to him either by the Probate Office or a District Probate Registry.[32]

Order 4, r 4 of the RSC provides that the indorsement of claim on a special summons shall be entitled SPECIAL INDORSEMENT OF CLAIM, and shall state specifically and with all necessary particulars the relief claimed and the grounds thereof. The indorsement of claim on a summary summons or a special summons shall be in such one of the forms in Appendix B, Pt III, as shall be applicable to the case, or, if none be found applicable, then such other similarly concise form as the nature of the case may require. Precedent No 2 in Appendix B, Pt III, s 2 of the RSC, provides as follows: **22–27**

> The plaintiff's claim is as the executor and trustee of the said will mentioned in the title hereof of XY, deceased, for the determination of the following questions arising (in the administration of the estate, and) upon the construction of the said will of the said testator, and in the events that have happened, viz (Set out questions in form which will enable them as far as possible to be answered "yes" or "no") and that the cost of the proceedings may be provided for.

Order 9, r 3 of the RSC provides that personal service shall be effected by delivering a copy of the summons to the defendant in person, and showing him the original or duplicate original, and Ord 9, r 12 provides that the person serving a summons shall, within three days at most after service, indorse on the summons the day and date of the service thereof; and every affidavit of service of such summons shall mention the date on which such indorsement **22–28**

---

28 Ord 54, r 2; see *Kilroy v Parker* [1966] IR 309.

29 Ord 83, r 2.

30 Ord 15, r 22(1) and (2).

31 Ord 83, rr 3 and 4.

32 *Ingall v Moran* [1944] 1 KB 160; *Creed v Creed* [1913] 1 IR 48; *Gaffney v Faughnan* [2006] 1 ILRM 481.

was made. Order 10, r 1 of the RSC provides that if it be made to appear to the court that the plaintiff is from any cause unable to effect prompt personal service, or such other service as is prescribed by the RSC, the court may make an order for substituted or other service, or for the substitution for service of notice by advertisement or otherwise. Order 12, r 2(2) provides that a defendant in proceedings commenced by special summons may enter an appearance thereto at any time, but shall not, without the leave of the court, be entitled to be heard in such proceedings unless he has entered an appearance. Order 38, r 1 provides that every special summons shall be returnable for such day as the Master shall fix, which, except in such cases where the parties consent to an earlier date, or where no service is required, shall be not less than seven days from the date of issue, and shall, where necessary, be served on the parties concerned at least four days before the return day. An affidavit verifying the claim indorsed on the summons shall be filed in the Central Office and notice of such filing shall be given to the parties concerned. Order 38, r 2 provides that the court may direct such other persons to be served with the summons as it may think fit. Order 38, r 3 provides that save in so far as the court shall otherwise order, proceedings commenced by special summons shall be heard on affidavit: provided that any party desiring to cross-examine a deponent who has made an affidavit filed on behalf of the opposite party may serve upon the party by whom such affidavit has been filed a notice in writing requiring the production of the deponent for cross-examination, and unless such deponent is produced accordingly his affidavit shall not be used as evidence unless by the special leave of the court.

22–29 Special Summons

SPECIAL SUMMONS
THE HIGH COURT

In the matter of 20... No....

Between A. B., Plaintiff,

and C.D., Defendant.
(or if not *inter partes*)
On the application of A.B.
To
of ... in the County of ...
This special summons is to require you to attend before the Master at the Four Courts, Dublin, on the ... day of ... 20... at ... o'clock in the forenoon at the hearing of this summons issued on the ... day of ... 20..., and if you do not attend in person or by solicitor at the time and place aforesaid, such order will be made, and proceedings taken as the Court may think just and expedient; and TAKE NOTICE that if you wish to attend and to be heard, you should first enter an appearance.
BY ORDER,
Chief Justice of Ireland,
the ... day of ... two

thousand and …
N.B.—This summons is required to be served not less than four days before the return day mentioned therein (exclusive of the day of service).

SPECIAL INDORSEMENT OF CLAIM

The plaintiff's claim is
(Signed)
Schedule of affidavit or affidavits intended to be used by the plaintiff (or applicant) on the hearing of the summons.
This summons was issued by the plaintiff (or applicant) who resides at (state address accurately) and is …
or,
This summons was issued by …, whose registered place of business is …,
solicitor for the plaintiff, who resides at …
and is ….
This summons was served by me at …
on the defendant on the … day of
… 20…
Indorsed the … day of … 20…
(Signed)
(Address)

SAMPLE SPECIAL INDORSEMENT OF CLAIM

For instance: The plaintiff's claim is as one of the next-of-kin of the above named X.Y., deceased, who died on [date] intestate for an order for the administration of the estate of the said deceased with all necessary and proper accounts, inquiries and directions.
(Indorsement of character in which defendant is sued.)
(Signed)

Or: The plaintiff's claim is as the executor and trustee of the said will mentioned in the title hereof of X. Y., deceased, for the determination of the following questions arising (in the administration of the estate, and) upon the construction of the said will of the said testator, and in the events that have happened, viz.:-(Set out questions in form which will enable them as far as possible to be answered "yes" or "no") and that the cost of the proceedings may be provided for.

The defendant is sued as [state nature of his interest, or capacity in which he is sued].
(Signed)

DEFENCE

Heading of defence
THE HIGH COURT
… 20 … No. …

Between A.B.,	Plaintiff,
and C.D.,	Defendant.

Defence.
Delivered on the … day of … , 20…, by G.H. of [registered place of business], solicitor for the defendant.

REPLY

Heading of reply
THE HIGH COURT
… 20… No. …
Between A.B., Plaintiff,
and C.D., Defendant.
REPLY.
Delivered on the … day of … 20… by E.F., of (registered place of business), solicitor for the plaintiff.
1. The plaintiff joins issue with the defendant on his defence save and in so far as the same contains admissions.
2. [as may be necessary].

NOTICE OF COUNTERCLAIM

[Title of action]

To the within-named X.Y.
Take notice that if you do not appear to the within counter-claim of the within-named C.D. within ten days from the service of this defence and counter-claim upon you, you will be liable to have judgment given against you in your absence. Appearance is to be entered [&c., as in Form No. 1].

NOTICE OF TRIAL (ORDINARY FORM)

[Title of action].

Take notice of trial of this [or of the issues in this ordered to be tried] [or as the case may be] for the … day of … 20… at …
Dated
(Signed)

22–30 In *Daly v Murphy*,[33] the proceedings commenced by way of a special summons issued on the 15th day of December 2015 and related to the estate of Joseph Daly deceased late of Thomond Lodge Nursing Home, Ballymahon in the County of Longford.

22–31 The deceased made a number of pecuniary legacies including *inter alia* a bequest in the sum of €15,000.00 to the plaintiff, a sum of €15,000.00 to Vera Daly, wife of the plaintiff, and sums of €10,000.00 each to Martin Daly and Ann Daly, the son and daughter respectively of the plaintiff and also made a bequest of €100,000.00 to the Administrator for the time being of

[33] [2017] IEHC 650.

the General Hospital in Mullingar and the deceased directed that the said sum was to be used for the benefit of patient facilities in the said Hospital.

The deceased concluded his will with a final bequest in the following terms: **22–32**

> I Give, Devise and Bequeath all the rest residue and remainder of my Estate of every nature and description and where so ever situate onto my Executor to apply same for such purposes as my executor in his absolute discretion shall think fit.

The net estate returned for probate purposes was in the sum of €922,941.00 **22–33** and the pecuniary legacies as made by the deceased totalled €257,000.00 so on the probate figures the residue of the deceased's estate is a sum in the region of €650,000.00.

In the prayer of the special summons the plaintiff seeks a determination as **22–34** regards the effect of the clause relating to the rest residue and remainder of the deceased's estate in effect as to whether or not the residue is to be distributed in accordance with the residual clause or does the residue fall to be distributed by way of intestacy.

The plaintiff claims a determination pursuant to Ord 3, r 2 of the Rules of **22–35** the Superior Courts of the following questions:

- (a) Does the residuary clause contained in the last will of the deceased named in the title thereof confer an absolute gift on the defendant?
- (b) Does the said residuary clause create a valid trust?
- (c) If the answer to (b) is in the affirmative what are the terms of the said trust?
- (d) Does the residuary gift fail?
- (e) Does the residue of the estate fall to be distributed on a resulting partial intestacy?

The plaintiff requests answers to the aforesaid questions in the following **22–36** terms:

- (a) No
- (b) No
- (c) No
- (d) Yes
- (e) Yes

and further if necessary claims an order pursuant to Ord 3, r 4 directing the **22–37** defendant to distribute to the plaintiff the share of the estate of the deceased to which he is by law entitled.

The plaintiff requests answers to the aforesaid questions in the following **22–38** terms:

- (a) No
- (b) No
- (c) No
- (d) Yes

(e) Yes

22–39 Further if necessary claims an order pursuant to Ord 3, r 4 directing the defendant to distribute to the plaintiff the share of the estate of the deceased to which he is by law entitled.

22–40 In that case, Gilligan J, having referred to s 90 of the Succession Act 1965, *Rowe v Law*,[34] *O'Connell v Bank of Ireland*,[35] *Black v Ann Sullivan Centre Ltd*,[36] *In the Estate of Stanley*,[37] *Howell v Howell* [38] and *O'Donohue v O'Donohue*,[39] stated that:

> 41. Accordingly, it follows that I answer the questions posed as follows:
> (a) No.
> (b) Yes.
> (c) Residuary to be distributed for charitable purposes.
> (d) No.
> (e) No."
>
> Thus the plaintiff's request for an order pursuant to O. 3 (4) of the Rules of the Superior Courts directing the defendant to distribute to the plaintiff a fuller share in the estate of the deceased is to be refused.

---

[34] [1978] 1 IR 55; see A. Keating, *The Construction of Wills* (2nd ed, Clarus Press, Dublin, 2017).
[35] [1998] 2 IR 596.
[36] [2016] IEHC 695.
[37] [2016] IEHC 8.
[38] [1992] 1 IR 290 at 292–293.
[39] [2011] IEHC 511.

CHAPTER 23

ACTIONS FOR BREACH OF TRUST AND ADMINISTRATION ACTIONS

INTRODUCTION

The primary guiding rule is that trustees must act honestly and in good faith, and comply with the terms of the will trust, and if they fail to do so, they may be liable for breach of trust.[1] A breach of trust may take the form of a wilful default, and this arises "only where that default can be truly characterised as a conscious breach of duty, the sense of conscious awareness that is dismissed."[2] Wilful default could not, however, encompass a situation where trustees, having considered the matter, opted not to pursue a particular course of action.[3] Decisions of trustees that are guided by an "improper motive" will always be a breach of trust.[4] However, a claim of breach of trust may be defeated where it is shown that the breach was caused or the issues relating to it were requested by the beneficiary, or that the beneficiary agreed or acquiesced in the breach. Actions relating to breach of trust may be commenced by the issuing of a plenary summons.[5] **23–01**

The Rules of the Superior Courts (Chancery and Non-Jury Actions and Other Designated Proceedings: Pre-Trial Procedures) (SI No 255 of 2016) amended Ords 22 and 63 of the Rules of the Superior Courts 1986 (the "RSC"), and the RSC as amended may be cited as the RSC 1986 to 2016. Order 63 of the RSC is amended by the insertion of a new Ord 63C and provides at r 2(1) that it applies to any proceedings the trial of which would, on service of a notice of trial (if required), be listed for trial in the Chancery List or the Non-Jury List of the Court. Order 99, r 1 of the RSC provides that the costs of, and incidental to, every proceeding in the Superior Courts shall be at the discretion of those courts. **23–02**

A beneficiary who alleges that the express trustees have committed a breach **23–03**

---

1 See *Greene v Coady* [2014] IEHC 38; See A. Keating, *Probate Motions and Actions Relating to Wills and Intestacies* (Round Hall, Dublin, 2017); A. Keating, *The Law of Wills* (2nd ed, Clarus Press, Dublin, 2018); A. Keating, *Succession Law in Ireland* (Clarus Press, Dublin, 2015); A. Keating, *Keating on Probate* (5th ed, Round Hall, Dublin, 2015); A. Keating, *Succession Law in Ireland: Principles, Cases and Commentary* (Clarus Press, Dublin, 2016).

2 See *Greene v Coady* [2014] IEHC 38.

3 *Greene v Coady* [2014] IEHC 38.

4 *Greene v Coady* [2014] IEHC 38.

5 Rules of the Superior Courts, Ord 1, r 2; Ord 5 r 1.

of trust must commence an action for the breach within a period of six years, unless the time is extended due to the presence of a vitiating element like fraud.[6] Where, however, there is a fraudulent breach of trust, the limitation period of six years may be extended.[7] Action for breach of trust may not be maintainable because of the beneficiary's *laches*.

23–04 An administration action may be instituted by beneficiaries issuing a special summons. Order 54, r 1 of the RSC provides that:

> The executors or administrators of a deceased person or any of them, and the trustees under any deed or instrument or any of them, and any person claiming to be interested in the relief sought as creditor, devisee, legatee, next-of-kin, or heir-at-law of a deceased person, or as *cestui que trust* under the trust of any deed or instrument, or as claiming by assignment or otherwise under any such creditor or other person as aforesaid, may take out a special summons for relief of the nature or kind specified in Order 3 (1) to (7) inclusive.

23–05 On the other hand, trustees may sue or be sued on behalf of the estate without joining any of the parties beneficially interested in the estate, unless otherwise ordered by the court.[8] Order 15, r 8 of the RSC provides that:

> Trustees, executors, and administrators may sue and be sued on behalf of or as representing the property or estate of which they are trustees or representatives, without joining any of the persons beneficially interested in the trust or estate, and shall be considered as representing such persons; but the court may, at any stage of the proceedings, order any of such persons to be made parties either in addition to or in lieu of the previously existing parties. This rule shall apply to trustees, executors and administrators sued in proceedings to enforce a security by sale or otherwise.

23–06 When referring to issues of costs in administration actions, Herbert J in *O'Connor v Markey*,[9] affirmed that the authorities referred to in *Vella v Morelli*[10] dealt with costs relating to probate issues regarding the due execution or revocation of wills and the testamentary capacity of a testator only, and stated that by contrast, in relation to the question of costs in administration action, "the instant application bore all the hallmarks of contentious litigation between beneficiaries which did not in any way touch upon the capacity of the testator or the state in which he left his testamentary papers", and so the issue of costs was not governed by *Vella v Morelli*.

23–07 In relation to the limitation of actions, s 126(1) of the Succession Act 1965

---

6 Statute of Limitations 1957, s 43(1).

7 Statute of Limitations 1957, s 44.

8 Ord 15, r 8; see A. Keating, *Probate Motions and Actions Relating to Wills and Intestacies* (Round Hall, Dublin, 2017); A. Keating, *The Law of Wills* (2nd ed, Clarus Press, Dublin, 2018); A. Keating, *Succession Law in Ireland* (Clarus Press, Dublin, 2015); A. Keating, *Keating on Probate* (5th ed, Round Hall, Dublin, 2015); A. Keating, *Succession Law in Ireland: Principles, Cases and Commentary* (Clarus Press, Dublin, 2016).

9 [2007] 2 IR 194.

10 [1968] IR 11; see A. Keating "Costs in Probate Actions" (2014) 19(4) CPLJ 94.

(the "1965 Act") provides that no action may be brought by a person entitled to receive a share or interest in the estate after the expiration of six years from the date on which the right to receive a share or interest accrued. However, in relation to actions brought by personal representatives on behalf of the estate, it appears the time limit for bringing such actions are governed by the Statute of Limitations 1957 (the "1957 Act").[11]

Actions for Breach of Trust

(i) Grounds

The following are grounds for actions for breach of trust: **23–08**

(i) Decisions by trustees "which are properly to be characterised as being ones that no reasonable of trustees could have made".[12]
(ii) Decisions that are guided by improper motives.[13]
(iii) Where the trustees' decision "is identified as one which no reasonable body of trustees properly informed and considering the decision could have made."[14]
(iv) The court will not to interfere with decisions by trustees "save for decisions which are plainly unreasonable".[15]
(v) Where the breach of trust amounts to wilful default and arises "only where that default can be truly characterised as a conscious breach of duty".[16]

(ii) Relative Considerations **23–09**

(i) A trustee is not liable for breach of trust after retirement unless the breach occurred during the time he or she acted as trustee.
(ii) If a trustee makes an unauthorised investment, he or she will have to replace the fund invested.
(iii) Any profit made on an unauthorised investment must be returned to the trust estate.
(iv) Where more than one of the trustees act in breach of trust, they may be liable for same jointly or severally.

(iii) Primary Defences to Claims of Breach of Trust by Beneficiaries **23–10**

(i) The breach was caused or requested by the beneficiary.
(ii) The beneficiary agreed or acquiesced in the breach.

Instituting Actions for Breach of Trust

Actions for breach of trust may be instituted by the issuing of a plenary summons out of the Central Office.[17] Under Ord 5, r 13 of the RSC, the **23–11**

---

[11] See *Drohan v Drohan* [1984] ILRM 179.
[12] See *Greene v Coady* [2014] IEHC 38.
[13] *Greene v Coady* [2014] IEHC 38.
[14] *Greene v Coady* [2014] IEHC 38.
[15] *Greene v Coady* [2014] IEHC 38.
[16] *Greene v Coady* [2014] IEHC 38.
[17] Ord 1, r 2; Ord 5 r 1.

issue of a summons in proceedings for breach of trust must be preceded by the filing of an affidavit made by the plaintiff or one of the plaintiffs in verification of the indorsement on the summons. The indorsement in the summons must show whether the plaintiff claims as creditor, executor, administrator, residuary legatee, legatee, next-of-kin, heir-at-law, devisee, or in any other capacity.[18] Order 9, r 3 of the RSC provides that personal service shall be effected by delivering a copy of the summons to the defendant in person, and showing him the original or duplicate original, and Ord 9, r 12 provides that the person serving a summons shall, within three days at most after service, indorse on the summons the day and date of the service thereof; and every affidavit of service of such summons shall mention the date on which such indorsement was made. Order 10, r 1 of the RSC provides that if it be made to appear to the court that the plaintiff is from any cause unable to effect prompt personal service, or such other service as is prescribed by the RSC, the court may make an order for substituted or other service, or for the substitution for service of notice by advertisement or otherwise. The defendant must deliver his defence and counterclaim within 28 days from the date of delivery of the statement of claim.[19] Where a counterclaim is filed, a reply to it will be governed by the same rules applicable to a defence.[20] Order 15, r 13 of the RSC also provides that the court may, at any stage of the proceedings,

> either upon or without the application of either party, and on such terms as may appear to the court to be just, order that the names of any parties improperly joined, whether as plaintiffs or as defendants, be struck out and that the names of any parties, whether as plaintiffs or defendants, who ought to have been joined, or whose presence before the court may be necessary in order to enable the court effectually and completely adjudicate upon and settle all the questions involved in the cause or matter, be added.

23–12 Plenary Summons

PLENARY SUMMONS.
THE HIGH COURT

… 20… No. …
Between A. B., Plaintiff,
and C.D., Defendant.

To the defendant …
of … in the County of …
This plenary summons is to require that within eight days after the service thereof upon you (exclusive of the day of such service) you in person or by solicitor do enter an appearance in the Central Office, Four Courts, Dublin, in the above action; and TAKE NOTICE that, in default of your so doing, the plaintiff may proceed therein, and judgment may be given in your absence.

---

18 Ord 4, r 10.
19 Ord 21, r 1(b).
20 Ord 23, r 5.

BY ORDER,
Chief Justice of Ireland,
the … day of two thousand and eighteen

N.B.—This summons is to be served within twelve calendar months from the date hereof, and, if renewed within six calendar months from the date of the last renewal, including the day of such date, and not afterwards.

The defendant may appear hereto by entering an appearance either personally or by solicitor at the Central Office, Four Courts, Dublin.

GENERAL INDORSEMENT OF CLAIM

The plaintiff's claim is …

(Signed)

This summons was issued by the plaintiff who resides at
[state address accurately] and
is, and whose address for
service is …
or,
This summons was issued by …, whose registered place of
business is …,
solicitor for the plaintiff, who resides at …
and is ….
This summons was served by me at …
on the defendant …
on the … day of … 20…
Indorsed the … day of … 20…
[Signed]
[Address]

INDORSEMENT OF CHARACTER OF PARTIES

For instance: The plaintiff's claim is as executor and trustee of C.D., deceased, for, &c.

MEMORANDUM OF APPEARANCE IN GENERAL

THE HIGH COURT

… 20… No. …
Between A.B., Plaintiff,
and C.D., Defendant.

Enter an appearance for C.D., the defendant in this action. Dated …
(Signed)
E.F.,
solicitor for the defendant.
The registered place of business of E.F. is …

[or C.D., the defendant in person.]
The place of residence of C.D. is ...
His address for service is ....
To the Registrar of the Central Office.
Take notice, that I have this day entered an appearance at the Central Office, Four Courts, Dublin,
for to the originating summons in this action.
[If statement of claim is required, add] The said ...
requires delivery of a statement of claim

Dated

(Signed)

To

(Signed)

STATEMENT OF CLAIM

Heading of Statement of Claim

THE HIGH COURT

... 20	No. ...
Between A.B.,	Plaintiff,
and C.D.,	Defendant.

Statement of claim
Delivered on the ... day of ... , 20... ,by E.F., of (registered place of business), solicitor for the plaintiff [or as the case may be].

DEFENCE

Heading of defence

THE HIGH COURT
... 20 ... No. ...

Between A.B.,	Plaintiff,
and C.D.,	Defendant.

Defence.
Delivered on the ... day of ... , 20..., by G.H. of (registered place of business), solicitor for the defendant.

REPLY

Heading of reply

THE HIGH COURT.
... 20 No. ...

Between A.B.,	Plaintiff,
and C.D.,	Defendant.

REPLY.
Delivered on the day of by E.F., of [registered place of business], solicitor for the plaintiff.

1. The plaintiff joins issue with the defendant on his defence save and in so far as the same contains admissions.
2. [as may be necessary].

NOTICE OF COUNTERCLAIM

[Title of action]

To the within-named X.Y.
Take notice that if you do not appear to the within counter-claim of the within-named C.D. within ten days from the service of this defence and counter-claim upon you, you will be liable to have judgment given against you in your absence. Appearance is to be entered [&c., as in Form No. 1].

NOTICE OF TRIAL (ORDINARY FORM)

[Title of action]

Take notice of trial of this [or of the issues in this ordered to be tried] [or as the case may be] for the day of … at …
Dated

(Signed)

Pre-Trial Procedures and Conduct of Trials

The Rules of the Superior Courts (Chancery and Non-Jury Actions and Other Designated Proceedings: Pre-Trial Procedures) (SI No 255 of 2016) amended Ords 22 and 63 of the Rules of the Superior Courts 1986 (the "RSC"), and the RSC as amended may be cited as the RSC 1986 to 2016. Order 22 of the RSC which deals with payments into and out of court and tenders was amended by SI No 255 of 2016 by the substitution of a new Ord 22, r 1(1). Order 63 of the RSC is amended by the insertion of a new Ord 63C and provides at r 2(1) that it applies to: **23–13**

(a) any proceedings the trial of which would, on service of a notice of trial (if required), be listed for trial in the Chancery List or the Non-Jury List of the Court;
(b) any other proceedings (not including proceedings admitted to the Commercial List under Order 63A, any proceedings required to be heard in the Competition List under Order 63B, personal injuries actions and jury actions) which the President of the High Court has for the time being designated in accordance with sub-rule (2) as proceedings to which this Order shall apply,

and a reference in this Order to "proceedings" shall be construed accordingly.
(2) Subject to sub-rule (3), the President of the High Court may from time to time designate any category of proceedings identified in such designation, or any proceedings having or involving any characteristics identified in such designation, as proceedings to which this Order applies.

23–14 At Ord 63C, r 3(1) it is provided that:

> The President of the High Court may, for the purposes of this Order, from time to time assign a Judge to be the Judge in charge of the List for any category of proceedings mentioned in, or designated in accordance with, rule 2, and any such assignment shall be published in the Legal Diary, provided that where the appropriate List Judge assigned in accordance with this rule is for any reason unavailable, another Judge may act in the place of the assigned List Judge.

23–15 In relation to pre-trial preparation, Ord 63C, r 4 provides that:

> A Judge may, at any time and from time to time, of that Judge's own motion and having heard the parties, or on the application of a party by motion on notice to the other party or parties, give such directions and make such orders, including the fixing of time limits, for the conduct of proceedings, as appears convenient for the determination of the proceedings in a manner which is just, expeditious and likely to minimise the costs of those proceedings.

23–16 The List Judge may make case management order under Ord 63C, r 6(1) and (2) in the following circumstances:

> (1) A List Judge may—
> (a) of that Judge's own motion and after hearing the parties in relevant proceedings,
> or
> (b) on the application of a party by motion on notice to the other party or parties at any time prior to the trial of the proceedings,
>
> where satisfied that the proceedings should, by virtue of their complexity, the number of issues or parties, the volume of evidence, or for other special reason, be subject to case management, make a case management order.
>
> (2) Where a case management order has been made, the List Judge shall fix a date for a case management conference, and may give any further directions for the completion prior to such conference of such, if any, steps in the proceedings (including the preparation of a case booklet in accordance with sub-rules (9) and (10)) as the List Judge considers appropriate.

23–17 In relation to pre-trial conferences, rr 9(1) and (2) provide that:

> (1) Where no case management order has been made in proceedings, the proceedings shall, on being set down for trial, be listed by the Registrar before the List Judge, or such Judge as the List Judge with the approval of the President of the High Court may nominate, for a pre-trial conference.
>
> (2) Where a case management order has been made in proceedings, the Judge chairing the case management conference shall fix a date for a pre-trial conference once all orders made or directions given in the course of the case management conference have been complied with.

23–18 Where no case management order is made by the judge, a pre-trial conference may take place under Ord 63C, r 9(1) as follows:

> (1) Where no case management order has been made in proceedings, the proceedings shall, on being set down for trial, be listed by the Registrar before the List Judge, or such Judge as the List Judge with the approval of the President of the High Court may nominate, for a pre-trial conference.

Under Ord 63C, rr 18 and 19: **23–19**

> 18. The costs of the hearing of any application for directions or orders in accordance with rule 4 shall, unless the Judge before whom that hearing takes place otherwise orders, be deemed to be costs in the cause.
>
> 19. The appropriate List Judge may prescribe requirements as to the form and content of bills of costs to be prepared in respect of relevant proceedings which have been made the subject of a case management order. Where the List Judge has not done so, such bills of costs shall be prepared in the manner prescribed by Order 99, rule 29.

Under Ord 63C, r 22(1): **23–20**

> (1) Documents required under or in accordance with this Order to be served, exchanged or inspected in proceedings (including any affidavit of discovery and copies of the documents (not including documents over which privilege is claimed) in any schedule thereto) may, where the President of the High Court by practice direction made in accordance with Order 63A, rule 31 (which practice direction may extend to proceedings to which this Order applies) permits, and on such terms and conditions and subject to such exceptions as the President of the High Court may by such practice direction specify, be served or exchanged, as the case may be, electronically.

The Rules of the Superior Courts (Conduct of Trials) 2015 (SI No 254 of 2016) which deals with the conduct of trials amended Ords 20, 21, 31, 36 and 39 of the Rules of the Superior Courts 1986 (the "RSC"), and the RSC as amended may be cited as the RSC 1986 to 2016. **23–21**

Costs in Actions for Breach of Trust

Order 99, r 1 of the Rules of the Superior Courts 1986 (the "1986 RSC") provides that the costs of, and incidental to, every proceeding in the Superior Courts shall be at the discretion of those courts. The Rules of the Superior Courts (Costs) 2008 (SI No 12 of 2008) (the "2008 RSC") inserts r 1A(1) immediately following r 1 of Ord 99 of the 1986 RSC. Rule 1A(1) provides that, notwithstanding r 1(3) and r 1(4): **23–22**

> (a) The Supreme Court, in considering the awarding of the costs of any appeal or any application in respect of an appeal, may, where it considers it just, have regard to the terms of any offer in writing sent by any party to any other party or parties offering to satisfy the whole or part of that other party's (or those other parties') claim or counterclaim the subject of the appeal, or application.
>
> (b) The High Court, in considering the awarding of the costs of any action (other than an action in respect of a claim or counterclaim concerning which a lodgment or tender offer in lieu of lodgment may be made in accordance with Order 22) or any application in such an action, may, where it considers it just, have regard to the terms of any offer in writing sent by any party to any other party or parties offering to satisfy the whole or part of that other party's (or those other parties') claim, counterclaim or application.

Rule 1A(2) of the 1986 RSC provides that "an offer in writing" includes any **23–23** offer made without prejudice save as to the issue of costs. Order 99, r 1(2) provides that no party will be entitled to recover any costs of or incidental to any proceeding from any other party to such proceeding, except under an order or as provided by the Rules of the Superior Courts. The 2008 RSC amended Ord 99, r 1(3) of the 1986 RSC by providing that: "Subject to sub-rule (4A), the costs of an action, question or issue tried by a jury shall follow the event unless the court, for special cause, to be mentioned in the order, shall otherwise direct." The 2008 RSC also amended Ord 99, r 1(4) of the 1986 RSC by providing that: "Subject to sub-rule (4A), the costs of every issue of fact or law raised upon a claim or counterclaim shall, unless otherwise ordered, follow the event." Order 99, r 1(4A) of the 1986 RSC, as a result of the amendment of the 1986 RSC by the 2008 RSC, now provides that: "The High Court or the Supreme Court, upon determining any interlocutory application, shall make an award of costs save where it is not possible justly to adjudicate upon liability for costs on the basis of the interlocutory application." Order 99, r 1(5) provides that where in any proceeding in the High Court or Supreme Court the costs of any party are ordered to be paid by another party, or by a fund or estate, those costs shall, if the High Court or the Supreme Court respectively so directs, include, in addition to the costs allowed on taxation as between party and party, all or any other costs, charge and expenses reasonably incurred for the purposes of the proceedings. The principles regarding costs may also be garnered and derived from former decisions of the courts. Such principles may also be reformulated by the courts.

The Limitation of Actions and *Laches*

23–24 A beneficiary who alleges that the express trustees have committed a breach of trust must commence an action for the breach within a period of six years, unless the time is extended due to the presence of a vitiating element like fraud.[21] While a claim against an express trustee for breach of trust will be statute-barred after six years from the date of breach under s 43(1) of the Statute of Limitations 1957, it will not be so barred where the breach

> was founded on any fraud or fraudulent breach of trust to which the trustee was party or privy, or the claim to recover trust property or the proceeds thereof still retained by the trustee or previously received by the trustee and converted to his own use.[22]

23–25 The type of behaviour envisaged by s 44 of the 1957 Act is one based on fraud only, and not negligence, and where a trustee, for instance, makes an incorrect payment through negligence, s 44 will not apply.[23] The limitation period of six years runs against a beneficiary from the date of breach of

[21] See Statute of Limitations 1957, s 43(1) and s 44.
[22] See Statute of Limitations 1957, s 43(1) and s 44.
[23] *Collings v Wade* [1896] 1 IR 34; see *Clarke v Crowley* (1930) 64 ILTR 1; *Re Irish Provident Assurance Co. Ltd* [1913] 1 IR 35.

trust.[24] But where a beneficiary is entitled to a future interest in the trust property, the limitation period will not commence to run until his future interest falls into possession.[25] Where, however, the interest of a beneficiary is statute-barred under s 43(1) of the 1957 Act, it cannot be revived on the grounds that the interest of another beneficiary still subsists.[26]

Actions for breach of trust may cease to be maintainable because of a beneficiary's *laches*. The doctrine of *laches* may be applied by a court of equity where: **23–26**

> [I]t would be practically unjust to give a remedy, either because the party has, by his conduct, done that which might fairly be regarded as equivalent to a waiver of it, or where by his conduct or neglect he has, though perhaps not waiving that remedy, yet put the other party in a situation in which it would not be reasonable to place him if the remedy were afterwards to be asserted, in either of these cases lapse of time and delay are most material.[27]

While lapse of time is essential to the doctrine of *laches*, it must also be coupled with circumstances that make it inequitable to enforce the claim.[28] A court of equity may also grant relief on the grounds of *laches* before the limitation period for the cause of action to which it relates has expired. Thus, either *laches* may be relied to bar a claim where there has been delay, or a time lapse would render it unjust in the circumstances to grant a remedy. **23–27**

Instituting Administration Actions

An administration action may be commenced by special summons in relation to the following matters: **23–28**

- (a) The determination of any question affecting the rights or interests of any person claiming to be a creditor, devisee, legatee or next-of-kin of the deceased or beneficiaries under a trust;
- (b) The payment into court of any money in the hands of the personal representatives or trustees;
- (c) Seeking a direction of the court ordering any of the personal representatives or trustees to do, or abstain from doing, any particular act in their character as personal representative, including the purchasing and vouching of accounts;
- (d) The approval of any sale, purchase or other transaction in connection with the administration of the estate of a deceased person or trust;
- (e) The determination of any question arising in the administration of any estate or trust or the ascertainment of any class of creditors, legatees, devisees, next-of-kin or others.

The personal representatives or any person claiming to be interested as **23–29**

[24] *Clarke v Crowley* (1930) 64 ILTR 1..
[25] Statute of Limitations 1957, s 43; see *Collings v Wade* [1896] 1 IR 34.
[26] Statute of Limitations 1957, s 43(2).
[27] *Lindsay Petroleum Co. v Hurd* LR 5 PC 211 at 239–240 *per* Lord Selborne.
[28] *Murphy v Attorney General* [1982] IR 241; see also *JH v WJH*, Unreported, High Court, Keane J, 20 December 1979.

a creditor, devisee, legatee, or next-of-kin of the deceased or trustees or beneficiaries under a trust may institute proceedings by means of special summons.[29] The personal representatives or trustees may sue and be sued as representing the estate of the deceased or trust estate without joining any persons beneficially interested in the estate or trust, as they will be considered as representing the estate unless the court orders that other persons also be made parties to the action.[30] In administration actions, the court may require the application to be supported by such evidence as it thinks fit, and it may not determine the issue of administration if it is of the opinion that the procedure by special summons in the matter is inappropriate.[31] Service out of jurisdiction of a special summons or notice of it may be allowed by the court whenever a will affecting land situate within the jurisdiction is sought to be construed.[32]

23–30 Order 15, r 8 of the RSC provides that:

> Trustees, executors, and administrators may sue and be sued on behalf of or as representing the property or estate of which they are trustees or representatives, without joining any of the persons beneficially interested in the trust or estate, and shall be considered as representing such persons ... .

23–31 Order 54, r 1 of the RSC provides that:

> [T]he executors or administrators of a deceased person or any of them, and the trustees under any deed or instrument or any of them, and any person claiming to be interested in the relief sought as creditor, devisee, legatee, next-of-kin, or heir-at-law of a deceased person, *cestui que trust* under the trust of any deed or instrument ... may take out a special summons for relief of the nature or kind specified in Order 3(1) to (7) inclusive.[33]

23–32 The persons to be named as defendants in any summons under Ord 54, r 1 "where the summons is taken out by executors, administrators or trustees or any of them" may include a creditor, devisee, legatee, next-of-kin or *cestui que trust*.[34] Under Ord 54, r 2(2) where the summons is taken out "by any person other than executors, administrators or trustees: the said executors, administrators or trustees" may be named as defendants. The court may also direct other persons to be served with the special summons as it thinks fit.[35]

---

29 Rules of the Superior Courts, Ord 54, rr 1 and 2; see also Ord 15, rr 23–25.

30 Rules of the Superior Courts, Ord 15, r 8. An executor may institute proceedings before probate of the testator's will is granted provided probate is granted before the hearing of the action (see *Ingall v Moran* [1944] 1 KB 160). This is because the executor derives his legal title from the testator's will. The grant of probate before the hearing is necessary only to prove that the executor is in fact the executor. An administrator's title to institute proceedings, however, depends solely on the grant of administration (see *Creed v Creed* [1913] 1 IR 48; *Ingall v Moran* [1944] 1 KB 160).

31 Rules of the Superior Courts, Ord 83, rr 3 and 4.

32 Rules of the Superior Courts, Ord 11, r 1(b).

33 See *In the Estate of Stanley* [2016] IEHC 8; *O'Byrne v Davoren* [1994] 3 IR 373.

34 Rules of the Superior Courts, Ord 54, r 2; see *Kilroy v Parker* [1966] IR 309.

35 Rules of the Superior Courts, Ord 83, r 2.

Where, however, there is some difficulty in ascertaining a beneficiary, or class of beneficiaries, or next-of-kin, the court may, in order to save expense or for some other reason, determine the question of construction before such beneficiaries or next-of-kin who have been ascertained by means of inquiry or otherwise, and for this purpose it may appoint one or more persons to represent the beneficiaries or next-of-kin.[36] It may also be added that, as an administrator derives his title from a grant of letters of administration, he or she will not be entitled to institute proceedings on behalf of the estate, or indeed, defend proceedings, before a grant of administration is issued to him either by the Probate Office or a District Probate Registry.[37]

Order 4, r 4 of the RSC provides that the indorsement of claim on a special summons shall be entitled SPECIAL INDORSEMENT OF CLAIM, and shall state specifically and with all necessary particulars the relief claimed and the grounds thereof. The indorsement of claim on a summary summons or a special summons shall be in such one of the forms in Appendix B, Pt III, as shall be applicable to the case, or, if none be found applicable, then such other similarly concise form as the nature of the case may require. **23–33**

Order 9, r 3 of the RSC provides that personal service shall be effected by delivering a copy of the summons to the defendant in person, and showing him the original or duplicate original. Order 9, r 12 provides that the person serving a summons shall, within three days at most after service, indorse on the summons the day and date of the service thereof; and every affidavit of service of such summons shall mention the date on which such indorsement was made. Order 10, r 1 of the RSC provides that if it be made to appear to the court that the plaintiff is from any cause unable to effect prompt personal service, or such other service as is prescribed by the RSC, the court may make an order for substituted or other service, or for the substitution for service of notice by advertisement or otherwise. Order 12, r 2(2) provides that a defendant in proceedings commenced by special summons may enter an appearance thereto at any time, but shall not, without the leave of the court, be entitled to be heard in such proceedings unless he has entered an appearance. Order 38, r 1 provides that every special summons shall be returnable for such day as the Master shall fix, which, except in such cases where the parties consent to an earlier date, or where no service is required, shall be not less than seven days from the date of issue, and shall, where necessary, be served on the parties concerned at least four days before the return day. An affidavit verifying the claim indorsed on the summons shall be filed in the Central Office and notice of such filing shall be given to the parties concerned. Order 38, r 2 provides that the court may direct such other persons to be served with the summons as it may think fit. Order 38, r 3 provides that, save in so far as the court shall otherwise order, proceedings commenced by special summons shall be heard on affidavit: provided that **23–34**

---

36 Rules of the Superior Courts, Ord 15, r 22(1) and (2).

37 *Ingall v Moran* [1944] 1 KB 160; *Creed v Creed* [1913] 1 IR 48; *Gaffney v Faughnan* [2006] 1 ILRM 481.

any party desiring to cross-examine a deponent who has made an affidavit filed on behalf of the opposite party may serve upon the party by whom such affidavit has been filed a notice in writing requiring the production of the deponent for cross-examination, and unless such deponent is produced accordingly his affidavit shall not be used as evidence unless by the special leave of the court.

23–35 Order 15, r 13 of the RSC also provides that the court may, at any stage of the proceedings,

> either upon or without the application of either party, and on such terms as may appear to the court to be just, order that the names of any parties improperly joined, whether as plaintiffs or as defendants, be struck out and that the names of any parties, whether as plaintiffs or defendants, who ought to have been joined, or whose presence before the court may be necessary in order to enable the court effectually and completely adjudicate upon and settle all the questions involved in the cause or matter, be added.

23–36 In *In the Estate of Stanley*,[38] Keane J stated that "it would be quite improper to issue proceedings impugning the validity of a trust in a non-trustee capacity without joining the other trustees of the relevant property or estate," and that a *legitimus contradictor* was necessary in such cases.

23–37

Special Summons

SPECIAL SUMMONS
THE HIGH COURT

In the matter of … 20… No. …
Between A. B., Plaintiff,
and C.D., Defendant.
(or if not *inter partes*)
On the application of A.B.
To …
of … in the County of …
This special summons is to require you to attend before the Master at the Four Courts, Dublin, on the … day of … at … o'clock in the forenoon at the hearing of this summons issued on the day of …, and if you do not attend in person or by solicitor at the time and place aforesaid, such order will be made, and proceedings taken as the Court may think just and expedient; and TAKE NOTICE that if you wish to attend and to be heard, you should first enter an appearance.
BY ORDER,
Chief Justice of Ireland,
the … day of … two
thousand and …
N.B.—This summons is required to be served not less than four days before the return day mentioned therein (exclusive of the day of service).

[38] [2016] IEHC 8.

SPECIAL INDORSEMENT OF CLAIM

The plaintiff's claim is
(Signed)

Schedule of affidavit or affidavits intended to be used by the plaintiff (or applicant) on the hearing of the summons.

This summons was issued by the plaintiff (or applicant) who resides at [state address accurately] and is ...

or,

This summons was issued by ... , whose registered place of
business is ...,
solicitor for the plaintiff, who resides at ...
and is ....

This summons was served by me at ...
on the defendant on the ...
day of ... 20...
Indorsed the ... day of 20...
(Signed)
[Address]

SAMPLE SPECIAL INDORSEMENT OF CLAIM

For instance: The plaintiff's claim is as one of the next-of-kin of the above named X.Y., deceased, who died on [date] intestate for an order for the administration of the estate of the said deceased with all necessary and proper accounts, inquiries and directions.
[Indorsement of character in which defendant is sued.]
(Signed)

Or: The plaintiff's claim is as the executor and trustee of the said will mentioned in the title hereof of X. Y., deceased, for the determination of the following questions arising (in the administration of the estate, and) upon the construction of the said will of the said testator, and in the events that have happened, viz.:-[Set out questions in form which will enable them as far as possible to be answered "yes" or "no"] and that the cost of the proceedings may be provided for.

The defendant is sued as [state nature of his interest, or capacity in which he is sued].
(Signed)

DEFENCE

Heading of defence

THE HIGH COURT
... 20 No. ...
Between A.B., Plaintiff,

and C.D., Defendant.
Defence.
Delivered on the … day of …, 20 …, by G.H. of (registered place of business), solicitor for the defendant.

REPLY

Heading of reply

THE HIGH COURT
… 20 … No. …
Between A.B., Plaintiff,
and C.D., Defendant.
REPLY
Delivered on the day of by E.F., of [registered place of business], solicitor for the plaintiff.
1. The plaintiff joins issue with the defendant on his defence save and in so far as the same contains admissions.
2. [as may be necessary].

NOTICE OF COUNTERCLAIM

[Title of action].

To the within-named X.Y.
Take notice that if you do not appear to the within counter-claim of the within-named C.D. within ten days from the service of this defence and counter-claim upon you, you will be liable to have judgment given against you in your absence. Appearance is to be entered [&c., as in Form No. 1].

NOTICE OF TRIAL (ORDINARY FORM)

[Title of action].

Take notice of trial of this [or of the issues in this ordered to be tried] [or as the case may be] for the day of at
Dated

23–38 In *In the Estate of Stanley*, an *ex parte* application was made to the court by the widow and daughter of the testator for an order setting aside a testamentary trust on the grounds that it was void for uncertainty. The two applicants, together with Donal Branigan and Vincent Murray, were appointed as executors and trustees of his will. The applicants did not, however, state whether they had brought the proceedings in their capacity as trustees or in some other capacity, such as that of the persons directly entitled to the trust property in the event that the trust is found to be invalid. Who then was to represent the trust as *legitimus contradictor*?

23–39 In his judgment, Keane J referred to the RSC Ord 15, r 8, which provides that:

> Trustees, executors, and administrators may sue and be sued on behalf of or as representing the property or estate of which they are trustees or representatives, without joining any of the persons beneficially interested in the trust or estate, and shall be considered as representing such persons; but the Court may, at any stage of the proceedings, order any of such persons to be made parties either in addition to or in lieu of the previously existing parties … .

It seemed to Keane J that: **23–40**

> It would be quite improper to issue proceedings impugning the validity of a trust in a non-trustee capacity without joining the other trustees of the relevant property or estate. While the applicants in this case have put the other trustees informally on notice of the present *ex parte* application, that cannot be sufficient since it leaves the applicants' claim without a *legitimus contradictor* and deprives the wider class of potential beneficiaries (comprising any person who may yet come within that class other than the applicants and, thus, will come within a separate class of beneficiaries without any evident residual or other claim to the trust property) of any representation of its interests in the face of the applicants' claim to orders that would, if granted, extinguish those interests.

He concluded that: **23–41**

> [T]he presence before the Court of Mr Murray and of Mr Branigan in the capacity of each as trustee of the trust at issue is necessary to enable the Court effectually or completely to adjudicate upon and settle the questions involved in the present proceedings. Accordingly, both in the exercise of this Court's supervisory jurisdiction and pursuant to the terms of Order 15, rule 13 of the RSC, I hereby Order that Mr Vincent Murray and Mr Donal Branigan be joined or added as defendants to these proceedings in the capacity of each as trustee of the trust at issue and I will adjourn the present application to afford the applicants (or plaintiffs, as it seems to me those parties should more properly be described), a reasonable opportunity to take the appropriate consequential steps in accordance with the RSC, if the present proceedings are to be maintained. It is for that reason that I do not propose to adjudicate at this stage on the application as it was presented to the Court.

Issues of Costs

The court, when awarding costs in administration actions, and construction suits, will first be guided by the principles set out in Ord 99 of the RSC. In relation to the issue of costs in administration actions, it was stated by Laffoy J in *Young v Cadell* that: **23–42**

> The factors which arise in a probate suit which justify the special rule in relation to costs which was reiterated in *Vella v Morelli*, the importance of ensuring that what are presented as testamentary documents are above suspicion and that legal costs are not a deterrent to pursuing *bona fide* beliefs or suspicions as to the validity of such documents, do not arise in administration suits, which, in the case of a death testate, proceed on the assumption that the testamentary document is valid, as was the case here.

In *O'Connor v Markey*, Herbert J, affirming that the authorities referred to **23–43**
in *Vella v Morelli* dealt with probate issues regarding the due execution or

revocation of wills and the testamentary capacity of a testator, stated that by contrast, "the instant application bore all the hallmarks of contentious litigation between beneficiaries which did not in any way touch upon the capacity of the testator or the state in which he left his testamentary papers", and so the issue of costs was not governed by *Vella v Morelli*. In *Rennick v Rennick*, the deceased died intestate and as the proceedings did not concern the testamentary disposition of property or execution of testamentary documents, *Vella v Morelli* and *Elliott v Stamp* were not relevant to the proceedings involving issues between beneficiaries arising out of intestacies.

23–44 In *Muckian v Hoey*, the applicants sought an order directing that the costs of their successful action be paid out of the estate.

23–45 Keane J stated:

> 10. The applicants submit that they brought their application by way of the special summons procedure under O. 3 of the RSC, as amended, to avoid the greater costs of a plenary action and point out that the first respondent did not object to that course, although she was undoubtedly entitled to do so, as her wilful default or misconduct in the administration of the estate was plainly in issue from the outset.
>
> 11. For my part, I do not accept that the first respondent could foreclose any possibility of a finding of wilful default on her part as administratrix by the simple expedient of not objecting to the use of the special summons procedure as the appropriate vehicle for seeking her removal from that position.
>
> 12. Nor do I accept that there is any absolute or inflexible modern rule whereby an administratrix is entitled to her costs of an administration out of the estate unless a finding of misconduct, expressed as such, is made against her. I do accept that there is an obvious public interest in the application of a general principle whereby, once there is a reasonable ground for litigation by an administrator, executor or trustee, and once that litigation is conducted bona fide, that party should have an order for his or her costs out of the estate or trust though unsuccessful in the action. The public interest concerned is a broader manifestation of that identified by Budd J in the narrower context of the circumstances surrounding the execution of wills in *In bonis Morelli: Vela v Morelli* [1968] I.R. 11 (at 34). That is to say, it is the wider public or community interest in the proper administration of estates and trusts generally. Administrators, executors or trustees should not be unduly deterred from seeking to have genuine problems or issues in the administration of any estate or trust judicially resolved because of the risk of a personal liability for the costs of the appropriate litigation.
>
> 13. There is another relevant principle. It is that an application which bears all of the hallmarks of a hostile lis inter partes – whether between beneficiaries under a will, under a trust or on an intestacy – may, depending on all of the circumstances, attract the unvarnished application of the usual rule that costs follow the event. That is the principle that I understand Herbert J to have identified in *O'Connor v Markey* [2007] 2 I.R. 194 and Laffoy J to have applied in *Rennick v Rennick* [2012] IEHC 589.

23–46 He went on:

> 18. Turning from an analysis of the applicable legal principles to a consideration of the factors relevant to the exercise of the Court's discretion under O. 99, r 1 (1) of the RSC in this case, I cannot ignore the following matters. In the face of the application to remove her as administrator, the first respondent chose to oppose it, as was her perfect entitlement. After a contested application, the first respondent

was found to have demonstrated a want of proper capacity to execute the duties of administratrix, amounting to a special circumstance warranting her removal from that position, and her removal was duly ordered. One of the findings that led to that conclusion was that, over the passage of many years and without any proper excuse, the first respondent has failed to produce a satisfactory distribution account, and has completely failed to account to each of the beneficiaries (including the applicants) for the relevant income, expenditure and interest associated with the property that comprises the estate. In those circumstances, to exercise the Court's discretion to order that the first respondent's costs of the unsuccessful defence of that application should be borne by the estate (and, thus, ultimately by the beneficiaries), rather than by the first respondent, would fly in the face, not only of fundamental reason and common sense, but also of justice. Indeed, the provisions of O. 99, r. 1(4), whereby costs should follow the event, provide strong support for an award of the applicants' costs of the action against the first respondent. Happily for the first respondent, the applicants' have made no such application, perhaps in the interests of conciliation, which is, of course, very much to be desired.

19. I must therefore refuse the first respondent's application for an order that her costs of the action be paid out of the estate.

Derived Principles

In *O'Connor v Markey*, Herbert J referred with apparent approval to the principles of Kekewich J in *Buckton v Buckton*, where the issue of costs in administration actions was considered. Kekewich J identified three types of administration action for the purposes of determining the issue of costs. **23–47**

(i) In administration actions where the applicants are the personal representatives or trustees seeking the court's direction in ascertaining the interests of the beneficiaries or to have some questioned determined which has arisen in the administration of the estate, costs of all parties as necessarily incurred for the benefit of the estate will be taxed as between solicitor and client and paid out of the estate.

(ii) Where the application is made by some of the beneficiaries but is made by reason of some difficulty of construction or administration that would have justified an application by the personal representatives or trustees, they will also be allowed their costs out of the estate.

(iii) But where a beneficiary "makes a claim adverse to other beneficiaries, and usually takes advantage of the convenient procedure by originating summons to get a question determined which, but for this procedure, would be the subject of an action commenced by writ and would strictly fall within the description of litigation" and "once convinced that I am determining rights between adverse litigants I apply the rule which ought, I think, be rigidly enforced in adverse litigation, and order the unsuccessful party to pay the costs."

(iv) In *Rennick v Rennick*, Laffoy J found that the principles in *Vella v Morelli* and *Elliott v Stamp* have no application to issues of costs in cases involving intestacies.

(v) In *Muckian v Hoey*, Keane J stated that:
"It is that an application which bears all of the hallmarks of a hostile lis inter partes – whether between beneficiaries under a will, under a trust or on an intestacy – may, depending on all of the circumstances, attract the unvarnished application of the usual rule that costs follow the event. That is the principle that I understand Herbert J to have identified in *O'Connor v Markey* [2007] 2 I.R. 194. and Laffoy J to have applied in *Rennick v Rennick.* [2012] IEHC 589."

23–48 Thus, the practice regarding the award of costs as described by Budd J in *Vella v Morelli* and confirmed by Kearns J in *Elliott v Stamp* is confined to probate actions only, and has no application to the question of costs in administrative actions involving disputes between beneficiaries in a will or intestacy, or *lites inter partes* between two beneficiaries under a will or intestacy. Issues of costs in probate, administration actions and equitable claims commenced by the appropriate civil bill in the Circuit Court are governed by similar principles.

Limitation of Actions

23–49 Section 123(1) of the 1965 Act provides that a personal representative in the capacity of personal representative shall not, by reason only of s 10 of the 1965 Act, be a trustee for the purposes of the 1957 Act. Section 124 of the 1965 Act provides that notwithstanding any rule of law, "trustee" in the 1957 Act shall not include a person whose fiduciary relationship arises merely because he is in possession of property comprised in the estate of a deceased person in the capacity of bailiff for another person. A trustee for the purposes of the 1957 Act does not include a person "whose fiduciary relationship arises by construction or implication of law and whose fiduciary relationship is not deemed to be that of an express trustee." The definition of trustee for the purposes of the 1957 Act is confined to express trustees only. Section 126(1) of the 1965 Act provides that no action may be brought by a person entitled to receive a share or interest in the estate after the expiration of six years from the date on which the right to receive a share or interest accrued. Under s 62(1) of the 1965 Act, no action may be brought against the personal representatives for their failure to distribute the estate of the deceased without leave of the court until the expiration of one year from the date of death of the deceased. Section 126(1), therefore, may be relied on by persons who have a share or interest in the estate and any action in relation to such share or interest must be brought against the estate within a time limit of six years, and the personal representatives may be the defendants for such purposes. As a result of the combined effect of s 62(1) and s 126(1) of the 1965 Act, it appears that no action may be brought against the personal representatives to distribute the estate of a deceased until the expiration of one year from the date of his death, and no action may be brought in respect of a share or interest in an estate after the expiration of six years from the date on which the right to receive such share or interest accrued. Section 127 of the 1965 Act provides that s 49 of the 1957 Act, which extends the periods of limitation fixed by that Act where the person to whom a right of action accrued was under a disability, will have effect in relation to an action in respect of a claim to the estate of a deceased person or to any share in such estate, whether under a will, on intestacy or as a legal right, as if the period of three years were substituted for the period of six years mentioned in s 45(1) of the 1957 Act.

23–50 It appears, however, that s 126 of the 1965 Act does not apply to actions brought by personal representatives as plaintiffs on behalf of the estate. In *Drohan v Drohan*, McMahon J stated that s 126(1) of the 1965 Act did not, however, apply to actions brought by personal representatives to recover land of the deceased. The plaintiff, as personal representative of the estate of the deceased, was entitled to rely on s 13(2)(a) of the 1957 Act, and the limitation period of twelve years to recover the land, and the action, therefore, was not statute-barred. The deceased was the registered owner of freehold land. He died intestate and a grant of letters of administration intestate was issued to his son, the plaintiff in the action. The defendant was the widow of another of the deceased's sons who was in possession of the land. The plaintiff issued a civil bill in the Circuit Court claiming to be entitled as personal representative to recover possession of the land from the defendant. The defendant pleaded that the plaintiff's action was statute-barred under s 126(1) of the 1965 Act which prescribed that an action must be brought within a period of six years. The plaintiff, however, relied on s 13(2)(a) of the 1957 Act which allowed for a twelve-year period to elapse before an action became statute-barred. McMahon J, in the course of his judgment, was of the view that s 126 (1) of the 1965 Act which amended s 45(1) of the 1957 Act was not applicable to the plaintiff's claim, and for support he referred to a similar English provision found in s 20 of the Limitation Act 1939 and an interpretation of that provision by the Court of Appeal in *Diplock v Wintle* and which was affirmed by the House of Lords *sub nomine* in *Ministry of Health v Simpson*. In *Diplock v Wintle*, it was held that s 20 of the Limitation Act 1939 did not include actions instituted by a personal representative on behalf of the estate. Approving of *Diplock v Wintle*, McMahon J was also of the view that s 45(1), as inserted by s 126(1) of the 1965 Act, did not apply to an action brought by a personal representative to recover land of the deceased from a beneficiary, or indeed a stranger, who held the land in adverse possession. Accordingly, he found that the plaintiff as personal representative of the estate of the deceased was entitled to rely on s 13(2)(a) 1957 Act, and the limitation period of 12 years within which to recover the land and the claim against defendant was therefore not statute-barred.

A similar question in relation to the limitation period for personal representatives to bring actions on behalf of the estate arose on appeal to the Supreme Court in *Gleeson v Feehan*. In that case, Finlay CJ found that the "plain and ordinary" meaning of s 126(1) of the 1965 Act was that those beneficially entitled could call upon a personal representative to give them their beneficial share or interest in the estate. The section does not, however, apply to an action taken by a personal representative against a stranger. In his view, the decision of McMahon J in *Drohan v Drohan* was correct. Any consideration of the provisions of s 13(2)(a) of the 1957 Act showed that they fitted precisely the form of action that was in question in the case before him. It was an action brought not by a person to whom it first accrued, but rather by a person who claimed through the person to whom the action first accrued. He was also satisfied "that no anomaly which could be said to occur could justify the interpretation of the sections otherwise than to make applicable to this cause of action s 13 (2) of the Act of 1957." In **23–51** the same case, McCarthy J, while agreeing with the observations of Finlay CJ, went on to state that he did not understand the decision in *Drohan v Drohan* to mean that s 45(1) of the 1957 Act as inserted by s 126(1) of the 1965 Act was confined in its application only to actions against a personal representative by those entitled to share in the estate. O'Flaherty J held that s 13 of the 1957 Act was clearly applicable to the case. He found that the language of s 126 of the 1965 Act was inappropriate to bar claims by personal representatives to the estates of deceased persons. It only applies to claims against a personal representative and has no application to a claim by a personal representative.

23–52 Section 71 of the 1957 Act is an express provision postponing the date of the accrual of the cause of action in cases involving fraud to the date when the fraud was, or could with reasonable diligence have been, discovered. The 1957 Act provides that where the action is either "based on" or "concealed by" the fraud of the defendant, the limitation period does not begin to run until the plaintiff either discovered the fraud or could, with reasonable diligence, have discovered it.

The Tracing of Property by Beneficiaries

23–53 Where it is discovered during the administration of the trust estate that trust property has come into the hands of a stranger, or that a trustee has used it for his own use and benefit, a beneficiary may elect to trace the property and seek its return. Tracing the property at common law may be undertaken if the property still remains in its original form and there is no difficulty in identifying it. Where, however, trust property is converted into money by the stranger or trustee and is mingled with other funds, tracing at common law will no longer be possible. This is where tracing in equity becomes relevant. Equity allows the tracing of property even though the property is converted into money, or where trust funds are mingled with other funds in the hands of a stranger or trustee. While this in itself may present little difficulty once the value of the trust property is known and the stranger or trustee has sufficient funds to satisfy the tracing, it may become more complicated where creditors seek payment of the money owing to them out of the same funds. Where other claims are made, the rule is that the tracing beneficiary will have a prior right to payment out of the funds, and other claims may then be discharged out of the residue. Where the trust funds are employed by a trustee to purchase property, the beneficiary has the option of taking the property purchased by the trust funds, or charging the purchased property with the amount of the trust funds expended on the purchase. A beneficiary may no longer have this option where other funds were also used to purchase the property, but he may still lodge a charge on the property for the amount of the trust funds spent on the purchase. The tracing process has its limitations, as it is dependent on the existence of a fund to be charged, and where no such fund exists, through dissipation or otherwise, the process ceases to work. It also cannot be used against a bona fide purchaser for value without notice.

CHAPTER 24

ACTIONS INVOLVING EQUITABLE PROPERTY RIGHTS

INTRODUCTION

Actions claiming the acquisition or creation of equitable property rights under equitable principles or doctrines may be instituted by the issuing of a plenary summons. Such claims may be founded on the equitable principles of proprietary estoppel, promissory estoppel or remedial constructive trusts, or the doctrine of secret and half-secret trusts, or the concept of *donationes mortis causa*, or pre-testamentary agreements to make mutual wills, contractual and equitable rights arising out of joint bank accounts. The court, when awarding costs in such actions, will be governed by the general principles of costs set out in Ord 99 of the Rules of the Superior Courts (the "RSC"), and as Clarke J in *Veolia Water UK plc. v Fingal County Council (No.2)*,[1] stated that, when awarding costs, it is first necessary to determine who was the winning party, in other words what was "the event" to which costs would normally follow under the rule in Ord 99 of the RSC. In relation to the limitation of actions against estates of deceased persons, s 8(1) of the Civil Liability Act 1961 (the 1961 Act) provides that on the death of the deceased all causes of action subsisting against him or her shall survive against his or her estate. Section 9(2) of the 1961 Act provides that no proceedings 24–01

> shall be maintainable in respect of any cause of action whatsoever which has survived against the estate of a deceased person unless either – (a) proceedings against him in respect of that cause of action was commenced within the relevant period and were pending at the date of death, or (b) proceedings are commenced in respect of that action within the relevant period or within the period of two years after his death, whichever period first expires.

Account may also be taken of the Rules of the Superior Courts (Chancery and Non-Jury Actions and Other Designated Proceedings: Pre-Trial Procedures 2016 (SI No 255 of 2016) which are also relevant. This statutory instrument amended Ords 22 and 63 of the RSC, and the RSC as amended may now be cited as the RSC 1986 to 2016. Order 63 of the RSC is amended by the insertion of a new Ord 63C, and provides at r 2(1) that it applies to any proceedings the trial of which would, on service of a notice of trial (if required), be listed for trial in the Chancery List or the Non-Jury List of the Court. In relation to pre-trial preparation, Ord 63C, r 4 provides that: 24–02

1 [2007] 2 IR 81; see *Naylor v Maher* [2018] IECA 32.

A Judge may, at any time and from time to time, of that Judge's own motion and having heard the parties, or on the application of a party by motion on notice to the other party or parties, give such directions and make such orders, including the fixing of time limits, for the conduct of proceedings, as appears convenient for the determination of the proceedings in a manner which is just, expeditious and likely to minimise the costs of those proceedings.[2]

Grounds for Actions Relating to Equitable Property Rights

(i) Proprietary Estoppel

24–03 Grounds for Action

- That the defendant made representations or assurances to the plaintiff regarding current or future interests in relation to land owned by the defendant;
- That the plaintiff placed reliance on such representations or assurances;
- That the plaintiff suffered a detriment on foot of his or her reliance on the representations or assurances made by the defendant by expending monies on the land;
- That the plaintiff suffered a detriment by working on the land free of charge or at a reduced rate due to his or her reliance on the representations or assurances made by the defendant.

(ii) Remedial Constructive Trusts

24–04 Grounds for Action

- That representations or assurances were made to the plaintiff by the defendant regarding a future interest in land belonging to the defendant;
- That the plaintiff placed reliance on such representations or assurances;
- That as a result of placing reliance on the defendant's representations or assurances the plaintiff suffered a detriment in the form of money expenditure on the defendant's land;
- That, and in the alternative, the plaintiff suffered a detriment by working free of charge or at a reduced wage on the defendant's land;
- That the defendant by will devised the land to another taking effect on the defendant's death.

(iii) Secret and Half-Secret Trusts

24–05 Grounds for Action

- That the testator intended to create a secret trust over property devised by him or her by will;

---

[2] See A. Keating, *Probate Motions and Actions Relating to Wills and Intestacies* (Round Hall, Dublin, 2017); A. Keating, *The Law of Wills* (2nd ed, Clarus Press, Dublin, 2018); A. Keating, *Succession Law in Ireland* (Clarus Press, Dublin, 2015); A. Keating, *Keating on Probate* (5th ed, Round Hall, Dublin, 2015); A. Keating, *Succession Law in Ireland: Principles, Cases and Commentary* (Clarus Press, Dublin, 2016).

- That the testator communicated his or her intention to the secret trustee/beneficiary of the devised property;
- That the secret trustee/beneficiary accepted the terms of the secret trust;
- That the alleged secret trustee denies (ii) and (iii) above;
- That a valid secret trust took effect on the death of the testator;
- That the estate of the deceased testator denies the existence of a valid secret trust.

(iv) Donationes Mortis Causa

Grounds for Action **24–06**

- That the donor intended to create a *donatio mortis causa* in favour of the donee;
- That the *donatio mortis causa* was made in contemplation of the donor's death;
- That the subject matter of the *donatio mortis causa* was delivered by the donor or his or her agent to the donee;
- That at the time of the donor's death, the donee had complete dominion over the subject matter of the *donatio mortis causa*;
- That the *donatio mortis causa* took effect on the death of the donor;
- That the estate of the deceased donor denies the existence of a valid *donatio mortis causa.*

(v) Joint Bank Accounts

Grounds for Action **24–07**

- That the deceased during his or her lifetime opened a joint bank account in his or her name and in the name of another person;
- That the deceased died leaving that other person him or her surviving;
- That the surviving account-holder was entitled as survivor to the monies remaining in the joint account;
- That the surviving account-holder had contractual rights to the remaining monies in joint account;
- That, and in the alternative, the surviving account-holder had an equitable property right to the monies remaining in the joint account;
- That the bank had a right of set-off on foot of an agreement entered into prior to the opening of the joint account;
- That the bank's right of set-off was not enforceable as it was based on negotiations entered into after the opening of the joint account.
- That the surviving account-holder was not subject to the bank's set-off after the death of the deceased account holder as same was negotiated after the opening of the joint account, and failed as a right of set-off.
- That the estate of the deceased joint account-holder denies the existence of a valid joint bank account.

(vi) Pre-Testamentary Agreements to Make Mutual Wills

Grounds for Action **24–08**

- That a pre-testamentary agreement was entered into by testators to make mutual wills benefitting one another;
- That, on the death of one of the testator, the pre-testamentary agreement took

effect, and was enforceable against the surviving testator by the creation of a constructive trust by equity;

- That the surviving testator acted in breach of his or her pre-testamentary agreement to make mutual wills;
- That a fraud was committed by the surviving testator owing to acting in breach of the pre-testamentary agreement to make mutual wills.

Instituting Proceedings

24–09 An action claiming equitable rights over property may be instituted by the issuing of a plenary summons out of the Central Office.[3] Order 9, r 3 of the RSC provides that personal service may be effected by delivering a copy of the summons to the defendant in person, and showing him the original or duplicate original, and Ord 9, r 12 provides that the person serving a summons shall, within three days at most after service, indorse on the summons the day and date of the service thereof; and every affidavit of service of such summons shall mention the date on which such indorsement was made. Order 10, r 1 of the RSC provides that if it be made to appear to the court that the plaintiff is from any cause unable to effect prompt personal service, or such other service as is prescribed by the RSC, the court may make an order for substituted or other service, or for the substitution for service of notice by advertisement or otherwise. The defendant must deliver his defence and counterclaim within 28 days from the date of delivery of the statement of claim.[4] Where a counterclaim is filed, a reply to it will be governed by the same rules applicable to a defence.[5] Order 15, r 13 of the RSC also provides that the court may, at any stage of the proceedings,

> either upon or without the application of either party, and on such terms as may appear to the court to be just, order that the names of any parties improperly joined, whether as plaintiffs or as defendants, be struck out and that the names of any parties, whether as plaintiffs or defendants, who ought to have been joined, or whose presence before the court may be necessary in order to enable the court effectually and completely adjudicate upon and settle all the questions involved in the cause or matter, be added.

24–10

Plenary Summons

PLENARY SUMMONS.
THE HIGH COURT

… 20… No. …

Between A. B.,	Plaintiff,
and C.D.,	Defendant.

To the defendant …
of … in the County of …
This plenary summons is to require that within eight days after the service thereof

---

[3] Ord 1, r 2; Ord 5, r 1.
[4] Ord 21, r 1(b).
[5] Ord 23, r 5.

upon you (exclusive of the day of such service) you in person or by solicitor do enter an appearance in the Central Office, Four Courts, Dublin, in the above action; and TAKE NOTICE that, in default of your so doing, the plaintiff may proceed therein, and judgment may be given in your absence.

BY ORDER,
Chief Justice of Ireland,
the day of two thousand and eighteen

N.B.—This summons is to be served within twelve calendar months from the date hereof, and, if renewed within six calendar months from the date of the last renewal, including the day of such date, and not afterwards.

The defendant may appear hereto by entering an appearance either personally or by solicitor at the Central Office, Four Courts, Dublin.

GENERAL INDORSEMENT OF CLAIM

The plaintiff's claim is

(Signed)
This summons was issued by the plaintiff who resides at …
[state address accurately] and
is, and whose address for
service is …
or,
This summons was issued by … , whose registered place of
business is …,
solicitor for the plaintiff, who resides at …
and is ….
This summons was served by me at …
on the defendant …
on the … day of … 20…
Indorsed the … day of … 20…
(Signed)
(Address)

INDORSEMENT OF CHARACTER OF PARTIES

For instance: The plaintiff's claim is as executor and trustee of C.D., deceased, for, &c.

MEMORANDUM OF APPEARANCE IN GENERAL

THE HIGH COURT

… 20… No. …
Between A.B., Plaintiff,
and C.D., Defendant.

Enter an appearance for C.D., the defendant in this action.

Dated …
(Signed)
E.F.,
solicitor for the defendant.
The registered place of business of E.F. is …
[or C.D., the defendant in person.
The place of residence of C.D. is …
His address for service is …].
To the Registrar of the Central Office.
Take notice, that I have this day entered an appearance at the Central Office, Four Courts, Dublin,
to the originating summons in this action.
[If statement of claim is required, add] The said …
requires delivery of a statement of claim

Dated …

(Signed)

To …

(Signed)

STATEMENT OF CLAIM

Heading of Statement of Claim

THE HIGH COURT
… 20… No. …
Between A.B., Plaintiff,
and C.D., Defendant.

Statement of claim
Delivered on the … day of …, 20…,by E.F., of [registered place of business], solicitor for the plaintiff [or as the case may be].

DEFENCE

Heading of defence
THE HIGH COURT
… 20… No. …
Between A.B., Plaintiff,
and C.D., Defendant.
Defence.
Delivered on the … day of …, 20…, by G.H. of [registered place of business], solicitor for the defendant.

REPLY

Heading of reply
THE HIGH COURT
... 20... No. ...
Between A.B., Plaintiff,
and C.D., Defendant.
REPLY.
Delivered on the ... day of ... 20... by E.F., of [registered place of business], solicitor for the plaintiff.
1. The plaintiff joins issue with the defendant on his defence save and in so far as the same contains admissions.
2. [as may be necessary].

NOTICE OF COUNTERCLAIM

[Title of action]

To the within-named X.Y.
Take notice that if you do not appear to the within counter-claim of the within-named C.D. within ten days from the service of this defence and counter-claim upon you, you will be liable to have judgment given against you in your absence. Appearance is to be entered [&c., as in Form No. 1].

NOTICE OF TRIAL (ORDINARY FORM)

[Title of action]
Take notice of trial of this [or of the issues in this ordered to be tried] [or as the case may be] for the ... day of ... 20... at ...
Dated ...
(Signed)

Costs of Actions

The court, when awarding costs in equitable claims against estates, will be guided by the general principles of costs set out in Ord 99 of the 1986 RSC. Order 99, r 1 of the RSC provides that the costs of, and incidental to, every proceeding in the Superior Courts shall be at the discretion of those courts. The Rules of the Superior Courts (Costs) 2008 (SI No 12 of 2008) (the "2008 RSC") inserts r 1A(1) immediately after Ord 99, r 1 of the 1986 RSC. Rule 1A(1) provides that notwithstanding r 1(3) and r 1(4): **24–11**

(a) The Supreme Court, in considering the awarding of the costs of any appeal or any application in respect of an appeal, may, where it considers it just, have regard to the terms of any offer in writing sent by any party to any other party or parties offering to satisfy the whole or part of that other party's (or those other parties') claim or counterclaim the subject of the appeal, or application.
(b) The High Court, in considering the awarding of the costs of any action (other than an action in respect of a claim or counterclaim concerning which a lodgment or tender offer in lieu of lodgment may be made in accordance

with Order 22) or any application in such an action, may, where it considers it just, have regard to the terms of any offer in writing sent by any party to any other party or parties offering to satisfy the whole or part of that other party's (or those other parties') claim, counterclaim or application.

24–12 Rule 1A(2) of the 1986 RSC provides that "an offer in writing" includes any offer made without prejudice save as to the issue of costs. Rule 1(2) of Ord 99 provides that no party will be entitled to recover any costs of, or incidental to, any proceeding from any other party to such proceeding, except under an order or as provided by the Rules of the Superior Courts. Order 99, r 1(3) provides that, subject to sub-rule (4A) of the 2008 RSC, the costs of an action will follow the event, unless the court otherwise directs. The 2008 RSC amended Ord 99, r 1(3) of the 1986 RSC by providing that: "Subject to sub-rule (4A), the costs of an action, question or issue tried by a jury shall follow the event unless the court, for special cause, to be mentioned in the order, shall otherwise direct." The 2008 RSC also amended Ord 99, r 1(4) of the 1986 RSC by providing that: "Subject to sub-rule (4A), the costs of every issue of fact or law raised upon a claim or counterclaim shall, unless otherwise ordered, follow the event." Order 99, r 1(4A) of the 1986 RSC, as a result of the amendment of the 1986 RSC by the 2008 RSC, now provides that: "The High Court or the Supreme Court, upon determining any interlocutory application, shall make an award of costs save where it is not possible justly to adjudicate upon liability for costs on the basis of the interlocutory application." Order 99, r 1(5) provides that where in any proceeding in the High Court or Supreme Court, the costs of any party are ordered to be paid by another party, or by a fund or estate, those costs shall, if the High Court or the Supreme Court respectively so directs, include, in addition to the costs allowed on taxation as between party and party, all or any other costs, charge and expenses, reasonably incurred for the purposes of the proceedings. The principles regarding costs may also be garnered and derived from former decisions of the courts. Such principles may also be reformulated by the courts.

24–13 In *Naylor v Maher*,[6] the plaintiff worked on the deceased's lands for minimal remuneration for a period of over thirty years. The deceased during his lifetime promised the plaintiff that he would devise his lands to him. In fact, the deceased made a will in 2005 under which he devised the lands to the plaintiff. He, however, made another will in 2006 by which he devised the lands to the defendant. The plaintiff submitted that the defendant was estopped from denying that the plaintiff had an interest in the lands. The deceased also made a bequest to the plaintiff of the sum of €150,000. O'Keeffe J found that the plaintiff's claim to the lands by way of promissory estoppel was established. In the Court of Appeal, Peart J in *Naylor v Maher*,[7] in relation to the question of costs, stated that:

24. Under Ord 99 of the Rules of the Superior Courts the normal rule is that

[6] [2012] IEHC 408.

[7] [2018] IECA 32.

costs will follow the event, unless the Court can be satisfied that there is some identifiable special reason why in the exercise of the court's discretion some other order should be made. Lengthy and complex cases often involve multiple issues only some of which are successfully argued. While the successful party will have succeeded, and in that sense the "event" for costs purposes has been achieved, nevertheless he/she may have failed on many issues that have occupied a significant number of days of hearing. In such circumstances the question arises as to what order for costs is fair to the losing party. The present case is such a case, where issues upon which the plaintiff has failed in the High Court occupied a great deal of time, and consequently added significantly to the costs incurred by the parties.

He further stated: **24–14**

25. The question of how costs should be awarded in such cases arose for consideration by Clarke J (as he then was) in *Veolia Water UK plc. v Fingal County Council (No.2)* [2007] 2 I.R. 81 in the High Court. He concluded that it was first necessary to determine who was the winning party, in other words what was "the event" to which costs would normally follow under the rule. There is no difficulty in the present case for the Court to conclude that the event for costs purposes was that the plaintiff succeeded in his primary claim that he had an entitlement to the lands. He went on to state that the Court should then consider whether it was safe to assume that the costs were increased by the successful party having raised issues upon which he did not succeed. Again, in the present case there is no difficulty in the Court being satisfied that the length of the trial, and therefore the amount of the costs, was greatly increased by the plaintiff's pursuit of the failed issues of duress/undue influence. At para. 13 of his judgment Clarke J stated:

> '13. … Where the matter before the court involved oral evidence and where the evidence of certain witnesses was directed solely towards an issue upon which the party who was, in the overall sense, successful, failed, then it seems to me that, ordinarily, the court should disallow any costs attributable to such witnesses and, indeed, should provide, by way of set-off, for the recovery by the unsuccessful party of the costs attributable to any witnesses which it was forced to call in respect of the same issue. A similar approach should apply to any discrete item of expenditure incurred solely in respect of an issue upon which the otherwise successful party failed.
>
> 14. Similarly, where it is clear that the length of the trial of whatever issues were before the court was increased by virtue of the raising of issues upon which the party who was successful in the ordinary sense, failed, then the court should, again ordinarily, award to the successful party an amount of costs which reflects not only that that party should be refused costs attributable to any such elongated hearing, but should also have to, in effect, pay costs to the unsuccessful party in relation to whatever portion of the hearing the court assesses was attributable to the issue upon which the winning party was unsuccessful.'

He concluded that: **24–15**

40. For all these reasons I would therefore dismiss the appeal, and affirm the order of the High Court, save to vary same by requiring the plaintiff as a condition of receiving a transfer of the entire lands, to execute a disclaimer in respect of so much of the bequest of €150,000 as he would otherwise receive, and also substituting for the costs made an order for 75% of the High Court costs in favour of the plaintiff, to be taxed and ascertained in default of agreement.

24–16 Derived Principles

(i) The court, when awarding costs in equitable claims against estates, will be guided by the general principles of costs set out in Ord 99 of the 1986 RSC.
(ii) It is first necessary to determine who was the winning party; in other words, what was "the event" which costs would normally follow under the rule.
(iii) Where the were multiple issues raised in an action, then consider whether the costs were increased by the successful party having raised issues upon which he or she did not succeed.
(iv) Where the length of the trial was increased by the successful party raising issues, that party may have to pay costs to the unsuccessful party in relation to whatever portion of the hearing the court assesses was attributable to the issue upon which the winning party was unsuccessful.

Maintainable Causes of Action Against Estates

24–17 Section 9(2) of the 1961 Act provides that no proceedings

> shall be maintainable in respect of any cause of action whatsoever which has survived against the estate of a deceased person unless either – (a) proceedings against him in respect of that cause of action was commenced within the relevant period and were pending at the date of death, or (b) proceedings are commenced in respect of that action within the relevant period or within the period of two years after his death, whichever period first expires.[8]

24–18 In *Corrigan v Martin*,[9] Fennelly J stated that s 8(1) of the 1961 Act governed all causes of action coming into existence right up to the point of death itself, and when referring to s 9(2)(a) and (b), that an action cannot be maintained unless the plaintiff can bring himself within one of the two sub-paragraphs. Referring to s 8(1) which applies to all cause of actions, Fennelly J stated that:

> The Oireachtas intended that provision to apply to all causes of action coming into existence right up to the point of death itself. It is unreal and almost metaphysical to distinguish between causes of action existing immediately prior to the death and those which matured on the death itself.

24–19 He went on to say that he was satisfied that

> the correct interpretation of the plaintiff's cause of action in the light of the section is that the obligation of the deceased was to perform the contract during his lifetime and not at the moment of his death. Hence, the cause of action was complete immediately before his death. It is unnecessary to decide how long before his death.

24–20 In *Prendergast v McLaughlin*,[10] O'Keeffe J found that the plaintiff's cause of action was primarily one based in contract or quasi-contract for breach of the deceased's promise to devise the lands to him. The breach could only

---

[8] See *Allied Irish Banks v Pollock* [2016] IEHC 581.
[9] Unreported, Supreme Court, 13 March 2006.
[10] [2009] IEHC 250.

have occurred during the lifetime of the deceased and the cause of action therefore accrued before the death of the deceased. He stated that:

> I also conclude, based on the agreed facts that the plaintiff's claim can alternatively be based on promissory estoppel or equity. As such it is not a claim arising after the death of the deceased but a claim subsisting at death, namely, the failure of the deceased to execute a will bequeathing the lands to the plaintiff during his lifetime. I do accept that the evidence relating to such cause of action emerged after death, the plaintiff's cause of action in contract, quasi-contract or in equity subsisted during the lifetime of the deceased. I reject the plaintiff's submission to the contrary.

When a cause of action has survived the estate of the deceased, s 9(2) of the 1961 Act provided two alternative periods in paras (a) and (b), and (a) did not apply as no action was pending the date of death of the deceased. The period provided under s 9(b) is the earlier of the relevant periods, being the expiry of the limitation period under the provisions contained in 1957 Act, or alternatively the period of two years from the date of death of the deceased. As the deceased died on 28 August 2003, proceedings ought to have been issued by 27 August 2005, the period of two years after the death of the deceased. The proceedings did not issue until 25 July 2006, and accordingly, O'Keeffe J held that the plaintiff's claim whether it arose in contract, quasi-contract, or in equity was statute-barred. **24–21**

In *Cavey v Cavey*,[11] the deceased testator who died on 18 December 2006 was the father of each of the parties to the appeal. The defendants/respondents were appointed executors in his last will and testament. Probate of the will was granted to the executors on 13 March 2008. The plaintiff/appellant initially commenced a first set of proceedings under s 117 of the Succession Act 1965 on 12 December 2008. The first proceedings were heard by Laffoy J on 23 April 2009, and were dismissed. The plaintiff/appellant appealed that decision to the Supreme Court but subsequently withdrew his appeal on 23 July 2010. Four days later, on 27 July 2010, he commenced second proceedings. The substance of his claim in the second proceedings arose out of a representation made to him by both of his parents to the effect that he would inherit the family home. He claimed to have acted on that representation and under the doctrine of promissory estoppel he was entitled to relief. **24–22**

The executors brought a motion before the High Court seeking to have the proceedings dismissed on the basis: **24–23**

(a) of an allegation that the proceedings were an abuse of process in accordance with the rule in *Henderson v Henderson* (1843) 3 Hare 100 and/or
(b) that the proceedings must invariably fail as being statute-barred having regard to the provisions of s 9 of the 1961 Act.

Herbert J held that the proceedings were statute-barred under s 9 of the 1961 **24–24**

[11] [2014] IESC 16.

Act, and that it was appropriate to dismiss the proceedings on that basis. He did not consider it necessary to determine whether the proceedings might also be considered to be an abuse of process under *Henderson v Henderson*. The plaintiff/appellant appealed to the Supreme Court against that decision.

24–25 In his judgment for the Supreme Court, Clarke J stated that:

> Assuming that all the necessary ingredients for a promissory estoppel can be established, then it follows that there was a legal obligation on a person, during their life, to make a will which complies with the promise made. While it is true that the person can make such a will at any time before death, it nonetheless follows that it is a failure to act during the lifetime of the deceased which gives rise to the cause of action.

24–26 Having referred to *Corrigan v Martin* and *Prendergast v McLaughlin*, Clarke J stated that:

> It seems to me that a significant distinction is made in s 9(2), so far as claims against an estate are concerned, between a cause of action which results from an act or omission of the deceased, on the one hand, and a cause of action which may exist against those in charge of the administration of the estate of the deceased, on the other. If Mr. Cavey had a cause of action in promissory estoppel at all, it can only be because he might be able to establish that his late father was in breach of a legally enforceable promise in respect of bequeathing the family home to him. If such could be established it would be a failure, during his life, on the part of his late father to make an appropriate will to comply with his promise that gives rise to the claim.

24–27 He continued:

> It seems to me that such a claim necessarily comes within the scope of the phrase "*a claim surviving against the estate of the deceased*" even if it is true that a deceased could have avoided such a claim being capable of being brought by complying with their promise to bequeath the relevant property up to the moment before their death.

24–28 He concluded:

> I am, therefore, satisfied that, on a proper interpretation of the effect of s 9 of the 1961 Act, a claim in promissory estoppel arising out of an enforceable promise by a person to leave property by will, is a claim which can properly be characterised as one which survives against the estate of that person in the sense in which that term is used in the section. It follows that the claim brought in these proceedings could only be maintained by Mr. Cavey if it had been commenced within two years of his late father's death. The claim not having been so commenced, it is clearly statute barred. It follows that Mr. Cavey's proceedings are bound to fail on that basis and should be dismissed.

24–29 In *Allied Irish Banks v Pollock*,[12] Baker J had to consider whether the proceedings were capable of being maintained against the estate of the deceased having regard to the provisions of ss 8 and 9(2)(b) of the 1961

---

[12] [2016] IEHC 581.

Act. In that case, the plaintiff sought judgment against the defendants arising from two loan facilities both of which were made in 2009 in the respective sums of €519,803.01 and €2,236,953.60. Both loans were accepted by the borrowers in the Bank's written form of acceptance and signed on 20 July 2009, and the monies were drawn down on 31 August 2009. The loans were secured over certain real property in the title of the first defendant and her now-deceased husband, Tom Pollock. Thomas Pollock died on 7 November 2010 and a grant of probate issued in his estate to one of his executors, William Roche, on 22 January 2015, the other executor, the third defendant, having renounced his right to probate. When the matter came on for hearing before Baker J on a motion for summary judgment, counsel agreed that the appropriate way to deal with the action against the estate of the deceased was to deal with the preliminary point of law arising regarding whether the action against the estate was statute-barred. The defendant argued that by virtue of s 9 of the 1961 Act, the claim against the estate was statute-barred, the proceedings not having been commenced within two years of the death of the deceased on 7 November 2010. Proceedings were commenced on 3 March 2015. No demand for payment was made at any time prior to 7 November 2010, and the plaintiff did not present any argument that any valid letter of demand was served until 4 February 2015, after a grant of probate had issued in the estate of the deceased. If the cause of action accrued only when demand was made, then the action was not one to which the provision of s 9(2) applied, the six-year time limitation provided by the Statute of Limitations 1957 was the relevant limitation, and the proceedings were not statute-barred.

Baker J stated that: **24–30**

> The case then comes down to a determination of two questions:
> (a) The date of the accrual of the plaintiff's cause of action against the second defendant, and whether the cause of action was subsisting at the date of the death of the deceased; and
> (b) Whether the proceedings are now capable of being maintained by the Bank against the second defendant having regard to ss.8 and 9(2)(b) of the Act of 1961, as amended.

She went on to state that: **24–31**

> 52. I cannot accept the argument of the plaintiff that taking the contract as a whole the loan facility was repayable only on demand. I consider in all the circumstances that it was repayable on or before 30th September, 2009, that it was a contract for a fixed term at the end of which the money became repayable in full, either from the resources of the borrowers or by refinance. There was, in those circumstances, no requirement that the Bank demand payment on 30th September, 2009.
>
> 53. As a consequence, I consider that the cause of action accrued on 30th September, 2009. The action therefore is one which existed at the date of death of the deceased, Thomas Pollock, who died on 7th November, 2010, and in respect of which the two-year time period provided by s 9 of the Act of 1961 applies.

She concluded that: **24–32**

> 61. The cause of action of the Bank against Thomas Pollock, deceased accrued on 30th September, 2009. Mr. Pollock died on 7th November, 2010 and as a result of the provisions of s 9(2)(b) of the Act of 1961, as amended, the action against the deceased was required to be brought within two years of his death. The action was one which, pursuant to s 8 of the Act of 1961, did subsist against the deceased and survived against his estate but only for the period of two years provided by s 9.
>
> 62. The action against the second defendant is barred by statute.

24–33 In *Reidy v McGreevy*,[13] Barron J held the view that whether a cause of action based on a constructive trust is one available against the deceased, and so capable of being barred after the lapse of two years from the date of his death, is dependent upon the facts of the case. But whatever the facts of the case, "the claim could not be maintained until the death of the testator because it could not have been ascertained until then," that he had failed to honour his promise. But he added that if the testator had repudiated his promise in his lifetime, this would have given rise to a cause of action at that stage. However, *Prendergast v McLaughlin*,[14] *Cavey v Cavey*[15] and *Allied Irish Banks v Pollock*[16] preferred Fennelly J's analysis of ss 8 and 9 of 1961 Act in *Corrigan v Martin*.[17]

---

[13] Unreported, High Court, Barron J, 3 December 1986.
[14] [2009] IEHC 250.
[15] [2014] IESC 16.
[16] [2016] IEHC 581.
[17] Unreported, Supreme Court, 13 March 2006.

Chapter 25

ACTIONS IN THE CIRCUIT COURT

Introduction

The Circuit Court has jurisdiction to hear and determine the following actions and proceedings: 25–01

1. an action in respect of the grant or revocation of a grant of representation of the estate of a deceased;
2. proceedings in respect of the administration of the estate of a deceased person or in respect of any share therein; and
3. any proceedings under ss 56, 115, 117, or 121 of the Succession Act 1965.[1]

The concurrent jurisdiction of the Circuit Court is dependent on the parties to the action signing a form of consent before or at any time during the hearing in the Circuit Court, otherwise the court will not have jurisdiction to hear the matter.[2] Furthermore, where the High Court is satisfied that the Circuit Court has jurisdiction in the matter, it may remit the case to the Circuit Court for hearing.[3] In the Circuit Court, the nature of the action will be indicated by the heading of the civil bill—for instance, where a probate action is intended to be commenced, the civil bill will be headed with the words "testamentary civil bill"; where a provision of the Succession Act 1965 is involved, the civil bill will be headed with the words "succession law civil bill"; or where an administration action is intended to be commenced, the civil bill must be headed "equity civil bill", as in the case of proceedings involving equitable matters. 25–02

Probate Actions by Testamentary Civil Bill

Probate actions in the Circuit Court may be commenced by issuing a testamentary civil bill seeking a grant of probate in solemn form, or the revocation of probate or letters of administration, and an equitable action may be commenced by the issuing of an equity civil bill.[4] The character in which the plaintiff claims must be stated in the indorsement, viz. executor, administrator, creditor, residuary legatee or devisee or next-of-kin, or in 25–03

---

1 Succession Act 1965, s 6.
2 Succession Act 1965, s 6(3).
3 Succession Act 1965, s 35(3).
4 Circuit Court Rules Ord.50 r 1(a); see Form 2G, Schedule of Forms, Circuit Court Rules; see Chapter 21: Actions Involving Trusts and Wills.

whatever other character.[5] Any person who has entered a *caveat* may be made a defendant to the proceedings.[6] Where proceedings are instituted for the revocation of a grant, the person seeking revocation will be the plaintiff, and the person to whom the grant was made will be the defendant.[7] Both the plaintiff and defendant must within 10 days of the entry of appearance file affidavits as to scripts, whether or not they have any testamentary scripts within their possession.[8] A party to the action will not be at liberty to inspect an affidavit as to scripts until he has first filed his own affidavit as to scripts, unless the court allows otherwise.[9] The filing of an affidavit verifying the claim of the plaintiff and specifying the names and addresses of the next-of-kin and of such persons as may be entitled to any interest in the assets of the testator must precede the issuing of the testamentary bill.[10] The defendant with his defence may give notice to the plaintiff that he intends to cross-examine the witnesses produced in support of the will only, and he may as a result not be liable to pay the costs of the plaintiff unless the court is of the opinion that there was no reasonable ground for opposing the will.[11]

25–04 Order 50 of the Circuit Court Rules 2007 (SI No 312 of 2007), in relation to probate actions in the Circuit Court, provides that:

> "1. (a) Any person desirous of taking proceedings in the Court for the purpose of obtaining a grant, or revocation of a grant, of Probate or Letters of Administration shall issue a Civil Bill in the form prescribed in Form 2G of the Schedule of Forms; such Civil Bill shall be headed with the words 'Testamentary Civil Bill'. On issuing a Testamentary Civil Bill the plaintiff shall, if he has not already done so, lodge a caveat in the Probate Office entitled in the estate of the deceased person. Following the issuing of the Testamentary Civil Bill, details of the lodgement of the caveat shall be endorsed thereon by the Probate Office prior to service thereof. Thereafter, the caveat lodged in the matter will continue in force until the Probate Office is satisfied that the proceedings have been completed whether determined, discontinued or otherwise. For the purposes of this Rule, 'the Probate Office' means the Probate Office or the relevant District Probate Registry.
>
> (b) The issue of a Testamentary Civil Bill shall be preceded by the filing of an affidavit made by the plaintiff, or, if more than one plaintiff, then by one of them, verifying the claim, and specifying the names and residences of the next-of-kin, and of such persons as may be entitled under an intestacy to any interest in the assets of the alleged testator or intestate in the said Civil Bill named.
>
> 2. In any such action the indorsement shall show whether the plaintiff claims as creditor, executor, administrator, residuary legatee, legatee, next-of-kin, heir-at-law, devisee, or in what other character.
>
> 3. Where any person shall have lodged a caveat against the grant of Probate or

5 Ord 50, rr 1(a) and 2; see Form 2H, Schedule of Forms, Circuit Court Rules.
6 Ord 50, r 3.
7 Ord 50, r 4.
8 Ord 50, rr 9 and 12; see Form No.28, Schedule of Forms, Circuit Court Rules.
9 Ord 50, r 11.
10 Ord 50, r 1(b).
11 Ord 50, r 12.

Letters of Administration, and proceedings are taken to obtain such a grant, that person shall be a defendant.

4. In proceedings for the revocation of Probate or Letters of Administration, the person applying for such revocation shall be plaintiff, and the person to whom such grant has been made shall be a defendant.
5. If upon the hearing of any Probate action it shall appear to the Judge that any person or persons not already a plaintiff or defendant therein ought to be made a party or parties to the suit, he may adjourn the proceedings and direct that such person or persons shall be made parties thereto by amendment of the Civil Bill.
6. Any of the next-of-kin of any alleged testator or intestate, or any beneficiary of any alleged testator, may appear at the hearing of any Probate action although he may not have been made a party to the same or served therein.
7. In any Probate action any defendant may propound a will by way of counterclaim.
8. Any party may rely on wills alternatively in his pleadings.
9. In Probate actions the plaintiff and defendant, within ten days of the entry of an appearance on the part of the defendant, shall respectively file affidavits as to scripts, whether they have or have not any script in their possession. Such affidavits shall be in the form set out at Form 28 in the Schedule of Forms with such variations as circumstances may require.
10. Every script in the custody or under the control of the party making the affidavit shall be annexed thereto, and deposited therewith in the office.
11. No party to the cause, or his Solicitor, shall be at liberty, except by leave of the Court, to inspect the affidavits as to scripts, or the scripts annexed thereto, filed by any party to the cause, until his own affidavit as to scripts shall have been filed.
12. The party opposing a will may with his Defence give notice to the party setting up the will that he merely insists upon the will being proved in solemn form of law, and only intends to cross-examine the witnesses produced in support of the will, and he shall thereupon be at liberty to do so, and shall not in any event be liable to pay the costs of the other side unless the Judge shall be of opinion that there was no reasonable ground for opposing the will."[12]

The following are grounds for challenging the validity of wills by testamentary civil bill: **25–05**

1. That the testator lacked testamentary capacity.[13]
2. That a severe form of physical illness affected the testator's mental powers when he or she executed his or her will.[14]
3. That the testator was subject to undue influence when he or she made his or her will.
4. That the will was procured by a beneficiary.
5. That the will was prepared and executed in suspicious circumstances.[15]
6. That the question of the righteousness of the transaction arises "when it is a question of knowledge and approval of the contents of a will the circumstances which are held to excite the suspicions of the court must be

---

12 Probate Office Update 2012.

13 Succession Act 1965, s 77; see A. Keating, *The Law of Wills* (2nd ed, Clarus Press, Dublin, 2018); A. Keating, "Testamentary Capacity" (2011) 16(3) CPLJ 46.

14 *Laaser v Earls* [2016] IECA 63.

15 See *Re Begley* [1939] IR 479 at 490; *Tyrell v Painton* [1894] P 151.

circumstances attending, or at least relevant to, the preparation and execution of the will itself."[16]

7. That the will was not duly executed in compliance with s 78 of the Succession Act 1965.[17]

25–06 Testamentary Civil Bill

FORM 2G

AN CHÚIRT CHUARDA

THE CIRCUIT COURT

CIRCUIT

COUNTY OF

TESTAMENTARY CIVIL BILL

BETWEEN

Plaintiff

AND

Defendant

You are hereby required within ten days after the service of this Civil Bill upon you to enter or cause to be entered with the County Registrar. at his Office at an Appearance to answer the claim of the Plaintiff herein.

And take notice that unless you do enter an Appearance, you will be held to have admitted the said claim, and the Plaintiff may proceed therein and judgment may be given against you in your absence without further notice.

And further take notice that, if you intend to defend the proceeding on any grounds, you must not only enter an Appearance, but also, within ten days after Appearance, deliver a statement in writing showing the nature and grounds of your Defence.

The Appearance may be entered by posting same to the said Office and by giving copies thereof to the Plaintiff or his Solicitor by post and the Defence may be delivered by posting same to the Plaintiff or his Solicitor.

Dated the
day of
Signed:
Plaintiff/Solicitors for the Plaintiff
To:
The Defendant/Solicitor for the Defendant

16 *Re R deceased* [1951] P 10 at 17.
17 See A. Keating, *The Law of Wills* (2nd ed, Clarus Press, Dublin, 2018).

INDORSEMENT OF CLAIM

1. X.Y., late of … in the County of … [description] died on the … day of … 20… having made his last Will whereby he appointed the Defendant executor of the said Will.

2. Probate of the said Will was on the … day of … 20… granted to the Defendant

3. The Plaintiff's claim is as [show interest] for the revocation of the said Grant of Probate upon the grounds following:

The Plaintiff's claim is for the grant of letters of administration of the estate of … in the County of … who died on the … day of … intestate.

Or

The Plaintiff's claim is for the revocation of Probate/Letters of Administration granted forth of Probate Registry on … in the matter of the estate of … in the County of …

4. The value of the estate of the said deceased at the time of the death of the deceased in so far as it consists of personal estate does not exceed

[INSERT DETAILS OF MONETARY BASIS OF JURISDICTION] and in so far as it consists of real estate does not exceed the rateable valuation of

[INSERT DETAILS OF RATEABLE VALUATION AS A BASIS OF JURISDICTION].

Plaintiff/Solicitors for the Plaintiff

FORM 28

AN CHÚIRT CHUARDA

THE CIRCUIT COURT

CIRCUIT

COUNTY OF

AFFIDAVIT OF SCRIPTS

BETWEEN

Plaintiff

AND

Defendant

of … [place of abode and description], the plaintiff of … [place of abode and description] the Defendant in this action, MAKE OATH and say as follows:-

1. No paper or parchment writing at any time made or written by or under the direction of late of … [place of abode and description] deceased, the deceased

in this cause, being or purporting to be a will, codicil, draft or copy of a will or codicil. or of any part of a will or codicil. or written instructions for a will or codicil, or for any part of a will or codicil, or having the form or effect of a will or codicil. or of a part of a will or codicil or other testamentary disposition of the said … has at any time, either before or since his death, come to the hands, possession, or knowledge, or under the control of me, this deponent, save and except the true and original last will (and one codicil or codicils, or draft copies, or as the case may be) said deceased hereunto annexed, the said will, bearing date the … day of … 20… (and the said codicil (or as the case may be) bearing date etc.) and also save and except [here add the dates and particulars of any other testamentary papers of which the deponent has any knowledge. information, or belief; and state the person or persons in whose possession same are; and the address *of* such person or persons], and also save and except the next hereinafter-mentioned papers [here describe the papers, with dates, etc.], which I verily believe are in the possession or under the control of … and I say that I have not, nor has any person for me, or by my consent or desire, or at all to my knowledge or belief cancelled, suppressed, or destroyed, or caused to be cancelled, suppressed, or destroyed, any paper or parchment writing, being or purporting to be a will, codicil, or part of a will or codicil, draft or copy of a will or codicil, or of any part of a will or codicil, draft or copy of a will or codicil, or of any part of a will or codicil, or written instructions for a will or codicil, or for any part thereof, or having the form or effect of a will or codicil or other testamentary disposition. or any part of a will or codicil or other testamentary disposition of the said deceased,

SWORN etc.

This affidavit is filed on behalf of

FORM 6A

AN CHÚIRT CHUARDA

THE CIRCUIT COURT

CIRCUIT

COUNTY OF

DEFENCE

BETWEEN

Plaintiff

AND

Defendant

Defence of the Defendant

of … delivered the … day of … by …

Defendant/Solicitor for the Defendant.
[Here insert details of the Defence]
[Here insert details of COUNTERCLAIM and reliefs sought by way of counterclaim if appropriate]

Dated this …

day of … 20…

To: The Plaintiff/Solicitor for the Plaintiff

And

The County Registrar

FORM 15A

AN CHÚIRT CHUARDA

THE CIRCUIT COURT

CIRCUIT

COUNTY OF

NOTICE OF TRIAL

BETWEEN

Plaintiff

AND

Defendant

Take notice of the trial of this action (or of the issues ordered to be tried as the case may be) for the day of next at the Courthouse at …

Dated this …
day of … 20…

Signed Plaintiff/Defendant/Solicitor for the Plaintiff/Defendant

To:

The Defendant/Plaintiff Solicitor for the Defendant/Plaintiff

In *Ahern v Greaney*,[18] the deceased died a bachelor farmer at his home and was survived by three sisters, Christina Greaney, Catherina Kelly and Margaret O'Donnell (the defendants/counterclaimants), one brother Michael O'Donnell and six children of his predeceased sister Marie Griffin. The plaintiffs, who were executors of the deceased testator's will, issued a testamentary civil bill seeking: **25–07**

(a) A declaration that the will of the deceased testator be propounded in solemn form of law,
(b) The will be admitted to probate,
(c) Further/other relief, and
(d) Costs.

---

18 [2017] IECC 1.

25–08 The defendants counterclaimed for an order:

(1) Refusing probate of the will,
(2) Declaring that the deceased died intestate,
(3) Other relief, and
(4) Costs.

25–09 The court had to decide whether or not the signature on the will was that of the deceased testator, or whether it was signed by another.

25–10 Judge O'Callaghan of the Circuit Court sitting in Limerick stated that:

> 56. Any suggestions that the deceased did not know or approve of the contents of the contested will as pleaded in paragraph 3(b) of the defence and in paragraph 15(b) of the Counterclaim are rejected by the Court. There is no evidence upon which to base such suggestions and this aspect of the Defendants' claim is dismissed.
>
> 57. 'Signed by the Testator in our presence and attested by us in the presence of him and of each other' is one of the examples of a valid attestation clause. The document used in this case has the following pre-printed version:
>
> 58. 'Signed by the said Testator/rix in our presence and then by us in his', which is also clearly an acceptable valid clause. The Defendants say the failure to delete the letters 'rix' is fatal to the validity of the clause though it is interesting to note that the example endorsed on the form is exactly the same. The court disagrees with the defendants' contention and holds that the failure on the part of the testator on both occasions to delete the letters "rix" does not invalidate the attestation clause.
>
> 59. Accordingly, this contested will, having a valid attestation clause, is entitled to benefit from the presumption of due execution.

25–11 He referred to the following case law:

> 41. In *Re Skerrington* (2005) EWCA (*sic*). The presumption of due execution should not be easily rebutted if a will on its face appears validly executed and has a full attestation clause.
>
> 42. *Wright v Rodgers* (1869) L.R. (*sic*). 'The Court ought to have in all cases the strongest evidence before it believes that a will with a perfect attestation clause, and signed by the testator, was not duly executed otherwise the greatest uncertainty would prevail in the proving of wills'.
>
> 43. The evidence must be positive and reliable.
>
> 44. In *Re Channon* (2005) EWCA. (*sic*).
>
> > 'What constitutes the strongest evidence in a particular case will depend on the totality of the relevant facts of the case and the Court's evaluation of the probabilities. The Court must look at all the circumstances of the case relevant to attestation. The more probable it is, from those circumstances, that the will was properly attested, the greater will be the burden on those seeking to displace the presumption …'.
>
> 45. The Irish courts have rejected the contention that there are any categories of civil cases to which a higher standard than that of proof on the balance of probabilities applies; though, where the allegations are serious, a court ought to apply the universal standard of proof in a more rigorous and exacting manner.

25–12 He concluded that:

> 62. I have come to my decision primarily based on my assessment of the evidence

given by the witnesses of fact taking into account my views of the strengths of the opinion evidence given by the expert witnesses.

63. I have taken into account, as I must, the presumption of due execution that applies in favour of the Plaintiffs and assessed the evidence in light of same. The burden of proof falls on the Defendants to rebut that presumption on the balance of probabilities. I do not accept that either Josie Ahern or Mary Mullane simulated the deceased's signature on the willform or that both ladies committed perjury while giving evidence to this Court. The Court holds that the defendants have failed to rebut that presumption of due execution.

64. Accordingly I dismiss the Defendants' Counterclaim and hold in favour of the Plaintiffs and make the following orders:

65. Declaration as per paragraph (a) and an Order as per paragraph (b) of the Plaintiffs' prayer in Testamentary Civil Bill dated 7th October 2014.

66. In all the circumstances I propose making no order as to costs though I will hear from Counsel should you wish me to order otherwise.

Administration Actions by Succession Law Civil Bill

Administration actions in the Circuit Court may be instituted by the issuing of a succession law civil bill. An administration action may also be commenced in the Circuit Court once it is established that that court has jurisdiction to hear the matter.[19] The action may be heard in the county where the testator or intestate at the time of his or her death had a permanent residence, unless the court orders otherwise.[20] Such an action may be brought by the personal representatives or trustees of a trust estate, or against the personal representatives or trustees, by a creditor, devisee, legatee, or next-of-kin or beneficiaries under a trust, and the indorsement must show the *locus standi* or interest the plaintiff has in the estate of the deceased or the trust estate. An order affecting the rights or interests of persons who are not parties to the action may also direct that they be served with notice of the order, and after receiving notice of the order will thereafter be bound by the proceedings.[21] A person served with such notice may within one month of service apply to the court to discharge, vary or add to the order.[22] **25–13**

The following are grounds for instituting administration actions by succession law civil bill: **25–14**

(i) The determination of any question affecting the rights or interests of any person claiming to be a creditor, devisee, legatee or next-of-kin of the deceased or beneficiaries under a trust;
(ii) The payment into court of any money in the hands of the personal representatives or trustees;
(iii) The seeking of a direction of the court ordering any of the personal representatives or trustees to do, or abstain from doing, any particular act in their character as personal representative including the purchasing and vouching of accounts;

---

19 Circuit Court Rules Ord 5, r 1.
20 Ord 2, r(c).
21 Ord 6, r 14.
22 Ord 6, r 14; see Chapter 23: Actions for Breach of Trust and Administration Actions.

(iv) The approval of any sale, purchase or other transaction in connection with the administration of the estate of a deceased person or trust;
(v) The determination of any question arising in the administration of any estate or trust or the ascertainment of any class of creditors, legatees, devisees, next-of-kin or others.

25–15 SUCCESSION LAW CIVIL BILL

FORM 2H

AN CHÚIRT CHUARDA

THE CIRCUIT COURT

CIRCUIT

COUNTY OF

SUCCESSION LAW CIVIL BILL

IN THE MATTER OF THE SUCCESSION ACT, 1965 AND IN THE

MATTER OF

THE ESTATE OF

BETWEEN

DECEASED

Plaintiff

AND

Defendant

You are hereby required within ten days after the service of this Civil Bill upon you to enter or cause to be entered with the County Registrar, at his Office at … an Appearance to answer the claim of … of … the Plaintiff herein.

And take notice that unless you do enter an Appearance, you will be held to have admitted the said claim, and the Plaintiff may proceed therein and judgment may be given against you in your absence without further notice.

And further take notice that, if you intend to defend the proceeding on any grounds you must not only enter an Appearance, but also, within ten days after Appearance, deliver a statement in writing showing the nature and grounds of your Defence.

The Appearance may be entered by posting same to the said Office and by giving copies thereof to the Plaintiff or his Solicitor by post and the Defence may be delivered by posting same to the Plaintiff or his Solicitor.

Dated the … day of … 20…

Signed

Plaintiff/Solicitors for the Plaintiff
To:
The Defendant/Solicitor for the Defendant

INDORSEMENT OF CLAIM

[Insert particulars of Plaintiff's claim and the basis upon which jurisdiction is claimed]

THE PLAINTIFF CLAIMS:

[Insert reliefs sought by the Plaintiff]

Plaintiff/Solicitors for the Plaintiff

FORM 6A

AN CHÚIRT CHUARDA

THE CIRCUIT COURT

CIRCUIT

COUNTY OF

DEFENCE

BETWEEN

Plaintiff

AND

Defendant

Defence of the Defendant

of … delivered the … day of … 20… by …

Defendant/Solicitor for the Defendant.
[Here insert details of the Defence]
[Here insert details of COUNTERCLAIM and reliefs sought by way of counterclaim if appropriate]

Dated this …
day of … 20…

To: The Plaintiff/Solicitor for the Plaintiff

And

The County Registrar

FORM 15A

AN CHÚIRT CHUARDA

THE CIRCUIT COURT

CIRCUIT

COUNTY OF

NOTICE OF TRIAL

BETWEEN

Plaintiff

AND

Defendant

Take notice of the trial of this action (or of the issues ordered to be tried as the case may be) for the day of next at the Courthouse at …

Dated this …
day of … 20…

Signed Plaintiff/Defendant/Solicitor for the Plaintiff/Defendant

To:

The Defendant/Plaintiff Solicitor for the Defendant/Plaintiff

Equitable Actions by Equity Civil Bill

25–16 Equitable actions in the Circuit Court may be instituted by the issuing of an equity civil bill. An equitable action may be brought by the personal representatives or trustees of a trust estate, or against the personal representatives or trustees, by a creditor, devisee, legatee, or next-of-kin or beneficiaries under a trust, and the indorsement must show the *locus standi* or interest the plaintiff has in the estate of the deceased or the trust estate. An order affecting the rights or interests of persons who are not parties to the action may also direct that they be served with notice of the order, and after receiving notice of the order they will thereafter be bound by the proceedings.[23] A person served with such notice may within one month of service apply to the court to discharge, vary or add to the order.[24]

25–17 The validity of a trust may be challenged by equity civil bill on the following grounds:

(i) That the subject matter of the trust was disposed of by the testator during

---

[23] Ord 6, r 14.

[24] Ord 6, r 14; see Chapter 24: Actions Involving Equitable Property Rights; Chapter 21: Actions Involving Trusts and Wills.

his or her lifetime, resulting in the failure of the trust under the doctrine of ademption.

(ii) That the objects of the trust predeceased the testator, resulting in the failure of the trust under the doctrine of lapse.

(iii) That the property of the lapsed trust forms part of the testator's residuary estate.[25]

(iv) That the object or beneficiary of the trust is a predeceased child of the testator who leaves issue him or her surviving and therefore the trust is not subject to the doctrine of lapse.[26]

(v) The words used by the testator fail to show that the testator intended "to create an obligation," or manifest an intention to create a trust.[27]

(vi) That the words used by the testator in creating the trust do not clearly state that the person appointed as trustee holds the property in trust for the named beneficiaries.[28]

The following are grounds for actions for breach of trust by equity civil bill: **25–18**

(i) Decisions by trustees "which are properly to be characterised as being ones that no reasonable of trustees could have made".[29]

(ii) Decisions that are guided by improper motives.[30]

(iii) Where the trustees' decision "is identified as one which no reasonable body of trustees properly informed and considering the decision could have made."[31]

EQUITY CIVIL BILL **25–19**

FORM 2B

AN CHÚIRT CHUARDA

THE CIRCUIT COURT

CIRCUIT

COUNTY OF

EQUITY CIVIL BILL

BETWEEN

Plaintiff

AND

Defendant

You are hereby required within ten days after the service of this Civil Bill upon you to enter or cause to be entered with the County Registrar, at his Office at an Appearance to answer the claim of … of … the Plaintiff herein.

---

25 See Succession Act 1965, s 91.

26 See Succession Act 1965, s 98.

27 *Chambers v Fahy* [1931] IR 17 at 21 *per* O'Byrne J; *Re Keyford* [1975] 1 All ER 604.

28 *Re Humphrey's Estate* [1916] 1 IR 21; *Re Sweeney* [1976-'77] ILRM 88.

29 See *Greene v Coady* [2014] IEHC 38.

30 *Greene v Coady* [2014] IEHC 38.

31 *Greene v Coady* [2014] IEHC 38.

And take notice that unless you do enter an Appearance, you will be held to have admitted the said claim, and the Plaintiff may proceed therein and judgment may be given against you in your absence without further notice.

And further take notice that, if you intend to defend the proceeding on any grounds, you must not only enter an Appearance, but also, within ten days after Appearance, deliver a statement in writing showing the nature and grounds of your Defence

The Appearance may be entered by posting same to the said Office and by giving copies thereof to the Plaintiff or his Solicitor by post and the Defence may be delivered by posting same to the Plaintiff or his Solicitor.

Dated the … day of … 20…

Signed

To:

Defendant/Solicitors for the Defendant

And

To: The County Registrar

Plaintiff/Solicitors for the Plaintiff

INDORSEMENT OF CLAIM

[Insert details of the Plaintiff's claim including the basis upon which jurisdiction is claimed]

THE PLAINTIFF CLAIMS:
[Insert reliefs sought by the Plaintiff]
Plaintiff/Solicitors for the Plaintiff

FORM 6A

AN CHÚIRT CHUARDA

THE CIRCUIT COURT

CIRCUIT

COUNTY OF

DEFENCE

BETWEEN

Plaintiff

AND

Defendant

Defence of the Defendant

of … delivered the … day of … by …

Defendant/Solicitor for the Defendant.
[Here insert details of the Defence]
[Here insert details of COUNTERCLAIM and reliefs sought by way of counterclaim if appropriate]

Dated this …
day of … 20…

To: The Plaintiff/Solicitor for the Plaintiff

And

The County Registrar

FORM 15A

AN CHÚIRT CHUARDA

THE CIRCUIT COURT

CIRCUIT

COUNTY OF

NOTICE OF TRIAL

BETWEEN

Plaintiff

AND

Defendant

Take notice of the trial of this action (or of the issues ordered to be tried as the case may be) for the day of next at the Courthouse at …

Dated this …
day of … 20…

Signed Plaintiff/Defendant/Solicitor for the Plaintiff/Defendant

To:

The Defendant/Plaintiff Solicitor for the Defendant/Plaintiff

Chapter 26

INTERPRETATIVE SOURCES OF LEGAL PRACTICE

Introduction

The interpretative sources of legal practice consist of the principles of interpretative construction, constructive interpretation, criteria and tests, formulated, or indeed, re-formulated, by judges in arriving at their decisions. Where the courts undertake an interpretative construction of a section of an Act of the Oireachtas, they may also formulate certain tests which must be satisfied before the provisions of the section become applicable to the circumstances of a case. In *Rowe v Law*,[1] for instance, the Supreme Court, when interpreting the provisions of s 90 of the Succession Act 1965 (the "1965 Act"), which provides that extrinsic evidence may be admissible to show the intention of the testator and assists "in the construction of, or to explain any contradiction in, a will," set down a twofold test which must be satisfied before such evidence may be deemed admissible.[2] The tests so formulated by the courts when conducting an interpretative construction of a section of an Act of the Oireachtas may be viewed as secondary interpretative sources of legal practice in cases involving the section. Principles of constructive interpretation may also be formulated by the courts in construction suits, as, for instance, in *Heron v Ulster Bank Ltd*,[3] where Lowry LCJ formulated six such principles of constructive interpretation of wills. Where, however, an issue is raised in a constructive interpretation of a will involving a rule of law and its application to determine the validity of a gift in the will, and where the gift is shown to have failed to satisfy the prerequisites of the rule, it may be deemed invalid, notwithstanding that such an interpretation "operates against or defeats" the intention of the testator.[4] As an interpretative construction of a rule of law may defeat a testator's intention as ascertained by the application of principles of constructive interpretation of wills, an interpretative construction of a rule of law may be viewed as a secondary interpretative source of legal practice—the primary source being, of course, interpretative formulations arising out of decisions relating to constitutional provisions. The principles of constructive interpretation applied for ascertaining the intention of a testator are made subject to an **26–01**

1 [1978] IR 55.

2 See *O'Connell v Bank of Ireland* [1998] 2 IR 596.

3 [1974] NI 44; see *Howell v Howell* [1992] 1 IR 290; *Corrigan v Corrigan* [2007] IEHC 367; *McGuinness v Sherry* [2008] I.EHC 134; *Corrigan v Corrigan* [2016] IESC 56.

4 See *Heron v Ulster Bank Ltd* [1974] NI 44; *Corrigan v Corrigan* [2007] IEHC 367; *Corrigan v Corrigan* [2016] IESC 56.

interpretative construction of a rule of law, and indeed, may be defeated by it, such principles may be viewed as tertiary sources of legal practice only.

Secondary Interpretative Sources of Legal Practice

26–02 A section of an Act of the Oireachtas may be subject to interpretative construction by the courts, and in such cases, the courts, when interpreting the provisions of the section, may formulate tests or preconditions before the provisions of the section become applicable to a case. In *Rowe v Law*,[5] for instance, the Supreme Court, when undertaking an interpretative construction of s 90 of the 1965 Act, which deals with the admissibility of extrinsic evidence showing a testator's intention, ruled that for such evidence to be admissible, it must not only show a testator's intention, but must also be of assistance to the court when conducting a constructive interpretation of a will, or that it helps to explain a contradiction appearing in a will. The interpretative construction placed on s 90 by the Supreme Court in *Rowe v Law* was later affirmed by the Supreme Court in *O'Connell v Bank of Ireland*.[6] In *Black v Ann O'Sullivan Centre*,[7] White J, when applying the *Rowe v Law* interpretative construction test, allowed the admission of extrinsic evidence to identify the person whom the testatrix intended to benefit by her will. White J stated that:

> 22. The extrinsic evidence is admissible in accordance with s 90 of the Succession Act 1965, to show the intention of the testator and to assist in the construction of her will to explain the contradiction in same. The extrinsic evidence does meet the two part test set out by the Supreme Court in *Rowe v Law* and approved in *In Re Collins O'Connell v Governor and Company of the Bank of Ireland.*

26–03 He went on to state:

> 24. The court is not rewriting the will or changing an ambiguous clause. It is reading the will with the assistance of the extrinsic evidence and giving effect to the intention of the will when it is clear that there was an error in that the testator's niece, Maureen Black, never had a daughter called Rosemary.

26–04 And at para 25, he stated:

> I am satisfied that the extrinsic evidence does meet the requirement of showing the intention of the testator and assisting in the interpretation of the contradiction in the will.

26–05 In *In the Estate of Courtney*,[8] Baker J applied the same *Rowe v Law* interpretative construction tests, and when doing so, allowed the admission of extrinsic of "direct or consequential evidence of the circumstances"

---

[5] [1978] IR 55; see A. Keating, *The Construction of Wills* (2nd edn, Clarus Press, Dublin, 2017); A. Keating *The Law of Wills* (2nd ed, Clarus Press, Dublin, 2018).

[6] [1998] 2 IR 596.

[7] [2016] IEHC 695.

[8] [2016] IEHC 318.

surrounding the making of a foreign will, and found that the general revocation clause in the testator's foreign will was limited in scope and effect to earlier foreign wills made by the testator.

Thus, the tests formulated by the courts when undertaking an interpretative construction of sections of an Act of the Oireachtas, may be viewed as a secondary interpretative sources of legal practice. **26–06**

In *O'Hagan v Grogan*,[9] the Supreme Court looked afresh at the nature of interests in estates during the administration of an estate. In her judgment, Macken J referred to s 10 of the 1965 Act, and stated that while the whole of an intestate estate vests in personal representatives, they do not hold the estate on their own behalf, but as trustees for the persons who were entitled to it by law. Section 10(1) of the 1965 Act provides that: "The real and personal estate of a deceased person shall on his death, notwithstanding any testamentary disposition, devolve and become vested in his personal representative." **26–07**

Section 10(2) provides that: "The personal representatives for the time being of a deceased person are deemed in law his heirs and assigns within the meaning of all trusts and powers." **26–08**

Section 10(3) provides that: "The personal representatives shall be the representatives of the deceased in regard to his real and personal estate and shall hold the estate as trustees for the persons entitled thereto." **26–09**

On an interpretative construction of s 10(1) and s 10(3), Macken J found that: **26–10**

> Under the provisions of s 10(1) of the Act of 1965 the whole of the intestate estate vests in the personal representative, who nevertheless does not hold the estate on his own behalf, but (under s 10(3)) as a trustee for the persons in law who are entitled to it, and he must act accordingly. Those persons have an immediate beneficial equitable interest in the estate by way of trust, which is nevertheless, subject to rights of the administrator, who has certain powers, including, for example, those for the purposes of disposition. The power to deal with the property of an intestate dates only from the date of grant, however, (as opposed to the position of an executor of a person who dies testate where the property vests on death).

Macken J went on to consider the effect of s 13 of the 1965 Act which provides that: **26–11**

> Where a person dies intestate, or dies testate but leaving no executor surviving him, his real and personal estate, until administration is granted in respect thereof, shall vest in the President of the High Court who, for this purpose, shall be a corporation sole.

When considering the role of the President of the High Court as a defendant **26–12**

---

9 [2012] IESC 8.

in a case, she referred to *Flack v President of the High Court*,[10] where Costello J stated that the vesting provisions in s 13 did not make the President of the High Court a trustee of the estate, nor did they impose any duty on him to perform in respect of the estate; his or her role was simply "a mere matter of necessary convenience and protection." This interpretative construction differed from that of Keane J in the Supreme Court case of *Gleeson v Feehan*,[11] who stated that the President of the High Court became the "true owner" of the estate of a deceased person for the period mentioned in s 13. The estate vested in him on the death of the deceased, and he divested himself only by the issuing of a grant of letters of administration to the person entitled under Ord 79 of the Rules of the Superior Courts. In *O'Hagan v Grogan*,[12] Macken J, when interpreting s 13, found that:

> The President, however, is not entitled, nor would his estate be entitled, to deal with or dispose of the estate, and s 13 imposes on him no powers, no duties and no obligations. It is precisely to avoid such an estate being left, in effect, in limbo, that s 13 vests the estate in him, *pro tem*. It, in a sense, "hovers" in the person of the President of the High Court for the time being, by means of a legal fiction, until something else happens.

26–13 The estate of a person dying intestate vested in the President as a corporation sole for the intervening period between the date of death and until a grant of letters of administration issued. But for the intervening period between the death of the deceased person, and the issuing of a grant of administration to the personal representative, the President, according to Macken J, is not entitled to deal with the estate or to dispose of it. The President fills the void between the death of the deceased and the issuing of a grant of administration so that the estate would not be left in "limbo". The estate vests in him *pro tem* only. The death of the deceased automatically vests the estate in the President, and a grant of letters of administration to the personal representative automatically divests the President of it. The President only holds:

> [A] bare estate in the property, but no sufficient interest against which adverse possession could be claimed, and the President has neither powers nor obligations in that regard, as is clear from the case law.

26–14 In *Flack v President of the High Court*, Costello J, when considering the role of the President as a defendant in the proceedings, stated that:

> The legislature did not make him a trustee of the estate which vested in him and he had no duty to perform and no obligation in respect of the estate. As was pointed out in relation to the vesting provisions of section 9 of the Administration of Estates Act 1925 in England (which are similar to those I am considering) these vesting provisions are a mere matter of necessary convenience and protection (see *Re Deans* [1954] 1 All E.R. 496 at 498). The President's position under the 1965 Act is exactly the same.

---

[10] Unreported, High Court, Costello J, 29 November 1983.
[11] [1997] 1 ILRM 522 at 538.
[12] [2012] IESC 8.

Macken J adopting the view of Costello J in *Flack v President of the High Court*, stated that: **26–15**

> The mechanism adopted in the Act of 1965, which mirrors previous legislation, is a mere "mechanism of convenience", as it is described in the case law, and to ensure that an estate has a temporary home pending the grant of administration.

There is no beneficial or other estate vested in the President, against which a claim to adverse possession can be made. He merely holds, on a temporary basis, a bare estate in the property in question. **26–16**

She went on to state: **26–17**

> I am fortified in my view that the President of the High Court does not hold any interest in the property which vests in him temporarily, sufficient to permit a third party to secure rights by means of adverse possession, by a consideration of his role in the devolution of the property upon administration apart from the fact that, as mentioned below, letters of administration are not granted to the Attorney General (or the Chief State Solicitor) by or on behalf of the President of the High Court, which would be the logical position, if the intestate estate vests in him in any real sense, when such property is eventually to vest in the beneficiary at the end of the administration, the President of the High Court plays no role in that either. He does not even assent to the vesting of such bare estate as is vested in him temporarily under the Act of 1965.

She also thought that had the decision of Costello J in *Flack v President of the High Court* been considered by the Supreme Court in *Gleeson v Feehan* "it is unlikely the learned Supreme Court judge would have made the statement found in the judgment as to the role of the President." **26–18**

When discussing the situation that existed when a grant issued, Macken J, focused on s 10 of the 1965 Act, and found that while the whole of the intestate estate vested in the personal representative, he did not hold it on his own behalf, "but as a trustee for the persons in law who are entitled to it, and he must act accordingly." She added that those persons "have an immediate beneficial equitable interest in the estate by way of trust, which is nevertheless, subject to the rights of the administrator, who has certain powers, including, for example, those for the purposes of disposition." Such an interpretation again differs from the view of Keane J, who, adopting the view of Viscount Radcliffe, stated that as the whole right of property vested in the personal representative, there was no need to distinguish between legal and equitable interests in an attempt to show that an equitable interest vested in beneficiaries. According to Keane J, once a grant issues, the whole estate vests in the personal representatives, and the beneficiaries will have no interest in the estate during the course of an administration of an estate. But according to Macken J, beneficiaries "have an immediate beneficial equitable interest in the estate by way of trust", although it is subject to the rights and powers of the administrator. **26–19**

Section 73(1) of the 1965 Act provides that, in the absence of next-of-kin, **26–20** the estate of a deceased person who dies intestate will pass to the State as the ultimate intestate successor. Under Ord 79, r 5(1)(m) of the Rules of the Superior Court 1986, a nominee of the State (the Chief State Solicitor or Solicitor for the Attorney General) may apply for a grant of letters of administration intestate by lodging the usual proofs for such grants, with the exception of an administration bond. Section 34(5) of the 1965 Act provides that the Chief State Solicitor or Solicitor for the Attorney General is not required to give an administration bond when applying for or obtaining administration for the use or benefit of the State. Section 65(1) of the 1965 Act provides that:

> Where administration of an estate is granted for the use and benefit of the State (whether to the Chief State Solicitor, the Solicitor for the Attorney General or any other person), any legal proceedings by or against the administrator for the recovery of the estate or any share thereof shall be of the same character and be instituted and carried on in the same manner, and be subject to the same rules of law and equity in all respects, as if the grant had been made to the administrator as a person beneficially entitled to a share of the estate.

26–21 Section 13(1)(a) of the Statute of Limitations 1957 (the "1957 Act") provides that:

> Subject to paragraphs (b) and (c) of this subsection no action shall be brought by a State authority to recover any land after the expiration of thirty years from the date on which the right of action accrued to a State authority or, if it first accrued to some person through whom a State authority claims, to that person.

26–22 Section 13(2) of the 1957 Act provides that:

> The following provision shall apply to an action by a person (other than a State authority) to recover land—
> (a) subject to paragraph (b) of this subsection, no such action shall be brought after the expiration of twelve years from the date on which the right of action accrued to the person bringing it or, if it first accrued to some person through whom he claims, to that person;
> (b) if the right of action first accrued to a State authority, the action may be brought at any time before the expiration of the period during which the action could have been brought by a State authority, or of twelve years from the date on which the right of action accrued to some person other than a State authority, whichever period first expires.

26–23 There are five State authorities listed in s 2(1) of the 1957 Act: a Minister of State, the Commissioners of Public Works in Ireland, the Irish Land Commission, the Revenue Commissioners and the Attorney General, and the list appears to be exhaustive. Section 3 of the 1957 Act provides that it will apply to proceedings by or against a State authority "in like manner as if that State authority were a private individual."

26–24 In *O'Hagan v Grogan*,[13] Macken J, when undertaking an interpretative

[13] [2012] IESC 8.

construction of ss 2 and 13 of the 1957 Act, and when referring to the role of the Attorney General as a State authority, stated that:

> The Attorney General is the legal representative of the State in all legal proceedings. The State does not, in general, act in its own name, independently of its Ministers or others officers, although it may, of course, do so. It acts through Ministers, including the Minister for Finance. The Attorney General falls into a different category to Ministers of State and those other parties mentioned expressly in s 2(1) of the Statute of Limitations. The Attorney General may hold property, qua Attorney General, although I do not know in what circumstances this occurs, but undoubtedly is also entitled to deal with the State's own property and in property to which it may become entitled, such as on an intestacy, by virtue of the unique position of the Attorney General as such legal representative. No limitation is placed on the scope of the Attorney General's role as a "State authority" in s 2(1), and he/she may act in more than one capacity, although always for and on behalf of the State, or on behalf of a Minister of State. The State itself is not separately represented in the list, although it must be accepted as a given, and, in the course of argument was accepted by counsel for the defendant, that it would be entitled to raise representation to the estate of Mrs. Dolan. But if it did so decide, it would act through the Attorney General, or the Chief State Solicitor. In circumstances where the State is the ultimate intestate successor to an intestate estate, as here, the Attorney General may act as a "State authority", and, as such, clearly is within the ambit of s 2(1) of the Statute.

The Chief State Solicitor, under s 65 of the 1965 Act, may institute proceedings for the recovery of the estate against persons who may be in adverse possession of it. But is he or she a State authority for the purposes of s 13 of the Statute? Section 13(1)(a) of the 1957 Act provides that **26–25**

> Subject to paragraphs (b) and (c) of this subsection, no action shall be brought by a State authority to recover any land after the expiration of thirty years from the date on which the right of action accrued to a State authority or, if it first accrued to some person through whom a State authority claims, to that person.

In *O'Hagan v Grogan*, the Chief State Solicitor argued that he was a State authority and referred to the Ministers and Secretaries Act 1924 (the "1924 Act"), s 6(1) which provided that there shall be vested in the Attorney-General the "business, powers, authorities, duties and functions" formerly vested or exercised by the Attorney-General for Ireland and Solicitor-General and any or all of them respectively, and the administration and control of the business, powers, authorities, duties and functions of the branches and officers of the public services specified in the Ninth Part of the Schedule to the 1924 Act. The Ninth Part of the Schedule includes the Chief State Solicitor's department and all local State Solicitors. However, Macken J stated that "even if the plaintiff, or any predecessor to him is—pursuant to the provisions of the Act of 1924—under the control of the Attorney General, he is not himself, a "State authority" within s 2(1)", and as a result the Chief State Solicitor was unable to claim a thirty-year limitation period for the recovery of the land from the defendant. She also stated that s 65 of the 1965 Act was not relevant when deciding on the correct limitation period to be applied. The Attorney General is one of the State authorities mentioned in s 2(1) of the 1957 Act, and as such is entitled to **26–26** institute proceedings for the recovery of State property, including property the State may become entitled as ultimate intestate successor under s 73(1) of the 1965 Act. Although s 65 of the 1965 Act expressly recognises the Chief State Solicitor as an appropriate person to apply for and be granted letters of administration intestate on behalf of the State, and may institute proceedings for the recovery of estate, he is not a State authority, and may not rely on the thirty-year limitation period for the recovery of the estate against a person in adverse possession of it.

26–27 An interpretative construction of statutory provisions may also involve the application of a legal doctrine, for instance, the doctrine of relation back. Under the doctrine of relation back, once a grant issues, the title of the personal representative to the estate of the deceased relates back to the date of the deceased's death, and by reliance on the doctrine, he or she may institute proceedings for any wrongdoing to the estate during the interval of time that existed between the date of death of the deceased and the issuing of the grant. Section 23 of the 1957 Act provides that an administrator of the estate "shall be deemed to claim as if there had been no interval of time between the date of the death of the deceased and the grant of letters of administration."[14] Otherwise, under s 24 of the 1957 Act, at the expiration of the limitation period for any person to bring an action, "the title of that person shall be extinguished." In *O'Hagan v Grogan*,[15] Macken J, when undertaking an interpretative construction of s 23 of the 1957 Act, and the recovery of land by the Chief State Solicitor as administrator of the estate, stated that

> if in the interval between the death of an intestate and the appointment of an administrator, a party has procured a lawful interest in lands the subject of the administration, that interest may be sufficient to bar its recovery by the administrator, when appointed, acting in the interests of those who, but for such event would have been entitled to the lands.

26–28 When referring to the facts of the case, she stated:

> In the result, time commenced to run against the estate for the purposes of adverse possession from either the date of death of Mrs Dolan, or the date of possession by the defendant. In either event, in this case, well more than 12 years passed before July, 2000. It does not follow, however, in the present case, that by reason of this interpretation of s 23 of the Statute of Limitations, the claim of the defendant to adverse possession is thereby determined. That issue at all times depends on the appropriate limitation period.

26–29 When referring to s 24 of the 1957 Act, Macken J stated that:

> The estate itself in the land is not extinguished, but title to that estate may well be, if a party has successfully established that he has adversely possessed the property for the relevant period.

---

14 [2012] IESC 8.
15 [2012] IESC 8.

Thus, if during the interval of time between the date of death of the deceased, and the issuing of a grant to the administrator, the period of limitation fixed by the 1957 Act had expired, the title of the administrator to the land will be extinguished against a person who has been in adverse possession of the land for the period of limitation prescribed by the 1957 Act. **26–30**

Therefore, where the courts undertake an interpretative construction of a section of an Act of the Oireachtas, they may also formulate certain tests which must be satisfied before the provisions of the section become applicable to the circumstances of a particular case, and such tests may become secondary interpretative sources of legal practice when determining similar issues in future cases. An interpretative construction of statutory provisions may also involve the application of legal doctrines. **26–31**

Tertiary Sources of Legal Practice

The courts may formulate principles of constructive interpretation, and such principles may be applied for the purposes of, e.g. ascertaining the intention of a testator in a construction suit. Such principles are, however, subject to an interpretative construction of a rule of law, and indeed, may be defeated by it, and as a result, principles of constructive interpretation may be viewed as tertiary sources of legal practice only. Six such principles of constructive interpretation of wills were formulated by Lowry LCJ in *Heron v Ulster Bank Ltd*,[16] and were later adopted and applied by the courts in this jurisdiction.[17] These principles have since become known as the Lowry Principles. The six principles are as follows: **26–32**

1. Read the immediate relevant portion of the will as a piece of English and decide, if possible, what it means.
2. Look at the other material parts of the will and see whether they tend to confirm the apparently plain meaning of the immediately relevant portion or whether they suggest the need for modification in order to make harmonious sense of the whole or, alternatively, whether an ambiguity in the immediately relevant portion can be resolved.
3. If ambiguity persists, have regard to the scheme of the will and consider what the testator was trying to do.
4. One at this stage must have resort to rules of construction, where applicable, and aids, such as the presumption of early vesting and the presumptions against intestacy and in favour of equality.
5. Then see whether any rule of law prevents a particular interpretation from being adopted.
6. Finally, and, I suggest, not until the disputed passage has been exhaustively studied, one may get help from the opinions of other courts and judges on similar words, rarely as binding precedents, since it has been well said that 'no will has a twin brother' (per Werner J in *Matter of King* 200 N.Y. 189, 192 (1910), but more often as examples (sometimes of the highest authority)

[16] [1974] NI 44; see A. Keating, *The Construction of Wills* (2nd edn, Clarus Press, Dublin 2017).

[17] See *Howell v Howell* [1992] 1 IR 290; *Corrigan v Corrigan* [2007] IEHC 367; *McGuinness v Sherry* [2008] IEHC 134; *Corrigan v Corrigan* [2016] IESC 56.

of how judicial minds nurtured in the same discipline have interpreted words in similar contexts.

26–33 Where a rule of law becomes an issue in a constructive interpretation of a trust or gift in a will, the courts may further undertake an interpretative construction of the rule when deciding on the validity of the trust or gift. Where the interpretative construction shows that the trust or gift has failed to satisfy the prerequisites of the rule, it may be deemed invalid, notwithstanding that such interpretation defeats or operates against the intention of the testator. In *Heron v Ulster Bank Ltd*,[18] Lowry LCJ also distinguished between a rule of law and a principle of construction when ascertaining a testator's intention, and stated that:

> Any rule the application of which is independent of the intention of the testator, and one which may operate against or to defeat that intention, is generally known as a rule of law. Any rule adopted by the court for ascertaining or effectuating the intention of the testator as declared in the will, and dependent, for its application to any will, upon whether it is consonant with or contrary to the whole will, is generally called a rule of construction.

26–34 In *Corrigan v Corrigan*,[19] McGovern J had to decide whether the testator in a devise of land in his will had intended to create a determinable fee of farmlands, and if he did, whether, as a matter of law, the determining event in the devise was void for uncertainty. He found that, as the determining event in the devise specified was void for uncertainty, the entire limitation failed, and the subject matter of the devise fell into the residuary estate of the testator.[20] When undertaking an interpretative construction of the rule of law relating to the creation of a determinable fee simple and its application to the devise in the will, McGovern J stated that at common law, the rule is that

> the testator cannot, in his will, create a determinable fee simple to the first named defendant and then provide that, in the event that a determining event occurs, the land is to pass to someone else. A testator cannot create a gift over to third parties after a determinable fee.

26–35 In that case, Clause 1 of the will contained the following devise:

> 1. I have 21 acres of land in Folio 13658 Co. Westmeath and I have been advised that said land or part thereof is rezoned for residential and/or industrial development. I direct my executors to hold the said lands upon the following trusts:
>
> (a) To allow my son Sean to hold and enjoy the profits of the land for his own benefit until there is acquisition of my lands for the purposes mentioned above. In such event the net proceeds of the sale of my land shall be divided equally amongst all my children and any section of the farm not so acquired shall become the absolute property of my son Sean.

26–36 At the time of the execution of the will, the land referred to in the bequest

[18] [1974] NI 44 at 52–53.
[19] [2007] IEHC 367; see also *Corrigan v Corrigan* [2016] IESC 56.
[20] See *Corrigan v Corrigan* [2016] IESC 56.

was zoned for agricultural use only. Later, however, certain parts of the land were rezoned for use as a special district for business and enterprise development.

McGovern J thought that the bequest only made sense in the light of the first part of the clause and seemed predicated on it. He stated that: **26–37**

> This can clearly be seen from the words '… until there is acquisition of my lands for the *purposes mentioned above'* (my highlights). On the face of it, it appears that the intention of the testator was that the first named defendant should hold and enjoy the profits of the lands until they were acquired for the development purposes which are stated to be residential and/or industrial. This would appear from the use of the words "to *allow* my son Sean to hold and enjoy the profits of the lands for his own benefit *until* …." (my highlights). In other words the testator expected the lands or part of them to be acquired for a value that would reflect the fact that they were zoned for residential and/or industrial development in that event the proceeds of sale would be divided equally among his children and the first named defendant would hold any part of the lands not so acquired.

On an interpretative construction of the common law rule, and when applying it to the devise in Clause 1 of the will, the determining event specified in the clause was void for uncertainty, and it followed therefore that the entire limitation failed, and that the subject matter of the devise fell into the residuary estate of the testator. **26–38**

Principles of constructive interpretation may, therefore, be viewed as mere discretionary and tertiary sources of legal practice only, which may, or may not, be applied by the courts, and insofar as wills are concerned, the Lowry Principles may, or may not, be applied by the courts when attempting to ascertain the testator's intention in a constructive interpretation of a will.[21] Further, it can be seen from *Corrigan v Corrigan* that an interpretative construction of a rule of law may prevail over a constructive interpretation of a will, even though it may have the effect of defeating a testator's intention. **26–39**

The Doctrine of *Ratio Decidendi*

The *ratio decidendi* of a case is the reason for a decision by a court, and such *ratio* may also be of binding force if made by a superior court, and as such may affirm a principle of law, or introduce a new one, or may create a corpus of principles, criteria or prerequisites. A *ratio* may also involve the formulation of tests or principles for future interpretation of a statutory provision, and may be of binding force in future cases involving that provision—for instance, the interpretative construction of s 90 of the 1965 Act by the Supreme Court in *Rowe v Law*[22] regarding the admissibility of extrinsic evidence when ascertaining the intention of a testator, formulated **26–40**

---

21 See *Howell v Howell* [1992] 1 IR 290; *Corrigan v Corrigan* [2007] IEHC 367; *McGuinness v Sherry* [2008] IEHC 134; *Corrigan v Corrigan* [2016] IESC 56; see A. Keating, *The Construction of Wills* (2nd edn, Clarus Press, Dublin, 2017).

22 [1978] IR 55; see *O'Connell v Bank of Ireland* [1998] 2 IR 596.

the tests to be applied when interpreting the section in future cases. A decision may also provide, in addition to the *ratio* of the case, a number of principles garnered from former decisions on a particular matter such as, for instance, *In the Estate of ABC, XC v RT*,[23] where Kearns J identified and summarised the principles derived from previous cases involving s 117 applications by children of testators, thereby creating a special jurisprudence for the guidance of judges when entertaining such applications. The *ratio* in a judgment may also provide a set of criteria—for instance, the Fennelly criteria in *Corrigan v Martin*,[24] which are to be applied in interpretative constructions of ss 8 and 9 of the Civil Liability Act 1961 regarding the periods of limitation for bringing actions against the estates of deceased persons.

26–41 A *ratio decidendi* of a case may also overrule a *ratio* formulated in a former case when made by a court of equal authority. The Supreme Court, when testing the correctness of a *ratio* in a former decision by that court, may decide to overrule it in order, e.g. to restore "equity to the high ground which it should properly occupy to ameliorate the harshness of common law rules on occasion rather than itself be an instrument of injustice."[25] In *Owens v Greene*,[26] the Supreme Court decided that a surviving joint bank account holder who had contributed to the account would not necessarily be entitled to the whole account as survivor, except where the survivor was the wife or child of the depositor or a person to whom the depositor stood *in loco parentis*. In the absence of evidence to rebut a resulting trust, the account may be treated as forming part of the deceased depositor's estate and vested in his personal representatives, and no assistance could be sought in equity, as equity would not assist a volunteer. Such accounts were viewed in Irish law as attempts to make testamentary gifts otherwise than by means of a testamentary instrument. The rule in *Owens v Greene* remained the law on the matter for 64 years, notwithstanding that during the course of that time, numerous negative criticisms were levelled at the rule by judges of the High Court who were willing but unable to overrule that decision of the Supreme Court. However, in *Lynch v Burke*,[27] O'Flaherty J in his judgment for the Supreme Court stated that opening of a joint bank account gave rise to a contract between the joint account holders and the bank. When overruling the decision in *Owens v Greene*, O'Flaherty J held that the concept of the resulting trust was devised primarily to defeat the misappropriation of property as a consequence of potentially fraudulent or improvident transactions, and was not to be used to defeat the clear intention of the depositor to benefit the surviving account-holder on death. The survivor had a legal interest in the monies on deposit either based on contract, or by virtue of a gift which was made subject to the contingency of the death of the depositor. He stated:

23 [2003] 2 IR 250.
24 Unreported, Supreme Court, Fennelly J, 13 March 2006.
25 *Lynch v Burke* [1996] 1 ILRM 114.
26 [1932] IR 225.
27 [1996] 1 ILRM 114.

> I believe that at law the niece had a legal interest in the monies on deposit either by reason of the contractual relationship of the parties or, in the alternative, as a gift which admittedly was not a completed gift in the conventional sense but is nonetheless one that should be upheld as being a gift subject to a contingency *viz.* that of the death of the donor which contingency does not disqualify it as being a proper gift.[28]

In *O'Meara v Bank of Scotland PLC*,[29] Laffoy J affirming the *ratio* in *Lynch v Burke*, stated that the legal effect of opening a joint bank account was that the bank became contractually bound to both account-holders and, as a matter of contract, between the surviving account-holder and the bank, the surviving account-holder became entitled to the balance in the account on the death of the deceased account-holder. **26–42**

[28] [1996] 1 ILRM 114 at 121.

[29] [2011] IEHC 402.

INDEX